PROTEST AND POLITICS

PROTEST AND POLITICS

THE PROMISE OF SOCIAL MOVEMENT SOCIETIES

Edited by Howard Ramos
and Kathleen Rodgers

UBCPress · Vancouver · Toronto

23 22 21 20 19 18 17 16   5 4 3 2

Printed in Canada on FSC-certified ancient-forest-free paper
(100% post-consumer recycled) that is processed chlorine- and acid-free.

Library and Archives Canada Cataloguing in Publication

    Protest and politics : the promise of social movement societies / edited by Howard Ramos and Kathleen Rodgers.

Includes bibliographical references and index.
Issued in print and electronic formats.
ISBN 978-0-7748-2916-8 (pbk.). – ISBN 978-0-7748-2917-5 (pdf). –
ISBN 978-0-7748-2918-2 (epub)

    1. Social movements. 2. Social movements – Canada. 3. Social movements – History. 4. Political participation. 5. Protest movements. 6. Social action. 7. Social change. I. Ramos, Howard, 1974-, editor II. Rodgers, Kathleen, 1974-, editor

HM881.P77 2015	303.48'4	C2015-900719-4
		C2015-900720-8

Canadä

UBC Press gratefully acknowledges the financial support for our publishing program of the Government of Canada (through the Canada Book Fund), the Canada Council for the Arts, and the British Columbia Arts Council.

This book has been published with the help of a grant from the Canadian Federation for the Humanities and Social Sciences, through the Awards to Scholarly Publications Program, using funds provided by the Social Sciences and Humanities Research Council of Canada.

UBC Press
The University of British Columbia
2029 West Mall
Vancouver, BC V6T 1Z2
www.ubcpress.ca

Contents

Acknowledgments

Considerable time and energy has gone into producing this volume and there have been many people along the way who provided support and assistance to the authors. The editors would like to thank everyone who contributed to this project.

To begin with, we would like to express our gratitude to the contributors to this volume. This project began with a workshop held at the University of Ottawa in May 2012. This event itself was a collegial occasion that led to the production of this volume, but equally notable is the fact that the workshop led to an enduring network of Canadian scholars from a wide range of perspectives dedicated to the study of social movements and activism. An edited volume is by nature a collaborative project and can only work when contributors are as committed to the outcomes as the editors; as we made repeated requests for revisions throughout the process, our contributors demonstrated this commitment by consistently responding with timely professionalism. And while they do not have papers in this volume we are also grateful for the participation and contributions of Karen Stanbridge and Rima Wilkes. We would also like to thank Nathan Young for his generous contributions to the workshop.

Kathleen Rodgers would like to thank Norah Rankin for her research assistance, as well as her support during the organization of the workshop.

Howard Ramos similarly acknowledges the research work done for this volume by Paul Pritchard and is thankful to NSPIRG (Nova Scotia Public Interest Research Group) for the loan of buttons used in the cover image.

We are also grateful for the entire team at UBC Press. In particular, we would like to thank Emily Andrew and Ann Macklem, as well as all of the staff at UBC Press for their work on this book. In addition, the three anonymous reviewers who challenged us with their in-depth and thoughtful comments have made valuable contributions to the final manuscript.

We also gratefully acknowledge financial support for this research from the Social Sciences and Humanities Research Council of Canada, the Aid to Scholarly Publications Program, as well as the support from the Faculty of Social Sciences at the University of Ottawa.

Moreover, insightful comments from our colleagues and students at the University of Ottawa and Dalhousie University provided us with encouragement for this project.

Kathleen would like to thank Raine, Liam, Darcy, and the rest of her family for their unfailing support and Howard would like to thank them and his own family for their patience and ongoing encouragement.

PROTEST AND POLITICS

Introduction

The Promise of Social Movement Societies

HOWARD RAMOS AND KATHLEEN RODGERS

Scholars, pundits, and policymakers have for many years lamented the steady decline in voter turnout in democratic countries around the world (Putnam 2000; Dalton 2002). Such trends have been documented in many advanced industrial societies, including the United States, the European Union, and Japan. Canada has been no exception. In the 2011 federal election, voter turnout was just 61.4 percent, which was up only slightly from the previous election, which set a record for the lowest rate in the nation's history. This is a far cry from the 79.4 percent turnout in the 1958 federal election (CBC News 2011) and is a sign of serious problems with the country's democratic political institutions. But to assume from these data that people are becoming either less political or apathetic would be incorrect. In fact, one doesn't have to look far to see the spread of contention and politics by other means around the world.

The "Arab Spring" saw unprecedented demonstrations across the Middle East and a sea change of power, with rulers in Tunisia, Egypt, Libya, and Yemen forced out of their positions. Contention spread throughout the region and has had long-lasting effects. The anti-austerity protests that swept across Europe are also evidence of the spread of such contentious politics. The Greek protests and the Spanish *Indignados* show that people are indeed still very political. The rise of the Occupy Movement, moreover, which spread from Canada to Wall Street and then the rest of the world, with protests in at least twenty-three different countries and all continents except Antarctica, is yet again evidence of politics by other means, as were the Quebec student movement (the "Maple Spring") or the unexpected rise and prominence of Idle No More. Such widespread mobilization has led some to claim that the transnational spread of protest during the 2010s rivals that of the late 1960s (Sidney Tarrow interview, in Stewart 2011). If that is indeed true, people are by no means politically apathetic. Instead, their discontent is increasingly expressed outside dominant institutions.

At the same time, states have begun to incorporate extra-institutional politics into their everyday operations. It has become standard practice for municipalities, politicians, and police forces to accommodate protesters by issuing permits for protest, setting up zones for demonstrations, and even offering resources for organizing dissent. This has led some to claim that public demonstrations have become so common that they are "a routine part of political bargaining" (Jenkins, Wallace, and Fullerton 2008, 12). The use of subpolitics rather than engagements with representative democracy and traditional avenues of party politics has been on the rise (Beck 1992; Castells 2004). This has meant that states and mainstream political actors regularly reach out to movements, non-governmental organizations (NGOs), and advocacy groups in their consultations, deliberations, and development of policies (Buček and Smith 2000). In effect, protest and contentious politics have become regularized.

Social Movement Society Thesis

David Meyer and Sidney Tarrow (1998) accounted for many of these trends by arguing that advanced democracies were becoming a "social movement society" (SMS). They observed that mobilization had changed from risky, contentious, and outside-of-the-state in the 1960s to predictable, accommodating, and partially incorporated into the state by the 1990s. More specifically, they raised three hypotheses, which we refer to as the "SMS thesis": (1) social protest moved from being a sporadic to a perpetual feature of contemporary life; (2) contentious action is more common and is used by a wider range of social actors; and (3) professionalization and institutionalization of social movements place them in the realm of conventional politics (Meyer and Tarrow 1998, 4).

Since their initial theorization of the concept, over 380 articles (according to Google Scholar at the time this chapter was being written) have cited their work, and many researchers have expanded upon the SMS thesis to add a fourth dimension: the institutionalization of state responses to social movements and protests in particular (Soule and Earl 2005, 346). Others have empirically examined the thesis and arrived at mixed results (e.g., Rucht and Neidhardt 2002; McAdam et al. 2005; Soule and Earl 2005; Jenkins, Wallace, and Fullerton 2008), sparking ongoing interest in seeing how the SMS thesis fits now, more than fifteen years later – in a context characterized by new waves of mobilization in the wake of the Great Recession.

During the spring of 2012, we organized a workshop in Ottawa, inviting scholars from across Canada and the United States to engage the SMS thesis. The goal of the workshop, and now this book, was to revisit the SMS thesis with new analysis and data to see whether it is still applied and to see what insights could be gleaned from Canadian movements in order to understand the relationships between movements and mainstream politics. We believe that this is an important endeavour as austerity measures have meant widespread cuts to social programs and a reshaping of contemporary politics. The goal of this edited collection of essays is thus not to provide a comprehensive examination of social movements in Canada but rather to see what Canadian social movements and scholars can contribute towards an understanding of the possibilities and realities of a social movement society.

Possibilities and Realities

As the Arab Spring, anti-austerity protests, *Indignados*, the Occupy Movement, the Maple Spring, and Idle No More all show, Meyer and Tarrow's argument (1998) still has much merit when trying to understand recent politics. The cases show that a *diffusion* of actions and movements has occurred in contemporary politics; that contentious tactics, as well as social movements, are more common; and that they tend to reach further – beyond the scope of locales or states – than they did decades ago. In addition, the cases show that the *form* of politics and movements has begun to change, with social movements, NGOs, and advocacy groups blending with mainstream political organizations to evoke change. This is seen with the toppling of dictators in the case of the Arab Spring, and, arguably, with the launching of the discourse of the 2012 US presidential election in the case of the Occupy Movement. As a consequence of both diffusion and changing forms of mobilization, the *institutionalization* of social movements and contentious politics has occurred. This has meant that movements have greater access to mainstream institutions, while at the same time those institutions are increasingly shaped by the subpolitics that surround them. Canada and its social movements appear to fit similar patterns of diffusion, form, and institutionalization. In fact, as a country, it has been an ideal-type case of a social movement society.

Widespread social movements and protest are far from new. In Canada one can readily cite as examples the social gospel and reform movement of the 1890s and early twentieth century, or the second wave of the temperance movement that influenced the United Kingdom, the United States, and Canada after the First World War, or the first wave of the women's movement that swept the world in the early twentieth century. During the post–Second World War period, however, and especially since the mid-1960s and 1970s, Canada has seen the rise of a wide range of social movements that have played a significant role in nation building (Pal 1993). Canada's Indigenous movements, for example, rose to prominence after widespread protest in 1969, laying the groundwork for the development of many national Indigenous organizations in the 1970s, including the Congress of Aboriginal Peoples, the Inuit Tapiriit Kanatami, and the Native Women's Association of Canada.[1] Indigenous organizations were not alone. During the same period, numerous influential Canadian social movements and advocacy organizations rose to prominence. The National Action Committee on the Status of Women (NAC), Greenpeace, and the Gay Alliance Toward Equality are just a sampling of organizations founded during this period.[2] In fact, the 1970s may have been a far more important decade for Canadian social movements and advocacy groups than the 1960s. The timing and spread of contention certainly fit the SMS model of diffusion.

Canada is an interesting case study because although these organizations participated in protest tactics and supported activists, many were also founded in part because of funds distributed by the Canadian Secretary of State, which aided pure advocacy organizations (see Pal 1993, 7), as well as other federal ministries (see Clément 2008a; Rodgers and Knight 2011). A prominent example can be seen in the founding of the Company of Young Canadians (CYC) in 1966 with the support of the federal government (Dickerson and Campbell 2008, 3), which in turn led some to label the group "government funded hell-raisers" (Brushett 2009, 247). Such practices continued into the 1970s and were amplified with the promotion of Prime Minister Pierre Trudeau's vision of creating a "just society." Much Canadian social justice mobilization has thus largely, despite some exceptions, been dependent on resources and opportunities provided by the state in an effort to build citizenship and the nation (Pal 1993). Again we find evidence for the SMS argument, where the form of mobilization has been blurred between those acting inside and outside of the state. As a result, although early mobilizing occurred during the 1960s and earlier (see Palaeologu 2009 for an edited volume on the decade), the 1970s were important because they were a decade of growth, prosperity, and opportunity for social justice organizations.

The Canadian state has been an important source of funding and opportunities for movements and social justice groups. As Lipset (1986, 1990) has argued, Canadians are less averse to collectiveness and the state than Americans.[3] This has meant that they are less likely to engage in voluntary activity, and in turn participate in a true civil society that is independent of state intervention. It has also meant that many organizations, as can be seen with the Indigenous, women's, and human rights movements, have depended on the federal government for "core funding" of their operations. In many respects, during the 1970s the government was anxious to avoid social unrest caused by unemployed baby boomers and funded a surge of new programs designed for students and youth. Programs such as the CYC, Opportunities for Youth (OFY), and the Local Initiative Program (LIP) served two functions: funding or creating social justice initiatives and offering jobs to young Canadians. The institutionalization of movements and the blurring of politics is clearly seen in how young, government-funded, organizations engaged political opportunities around nation building.

The process of patriating Canada's Constitution during the early 1980s sparked the emergence of unprecedented political opportunities for social movements, advocacy groups, and others seeking social justice (Pal 1993). The federal government openly solicited input from Indigenous organizations, the women's movement, and countless other interest groups. Miriam Smith (2005a, 146) argues that "prior to the 1982 Constitution, legal opportunities were limited for interest groups and social movements." In fact, Section 15 of the Constitution recognized "equal rights," offering new opportunities for mobilization around race, religion, sex, and ability, and leading to a questioning of the lack of protections and rights for many others, such as the lesbian, gay, bisexual, and transgendered (LGBT) communities. In her other work Smith (2005b, 2007) notes that the Constitution was the basis of much mobilization by LGBT organizations in the 1980s and 1990s. It was also central to the success of the movement in gaining recognition of same-sex marriage in 2005 through the Civil Marriage Act. The same section also played a key role in the lobbying for an apology by

Japanese Canadians interned during the Second World War and led to the founding of the Canadian Race Relations Foundation. The Constitution has played such a central role in Canadian social justice mobilization that conservatives lament that its use by movement organizations has led to a "Charter revolution" in which the Supreme Court has become activist and overly influenced by "special interests" (Morton and Knopff 2000). Since patriation, the Constitution has been used by those concerned with the access to and the right to abortion, Indigenous rights, LGBT rights, bilingualism, and prisoner voting. It is a central tool for social justice.

During this period, the Canadian state even promoted the use of the courts by social movement and advocacy organizations. This can be seen through the funding of the Court Challenges Program (CCP) between 1985 and 1992 and then again between 1994 and 2006, to provide financial assistance and support for cases dealing with equity rights under the Constitution. As Bashevkin (1996, 229) found, many feminists credited the program with the successes of NAC during its peak years of prominence in the late 1980s. The program was also important in the same-sex marriage fight in the 2000s as seen through its use by Egale, one of Canada's leading LGBT organizations; in turn, the CCP sought out Egale's expertise in preparation of Case Development Reports and legal analyses of decisions (Egale Canada 2011). As a result, unlike in other countries, where close ties between mainstream political institutions and movements has been lamented as a form of co-optation (Piven and Cloward 1979), this has not been the case in Canada. From the very outset, Canadian movements and social justice organizations have tended to rely on the state for their very existence, and they were given room to challenge the state and promote social change. The state, moreover, has depended on movements and NGOs to help deliver services and build a Canadian nation that is distinct from others – one that is socially just.

This historical trajectory of the relationship between the Canadian state and civil society actors clearly fits the main propositions of the SMS thesis. It is less clear, however, whether this relationship will continue into the future. Neoliberal policies took root in the late 1980s and have only become more prominent since. As a result, the relationship between advocacy groups and the federal government became increasingly antagonistic. Core funding to organizations was increasingly scrutinized and the cabinet position of the Secretary of State ended in 1996. The responsibilities for funding advocacy organizations were dispersed to other ministries and have increasingly diminished, leading to a true attack on the interdependence between organizations and the state in recent years.

As Sylvia Bashevkin (2009, 137) notes, with respect to the women's movement, in 2006 the federal government cut the budget of Status of Women Canada, a federal agency overseen by the Minister for Status of Women, by $5 million, or about a fifth of its budget at the time. Similar cuts were seen in other government agencies and affected a wide range of organizations. The fate of the Canadian women's movement is so precarious that as we write the once-prominent NAC, which hosted national election leadership debates in 1984 (Bashevkin 1996, 219), no longer even maintains a website. As one representative of a women's organization commented in this context: "After all of the assaults we have suffered over the years with the chipping away at the funding and program mandates and all of that, this was like the axe in the chest ... you just felt the collective wind being knocked out of us ... it was a palpable feeling of defeat" (Rodgers and Knight 2011).

In 2006, the Conservative government continued to cement neoliberal policies that were promoted by previous governments in the 1990s and 2000s, and ultimately cut funding to the CCP. This again affected the promotion of women's rights, and was followed by a range of attacks on social justice organizations more generally. In 2012, for instance, the federal government introduced restrictions to the ability of charitable foundations to fund political activities. The government also increased sanctions against charities that do not comply with the "10 percent rule," which mandates that no more than that amount can be used for political advocacy by a given charity (Waldie 2012). This now means that charities have to be cautious about formally supporting well-known direct action groups like Greenpeace or advocacy groups like Amnesty International for fear of sanctions.

The Conservative government also attacked NGOs critical of its policies. The Minister of Natural Resources, for instance, attacked Tides Canada, a Vancouver-based charity, when it opposed the Northern Gateway pipeline, and the Minister of Citizenship and Immigration attacked No One Is Illegal, which defends the rights of temporary foreign workers and illegal migrants. The situation has gotten so bad that it even led long-time and famed environmentalist David Suzuki to leave the board of the charity bearing his name to avoid undermining its work in the wake of Conservative bullying (S. McCarthy and Moore 2012). Other organizations, such as ForestEthics, which targeted the Canadian energy industry by encouraging large US firms to avoid the use of fuel derived from Alberta oil sands, have opted to give up their charitable status in order to ensure their ability to take a critical stance towards the federal government.

Public support for advocacy organizations also appears to be falling. The 2006 decision to cut funding to the CCP was met with little public outcry, and recent national polling shows that one of the most popular 2012 federal budget items was the requirement that charities provide more information on their political activities and their funding by foreign sources. Eighty percent of Canadians voiced their support of these policies (Brennan 2012). Polling by Nanos Research for the *Globe and Mail* and *La Presse* (Mackrael 2011), however, found that 58 percent of Canadians who were aware of the Occupy Movement protests were favourable or somewhat favourable towards them. What do these conflicting patterns mean for the SMS argument?

We believe that trends witnessed in the Canadian case provide opportunities to refine the SMS position in at least three areas. First, Canadian mobilization raises questions about the timing of the emergence of an SMS. Second, the Canadian case also raises questions about the usefulness of the social movement literature's treatment of movements as unique and separate from other forms of politics. The SMS argument notes a recent blurring of political space, but we believe that this is an artefact of much of the literature rather than a historical fact. Last, the Canadian case calls into question the notion of a singular social movement society, versus plural social movement societies. One of the reasons Canada invested in legislating equity policies and building its civil society as a part of nation building was the threat of Quebec nationalism. Likewise, the changes Canadians are witnessing with respect to social justice in the country reflect the regionalism of Canada and the rise of Alberta-based politics associated with extreme neoliberal policies. They do not reflect the significant differences seen in attitudes and actions in British Columbia, Ontario, or Quebec, which have all seen much mobilization in recent years. They also do not reflect the increasingly transnational ties that foster mobilization. Let us briefly elaborate on each of these observations.

Timing

Although Meyer and Tarrow (1998) popularized the notion of social movement society and used it to understand the changes from the 1960s to the new century, one can cite the acceptance and spread of widespread mobilization in earlier times. As we noted above, the social gospel and reform movement, the temperance movement, and the first wave of the women's movement all point to elements of a social movement society long before the end of the twentieth century. Others, such as Rucht and Neidhardt (2002, 7), moreover, claim to have used the concept with caution much earlier than Meyer and Tarrow. They also cite similar concepts by Etzioni (1970) ("demonstration democracy") or Pross (1992) ("protest society") as evidence of earlier realizations that protest had become a feature of routine politics. These observations parallel the comments by Jenkins and colleagues (2008) cited above but came almost thirty years earlier. In their reflection on the state and emergence of the social movement literature McAdam and colleagues (2005, 2) note that one of its deficiencies has been its tendency to be ahistorical, which the comparison to Etzioni (1970) and Jenkins and colleagues (2008) accentuate. McAdam and colleagues (2005) also note that the social movement literature has tended to focus on disruptive politics in public settings, national campaigns, urban-based protest, and struggles by disenfranchised groups. Their analyses of contentious action in and around Chicago show that such a focus misses much of the mobilization that goes on. Some of this suggests that the Canadian case may not be so exceptional after all, and that the roots of the SMS came earlier than originally thought. The historical applicability of the SMS thesis thus warrants further investigation.

Political Space

Others have shown that the blurring of political action and form, from protests outside the mainstream system to lobbying inside it, has been a feature of most modern politics. The social movement literature's tendency to denote a unique space separate from other forms of politics does little to advance our understanding of social change, and instead does more to advance the careers of those in the area. That said, many contributors to the social movement literature have shown how different tactics and forms of mobilization are often interrelated. Haines (1995), for instance, showed that the radical actions of more militant African American activists in the 1960s benefited the more moderate organizations of the period and even led to increased financial support for them. Suzanne Staggenborg (1998) showed the importance of culture and communities in women's mobilization, especially in periods of abeyance or when political opportunities do not promote mobilization. And the resource mobilization approach introduced by McCarthy and Zald (1977) focused on professionalization, entrepreneurs, and resources. It didn't highlight chequebook activism per se, but certainly showed that many advocates of social change participate through formally organized institutions of civil society. As Goldstone (2004) rightly notes, much mobilization has been by groups of influence and not the disenfranchised. He shows a strong relationship between the growth of normal democratic politics and social movements, leading one to ask whether in fact social movements are synonymous with democracy. This might account for why Corrigall-Brown (2012) found that two-thirds of Americans in her analysis claim to have belonged to a social movement organization. Again, we find that the Canadian case is not unique and that these observations both support the SMS model and contradict it. They are the outcome observed in the SMS thesis, but they are far from new or the end result of a move from radical to institutionalized politics. Again we find a point for further elaboration. The blurring of political action and form has likely existed as long as groups have become political.

Social Movement Societies – Plural

Something that may be somewhat unique to the Canadian case is the extent to which one might think of social movement societies – plural rather than singular. This is in part because much of the mobilization witnessed in the country in the postwar period, especially during the 1960s and beyond, has been linked to Canadian nation-state building (Pal 1993). While the notion of a "just society" was advocated by Pierre Trudeau as early as his first election campaign to become prime minister in 1968, it is equally tied to threats against the Canadian state. As Soule and Earl (2005) note, mobilization and the SMS thesis are inherently linked to the political context examined. If one is to take that seriously, with respect to the Canadian case it is paramount for one to account for the role of Quebec and Quebec nationalism in the building of social movement societies within the country. Clément (2008a) has noted rightly that much of the work on Canadian mobilization has ignored francophone insights. One must also account for the ongoing role of colonization with respect to First Nations and the fact that Canada is an officially multicultural society. All of these have meant that mobilization and political action and form have largely been regional, and much has been identity-based. This can be seen in the widespread protests by Quebec students in 2012. It can also be seen in the province's continued election of separatist or left-of-centre federal parties. And it can be seen in the continued success of many movements in that province when they are threatened elsewhere. The ongoing strength and prominence of the Fédération des femmes du Québec (FFQ) is just one example.

The importance of new information technology, such as the Internet and social media and their widespread use in Canada, has also meant that mobilization is increasingly transnational. This is amplified by the large number of diaspora communities living in the country. It has meant that Canada, to use the language of Tarrow (2005), is filled with "rooted cosmopolitans" who act in the name of foreign causes within the country and also support them from abroad. One can readily point to Tamil immigrants who shut down the Gardiner Expressway, a major highway running through Toronto, in 2009 to protest the harsh repression of their people in Sri Lanka (Jeyapal 2013). The importance of the Internet and social media in mobilization can also account for the role that Vancouver-based Adbusters played in sparking the Occupy movement and the rapid spread of Idle No More. It also partially accounts for some of the contradictions found between, on the one hand, high levels of support for mobilization and, on the other, approval of cuts to state funding of organizations and the role they play in mainstream politics. That is, we live in an era of media, political, and cultural solitude – what David Meyer and Amanda Pullum call silos (see Chapter 1). We may in fact communicate, challenge power, and appreciate identities around one another with fewer chances to engage one another.

For at least these three reasons (timing, political space, and societies in the plural), we believe it is important to critically ask whether Canada fits the SMS thesis and whether the country can be used as a case to extend and refine the SMS argument. We also believe that the SMS thesis should be engaged in the Canadian context because of the rapid changes in relationships between social movements, advocacy groups, and the Canadian state witnessed in recent years. Only with analysis and systematic engagement can those changes be fully understood.

An Outline of This Book

Many of the chapters in this volume expand upon our insights on the timing of the SMS argument, the theorizing of political space, and the notion of social movement societies, plural rather than singular. They also expound on the SMS thesis, test its assumptions, and contribute to social movement theory by identifying mechanisms of social movement societies and approaches to understanding contemporary mobilization. The goal of this book is to assess the SMS thesis, and this is done by looking at four issues: (1) the role of political and historical context; (2) the dimensions of state and movement dynamics and processes; (3) how people participate in contentious politics; and (4) the role of the production of knowledge and culture.

The first chapter consists of David Meyer and Amanda Pullum's reflections on the SMS thesis. Like us, they recognize that much has changed since Meyer and Tarrow initially conceived it. They pay special attention to the rise of nativist, fundamentalist, and conservative identity-based movements, as well as the rapid rise of Web 2.0 technology or changes in mass communication, and the costs and consequences of institutionalizing mobilization in changing both movement and mainstream politics. They examine these issues through a discussion of American populism and the Tea Party and Occupy movements. Many of their insights accord well with other chapters in the volume. Others, such as Tina Fetner, Allyson Stokes, and Carrie Sanders in Chapter 2 or Philippe Couton in Chapter 6, recognize the role of nativist politics and populism. The role of new technologies is engaged by Jim Conley in Chapter 10 and Mark Stoddart in Chapter 13, and institutionalization is analyzed by Dominque Clément in Chapter 3, Dominique Masson in Chapter 4, and Catherine Corrigall-Brown and Mabel Ho in Chapter 5. Chapter 1 thus offers an ideal point of entry into the role of historical and social context as well as the other chapters of this book.

The political and institutional history of mobilization is examined further in Chapters 2, 3, and 4. All three chapters show that the existence of social movement societies spans a greater period than the 1960s generation, and that the relationship between movements and states can be more complicated than the asymmetrical and confrontational position identified by many social movement scholars. The religious right in Canada and the United States is examined by Fetner, Stokes, and Sanders in Chapter 2. Through comparative analysis, they look at the influence of historical forces on social movements and the role of the institutional infrastructure of media on mobilization. More specifically, they show how larger media organizations, reaching a wider audience and with less restrictive policies, benefited the American religious right, compared with the narrower field of media in Canada, where the religious right saw less success. In Chapter 3, Clément also offers a historical account of mobilization, looking at the human rights movement in British Columbia. He shows how the women's movement and human rights activists were key players in the development of what he calls the "human rights state." They were important actors in the creation of policies, laws, and sections of the Constitution – all of which show that movements and NGOs are important subpolitical actors. They both influence states and are looked upon by states to implement and develop policy. The relationship between movements and the state is examined yet further by Masson in Chapter 4. She too looks at the women's movement, but focuses on Quebec. In doing so, she shows, like Fetner and colleagues and Clément, that historical and political forces shape the mobilization of movements even as movements shape those forces. She argues that it is essential for social movement scholars, and those looking at social movement societies in particular, to revise their understanding of the relationship between movements and states. The relationship is by no means one-sided, and movements are important political actors.

The relationship between movements and the state is examined further in Part 2, "State Dynamics and Processes." The chapters in this part show, as we have argued, that the political space of the SMS thesis needs expanding. In Chapter 5, Corrigall-Brown and Ho look at the role of state funding in the Canadian environmental movement. They expand upon some of the insights offered by Masson and others in Part 1, on political and historical context and the role of government funding. More specifically, they compare the media activism of the World Wildlife Fund and Greenpeace before and after changes in government and recent cuts to funding for environmental groups. They show that the organizations had different responses, pointing to the need to look not only at context but also at the properties of organizational actors. Their chapter is followed by Philippe Couton's analysis of immigrant mobilization and socio-economic integration in Chapter 6. The role of immigrants in politics has been receiving increasing attention. Arguably, changing demographics as a result of immigration are shifting the way in which politics are conducted worldwide. Couton, moreover, changes the focus of social movement outcomes from direct political changes in mainstream institutions to how mobilization also shapes economic power. In doing so, he expands the analysis of SMS from looking at the relationship between movements and states to looking at movements and broader forms of power. As with the other chapters in Part 2, Lesley Wood's focus in Chapter 7 is on the relationship between movements and the state. She looks at the diffusion of a dual model of policing protests in the post-9/11 context. Her chapter challenges the nature of social movement societies – it finds that although protest is possibly becoming routinized, it is by no means less radical, and the relationship between some activists and the police is increasingly suspicious.

How people participate in social movement societies is examined in the chapters of Part 3. In Chapter 8, Suzanne Staggenborg synthesizes a number of the insights of the earlier chapters by looking at the role of social movement communities in the SMS argument. Like Fetner, Stokes, and Sanders, she argues that it is important to consider the prefigurative elements that support movements, and like Masson and Corrigall-Brown and Ho she contemplates the role states play in those communities. She does this by comparing the World March of Women in Quebec with G-20 protests in Pittsburgh. She argues that social movement scholars need to move beyond merely counting and documenting protests to also consider the conditions that induce them. Judith Taylor follows this in Chapter 9 with an analysis of a local movement against dirty diesel trains in Toronto. She assesses how and why local activists participate in everyday mobilization, and theorizes why many prefer "gentle activism" or "contention in disguise" rather than more overt and radical action. In Chapter 10, Jim Conley examines these issues further by introducing concepts of French pragmatic sociology. Specifically, he shows how people escalate grievances along orders of worth, moving analysis beyond more simplistic frames of injustice. His analysis effectively shows, moreover, how Web 2.0 is used in the negotiation of a local grievance in Toronto between a cyclist and a driver. It shows, like the other chapters in Part 3 and our own observation, that the SMS thesis demands more complex notions of both movements and societies. Similar arguments are made by David Tindall and Joanna Robinson in Chapter 11. They question how "membership" in movements is understood and analyzed. Specifically, they examine whether or not it is safe to assume that belonging to an organization is the same as being active in public protests. In doing so, they empirically test one of the main claims of Meyer and Tarrow's initial SMS thesis (1998) – that activism is becoming more common and widespread.

Part 4 looks at how people participate; it does so contemplating the role of knowledge and culture and how it factors into the SMS argument. The chapters here go beyond our look at societies, plural, in the SMS by offering insight into how culture shapes those societies. These chapters accord well with earlier chapters that look into what generates social movement societies, such as Clément looking at subpolitics, Masson looking at relations, or Staggenborg's consideration of communities. In Chapter 12, William Carroll analyzes the scale of the SMS and looks at how knowledge production is generated among organizations of the global North and South. He looks at how organizations make claims and generate counter-hegemonic information. In Chapter 13, Mark Stoddart looks at the cultural work of two local environmental movements in British Columbia and Nova Scotia. Like Staggenborg, he urges social movement scholars to step outside of their usual spaces of analysis – national movements and "factual" counts of mobilization. In Chapter 14, Randolph Haluza-DeLay also looks at the cultural work of movements. Examining how environmentalists frame their mobilization and Albertan identity, he shows the importance of looking at challenging socio-hegemonic norms in addition to focusing on institutional changes.

We wrap up the book in the Conclusion by revisiting the SMS argument and considering how our collective work contributes to the promise of social movement societies. It is our hope that you will find the chapters in this edited collection both thought-provoking and useful to your work.

Notes

1 The Congress of Aboriginal Peoples was originally founded in 1971 as the Native Council of Canada. It currently represents Indigenous peoples living off Indian reserves. The Inuit Tapiriit Kanatami was founded in 1971 as the Inuit Tapirisat of Canada. It represents Inuit peoples living in Northern Canada. The Native Women's Association of Canada was founded in 1973 and represents Indigenous women.

2 Interestingly, all three organizations were founded in 1971.

3 He is not without his critics. See, for example, Baer, Grabb, and Johnston 1990.

PART 1

POLITICAL AND HISTORICAL CONTEXT

1

Reconsidering the Social Movement Society in the New Century

DAVID S. MEYER AND AMANDA PULLUM

Don't look back, legendary pitcher Satchel Paige warned, something may be gaining on you. What's true for baseball must be at least as true for social science, where the careers are longer and almost everything is in print. It's always dangerous to think seriously about what we've said in the past, particularly if one is prepared to prognosticate (Tetlock 2005). The risks of overconfidence, naiveté, and just plain ignorance are evident. We therefore approach a re-examination of the social movement society with some trepidation.

More than fifteen years ago, when one of us (David Meyer) and Sid Tarrow thought about the social movement society, they extrapolated from what they saw around them to imagine a world in which social movement politics were ubiquitous. At one level, it's easy to make a claim about the frequency, diversity, and importance of social movements since then, pointing to, for example, the colour revolutions across Eastern Europe, the mobilizations against austerity across all of Europe, anti-immigrant campaigns, the Arab Spring, and the Tea Party and Occupy movements in the United States.

That there is plenty of mobilization in the streets, and not just in the wealthy countries, suggests that Meyer and Tarrow got at least some things right in *The Social Movement Society* (1998). At the same time, they situated their analysis in a larger understanding of the politics of advanced industrial societies that emphasized the flexibility and resilience of those states, and the availability of multiple reliable paths towards the political institutionalization of dissent. This understanding is well worth re-examining. It's also completely appropriate to look at the magnitude of economic, technological, and political challenges that have emerged in the first part of this century, which have been more extensive than Meyer and Tarrow imagined at the end of the last one. They wrote after the end of the Cold War, but before the World Trade Center attacks and the emergence of intense battles in Western societies around fundamentalist religious movements, particularly Islamic movements. They wrote when technological changes in communication and transportation were proceeding rapidly, but could not anticipate how far those developments would go and have gone. And they wrote before the global economic slowdown in 2008, which radically changed the character of claims and constituencies animating social movements. It's time to re-think and update their initial ideas.

Towards that end, we appreciate the opportunity to conduct this re-examination publicly and collectively, in sight of thoughtful colleagues. To start, in this chapter we will briefly summarize the claims of the social movement society approach, emphasizing and extending some of the arguments that we realize, in retrospect, could have been made more clearly. We then want to point to a few things that Meyer and Tarrow didn't anticipate, specifically the magnitude of nativist challenges in advanced industrial states, often focused in campaigns against immigrants and immigration; the stress on the euro (direct) and the concomitant stress on the European Union (less direct so far); the appropriation of public spaces by challenging movements; and the magnitude and consequence of technological advances and their impact on the nature of social movement politics. Having summarized these broad issues, we will discuss them as seen in the contending cases of two populist movements in the United States, the Tea Party and Occupy movements, paying particular attention to the dilemmas of institutionalization.

The Social Movement Society

We begin with an acknowledgment of a basic approach to social protest that emphasizes the ongoing connections between movements and the world around them, closely tied to political process accounts of movements (Meyer 2004). The premise is that the history of social movements is less a break from more institutional politics than a continuation of those processes by additional means (see, for example, Chapters 2, 4, and 7). Although some activists are committed to particular movement forms or specific definitions of issues that essentially force their politics outdoors, most people engage in movement politics only when they won't get what they want without it, and protest politics represent at least the possibility of influence (Meyer 2007).

Meyer and Tarrow (1998) invoked the social movement society idea based on their understandings of movement politics in relatively open polities with relatively well-developed economies, thinking of North America and Europe. Implicitly, they were agnostic about how protest politics might develop in authoritarian states and poorer societies; explicitly, they were silent. The Arab Spring and the people power movements in Southeast Asia offer the opportunity to extend and refine the social movement society hypothesis (Alimi and Meyer 2011). For the moment, we will leave those questions to others. For now, we will retreat to use the cases we know best to explain the conceptions underlying the social movement society.

The history of social movements in the United States is animated by fights for political inclusion lodged by (and on behalf of) groups without the political access or resources to exercise influence without protest. For the most part, the largest movements of the first two centuries of American life represented people who were visibly excluded, most notably property-less workers, African Americans, and women. (To be sure, populist conservatism and nativism have episodically mobilized in opposition to the threats from those rising constituencies.) Sometimes, smaller numbers of people challenged government on other issues: progressives pushed for urban reform and government transparency (Stromquist 2006); pacifists campaigned against war and imperialism (Chatfield 1992); and, led by feminists, reformers advocated (successfully) for temperance (Szymanski 2003).

After the Second World War, however, large and sometimes sustained mobilizations by groups composed of people who ostensibly enjoyed access to mainstream American life and politics emerged with greater vigour, size, and frequency. Anti-nuclear weapons, environmental, and anti–Vietnam War campaigns, to name a few, were animated by middle-class white people who claimed that they lacked meaningful access to decisions that affected their lives. In effect, their efforts argued that the availability of conventional democratic remedies for redress (party activism, election campaigns, lobbying, and more routine civic engagement) were insufficient. On the left and the right, activists identified similar categories of culprits: self-interested politicians who ignored them; well-established interest groups who looked after narrow concerns; non-responsive government; and mobilized opponents.

Over the last fifty years, in the United States, and indeed in other wealthy countries, it seems that the routine means of access to political influence have been inadequate and unsatisfying for virtually everyone involved. Liberal democratic states face new economic and governance challenges that make it very hard for them to satisfy any claimant. The culprits include the growth of the administrative state and the decline of meaningful political parties (Ginsberg and Shefter 2002). Thus, we have seen the permanent establishment of groups that represent interests that are only occasionally visible to the larger public (e.g., various corporate and trade associations; peace concerns; abortion rights [for and against]; gun rights [for and against]).

Ironically, the growth of mobilization leads to more mobilization, through demonstration effects and countermobilization. Advocates who see activists get what they want through protest are likely to take to the streets themselves. Opponents of the reforms social movements effect are likely to mobilize as oppositional movements (Meyer and Staggenborg 1996). Moreover, as more diverse groups take to the streets to influence policy – on multiple sides of any issue – it is harder and harder for government to take the initiative or, more generally, to govern, thus spurring more frustration – and the basis for more diverse and continual mobilization.

The concept of a social movement society was an effort to unify a series of observations about protest politics, and to make sense of a trend that had developed over the last half of the twentieth century. Provocatively, Meyer and Tarrow (1998) asserted that their observations reflected the nature of social movements and politics for the twenty-first century. Let us summarize the social movement society's basic claims, and then suggest what Meyer and Tarrow may have missed.

Previous understandings of social movements have viewed social protest as an effort to even the odds by those who are poorly positioned to make claims effectively through conventional politics (e.g., Lipsky 1970; Tilly 1978). The disadvantaged could use disruption to bring attention to their cause, to engage latent support, and to mobilize countervailing resources. In relatively closed or repressive polities, this meant that anyone outside the ruling group might try to launch protest movements. In advanced industrialized democracies, however, people who were disadvantaged politically, economically, or socially were the ones who would use protest to try to make gains. Either way, movements were a tool for enhancing democratic participation in politics. Meyer and Tarrow challenged this understanding.

First, they argued that the tactics that defined social protest movements in the past had spread across causes and constituencies through a process of diffusion (Givan, Roberts, and Soule 2010). Specifically, demonstrations and rallies, pickets and petitions, and citizen lobbying were no longer confined to groups that could be readily defined as "excluded." Very directly, they challenged the "polity model" (Tilly 1978; Gamson 1990), which viewed social protest as a strategy for those poorly positioned to get what they wanted otherwise, and that would give the excluded ones access, if not direct results. It's not just the white middle class that picked up the picket sign, but even elected officials and representatives of affluent constituencies. Well-heeled interests were increasingly willing to take up the challenge of protest politics, not as a substitute but as an add-on to other tactics of influence. As a corollary, Meyer and Tarrow noted that participating in protest tactics was no longer as stigmatizing, and changes in attitudes spurred changes in activism. Such tactics were also less of a break from more conventional influence strategies, such that lobbyists would hold rallies while movement activists would organize citizen lobbying campaigns. There would be little separation between movement politics and more conventional interest group advocacy.

Second, Meyer and Tarrow argued that as new groups took on social movement styles of politics, movements would become less episodic and more sustained. This doesn't mean, of course, that demonstrations would become continual, but that the efforts to promote particular visions of social good using a range of movement tactics would not end with defeat or victory but would instead continue through more ambiguous outcomes. Ongoing movements would develop the facility to shift foci and emphases over time, in responses to changes in political opportunities, continuing their campaigns across a range of issues.

Third, to coordinate ongoing campaigns, social movements would rely upon formal organizations and networks of movement professionals, skilled at organizing, fundraising, and communications, and expert in sets of relevant issues. Formalized organizations would be more engaged in conventional politics as well as movement tactics, more opportunistic in response to less visible shifts in politics and policies, and, of course, to the survival of their organizations as well as their causes (J.D. McCarthy and Zald 1977; Staggenborg 1988). This means that movement infrastructure becomes permanent rather than ad hoc and improvised (see Chapters 3, 4, and 5). Formal organizations will increasingly rely on approaches and political strategies that they've invested in previously, even in the absence of evidence that they are likely to be effective (e.g., Meyer and Boutcher 2007). Moreover, well-established organizations develop relationships with one another, negotiate coalitions for particular campaigns, and share intelligence as well as resources and professional employees. Professionalization has led to increased dependence on financial resources for organizing movements and for supporting a permanent infrastructure as opposed to an urgent episode of contention. To some degree, this has always been the case, but Meyer and Tarrow argued that in the contemporary period it would be even more prevalent.

Fourth, because movement struggles aren't the province of the excluded and marginal and because campaigns last a long time, less disruptive tactics become more frequent, generally supplanting more disruptive tactics (McAdam, Sampson, Weffer, and MacIndoe 2005). On this point, it's important to emphasize that both movements and authorities have learned from the past, and continue to learn. Organizers will negotiate the contours of a demonstration or other event with police, planning timelines, boundaries, arrests, and publicity. Local police departments have generally become more adept at controlling demonstrations of dissent without resorting to overt violence or mass arrests, albeit with frequent exceptions.

Fifth, diversification of claims and claimants, professionalization of movement advocacy, negotiations with police, and increased tolerance have all contributed to make protest more frequent and consequently less disruptive (see Chapters 4, 5, and 7). Meyer and Tarrow speculated on the political consequences of this mood, wondering whether the dependence on financial resources and permanent organization would crowd out the interests of less-resourced interests, paradoxically meaning that even the social movement would become the province of the relatively advantaged.

More generally, however, they noted that the implications of such changes were largely unexplored, and posed fundamental questions about contemporary democracy. They asked whether the social movement society represented an increased democratization of political life in advanced industrialized societies or the effective neutralization of a tactic that had sometimes been useful to those without other access to political influence. They suggested that the more crowded social movement landscape made it harder for any new cause or constituency to break through the clutter of movements. If social movements become a part of routine politics, they asked, can they also be an effective means of redress for those normally excluded from mainstream politics?

What Meyer and Tarrow Missed

Meyer and Tarrow's observations were based on an understanding of movement politics of the past. Because social movements, particularly the civil rights and women's movements, had demonstrated influence, other claimants adopted their strategies. Taking emulation, institutionalization, professionalization, social learning, and generational change together, in a context of relative affluence, the social movement society became the dominant polity model in advanced liberal democracies. More than fifteen years later, however, there are elements to the social movement society that Meyer and Tarrow didn't take as seriously as they might have. This is an opportunity to examine what they missed.

First, they wrote about a left-leaning politics in the classical sense, based on organization, advocacy, and democratic political structures that enjoyed substantial legitimacy. They did not discuss challenges to liberal governance altogether. Meyer and Tarrow's articulation of the social movement society doesn't mention religious fundamentalist movements, including Islamism in Europe as well as the Middle East and North Africa, evangelical Christianity in the United States, and the romantic identity-based nationalist campaigns in both Europe and North America. Although it may be possible to interpret such campaigns as cloaks for old-style materialist interests, the battles are not articulated in that way; rather, the rhetoric is about race and nation in tones that make those committed to liberal democratic governance queasy. The fundamentalist challengers start with no inherent respect for democratic structures of procedures, seeing absolute truths that must be protected regardless of the assent of the majority. The protests they lodge are less appeals to authority than assertions of alternative authorities.

Second, although Meyer and Tarrow recognized the advent of new media and means of communication, which created a smaller world, they did not foresee the extent to which new technologies, social networking sites, and communication channels such as Twitter, Facebook, and YouTube would fundamentally change the terrain for social movements and democratic politics more generally. This is not to say that new technologies created new movements, but rather that the availability of additional means to publicize and organize movements altered what was possible for activists. The old understanding of media and social movements (e.g., Gans 1979; Gitlin 1981; Ryan 1991) viewed mainstream media as the necessary interlocutor between movement challengers and the political mainstream. Activists staged events to project their claims and their identities to a broader audience, depending upon mainstream media to project those concerns.

Although mainstream media still matter, activists have developed ways to get around them. Let us cite a few examples.

Because access to the World Wide Web is relatively easy and cheap (although certainly not universal), and online storage and display space is effectively unlimited, activists now enjoy the capacity to articulate their ideas to a much wider range of potential sympathizers. Consider, for example, the recent case of WikiLeaks. Although WikiLeaks founder Julian Assange negotiated with mainstream media outlets, including the *New York Times* (Zetter 2011), to report on hundreds of thousands of pages of US intelligence documents, he was able to post those documents himself on a website accessible to other media outlets and virtually anyone with an Internet connection. Compare this with an eventful leak decades earlier, when Daniel Ellsberg released the Pentagon Papers to major national newspapers. Ellsberg spent months smuggling and photocopying documents and negotiating with national papers for publication, and the US government could attempt to squelch the information by enjoining publication (Franklin 2001). Such a course of events is unimaginable today.

Since there are now a far greater number of outlets for information, each individual outlet has become less consequential for mainstream politics. No source or site enjoys the same dominance that large television networks or national newspapers did decades ago. The growth of new media has accompanied the atrophy of the old mainstream media and its dominance over conventional political understanding. Activists are no longer dependent upon getting into the *New York Times* or CBS News to get their message out; they have alternative outlets. But today no single outlet commands the attention that older outlets once claimed. Increasingly, people can read the news they want to read, often selected and digested with an eye to a particular audience, as a "narrowcasting" model has pushed out "broadcasting." There is no longer a singular mass media or mass public as earlier scholars suggested. This means that dissident positions may be able to find an audience more easily than in the past (Earl and Kimport 2011). It also means that dissident positions, including nativist and racist diatribes as well as disputed claims against science, cannot be effectively dismissed. As a whole, these changes are likely to have broadened and cheapened public discourse.

The growth of new media has changed the calculus for organizers seeking to get their message out. The new media have also dramatically changed the nature of recruitment to activism. The old saw in organizing, supported by data (Rosenstone and Hansen 1993), was that the most likely prospects for movement engagement were already engaged – in community organizations, churches, and social groups. People who had already committed to something were more likely to commit to something else; moreover, they were more likely to be asked. The online engaged are more accessible and less visible. Online social sites are different in some critical ways from social spaces located in the physical world. Online media also offer the prospects of different kinds of engagement. Moveon.org, for example, has been very successful in using the Internet to raise money, but much less successful in mobilizing other kinds of activism. Change.org posts petitions every day, it seems, but it's not clear that the kind of action encouraged is anything more than clicking affirmation. One question is whether Internet-based activism is limited to the Internet ("what happens on Facebook stays on Facebook"), or whether it can inspire other kinds of action in the non-virtual world.

We know, however, that social networking and digital communications technologies can play a key role in mobilization and protest. The Arab Spring protesters of early 2011, for example, relied heavily on social media tools such as Twitter to spread information widely and rapidly. Castells (2012) argues that the Internet has created a common "space of autonomy" within which activists can share feelings of outrage and transition to hope through democratic consensus building, creating non-hierarchical social networks like those built by Occupy protesters.

We're struck, however, by several questions about online activism that have, to our knowledge, escaped scholarly scrutiny thus far. The first is about siloing – that is, the ability of people to insulate themselves from the news they don't like and to accept their own distinct sets of facts. If this is indeed the case, it should produce more volatile and less stable politics, with little prospect for compromise or conciliatory governance, much less wise policy. The second is about the relation of virtual to actual activism (see Chapter 13). The third is about the effect on the rest of our civic life of the pugnacious rhetoric that characterizes online discussions and comments. And finally, issues of surveillance, data mining, filtering, and other forms of online repression have arisen as governments recognize the utility of social media technologies for mobilization. More generally, we want a better sense of how the public sphere has changed.

Finally, we find the issues attendant on the process of institutionalization continually fascinating and theoretically underdeveloped. In discussing institutionalization, Meyer and Tarrow (1998) identified two distinct but interrelated processes. The first is the establishment of a set of relationships with mainstream political and social institutions, particularly regarding the government (Clemens 1997). External institutionalization entails setting up a relationship with authorities that allows the costs of making claims to be reduced, stabilized, and predicted, so that the process of representing a set of concerns or constituents becomes routine. The second, internal institutionalization, means building an infrastructure that can sustain claims making. This usually entails professional staff, offices, a reputation, and a financial and organizational infrastructure: fundraising, mailing lists, press officers, and so forth. Questions surrounding institutionalization, as identified in *The Social Movement Society*, particularly its costs and consequences, are critical to understanding the nature of social protest in contemporary politics. It is to those issues that we turn in the context of discussing different strategies displayed by two contemporary populist movements in the United States: the Tea Party and Occupy.

Contemporary American Populism: The Tea Party

The Tea Party movement provides a fascinating case of right-wing populism in the social movement society, and an illustration of much that is well established within social movement theory. Tea Party activists attacked the policies of the Obama administration, claiming a democratic lineage traceable to the founders of the American republic. Employing the usual social movement repertoire, including demonstrations, lobbying, litigation, and electoral activism, they charged that the Obama administration's efforts, particularly on health care, violated both the US Constitution and basic notions of democracy. They believed that the America they knew and loved was being stolen away, and Obama's election was one step in this theft (Parker and Barreto 2013). Since the passage of a first round of health care reform, a variety of Tea Party organizations have sought to maintain their efforts and focus attention on new issues.

The Tea Party's sudden emergence and generally unexpected mobilization led to a flush of attention. When directed to the mid-term elections, mainstream media coverage was extensive and often hyperbolic, as reporters and analysts tried to make sense of an ostensibly new force in American politics. Contemporary political figures with all kinds of axes to grind seized upon the Tea Party to find: authentic American democracy; horrific American nativism; regular citizens newly engaged in politics; marginalized crazies newly legitimized; an AstroTurf lobby for wealthy interests; or a backlash against government intrusions on health care, bank bailouts, gun regulation, and taxation; or antipathy to the election of the first Black president.

An analyst can find evidence to support any of these claims. Given the sloppy and diverse nature of social movements in America – and elsewhere – it really isn't surprising that we can use any volatile social movement as a kind of Rorschach test in which we tag it with our preferred political interpretation. This, of course, *isn't* new.

Like most movements in the United States, the Tea Party is diverse and divided. From the start, however, the organizations within it have worked actively to enter and transform mainstream political institutions. In the electoral realm, Tea Partiers exercised tremendous influence in the Republican primaries in 2010, sometimes nominating candidates who were notably weaker in the general election than the mainstream Republican politicians they defeated. In the newly Republican House of Representatives, true believers battled pragmatic conservative politicians in the debt ceiling debacle – all within the Republican Party.

Tea Party activists, journalists, and public opinion pollsters claim that the Tea Party represents people not normally dependent upon social protest to try to get what they want from the political process, but polls consistently show Tea Party supporters to be better educated, more affluent, and whiter than the American population at large – not unusual for some kinds of social movements (New York Times/CBS News 2010); those are exactly the people who animate protest campaigns in the social movement society (Meyer and Tarrow 1998). Note, however, that the research tool of public opinion surveys can tell us only about how members of the public respond to a movement like the Tea Party, and not about those who actually turned out at Tea Party events and engaged in claims making.

Like most American movements, the Tea Party consists of multiple organizations and more or less loosely associated individuals who agree on some things and disagree on others. For participants, the Tea Party is about more than its expressed claims – which have been mostly vague – but participants disagree about what the rest is. This isn't unusual for movements in the United States. The Tea Party's success in sustaining itself and exercising influence on politics and policy will reflect the extent to which activists and organizations are able to agree to cooperate on proximate goals and strategies (Meyer and Corrigall-Brown 2005).

The Tea Party movement emerged in the wake of Barack Obama's taking office, aroused initially in opposition to the bank bailouts (and the threat of debt relief for some homeowners), and then focused intensively on the Affordable Care Act health care reform. Tea Partiers took to the streets largely because they saw little prospect of getting what they wanted through institutional politics. There's some sense here. Barack Obama, running on a platform that emphasized health care reform and increased taxes on the wealthiest Americans, was elected with a decisive margin in 2008. On Obama's coattails, Democrats picked up nine seats in the US Senate, going from a bare majority dependent upon the support of two independents to a filibuster-proof sixty votes (after Senator Arlen Specter, long-time Republican from Pennsylvania, changed parties). Democrats also picked up twenty-one seats in the House of Representatives, creating a margin of sixty-nine votes. This meant that the liberal wing of the Democratic Party enjoyed firm control of the House, and that the centre of gravity in the Senate had shifted substantially to the left as well.

The Tea Party movement provides a clear case of a constituency mobilizing in response to bad news, that is, perceived exclusion, and the threat of unwanted policy initiatives (Meyer 2002). The Tea Party represents the mobilization of conservatives in the face of defeats and threats, and the absence of viable institutional alternatives for influence. Tea Partiers started protesting *after* they'd lost at the polls, clearly demonstrating a failure in conventional politics. They succeeded in mobilizing when demonstrations seemed like the only way to gain influence. After the 2010 elections, however, when the Republicans took control of many state legislatures and governorships as well as the House of Representatives, the dynamics of protest mobilization became more complicated, and Tea Party mobilization at the grassroots declined substantially as conventional means of politics became – or at least appeared to become – more promising.

In the movement's early days, Tea Partiers were able to mobilize aggressively without worrying much about working in concert with conservative politicians in government. Untethered by the responsibility of governance, conservative rhetoric was untempered. The centre of gravity understandably shifted from the minority leaders in the House or Senate – who really couldn't do much more than talk – to advocates who were better talkers and better positioned to speak more clearly and more provocatively. Radio and television personalities, particularly Rush Limbaugh and Glenn Beck, became the most colourful, prolific, and provocative opponents of the Obama administration. The hundreds of Republican legislators were a less promising target for influence than the more diffuse politics of the streets and social movements. This is a clear case in which interests and advocates who would normally work through lobbying and electoral politics were essentially forced out into the light, with politics outdoors and the more polemical rhetoric that flourishes in such settings.

Although Tea Partiers mobilized in response to perceived (and real) exclusion, the movement was not created *de novo* but rather was facilitated by well-resourced and experienced professionals. Large business interests organized against some of what later became the Obama administration's initiatives years before Obama came to power. Most notably, FreedomWorks (fronted by former House Republican leader, Dick Armey), the libertarian Club for Growth, pro-business Americans for Prosperity, and American Majority were all established long before Obama's election and funded by very wealthy sponsors who sought both to promote an ideological vision and to protect a financial interest. As Jane Mayer's profile (2010) of the billionaire Koch brothers notes, the promotion of a conservative ideology with hundreds of millions of dollars serves business concerns worth many times that. Americans for Prosperity and FreedomWorks had grown out of Citizens for a Sound Economy in 2004, and other Koch initiatives had been operating for decades before that.

This is not to say that the people who assembled in town meetings across the United States to shout at members of Congress who might support health care reform were insincere. Rather, we want to emphasize that coordinated campaigns and social movements more generally are not spontaneous affairs but are organized. Well-heeled financiers and professional organizers dedicated themselves to stoking activism in the town halls, at the National Mall in Washington, DC, and in the streets more generally, and activists at the grassroots may not know – or have reason to care – about these larger business interests. Conservatives were also adept in using websites and social networking, conservative radio shows, and Fox News to promote their analyses and their activities. Personalities like Glenn Beck or Rush Limbaugh were vital in spreading the Tea Party's claims, and their programs were discussed in detail among local Tea Partiers. Beck modelled his broadcasts after lectures (complete with a schoolroom-like set) and encouraged his viewers to have these conversations about what they had learned, often a reimagining of American history that fit with Tea Party ideals (Lepore 2010). Frustrated citizens with grievances about taxes or health care found support – material, organizational, and ideological – for their opinions. Populist mobilization was dependent upon the support and coordination of large money interests that had opportunistically seized upon popular antagonism to specific policies to advance much larger claims about the role of government in the economy.

The key issue here is that large established interests found common cause with populist anger, and lacked alternative approaches to influence. Groups like FreedomWorks invested in grassroots mobilization because it was their best opportunity to express their claims visibly and effectively. For example, Tea Partiers have joined in anti-union protests, both in Wisconsin and elsewhere (Boven 2011). In Madison, Sarah Palin told Tea Party rally attendees – and by some accounts, a larger number of pro-union counter-protesters – that Wisconsin governor Scott Walker's policies curtailing public employees' unions were intended "to save your jobs and your pensions" (Kertscher 2011). The rally, however, was organized by Koch-funded Americans for Prosperity (AFP), and videos show Palin speaking from behind a podium draped with an "I am AFP" sign (Benen 2011). Meanwhile, FreedomWorks lists opposition to the Employee Free Choice Act and promotion of school voucher systems – with a jab at teachers' unions – among its second-tier concerns (FreedomWorks 2011).

A generalized disapproval of government spending and a continuing national fiscal crisis could explain Tea Partiers' opposition to public unions, but there's more than one way to balance a state budget, and unionized employees are most often the lower- and middle-class "ordinary" folks that Tea Partiers claim to represent. However, it's not hard to argue that big businesses have always had a vested interest in union busting. The alliances between the grassroots and their business sponsors, however, are something that cannot be taken for granted, but must be renegotiated from issue to issue. Sometimes these negotiations are successful, but there are also some ideological disconnects between grassroots Tea Partiers and the larger, well-funded organizations that promote their own interests through Tea Party campaigns.

Nationally, the Tea Party has been represented by several different organizations that share some short-term concerns but offer very different visions of the future. Within such a movement coalition, groups can share a common short-term agenda but differ in their analyses and in affiliated issues that matter to them. For example, the Nuclear Freeze movement represented a coalition that spanned absolute pacifists, far-left groups, and advocates of an older tradition of nuclear arms control (Meyer 1990). Such a coalition functions only in opposition, and fragments when political authorities start to respond in any way. This is partly a function of apparent reductions in threats and grievances, but also in response to the availability of ostensibly more direct and promising strategies for political influence.

Of all the national groups, the Tea Party Patriots seems to embody best the conservative democratic ethos the movement claims. Organized by a few experienced activists, it styled itself as something of a clearinghouse for conservative grassroots politics. Claiming more than 2,500 local affiliates, the group's initial goal was to support grassroots activism. Articulated in terms of limited federal government, free markets, and fiscal responsibility, it also prizes personal liberty and the rule of law. The Tea Party Patriots have self-consciously tried to develop a model of organization based in the grassroots, immune to co-optation or decapitation (Rauch 2010). The activist leaders read and recommend iconic community organizer Saul Alinksy as a model for grassroots organizing, and explicitly reject the notion of building a stable Washington-based institutional structure. They have also suffered from fundraising difficulties, and have, over time, become a more formal organization.

After the 2010 election, and facing sustained fundraising difficulties, the Tea Party Patriots announced the receipt of a $1 million gift from an anonymous donor at the National Press Club. Criticizing the legitimacy of other groups using the Tea Party appellation, they announced that they would support Tea Party electoral efforts without giving donations to candidates or consultants, or endorsing specific candidates. They also announced that former Congressman Ernie Istook would join the group as an adviser, as part of their effort to establish a permanent presence in American politics. About a year later, co-founder Mark Meckler was forced out of the organization, complaining that his one-time ally Jenny Beth Martin had succeeded in gaining control of the national organization and had steered it into too close an alliance with the Republican Party (Fox News 2012).

In contrast, the Tea Party Express is a somewhat older group established by a long-time Republican political consultant, Sal Russo. Originally called "Our Country Deserves Better," the group was renamed by Russo when grassroots Tea Party activism took off. It is far more focused on candidates than on any particular policy position, save for safe positions against taxes and against the "nationalization of industry." The group funnelled money and expertise into several Congressional campaigns, notably those of Republican Senate candidates Joe Miller (Alaska), Ken Buck (Colorado), and

Sharron Angle (Nevada). The largest independent group supporting Republican candidates in 2010, it spent over $5 million on the primary campaigns of candidates it endorsed. More than half of this money went to consulting firms controlled by Russo or his wife.

The Tea Party label became a catchall for conservatives who disagreed among themselves about both substantive and strategic matters. The 2010 election provided a focus as well as a source of unity and division. Candidates must articulate policy preferences on the whole range of issues that often separate Tea Partiers into libertarian and social conservative camps, and battles were waged between pragmatists and ideologues in the Republican Party. Nonetheless, Tea Partiers claimed much of the credit for the large Republican victories in 2010.

But movement candidates virtually always disappoint in office. If they hold to the purist rhetoric, they will be unable to make inroads in Congress. If they eschew pork barrel politics, they will disappoint constituents who *know* that other elected officials deliver earmarks to their districts. If they compromise on principle to make deals, they will alienate many of the people who put them in office, because they will become the successful institutional politicians they railed against. This is a feature of the institutional design of the United States, and one that challenges all social movements. The nature of representative democracy, especially as embodied in American politics, necessitates the kinds of compromises that populists at the grassroots view as anathema.

After those elections, however, Tea Party activists found themselves trying to promote a populist, grassroots image while advocating policies that benefit business interests and wealthy funding organizations, and dealing with a conflict among conservatives that had been institutionalized in the House of Representatives. At its heart, this is not a new situation; activists on the left and right often find themselves trying to balance the need for fundraising and material resources with the need to craft a message that will enable them to recruit and maintain a rank-and-file membership. The rhetoric that we've heard thus far, however, suggests that rather than striking a balance between these concerns, the Tea Party's message at the grassroots often differs from the policy proposals and stated concerns of its largest, wealthiest organizations, such as Americans for Prosperity and FreedomWorks. The national organizations invested heavily in a Washington presence and the Republican presidential nomination, while groups at the grassroots, generally and understandably, atrophied. By the time Congress reconvened in January 2011, the Tea Party had a large presence in the newly Republican House of Representatives and the Republican Party more generally, several well-established organizations focused on Washington, a faltering set of local groups, and a strong focus on replacing President Barack Obama with someone more responsive to their interests.

The Republican presidential hopefuls aggressively sought to cultivate the support of Tea Party groups, both nationally and in each state, but in the process redefined what the Tea Party meant. For all of the seemingly viable candidates save Congressman Ron Paul, Tea Partiers were social conservatives, not libertarians, committed to an aggressive US military policy. Although the rhetoric about limiting government was recurrent, these pragmatic politicians were reluctant to criticize Medicare or Social Security – programs from which many Tea Partiers benefited, and which they often supported (Skocpol and Williamson 2013). These legislators were willing to use the powers of government to enforce a social orthodoxy. (Ron Paul, who mostly articulated libertarian policies domestically and abroad, found a ceiling on his support within the party, and was ultimately reluctant to support the Republican presidential nominee.) One after another, conservative alternatives to Mitt Romney cultivated support from Tea Partiers, and one after another they faltered for other, related reasons. Essentially, all failed to defeat him because they were far less successful as pragmatic politicians, raising money, organizing a campaign, and cultivating the support of mainstream political interests; in different ways, all of the challengers to Romney had failed in conventional politics or just hadn't achieved very much. One of the ironies of the Tea Party's drive towards institutionalization is how poorly the presumptive Republican nominee represents the interests they articulated. Indeed, the march to mainstream institutions has re-established the Republican electoral coalition based on social conservatives and economic conservatives, and Governor Romney struggled to unite that coalition in exactly the same way that every Republican candidate since Ronald Reagan has. Despite the influence on rhetoric the Tea Party exercised, it has been firmly incorporated in the mainstream politics that its adherents challenged.

Contemporary American Populism: Occupy
The Tea Party's victories set the stage for the emergence of an alternative populism, represented by the Occupy movement. Occupy has confronted the same dilemmas of institutionalization that occupied the Tea Party, but

its activists have made mostly different decisions, so far. It remains to be seen whether the outcomes of those decisions will be appreciably different, much less better.

The conservative Republican victories in 2010, at both the state and national level, dramatically swung the debate on policy far to the right. With the country facing large budget deficits, increasing health care costs, and sustained high unemployment, the national debate focused on the deficit; at the same time, the Republican House refused to consider any increases in taxation, proposing instead tax cuts and often unspecified cuts in spending. At the state level, newly elected Republican governors implemented agendas centred on spending cuts, which resulted in layoffs in state services, particularly public education, increased tuition at public universities, salary cuts for state workers, and assaults on labour unions.

The Occupation idea was not new; indeed, it was the central tactic of the colour revolutions of the 2000s, starting with the Bulldozer Revolution in Serbia, and of the Arab Spring protests. In Southern Europe, citizens rallied to protest austerity budgets, staging large and often disruptive demonstrations against cuts in state services. Although Occupiers frequently cited Egypt's Tahrir Square as inspiration, more similar to Occupy were the campaigns for social spending that resulted in the Israeli Summer – a series of demonstrations in 2011 against the country's rising cost of living – and the marches in Madison, Wisconsin, organized in opposition to Governor Scott Walker's drive to end collective bargaining for most state workers.

Kalle Lasn, an activist provocateur who edits *Adbusters,* an anti-consumerist magazine, floated the idea for an "occupation" of Wall Street in the middle of 2011, calling on activists to assemble in the financial centre of America, agree upon one demand, and stay until it was met. Lasn produced a beautiful poster, featuring a ballerina on the iconic Wall Street bull and a date, 17 September 2011. The idea was taken up by local anarchist activists who were generally distant from other political reform efforts on the left.

The initial march and demonstration was small, far less than the 20,000 predicted, with disjointed and poorly articulated politics, save for a recurrent concern with the 99 percent and an opposition to the disproportionate political and economic influence of the other 1 percent. After a faltering march, activists encamped in Zuccotti Park, a private concrete space kitty-corner to the financial centre. They established a functioning community of sorts, living on donated food and using the restrooms of local merchants. They also established a modern press centre, consisting of a floating group of Web programmers and bloggers using laptop computers. The Occupation also established a mode of decision making based in anarchist practice – a General Assembly that met twice daily, discussing all kinds of issues and applying a consensus model. Episodically, they left Zuccotti Park to stage actions at targets throughout New York City, most notably the homes of powerful bankers like Jamie Dimon, chief executive officer of JPMorgan Chase.

Initially, the Occupation hobbled along, buoyed into the mainstream media by occasional visits by celebrities, some affiliated with liberal causes. Although the mainstream media didn't give much coverage to the Occupation, activists used websites, blogs, Twitter, and other social media to propound a message of opposition to inequality. These technologies were crucial to getting the word out among activists, but did not reach deeply into the American political mainstream. The key event that enabled the site to grow into a national movement was a social control error by the New York Police Department. Occupiers staged a march across the Brooklyn Bridge. When many of them strayed into the traffic lanes, police arrested 700 Occupiers, bringing mainstream national attention to the encampment at Zuccotti Park. In reviewing videos and testimonies from the event, it appears that some activists were trying to provoke a confrontation with the police, while some police led demonstrators into the traffic lanes.

With national attention came efforts at emulation across the United States – and, indeed, around the world. Activists staged Occupations of public spaces in every major city in the United States and hundreds of smaller locales. The consensus-based General Assembly model was broadly adopted, along with some of the affectations that developed in Zuccotti Park. The Human Microphone, for example, a process of repeating the comments of each speaker in bites of a few words, also spread, even though the strictures regarding amplification didn't hold everywhere. Importantly, well-established activist groups in some cities adopted the Occupy name, placing their own politics underneath the umbrella of a larger campaign against inequality.

The Occupations became a trap for the movement, albeit one that provided something of a coherent identity and the chance to proffer broader claims. Labor unions and environmentalists visited the camps, holding their own events in the physical and media space the Occupations had opened. On the Web, activists offered proposals for rectifying gross inequality. Lasn himself called for a tax on financial transactions. More significantly, the

dialogue opened by the Occupations allowed others to discuss the substance beneath activist complaints. Sympathizers told their stories on the
Web, posting photos of handwritten or typed tales of hardship based on
unemployment, underemployment, foreclosure, student debt, and the lack
of health insurance on Tumblr and other social media sites. These messages,
usually signed with "I am the 99%," quickly went viral, leading *TIME* to
name the slogan the top Internet meme of 2011 (Carbone 2011). The phrase
became an integral part of the national dialogue about inequality. Mainstream media gave more prominent attention to reports on poverty from
the Congressional Budget Office or the Census Bureau. Many local officials
announced support for the goals of the movement – even as they too
redefined it. Occupy's concerns were institutionalized rhetorically, carried
by institutional allies, even as the Occupiers themselves were still outside in
the parks.

In the encampments, however, consensus norms and procedures made it
impossible to agree upon one demand, or even a set of them, beyond the
desire to stay in the encampment. While some Occupiers were extraordinarily well educated and politically motivated, many camps also became a
haven for the homeless. Maintaining some kind of order in the Occupations
was extremely difficult, and a few reports of violent crime within some
camps got massive attention. Perhaps most significantly, consensus norms
made it impossible for the activists to make any kind of deal with authorities. In Los Angeles, for example, Mayor Antonio Villaraigosa saw himself
as an ally of the movement, and tried to negotiate a deal to get Occupy LA
to vacate the lawn in front of City Hall. He offered office space in City Hall,
farm space, and shelter beds. There was no one, however, who could make
and enforce a deal within Occupy. Many of the activists were acutely aware
of the dangers of institutionalization, and enforced governance norms that
made "selling out," that is, compromise with authorities, impossible.

Although the concerns of the Occupiers centred on inequality, activists
had very different ideas about remedies. Some articulated an anti-government
ethos and envisioned themselves as building a new world from the bottom
up, starting in public spaces. Others thought that a government that could
bail out the financial industry could do something similar for homeowners
with mortgages they couldn't afford or underemployed college graduates
with large debts. Still others sought to resurrect stricter rules and regulation
of the financial industry by the federal government. The decision-making
processes in place in the camps made it impossible to agree on disputes

about the appropriate role of government in fighting inequality, and mostly the encampments focused on maintaining themselves.

By the end of the fall of 2011, local officials had cleared the camps, mostly with police force. When activists tried to reoccupy the same sites, police closed parks or prevented people from entering when they were carrying tents or stoves. When the Occupations ended, Occupy activists had to confront the dilemmas of organizing their efforts and their politics in the absence of an actual Occupation. Some activists have worked hard to find other things to occupy, including parks and vacant buildings, but local officials have stifled these efforts. At the same time, mainstream politicians have attempted to pander to the concerns represented by Occupy, even as they redefine them in their own terms. Running for the US Senate in Massachusetts, Elizabeth Warren has emphasized her long record of crafting regulatory rules and agencies to protect consumers from large banks. Representative Ted Deutch (Florida) introduced a constitutional amendment banning corporate money in political campaigns, helpfully titled "Outlawing Corporate Cash Undermining the Public Interest in our Elections and Democracy (OCCUPIED)." And President Barack Obama, seeking a campaign mode for re-election, increasingly lifted the language of Occupy in pressing for fair taxation and support for students. They lifted the spirit of Occupy to benefit from its support.

Unsurprisingly, in the absence of Occupations the movement faced a critical opportunity to define itself, which was no easy feat. The anarchist segment of the movement has staged civil disobedience and direct action efforts on city streets, in bank lobbies, and to stop foreclosures. Across the states, students and labour unions, fighting against budget cuts and tuition hikes, have continued their protest and lobbying efforts but taken on the Occupy label. Several Occupiers have announced campaigns for elective office. And new organizations have sprung up, often coalitions of existing organizations, to stage demonstrations at the annual meetings of large corporations. The obvious risk for Occupy is that all of these efforts don't add up to a coherent whole, and without formal organization, Occupy will yield attention and direction to the scores of activist groups that operated before the movement emerged, including Moveon.org, labour unions, environmentalists, and other advocates.

For the most part, because Obama did not face a challenge for the Democratic nomination, Occupy was spared the dilemmas of electoral participation that Tea Partiers wrestled with. By the fall, however, the election crowded out political attention to much else. Occupiers, like their opponents on the other end of the political spectrum, were confronted with the responsibility of voting, likely by choosing the less offensive candidate.

Conclusion

The Tea Party and Occupy movements represent different manifestations of the social movement society, both growing in response to the widespread perception that dramatic action is needed to get mainstream politics to respond to their concerns. These movements highlight the shortcomings we've identified in Meyer and Tarrow's vision of the social movement society. Occupy and the Tea Party reinterpret American democracy and offer alternative ideas of the relationship between government, citizens, and corporations. Like many of their modern social movement counterparts, they make extensive use of online resources and niche news outlets to educate and mobilize supporters. They flourish in an atmosphere of political exclusion, and in the very real crisis of sustained economic and political underperformance. They also represent two different articulations of the risks that attend political institutionalization.

Democratic rhetoric animates the Tea Party, as it does many social movements, for obvious reasons. Activists claim that government has been unresponsive to their needs, values, and concerns. They argue that citizens like themselves should play a critical role in making (or stopping) policies that affect their lives – thus, embodying democracy. They employ the Constitution as a justification for their claims, arguing that their efforts hark back to a better time for people like themselves. Without allies in power, the only meaningful expression for their concerns is through grassroots activism – which, with increasing frequency, focuses on the electoral process.

In the contemporary social movement society, however, we've seen that substantial sponsorship is necessary to build the infrastructure of a movement, even one that emphasizes democratic participation at the grassroots. If those sponsors are comfortable employing grassroots activism to serve their own ends, their willingness to allow the grassroots to define their efforts is not yet apparent. When social movement activism becomes widely diffused, used by the advantaged as well as the excluded, it may be that viable paths towards influence for the excluded have become even harder to find and follow. Since 2010, the institutional strategy has produced ongoing disappointment for Tea Partiers at the grassroots. There is a democratic irony here. Mobilization to take back American politics, shifting it towards activists' vision of democratic control, is contingent upon the sponsorship of interests that want only to use those people and that mobilization for their own ends – which often, for good and ill, have little to do with democracy.

Occupy's emergence called into question the necessity of large resources for staging a social movement. The Occupations were really organized at the grassroots level, and directed by local communities that were defined largely by volitional participation in those communities (see Chapters 8 and 9 for further discussion of the role of communities). Taking a cue from their colleagues in the Arab Spring protests, Occupy effectively used social media to bypass mainstream media in cultivating and projecting a message, one that enabled it to spread without elite sponsorship. But the focus on a particular physical space and tactic and the norms of consensus presented constraints, constraints that have begun to erode. Occupy has since faced the challenge of sustaining and targeting a political effort that can influence policy, as well as the ever-present dilemma of finding a way to participate in mainstream politics without being eaten by it. The antipathy towards formalization has meant a fading public profile and forfeiture of the political debate to mainstream political actors.

Taken together, the two populist movements illustrate two dark sides of institutionalization. For the Tea Party, monied interests, formal organizations, and mainstream politics have captured the energy, redefining a movement in terms of conventional electoral politics and neglecting the grassroots. For Occupy, the resistance to formalization has highlighted the difficulties of sustained mobilization without professionalism and resources, and the claims of the movement have been appropriated and softened by mainstream politicians. It's not clear which of these strategies represents the best choice for activists, or even whether there is a good choice at all.

2

Evangelical Radio

Institution Building and the Religious Right

TINA FETNER, ALLYSON STOKES, AND CARRIE B. SANDERS

Meyer and Tarrow (1998) and Meyer and Pullman in Chapter 1 argue that a social movement society (SMS) is one in which protest has been institutionalized, routinized, and professionalized. Their emphasis on the way that social contexts have adapted to formerly disruptive protest tactics calls to mind the malleability of social institutions that interact with protesters, such as states and their various agencies, educational institutions, media, and so on. Societies can adapt to protest, this perspective argues, and defang movements at the same time, allowing for the co-optation of movement claims, the relocation of protesters to out-of-the-way spaces, or the dismissal by news media of protest as no longer being news. Among the many insights that this perspective contains is the idea that the contexts in which social movements operate are neither singular nor static. Historical changes matter to the SMS model, something that is underexamined by Meyer and Tarrow (1998) and merely alluded to in Chapter 1. This perspective therefore calls out for a comparative empirical approach that considers differences across cultural, historical, or geographic contexts.

Our chapter thus takes on a comparative project, which has largely been absent from the scholarship in the SMS tradition. We consider the effect on social movements of policy structures that are not obviously or intentionally related to these movements, to seek clarity on the role of historical forces on social movements. We select for our cases two articulations of a single movement, the religious right, in Canada and the United States. We ask why this movement has played so prominent a role in US politics but has struggled to achieve its policy goals in Canada. We examine historical differences between conservative evangelical Christian media development in these two countries. By examining a single movement in comparative perspective, we hope to produce new insights for social movement theory. In particular, we focus our comparative lens on the role of institutional infrastructures in providing support to social movement activity. The historical processes that produce social movement societies are situated in particular geographic, political, and bureaucratic systems. It stands to reason that variations in political context will yield differences in the amount or qualities of the institutionalization processes that are the hallmarks of social movement societies.

Canada and the United States are similar on many fronts, and both countries are considered by social movement scholars to be social movement societies. By examining a movement common to both countries we can explore historically contingent institution-building practices while holding more or less constant many other variables, such as the movement's central claims, policy goals, rhetorical strategies, collective identity, and so on. In doing so, we reveal the historical variation in institution building by conservative evangelical Christian communities that predated the religious right in each country. In particular, we consider the disparity in the establishment and growth of media institutions between communities in Canada and the United States. We then consider the role of these media institutions in providing disparate supports to the social movement once it emerged in the late twentieth century.

As we consider similar movements in similar countries that rest on quite different institutional foundations, we call upon the SMS theoretical framework to expand its view somewhat to consider historical processes that predate movement emergence. As Howard Ramos and Kathleen Rodgers argue in the Introduction to this volume, there is room in social movement society theory to consider differences across political contexts – that is, to envision multiple social movement societies with different characteristics and complexities. The case we offer here exemplifies the need for both historical and comparative analyses to flesh out the variations among different social movement societies.

The religious right is a nationwide movement in both Canada and the United States, emerging around the same time, towards the end of the 1970s, in both countries. Although the movements' policy goals, collective action frames, and constituencies are very similar in the two countries, there has been a marked difference in terms of how much influence these movements have had on political discourse and policy outcomes. Seeking to discover how these movements have divergent impacts, we trace their historical roots to the conservative evangelical Christian communities from which they emerged. We find in these histories a significant divergence in community development and institution building in the period from 1920 to 1950, and we explore that divergence here. In this chapter, we focus on the development of radio broadcasts in these communities, finding that the bureaucratic policy contexts in the two countries shaped the growth of Christian radio substantially. We argue that, decades later, the historical trajectories produced by these policy contexts led to divergent institutional infrastructures for the Canadian and American religious right movements.

Institutional Infrastructures

Social movement scholars have long understood the role of organizational and institutional supports for social movements. They have shown, for example, how the Black churches of the civil rights movement provided meeting spaces, leadership training, and a place to practise non-violent civil disobedience (Morris 1984; Polletta 2002). They have also demonstrated that organizations are key to cultural outcomes such as collective identity and movement rhetoric (Minkoff 1995). This scholarship has also shown that organizations need not be dedicated to social movement activity in order to support movement goals. John D. McCarthy (1996) coined the term "mobilizing structures" to capture the way that churches, volunteer organizations, local community groups, and so on can facilitate the activism of a social movement. In fact, Campbell and colleagues (2005) argue that social movement organizations themselves are not as important as the wider field of organizations in which they operate. And some movement scholars consider this network of interested parties to be the core of activism, as opposed to dedicated movement organizations (e.g., J.D. McCarthy, Smith, and Zald 1996; Diani 1997, 2003).

Andrews's concept (2001, 2004) of *institutional infrastructure* best captures the multidimensional nature of the supports that organizations offer social movements, including resources, training, meeting space, and volunteer personnel. Andrews argues that while the importance of institutional supports in social movement activity is widely accepted by social movement scholars, less attention is paid to variation among different institutional infrastructures. The concept of movement infrastructure calls upon students of social movements to seriously consider the sum total of organizations and resources that offer supports to activism rather than to focus on one or two key organizations or resources. Such an examination is an approach that very much considers as the unit of analysis social movement societies, or broader contexts, rather than movements in isolation.

Data, Method, Analysis

We use secondary sources to establish the historical record of conservative evangelical Christian community development in the United States and Canada. Much has been written by historians, religious studies scholars, and sociologists of religion to establish the path that evangelicalism took in each of these countries. These works, usually in the form of book-length monographs and edited volumes, document the growth of these communities, the main sources of conflict and belief, and the expansion and decline of various denominations, sects, and neighbourhood churches. Historical scholars approach secondary materials with a skeptical eye, keen to expose any biases that the original authors may have or to reveal any contradictions between various histories (Amenta 2003). To ensure a robust and well-informed historical record, we engaged in an extensive library search of secondary sources. The literatures on evangelical history in Canada and the United States are largely separate from each other, but they are substantial. To complement this literature, we draw on several primary data sources, including the Aird Report, which stemmed from the Royal Commission on Radio Broadcasting in Canada and a public notice from the Canadian Radio-television and Telecommunications Commission (CRTC). In our analysis, we use a comparative lens to seek information about how these two cases overlapped and where they diverged, paying special attention to community development and institution building.

We rely on historical institutionalism to provide a theoretical framework for our analysis. This perspective understands social policy to be dependent upon those policies that preceded it, setting up a path dependence by structuring the choices of political actors in any given time period. Precisely, this tradition argues that social change is limited by the historical paths that policymakers have created through earlier actions (see, for example, Skocpol 1992). We take Andrews's concern (2004) for the process of movement building seriously, and we contend that scholars should extend their analyses to the historical infrastructure-building activities that precede the emergence of a movement. An SMS perspective requires careful thought about the political contexts in which movements develop. We question whether the political contexts that exist prior to the emergence of social movements also shape movements and their potential to achieve political gains. Below we take a historical, comparative approach to explore differences in movement infrastructure by considering the paths of community development and the establishment and growth of organizations and their resources prior to movement emergence.

Case Selection and Historical Overview

We use a comparative case study, selecting as our pair of cases the religious right movement in Canada and the United States. In selecting this pair of movements in neighbouring states, we employ an approach that selects similar cases to highlight variations between cases. Lipset (1990) argues that Canada and the United States are excellent cases for comparison because both their political histories and their contemporary social and cultural contexts are so similar. Because these cases have so much in common, they are akin to a natural experiment in which a good deal of variation is held constant. Thus, they are well positioned to reveal the causal chain of events where their paths do diverge.

We thus begin with the current religious right movements and trace them backward through time to the communities and social spaces from which they emerged – conservative evangelical Christian communities. Although some in the religious right may claim to represent a wide swath of religious conservatives, especially Catholics, a deeper view into the history of this movement reveals the primacy of conservative evangelicalism in the movement's leadership, its rhetoric, and the organizations that constitute it. Thus, we focus exclusively on conservative evangelical Christian communities, leaving Catholicism for other analyses (please see Fetner 2008 for a more rigorous discussion of evangelicalism and the religious right). Like a genealogist tracing a family tree back through generations, we work backward to find those moments when these communities branched off from each other and began to take different paths. For this chapter, we do not follow Lipset's path (1990) all the way back to the American Revolution, as he does for his classic work explaining value differences in the United States and Canada. Instead we explore the period that is more crucial to our cases: the first half of the twentieth century, especially the period from 1920 to 1950, when evangelicalism was redefining itself in both countries. This period is particularly important to our study of media institutions, as the expansion of radio broadcasting created new opportunities for religious communities of all stripes to voice their views.

The work presented in this chapter is part of a larger project that uses this historical approach to trace a wide variety of differences in the Canadian and US evangelical communities. Elsewhere, we argue that the "modern controversy," in which new discoveries in science have called into question the Bible's historical accuracy, has led to differences in community building among evangelical Christians in the United States and Canada, in terms of both scope and form (Fetner and Sanders 2011, 2012). In the United States, debates over modernity led to major splits within denominations, a general move away from denominations to independent churches, and divisions among so-called fundamentalists, who retained a core belief in the literal truth of the Bible. In Canada, the modern controversy coincided with a major reorganization of denominations, especially the unification and liberal vision of the United Church of Canada. This move consolidated and strengthened Protestant Canadians, including those who retained a belief in the literal truth of the Bible. The establishment of the United Church of Canada provided an important denominational home for these biblical literalists at a time when US literalists were breaking into different factions of those who at the time called themselves fundamentalists, but whom we now call conservative evangelical Christians.

Thus, in Canada most people who identify as evangelical would not be counted as conservative evangelical Christians. This produces a good deal of confusion regarding terminology. We seek to clarify matters by using the term "conservative evangelical Christian" to capture those "fundamentalists" of the United States who later adopted the term evangelical, as well as a much smaller group of Canadians who did depart from mainline denominations to form new churches, Bible institutes, and missionary organizations. These conservative evangelical Christians have in common a belief in biblical literalism and a distrust of both secular institutions and mainline faiths. However, worship practices and specific theological claims, such as end-times philosophies, vary widely among conservative evangelical Christians (Reimer 2003).

Our overarching argument is that these histories of evangelicalism, which diverge during the era of the modern controversy, placed the conservative evangelical Christian communities of Canada and the United States on different paths of institutional development, especially during the decades between 1920 and 1950 – the heyday of Christian radio and of evangelical community development in general. There is no evidence to suggest that the institutional development of this era was intended to support the religious right of the future, which would emerge as a social movement in the late 1970s. When the movement did emerge in both Canada and the United States, however, activists would find that the institutional infrastructure upon which each movement relied were markedly different in size, strength, and density of network.

Elsewhere, we focus on para-church organizations in general (Fetner and Sanders 2011). In this chapter, we focus specifically on one of several key differences between the evangelical communities in Canada and the United States: radio broadcasting. In the latter country, evangelical Christian radio was a widespread cultural enterprise that evolved into a multimillion-dollar industry, eventually supporting media conglomerate organizations that were highly influential for the religious right. In Canada, relatively little evangelical radio was produced, most of it emerging decades after the heyday of Christian radio in the United States. Coming from a historical institutionalist perspective, we interrogate the policy structures that governed evangelical Christian radio. Although coming decades prior to any recognized social movement activity, the policy choices of Canadian as opposed to American bureaucrats created a starkly different set of institutions – in this case cultural institutions – upon which later movement organizations would rest. As noted in Chapters 4 and 6, policy decisions by governments influence the emergence and types of movements that get formed – a central blurring recognized in the SMS thesis.

United States

Christian evangelicalism in the United States has been intimately connected with radio since its inception (Ostling 1984). Evangelical ministers broadcast their services, expanding their audiences dramatically. Revivals in particular were well suited for radio, filled with music, inspiring rhetoric, and theatrical grandeur (Young 2007). From 1920 on, evangelical Christian radio broadcasts became a staple of the airwaves. American audiences grew into the millions, making evangelical Christian radio broadcasters celebrity figures well before the advent of televangelism. Christian radio broadcasting continues to be an important cultural institution of American evangelicalism today (Ostling 1984).

Finke and Stark (2005, 218–24) point to the role of broadcast policy in the United States in shaping evangelical radio. The Federal Communications Commission (FCC), which regulates the airwaves, promoted religious radio programming by categorizing it as public service broadcasting. Since the FCC began regulating radio stations in the 1920s, it had required some percentage of time to be dedicated to public service broadcasting. That these free broadcasting spots could be assigned to religious organizations in addition to other public interests meant that there was a long lineup of churches, pastors, and religious organizations of all stripes to broadcast their messages on the radio. How to choose between these religious broadcasters became a problem, but it was one that the FCC did not take on. Instead, this selection was managed by national broadcast companies and by local radio station owners themselves.

Mainline Protestant churches wanted the lion's share of this free air time, and there was a time when it seemed that they might keep conservative evangelical programming off the US airwaves altogether. The Federal Council of Churches advised national broadcasters to give its free public-interest programming slots to its member churches, and further advised them not to sell any paid airtime for religious broadcasts. Neither NBC nor ABC sold time to religious broadcasters, and CBS did so for only four years, from 1927 to 1931. Despite this attempt to prevent evangelical churches from reaching radio audiences, a fourth network, the Mutual Broadcasting System, did sell airtime to evangelicals, providing them with access to a national network.

Evangelical programming turned out to be some of the most successful religious broadcasts, drawing "millions of listeners" (Finke and Stark 2005, 219) to programs such as Charles E. Fuller's "Old-Fashioned Revival Hour" and the Seventh-Day Adventists' "Voice of Prophecy." The Mutual Broadcasting System was under much pressure to change, however. In 1944, the network revised its policies to limit religious programming to thirty-minute shows that aired only on Sundays, when most listeners would be in church. Finally, in a policy particularly directed at evangelical broadcasts, the network forbade solicitation of donations on the air. By then, however, evangelical radio had already become established as a major cultural institution.

By the mid-1940s, evangelical radio broadcasting – especially shows that solicited funds directly from their listeners – had become a multimillion-dollar industry. Finke and Stark (2005, 221–22) cite a report claiming that in 1943, the Mutual Broadcasting System received over $3 million from sales of airtime to religious broadcasts, out of its total airtime revenues of $12 million. The broadcasters themselves were profiting at unknown levels beyond the $3 million that they paid to buy broadcast time, but clearly it was a large enough revenue stream that evangelical broadcasters came together in response to Mutual's new rules. Two actions in particular are of interest for our discussion of institution building: the invention of syndication and the formation of the National Religious Broadcasters (NRB) (Finke and Stark 2005, 223).

The exclusion of evangelical programming from national radio networks forced evangelical broadcasters to be creative in reaching radio audiences. Having built a national audience that routinely donated millions of dollars to radio programs, they performed an end run around network gatekeepers. Instead of broadcasting their shows through networks, evangelical broadcasters invented syndication (Finke and Stark 2005). They recorded their live shows, pressed transcription disks, and then sold these disks directly to local radio stations around the country. Thus, one show could be adopted by hundreds of local stations without any support from a network. This practice became widespread in radio, was later copied by television and print media, and remains a standard practice today.

The National Religious Broadcasters was formed under the auspices of another key conservative evangelical organization: the National Association of Evangelicals. This umbrella group sought to unite a fractured and dispersed set of evangelical denominations and independent churches by downplaying disputes over theological philosophies, worship practices such as glossolalia, and even racial divides. The association is one of the main institutional foundations of the conservative evangelical Christian community in the United States, not least because it created a network within which many additional organizations and networks were developed. The NRB was one of the largest and most successful of these. It lobbied to redress inequalities of access to radio airtime on behalf of evangelical broadcasters. Eventually, in 1960, the FCC expanded its definition of public service programming to include religious broadcasting that had paid for its airtime. This ruling encouraged local stations to substitute paid religious programming for those time slots that they had previously been mandated to give away for free. Evangelical broadcasters, having developed a highly successful model for paid programming, took most of these slots, while mainline denominations, who had become accustomed to getting their airtime for free, were virtually shut out under these new rules (Finke and Stark 2005).

As television became more and more popular after the Second World War, evangelical broadcasters were at the forefront. Some radio broadcasters became hosts of television shows. Oral Roberts is an excellent example. A crusading faith healer and advocate of the prosperity gospel, Roberts began his radio broadcasts in 1947 and moved to television in 1954 (Harrell 1985). His weekly shows reached national and then international audiences. Over the next thirty years, Roberts built a media empire that gained $120 million in annual revenues, expanding to build the Abundant Life Prayer group, a twenty-four-hour call centre that claims to have received over 24 million calls, according to www.oralroberts.com. Oral Roberts University was started in 1963. His television broadcasts expanded from his live services to include other evangelical entertainment, including popular gospel and country music singers. Famously, in 1977 Roberts claimed to be visited by a 900-foot Jesus who commanded him to build a hospital. He raised over $9 million in one 1984 fundraising campaign in which he claimed that God might "call him home." According to a *New York Times* obituary, "Oral Roberts University estimated that Mr. Roberts, its founder and first president, had personally laid his hands on more than 1.5 million people during his career, reached more than 500 million people on television and radio, and received millions of letters and appeals" (K. Schneider 2009). His ministries employed over 2,300 people at its peak in the 1980s.

Oral Roberts is just one example of many US conservative evangelical Christians who took advantage of the loose regulatory environment for radio broadcasting to build massive media empires that launched multiple, long-lasting institutions, raised hundreds of millions of dollars of revenue, and spread the culture of conservative evangelicalism to a massive and growing audience. The National Religious Broadcasters group has continued working on behalf of conservative evangelical Christian radio and television broadcasters to form a dense network, to continue lobbying for an evangelical-friendly policy environment, and to provide support for this wing of the evangelical community in the United States. As we discuss next, Canada's history tells quite a different story.

Canada

The story of religious broadcasting in Canada is primarily one of stewardship through government regulation. Christian evangelicalism and radio have not been as closely and consistently interconnected as in the United States, and there have been fewer prominent religious personalities in Canadian media (Reimer 2003). Some, like Pierre Berton (1965), blame this on the unwillingness of churches to embrace modern telecommunications technologies. Others argue that the major barrier to religious broadcasting in Canada has been restrictive broadcast policies (Cook and Ruggles 1992; R. Johnston 1994; Fortner 2005; Faassen 2011). This was not always the case, however. When radio first appeared in Canada in the 1920s, religious broadcasting was quite common (Nolan 1989). Many religious broadcasts were simply local church services being broadcast as they were delivered on

Sunday morning. In 1924, *Maclean's* reported: "Every Monday, these radio
stations receive sheaves of letters from aged folk, the sick and invalids
– shut-ins who were not able to attend service but who heard everything
clearly and beautifully as if they had been in church" (E. Johnston 1924).

Throughout the 1920s, the Department of Marine and Fisheries regulated radio in Canada by issuing licences to broadcasters through its minor
wing, the Radio Branch (Faassen 2011). This agency was reluctant to issue
broadcasting licences to religious groups, preferring local stations to take
responsibility for any religious broadcasting. That said, the branch did
issue a few licences for religious broadcasting, but the bureaucrats were
clearly nervous about this decision, as it put them in a position of having
to mediate conflicts between religious factions (R. Johnston 1994).

In 1927, for example, one religious broadcaster, the International Bible
Students Association (IBSA, now known as the Jehovah's Witnesses) caused
so many complaints to the regulatory body that a special commission was
called. The IBSA used its five licences to broadcast attacks against the
mainline Protestant and Catholic churches, to sell air time to the Ku Klux
Klan, and to overlay an IBSA service onto the broadcast of a service by a
popular Toronto cleric, Reverend William Cameron, who had gone over
his allotted time. The Radio Branch reported receiving eighty bags of mail
complaining about the IBSA's actions (R. Johnston 1994, 390). When the
branch tried to resolve the controversy by allowing the licences of the IBSA
to expire without renewal, it drew another storm of complaints against
government censorship of religious minorities.

The following year, the Canadian government formed the Royal Commission on Radio Broadcasting. This came to be known as the Aird Commission for its chair, John Aird. The Aird Commission is known in collective
memory for producing the Aird Report (Aird 1929), which made recommendations to establish public radio in Canada and to create the Canadian Radio Broadcasting Corporation (CRBC; later renamed the Canadian
Broadcasting Corporation). In addition, the Aird Report emphasized that
radio should promote a uniquely Canadian culture rather than simply
broadcast American programs. The report outlined suggestions for regulating particular kinds of broadcasting, such as educational, international, and
religious broadcasting (Bird 1988). This kept most American evangelical
radio broadcasts from Canadian radio stations (although there were many
Canadians who lived close enough to US stations to receive these broadcasts on their radios).

Regarding religious broadcasts, the Aird Report recommended that guidelines be established "prohibiting statements of a controversial nature or one religion making an attack upon the leaders or doctrine of another" (Aird, Bowman, and Frigon 1929, 13). In addition, the report recommended "that competent and cultured announcers only should be employed" (ibid.). Finally, it recommended against allowing direct advertising on the radio, favouring only the indirect advertising of sponsored shows. These regulations were very heavy-handed relative to US regulation of radio, seeking a great deal of governmental oversight not only over which religious organizations would be granted licences but also over the content of the radio broadcasts themselves. The requirement for uncontroversial, "cultured" dialogue that makes no attacks on the beliefs of others has laid out very clear principles of Canadian culture. The Aird Report set religious broadcasts in Canada on a very different path from that in the United States, where broadcasters developed a strongly fundamentalist character with a fire-and-brimstone preaching style and direct appeals for donations from listeners. The Canadian regulations called for broadcasts with a much more reserved tone. In addition, by explicitly criticizing direct advertising, the Aird Commission ensured that Canada would not develop the resource-rich evangelical media empires that sprang up in the United States.

While the Canadian government did grant the Canadian Radio Broadcasting Corporation the right to close down or expropriate private stations, the CRBC chose not to do so. The effect was a small and geographically uneven set of religious broadcasts that allowed a few conservative evangelical voices on the radio. Thus, Canadian radio did include religious and even conservative evangelical broadcasts, although they were not as numerous or as profitable as their counterparts to the south.

The Antigonish movement in Nova Scotia was one example of religious radio broadcasting in Canada. Based at St. Francis Xavier University, it took to the airwaves to disseminate its messages of adult education and social justice (Alexander 1997). Fathers Jimmy Tompkins and Moses Coady, along with other Catholic priests, used this small radio station (CJFX) to launch a movement in the Maritime provinces that addressed the problems of poverty and debt. These broadcasts were crucial to the development of cooperatives and credit unions in the first half of the twentieth century (Dodaro and Pluta 2012). Other examples emerging from the Catholic Church could be found in Quebec at that time. Of course, although an important part of Canada's religious broadcasting history, the Antigonish movement and other Catholic denomination broadcasts were far removed from the conservative evangelical movement of the day.

Much closer to the pioneers of American evangelicalism was Baptist preacher T.T. Shields. A self-professed fundamentalist and ardent believer in biblical literalism, Shields led the Jarvis Street Baptist Church in Toronto (Priest 2005). He was one of the key Canadian figures in conservative evangelicalism who made a name for himself by aggressively scrutinizing his fellow Baptists for any signs of liberalism or modernism (Tarr 1967). As part of his ministry, Shields hoped to create a "fundamentalist superstation" that would reach an international audience, but he failed to raise the capital required, settling for a weekly broadcast of his Sunday services (R. Johnston 1994). Shields did manage to deliver a fundamentalist message over the airwaves from his Toronto pulpit, but his radio endeavours could not break even financially and he closed down his radio wing after only one year (R. Johnston 1994, 400). It is not clear whether the Canadian regulatory prohibition on soliciting donations was the main cause of Shields's financial difficulties, but it certainly did cut off a revenue stream that was important to the successful American fundamentalists on the radio in his day.

Shields was the most prominent conservative evangelical Canadian preacher in these early radio days, but it was William "Bible Bill" Aberhart of Alberta who had the most successful radio career. Aberhart was a Baptist minister, and he broadcast his sermons in 1929 to an audience of 350,000 across Western Canada, including fiery attacks on those who sought to reconcile their Christianity with science or other forms of modernism (R. Johnston 1994, 387; Stackhouse 1999, 39). He launched a successful political career as well, becoming premier of Alberta in 1935 at the head of the Social Credit Party that he founded. His successor, Ernest Manning (father of prominent conservative politician and lobbyist Preston Manning), also broadcast on Aberhart's Prophetic Bible Institute Sunday radio hours, a practice he continued for decades.

Aberhart was a prominent character in conservative evangelical Christian radio, and his legacy is as close a rival to the evangelical radio of the United States as any in Canada. And yet his evangelicalism and the politics of his Social Credit Party stood in stark contrast to the evangelicalism that was prominent in the United States at the time. US-style evangelicalism's staunch aversion to secular politics, shared in large measure by Canadian evangelicals, was disregarded by Aberhart, who sought political solutions to the real-world problems that he saw around him in Alberta

(Stackhouse 1999). And unlike conservative evangelicalism's focus on individuals' personal salvation, the problems Aberhart sought to address were communal problems. His concern for the plight of farmers inspired the creation of the Social Credit Party; he imagined a class of people treated unfairly by an economic and political system and encouraged deep engagement with the secular sphere.

Russell Johnston (1994, 399) argues that Aberhart's broadcasts "lost their edge" as they continued through his political career, which was cut short by his untimely death in 1943. Other scholars claim that Aberhart's political success cost him his evangelical following (Finkel 1989; Stackhouse 1999). Using electoral statistics, Grayson and Grayson (1974) find that urban religious fundamentalists accounted for a small proportion of the Social Credit Party's total support. They argue that economic rather than religious appeal may offer a better explanation for the rise of Social Credit (see also Boudreau 1975). Perhaps more relevant to our analysis, his broadcasting may have launched a great political career, but it failed to build him a multimillion-dollar media empire, as was the case with his US contemporaries. While Aberhart definitely built a strong institutional basis for evangelical conservatism in the Canadian West, it was small relative to the American media empires built by conservatives. In addition, its close connection with the political party structure gave it a very different character from the for-profit, stand-alone conservative evangelical institutions built in this era in the United States.

In 1938, the CBC established a National Religious Advisory Council, with members drawn from several mainline denominations (Fortner 2005). This allowed for a small amount of religious programming, Catholic and mainline Protestant, free of charge. At the same time, the Canadian government allowed its licences to religious radio stations to expire. State-sponsored religious radio was governed by committee, while the for-profit model of evangelical broadcasting in the United States was limited to the small number of private, local stations (Armstrong 2010). Even as late as 1968, Canadian policy reaffirmed its distrust of religious programming. The Broadcasting Act of 1968, which is known for establishing the CRTC, included a regulation of religious broadcasting. Section 3(d) of the act stated that "the Canadian broadcasting system should provide a reasonable opportunity for the public to be exposed to the expression of differing views on matters of public concern" (Darling 1993). In order to achieve this objective, individual licensees were required to be "balanced," a goal that the commission deemed unlikely to be fulfilled by single-faith denominational stations, since these types of stations by definition would be one-sided and predisposed towards one point of view (Salter and Odartey-Wellington 2008; Grant and Buchanan 2010). For this reason, the CRTC refrained from issuing licences to any religious broadcasters until 1983. This has had a long-lasting effect. Even as late as 1993, for example, religious broadcasters complained of difficulty in purchasing airtime on conventional stations and of being relegated to marginal time slots (Darling 1993).

Other than the large audiences of Aberhart, most evangelical broadcasting in Canada was small in scope and scattered about the country. The majority of religious broadcasts in the early days of radio in Canada were ecumenical and entertaining to a wide audience, as Canadian regulations intended. The Aird Commission created quite different cultural programming from that found in American religious radio. Of course, many Canadians living along the US border could pick up American radio signals, and in some cases American evangelical shows were rebroadcast in nighttime slots on Canadian stations. In terms of institution building, however, the stricter regulatory framework of Canadian broadcasting prevented much growth of a uniquely Canadian set of conservative evangelical Christian media organizations. Prohibitions against on-air fundraising snuffed out the lucrative opportunities that were present in the United States.

The regulation of Canadian broadcasting has consistently aimed to achieve a cohesive national identity and culture and to resist "Americanization" (Vipond 2000). These intentions have limited the ability of religious broadcasters to spread their messages, especially if these messages reflected a single-faith perspective and were not appropriately "balanced." Historically, since frequencies were limited and the airwaves were deemed public property, access and licensing were seen as rightfully determined by representatives of the public rather than market forces. Those who obtained licences to broadcast over the public airwaves, then, became public trustees who were held accountable for ensuring that their frequencies were used in responsible ways, and not to express narrow or singular perspectives (Vipond 2000). Combined with restrictions on the ability to solicit donations on air, this limited the broadcasting of conservative evangelical viewpoints.

Institutional Infrastructures and Cultural Resources

The SMS perspective reminds us to consider the extent to which activism is institutionalized. We adopted a historical lens for viewing SMS theory in order to consider the processes and especially the extent of institution-alization that was present in the earliest days of – or in our case, decades before – movement emergence. Our comparative frame reveals two divergent paths to institutional development, based on the peculiarities of the regulatory framework of radio broadcasts. Widely divergent approaches to broadcast policy in Canada and the United States led to enormous differences in the scale of conservative evangelical Christian religious broadcasting in these two neighbouring countries, creating significant differences in the *extent* of institutionalization and mobilization of evangelical Christian communities.

Beginning with radio broadcasts and continuing into television, the kind of wide-open field of religious broadcasting that existed in the United States was simply not available to conservative evangelical Christian groups in Canada. This set of institutions, established well before the emergence of the religious right, formed an important part of the institutional infrastructure for this movement. In the United States, this infrastructure of media organizations is large and rich, with massive audiences and densely networked organizations. In Canada, the media wing of this institutional infrastructure was much smaller, less resource-rich, with smaller audiences and fewer organizations. There were fewer media-related corporations for Canadian religious right activists to rely on, and this may well have reduced the Canadian audience for the religious right's agenda, considering that widespread media exposure in the United States was one tool for evangelicals to spread their message and expand their constituencies. These foundations left the two similar social movements with starkly contrasting institutional supports and forms and salience of mobilization.

As we move forward in time to the emergence of the religious right in the late 1970s and early 1980s, we see the same movement emerge in both Canada and the United States. In the latter, the Reverend Jerry Falwell, a famous televangelist with a large following, formed a partnership with a set of Republican Party insiders from Washington, DC, to create the Moral Majority. They used Falwell's extensive mailing list of contributors to solicit direct-mail donations to support a social movement organization's attempt to legislate conservative evangelical Christian values in Congress, and Falwell used his television show to convince his audience to support this legislation. All of the institutional infrastructure that this movement organization relied upon was the historical product of religious radio broadcasting in the United States. Although Canadian religious right activists were similarly interested in socially conservative legislation, their movement organizations did not rest on a similar institutional infrastructure. They could not harness a similarly broad audience through an infrastructure of media organizations.

A social movement society is one in which the practices of activism have been institutionalized and routinized. We argue that the SMS theoretical framework should include within its view of institutionalization those historical practices of organizational development and institution-building projects that take place prior to movement emergence. The comparative analysis presented here demonstrates that the work done by conservative evangelical Christians in the first half of the twentieth century produced different levels of institutionalization in the Canadian religious right vis-à-vis the US movement. Our research suggests that there are multiple elaborations of SMSs, each articulated somewhat differently from the others given particularities of different historical and political contexts. This finding is line with the position held by Ramos and Rodgers in the Introduction to this volume, that it is fruitful to think of societies plural – or in this case historical trajectories plural – and it elucidates the historical underpinnings of the important relationship contemporary movements have with states, as illustrated in Chapters 4 and 6. Our work supports these efforts to improve our understanding of multiple social movement societies and the bureaucratic, organizational, and political histories that produce them.

While both Canada and the United States may be understood by scholars to be social movement societies, the rapid proliferation of religious media organizations in the United States created a denser, stronger institutional infrastructure for its religious right social movement than in Canada. The social movement societies vary in terms of both the degree and quality of institutionalization. They provide disparate amounts of routinized, institutionalized support for the religious right movements that they host. Our focus here on the historical differences in how policy interacted with organizational growth brings our attention to the pre-movement institution-building practices of communities. This example is but one of many ways in which social movement societies vary in their articulation relative to a given social movement. Future research on social movement societies – especially those with a comparative lens – will surely reveal many more.

3

The Social Movement Society and the Human Rights State

DOMINIQUE CLÉMENT

The diffusion and institutionalization of protest are defining features of the social movement society. One of the most visible manifestations of institutionalization is the way some social movements help create, promote, and enforce the law. Human rights law in Canada exemplifies this phenomenon. Laws that bind the state to enforce human rights principles, as well as human rights agencies and social movement organizations (SMOs) that enforce these laws, constitute the "human rights state." The backbone of the Canadian human rights state is a series of provincial and federal human rights statutes as well as the Canadian Charter of Rights and Freedoms. In this chapter, I explore how the human rights state exhibits many qualities associated with a social movement society.

The human rights state in Canada, I argue, depends on the participation of non-state actors. SMOs play multiple roles in implementing human rights law: campaigning for legislation and future reforms; drafting statutes; enforcement; educating the public; keeping the government accountable; acting as a liaison between human rights agencies and the community; and training staff and providing a pool of recruits for human rights agencies. The first section of this chapter explains the methodology and the choice of case studies. The second documents the role of social movements in the creation of the modern human rights state. The human rights state, as we shall see, evolved alongside the social movement society. The third section places the human rights state in a national and contemporary context, and documents how social movements continue to shape (and are shaped by) the human rights state. The final section addresses the central themes of the social movement society thesis.

Methodology

Human rights legislation is one of the great legal innovations of the twentieth century. These statutes prohibit discrimination in employment, services, and accommodation, as well as unions, business associations, and the display of signs. They ban discrimination on the basis of sex (sexual harassment, pregnancy), age, physical and mental disability, marital status, pardoned conviction, sexual orientation, family status, dependence on alcohol or drugs, language, social condition, source of income, seizure of pay, political belief, and gender identity and expression. Specially trained human rights officers investigate complaints and attempt informal conciliation. When conciliation fails, boards of inquiry can impose settlements, such as requiring offenders to pay a fine, offer an apology, or reinstate an employee. Human rights commissions or tribunals are specialized government agencies that are more efficient and accessible than courts, and absorb the cost of resolving complaints. They are also given the resources to pursue vigorous human rights education programs (Clément 2014). While the Charter is binding on governments, federal and provincial human rights law applies to private as well as public activities.

There are many parallels between the human rights state and the social movement society thesis. First, if protest is broadly defined to include such SMO activism as lobbying, litigation, letter writing, research, or media campaigns, then the human rights state has facilitated the diffusion and proliferation of protest. The diffusion of protest is apparent in the way new constituencies, from sexual minorities to people with disabilities, have organized into SMOs around human rights reform. Second, many of these new SMOs have become integrated – institutionalized – into the human rights state. The human rights state provides people with a unique access point for influencing state policy and, in doing so, redirects protest into an institutional framework. Third, institutionalization has facilitated the professionalization of SMOs. The human rights state has encouraged the formation of a host of new SMOs staffed with professional activists, and the line between civil servants and activists has become increasingly blurred. Fourth, this process constitutes a new form of governance. Through the human rights state, SMOs have become part of the lawmaking and enforcement process. Finally, social movements have also been at the forefront of challenging limited conceptions of human rights. SMOs are increasingly framing a host of new grievances as human rights violations. The human rights state exemplifies Hank Johnston's description of a social movement society as "an extension of the state's role into areas where it had been minimal or absent ... a society infused with state agencies, interjecting themselves more deeply into daily life" (H. Johnston 2011, 69).

British Columbia is the ideal context for exploring the human rights state as a case study of the social movement society. The province has a long history as a locus of social movement activism and human rights policy innovation. It was host to the country's first gay rights organizations, Greenpeace, dozens of civil liberties groups and Aboriginal peoples' advocacy groups, and dramatic student protests in the 1970s (Clément 2005). The women's movement, in particular, flourished in British Columbia. There were at least 76 advocacy groups, 46 women's centres, 15 transition houses, 12 rape crisis centres, 36 service-oriented organizations (health centres, self-defence programs), and 20 artistic initiatives (women's music festivals, bookstores) in the 1970s (Clément 2008b). Because the majority of human rights complaints throughout the 1970s and 1980s involved sex discrimination, I focus especially on the role of the women's movement in the human rights state. Moreover, the province has a history of being a site of contestation over human rights law and has sparked national debates. British Columbia was one of the first jurisdictions to enact human rights legislation, the first to prohibit sex discrimination, the first to set precedents in areas such as gay rights and sexual harassment; in 1974 it introduced the country's most progressive human rights legislation. Ironically, the province has also historically led the way in passing the most *regressive* human rights legislation in Canada.

This chapter draws on extensive archival research, including newly released materials secured through the British Columbia Freedom of Information and Protection of Privacy Act. Because there is no single collection of records for the human rights branch or commission, this project draws together multiple collections, including the University of Victoria Archives' Human Rights Boards of Inquiry records and the Ministry of Attorney General Human Rights Branch collection; *Labour Relations Bulletin; Canadian Human Rights Reporter;* and over a dozen SMO archival collections. The University of Victoria Archives and the University of British Columbia

Rare Books and Special Collections have among the best collections on the women's movement in Canada. This chapter also draws on provincial government publications relating to human rights policy, interviews with activists and key figures in the human rights bureaucracy, and a survey of the websites of several major SMOs to sample how they are framing their grievances using human rights.

Social Movements and the Human Rights State

The first anti-discrimination laws in Canada appeared in the 1940s and, between 1962 and 1977, every jurisdiction introduced expansive human rights legislation. Ontario's 1944 Racial Discrimination Act prohibited the display of discriminatory signs and advertisements, and three years later Saskatchewan passed its Bill of Rights. These initiatives were largely ineffective, however. Even the premier of Saskatchewan acknowledged that the law was primarily educational (Patrias 2006, 284). Ontario led the way again when it passed the country's first Fair Employment Practices Act in 1951, followed soon after by a Fair Accommodation Practices Act and the Female Employees Fair Remuneration Act in 1953. These laws required equal pay for women and banned racial, ethnic, and religious discrimination in employment and accommodation. Most other jurisdictions introduced similar legislation. British Columbia's Equal Pay Act was passed in 1953, followed by the Fair Employment Practices Act (1956) and the Fair Accommodations Practices Act (1961).

Social movements were at the forefront of these initiatives. By the 1950s, organizations as diverse as the United Nations Association, Canadian Association of Social Workers, YMCA/YWCA, Toronto Social Planning Council, University of Toronto Faculty of Social Work, Fellowship of Reconciliation, Canadian Council of Christians and Jews, Japanese Canadian Citizens' Association, and the Canadian Association for Adult Education were engaging in public education campaigns and lobbying for fair practices legislation (Sohn 1975, 78–82). The most prominent SMOs were the Association for Civil Liberties and the Jewish Labour Committee (JLC) (Lambertson 2001). Both organizations led large delegations of unions, ethnic and racial minorities, students, and religious organizations before Ontario premier Leslie Frost. These delegations, which also helped draft the law, were a critical factor in convincing the premier to introduce the Fair Employment Practices Act (Lambertson 2001). Meanwhile, the labour movement led campaigns to extend the human rights state throughout Canada. As the federal Department of Labour acknowledged in 1964, "it can be stated without qualification that the history of fair employment practices legislation in Canada testifies to the effectiveness of the fundamental educational groundwork carried on by labour" (Canada, Department of Labour 1960, 4).

Securing the legislation was only the beginning. SMOs became essential to enforcing the law. Vancouver's JLC committee was typical: it produced educational programs (films, public lectures, literature, an annual race relations institute seminar); wrote briefs to the provincial government; prepared test cases to investigate allegations of discrimination; issued press releases and spoke on local radio; and investigated complaints (VLCHR 1952, 1960–71, n.d.a). One of the Vancouver committee's earliest successes was to convince the Downtown Hotel in 1959 to stop refusing service to blacks. The hotel owner refused initially, but yielded when the committee secured a promise from the British Columbia Automobile Association to remove the hotel from its "approved" ranking (VLCHR 1959).

The government did nothing to publicize its anti-discrimination legislation. Instead, it was the British Columbia Federation of Labour that produced a "Guide to Employers" and distributed it across the province. The federation also hired William Giesbrecht as a human rights worker. One of his first projects was a survey of job advertisements and applications. Employers routinely asked prospective employees about religious preference, nationality, race, or place of origin. Giesbrecht identified cases of discrimination and forwarded the results to the director responsible for the legislation (VLCHR 1960–71, n.d.b). In cases when the director delayed responding to an individual complaint, Giesbrecht lobbied to have the complaint pursued (BC Federation of Labour 1964 to 1969). In several cases he convinced large companies to revise their application forms, and it was not uncommon for Giesbrecht to meet with a landlord or a cemetery manager and convince them to stop discriminating against blacks or Jews (VLCHR 1960–71; BC Federation of Labour Human Rights Committee 1961). In this way, non-state actors were integral to the human rights state.

Unfortunately, anti-discrimination legislation was largely ineffective. Only six complaints were filed under British Columbia's Fair Employment Practices Act (1953–69), and only three under the Public Accommodation Practices Act (1961–69). Equal pay legislation was equally ineffective. Only thirty-three women successfully applied for restitution under the Equal Pay Act (BC Department of Labour 1959–63). Across Canada, the impact of anti-discrimination legislation was similarly dismal: the law was not adequately enforced, individuals had to take the initiative themselves to pursue a complaint, and the remedies were weak (*Toronto Star* 1961; Eberlee and Hill 1964, 451; Langer 2007, 4). The human rights state remained an unfulfilled promise.

It was the Vancouver Civic Unity Association that likely convinced the government to introduce its first Human Rights Act in 1969 (D. Anderson 1986, 60–61). The legislation did little more than consolidate existing laws into a single statute, however. The British Columbia Federation of Labour insisted that the "legislation is not a human rights bill and is only designed to catch votes rather than protect the human rights of the citizens of the province" (*The Province* 1969). By the 1970s, newly emerging social movements, rather than organized labour, were at the forefront of mobilizing for reform. One of the leading SMOs was the Vancouver Status of Women (VSW). Established in 1971, the VSW "dealt only in women's rights," and its key objective was to "foster public knowledge of the rights and status of women in Canada." By 1978, the VSW had over 800 members, a half-dozen full-time staff, and a budget of over $90,000 (Brown 1989, 98). It prepared briefs and lobbied the government, assigned volunteers to attend all-candidates meetings during elections, and flooded the media with press releases (VSW 1973, 1978). The Status of Women Action Group (SWAG), British Columbia Federation of Women, Young Women's Christian Association, Vancouver Women's Caucus, and NDP Women's Rights Committee also lobbied for human rights legal reform (D. Anderson 1986; Brown 1989). After the New Democratic Party defeated the Social Credit Party in 1972, the government introduced a new human rights statute. Rosemary Brown, the VSW's first ombudswoman and a key figure in the organization, helped draft the 1974 Human Rights Code (Brown 1989). Fourteen SMOs attended a workshop hosted by the British Columbia Civil Liberties Association (BCCLA) and produced several recommendations that provided the foundation for the new legislation.

The NDP's Human Rights Code embodied the best aspects of the Canadian human rights state: professional human rights investigators, public education, a commission promoting legal reform and representing complainants before formal inquiries, jurisdiction over the public and private sector, a focus on conciliation over litigation, independence from the government, and an adjudication process as an alternative to the courts. British Columbia had gone even further than the already expansive Canadian standard. Instead of restricting the legislation to a set of enumerated grounds, discrimination was prohibited unless the accused could demonstrate *reasonable grounds*. As a result, the province set precedents in areas such as a sexual orientation, pregnancy, physical appearance, and sexual harassment. It was, without a doubt, the most progressive human rights law in Canada (Clément 2014).

Social movements were soon involved in every aspect of the human rights state in British Columbia. The Human Rights Code facilitated the expanding role of SMOs in developing and enforcing state policy. In this way, the central features of the social movement society became manifest: the proliferation and diffusion of protest, institutionalization, professionalization of social movements, and new forms of governance. For instance, there was no such thing as a human rights investigator in British Columbia in 1974; the Social Credit government had used overworked Industrial Relations Officers (labour mediators) to investigate human rights complaints. In contrast, the new Human Rights Branch hired and trained dozens of human rights officers. SMOs were a fruitful source for recruiting staff: all three directors of the Human Rights Branch between 1974 and 1984 had been involved with women's rights organizations, and the investigators had been active in women's groups, the BCCLA, Aboriginal Friendship Centres, disability rights organizations, and Indo-Canadian community groups. Fourteen staff were asked in 1981 about their ties to community groups: at least fifty-two SMOs were mentioned, including associations as diverse as the National Black Women's Congress, Greenpeace, and the Elizabeth Fry Society (AG HRB 1981a). The distinction between human rights investigators and activists became increasingly blurred (AG HRB 1981b). For instance, it was not uncommon for human rights investigators working for the government to participate in symposia organized by the BCCLA or VSW that led to resolutions calling for legislative reform, or they might organize public seminars on topics such as the resurgence of the Ku Klux Klan.

The integration of social movements was also apparent in the way they often supplanted the state in enforcing the law. SWAG initiated at least two equal pay cases that had widespread ramifications. At times, the VSW was more effective than the government's own staff. Its full-time ombudswoman prepared numerous human rights complaints and was responsible for initiating the largest equal pay case in the province's history. The ombudswoman often adopted the role of a government official. For example, in 1972 she met with managers of the Hudson's Bay Company and convinced them to voluntarily raise the salaries of female sales clerks to comply with the legislation (VSW 1972). The ombudswoman also provided free legal counsel to complainants at hearings.

SMOs such as the VSW engaged in a wide array of activities to enforce the legislation: documenting cases of discrimination; producing surveys or conducting research on issues such as equal pay (e.g., documenting employers' pay scales) to initiate inquiries; identifying large employers who were violating the legislation and mailing them letters with a copy of the statute; sending volunteers to individual employers to discuss hiring and management practices (e.g., department stores that rarely hired women); drawing the media's attention to deficiencies in the legislation, including delays and poorly trained investigators; organizing and inviting investigators to conferences on human rights; lobbying government departments on policy issues (e.g., gender stereotyping in textbooks); promoting awareness of board of inquiry decisions through press releases and newsletters; securing federal government funding to promote human rights in the province; and writing to the Human Rights Branch to support specific cases and to prod investigators to advance an inquiry (SWAG 1972; VSW 1976a; Victoria Human Rights Council 1979; BC Department of Labour 1981; BC Federation of Women n.d.).

The Human Rights Commission, which was responsible for human rights education, depended heavily on SMOs. The commission provided grants to SMOs to host conferences, conduct research on issues such as mandatory retirement, or produce educational materials (AG HRB n.d.). Some of the SMOs responsible for human rights education included the Vancouver Island Multicultural Association, Women Against Violence Against Women, Canadian Council of Christians and Jews, Associated Disabled Persons of BC, Surrey Delta Immigrant Services Society, Committee for Racial Justice, Vancouver Native Police Liaison Program, and Vancouver Gay Community Centre Society (Renate Shearer 1979–83). By the early 1980s, SMOs were essentially carrying out the commission's statutory mandate.

SMOs were especially important in rural British Columbia. Human rights investigators actively courted their support. Investigators drove throughout the region meeting with women's groups, Aboriginal Friendship Centres, and church groups, among others. Given the difficulty of patrolling large swaths of territory, they often relied on SMOs to spread awareness of the law. In Prince Rupert, for instance, the security guard at the local Hudson's Bay Company routinely followed Aboriginal men when they visited the store, often little more than a few feet behind. Furious at the company's policy, the leaders of the local Aboriginal Friendship Centre asked a human rights investigator from Prince George to visit in the summer of 1978.

Within a day, he convinced the store manager to change the policy (Andison 2010). By the early 1980s, the Human Rights Branch was insisting that all officers spend at least 10 percent of their time working with community groups.

Social movements became essential to the human rights state in almost every aspect: staff recruitment, drafting of legislation, enforcement, education, chairing of inquiries, and outreach to rural areas. The focus on administering human rights legislation invariably facilitated the professionalization and institutionalization of social movement organizations. The human rights state also constituted a new form of governance in the way non-state actors played a role in creating and enforcing state law. However, because the NDP government lasted for a only few short years (1972–75), it fell to the Social Credit Party (Socreds) to enforce the Human Rights Code. The Socreds, a right-wing political party with close ties to business, were opposed to the NDP's expansive legislation that restricted the right of employers to hire or fire employees (Clément 2014). Their administration of the Human Rights Code is an ideal case study of how social movements adopt the role of state actors when governments inhibit the application of law.

The Socreds did everything in their power to undermine the human rights state until they eliminated the Human Rights Code in 1984. Ministers obfuscated or lied outright, delayed appointments, were recalcitrant in approving boards of inquiry, replaced human rights investigators with untrained Industrial Relations Officers, cut funding, reduced regional offices, and appointed inexperienced people to the commission (Legislature of British Columbia 1977). *Vancouver Sun* columnist Allan Fotheringham suggested that "the whole range of names on the commission demonstrates Williams' desire to make the commission so bland as to be ineffectual" (Fotheringham 1978). One member, Jock Smith, had previously been the target of two complaints for violating the code (Hume 1979a, 1979b). Meanwhile, the backlog of complaints was growing. The director of the Human Rights Branch estimated in 1982 that they were receiving 42 percent more cases than they were capable of handling (BC Department of Labour *Annual Report* 1982). SWAG expressed a common grievance with the Socreds' management when it insisted that the "B.C. Human Rights Commission is an embarrassment and a bad joke. They have done nothing except show their appalling ignorance and insensitivity to human rights" (SWAG 1979). Social movements protested the government's inaction, interference, and cutbacks. Throughout the late 1970s, the VSW campaigned against the Social Credit government's obstinacy in appointing new human rights officers, going so far as to organize a province-wide "day of mourning" on 10 December 1976, International Human Rights Day (VSW 1976b). After the Human Rights Commission embarrassed itself in a public meeting where its members made lewd comments about women and homosexuals, several SMOs organized a petition campaign to have them dismissed (AG HRB 1979). Two hundred women mobilized in 1975 for a protest in downtown Vancouver on Mother's Day, with participation as diverse as the British Columbia Federation of Women, Women's Bookstore, SORWUC (a female labour union), Women's Health Collective, Child Care Federation, and Vancouver Rape Relief (BC Federation of Labour 1975). In 1976, the largest mass rally at the Legislature in the province's history thus far featured a host of women from across the province protesting, among other issues, deficiencies in the administration of human rights law (Anonymous 1976). A year later, SMOs successfully lobbied the Minister of Labour to appoint outstanding boards of inquiry (D. Anderson 1986, 81). They also answered the Human Rights Commission's call in 1981 for briefs on amending the Human Rights Code. The commission's hearings attracted dozens of SMOs that provided documentation of government mismanagement (BC Human Rights Commission 1983a, 1983b). Among the diverse array of SMOs participating in the hearings were the Okanagan Women's Coalition, BC Coalition of the Disabled, BC School Trustees Association, Social Planning and Review Council of BC, BC Association for the Mentally Retarded, and Vancouver Labour Council.

In 1982, the Socreds began preparing to replace the Human Rights Code. A secret memorandum to cabinet outlining the proposed changes noted that "there may be a lobby of resistance to substantive changes to legislation" (BC Department of Labour *Annual Report* 1982). It was a profound understatement. The first attempt, in 1983 (Bill 27), was so widely condemned in the press and by a coalition of SMOs that the government retracted the bill. A year later, the Socreds inserted the same bill into a large omnibus bill that contained thirty statutes implementing widespread budget cuts. Once again, dozens of SMOs were critical of the amendments (*Sisterhood* 1983; Legislature of British Columbia 1984; Solidarity Coalition 1984).[1] Criticism of the reforms came from organized labour, civil libertarians, feminists, racial and ethnic minorities, religious organizations, and seniors' groups (Clément 2014). The Canadian Association of Statutory

```
MERCHANT ID 030000097004        C
CLIENT ID 9801            SLIP# 2622
TERMINAL ID 004           TRACE# 00253546

** PURCHASE              **      41.81
DEBIT # ************6161
ACCOUNT Chequing          RESP 000
DATE 09/14/2016           TIME 13:02:33
AUTH # 130233             REF # 00000064
APPL.: Interac
AID: A0000002771010
TVR: 8080008000           TSI: 7800

              APPROVED

BY ENTERING A VERIFIED PIN, CARDHOLDER
AGREES TO PAY ISSUER SUCH TOTAL IN
ACCORDANCE WITH ISSUER'S AGREEMENT WITH
CARDHOLDER

           CUSTOMER COPY
----------------------------------------
    *** Customer Copy ***
2622 0938 004   4      09/14/16 01:02PM
```

Human Rights Agencies (CASHRA) described the act as a "tragic mistake" and insisted that it be reversed ("Ottawa Steps Up" 1983; Palmer 1987). Opposition to the reforms also became a prominent component of the platform of the Solidarity Coalition, a diverse coalition of SMOs campaigning against the Socreds' fiscal restraint package (Palmer 1987).

Despite the Solidarity Coalition's mass mobilization on a scale rarely seen in the province's history, activists were unable to prevent the Socreds from gutting the human rights state. The "reasonable cause" section was removed, the maximum possible fine was reduced from $5,000 to $2,000, the Human Rights Commission was eliminated, and the process for submitting complaints was streamlined to allow bureaucrats to dismiss complaints without an investigation. Human rights investigators were fired and replaced with overworked Industrial Relations Officers with no human rights training (Black 1994). Not a single member of the government defended the legislation in the legislature (Legislature of British Columbia 1983). As R. Brian Howe and David Johnson (2000, 158) suggest, "this was the furthest any Canadian government has ever gone in restructuring its human rights policy."

The human rights state has remained contested in British Columbia since 1984. The NDP returned to power and reintroduced expansive human rights legislation in 1992, only to have the Liberal Party defeat them and change the law again in 2002. In this way, though, the province was an exception in Canada. Throughout most of this period, human rights legislation had widespread support across the country, and social movements became an integral component of the human rights state. As R. Brian Howe insists, activists' views have "considerable policy influence either because of the substantial political pressure they represent or because they provide legitimacy for what commissions themselves want to do" (Howe and Andrade 1994, 4). Rosanna Langer (2007, 9) argues that SMOs "provide human rights expertise and play a collaborative role in advancing rights discourse in the community at large." SMOs are especially important in developing policy: "As an example, the OHRC Strategic Plan 2001-2004 Backgrounder details policy development in the area of gender identity, synthesizing research, consultation with the transgendered community, meetings with selected officials and health professionals, development of a discussion paper, and incorporation of feedback in the discussion paper, culminating in Commission approval of its Policy on Gender Identity" (Langer 2007, 111). The participation of SMOs has evolved into a cooperative process that involves developing values, administrative frameworks, and patterns of communication with the state.

Moreover, social movements have contributed to an expansion of the scope of human rights. Debates surrounding the proposed Charter of Rights and Freedoms in 1980–81, for instance, reveal how social movements transformed rights talk in Canada (Fudge 1989, 445–48; J. Kelly 2005, 63–73; James 2006, ch. 6; Clément 2008a, 158–60). Hundreds of SMOs participated in public hearings on the Charter. Women's groups raised the possibility of a human right to learning and training, an annual income, parental leave, and day care. Ethnic minorities demanded recognition of a right to culture and identity. SMOs representing disabled people spoke of a human right to employment, protection against unemployment, healthy working conditions, and an adequate standard of living, health care, education, social insurance, and privacy. Sexual minorities sought a human right to full and equal participation in public and private life. Aboriginal peoples insisted on the right to self-determination and to control of natural resources, economic development, and education.[2] It was not the nature of the grievances that was significant – Aboriginal peoples had been campaigning on these issues for generations – but that activists were now articulating these grievances using the language of human rights.

Human rights has evolved into the dominant discourse most social movements use to articulate grievances. Egale Canada, for instance, believes that there is a human right to "a safe learning environment." They also insist on the inclusion of gendered identity in human rights legislation, as well as equal marriage rights and benefits for sexual minorities.[3] The Assembly of First Nations (AFN) and the Ontario Coalition Against Poverty (OCAP) are continually mobilizing around socio-economic rights. Whereas the latter wants recognition for the rights of the disabled poor to improved public and private services, the AFN is insisting on Aboriginal peoples' human rights to clean water, natural resources, self-determination, culture, language, education, land, and the environment.[4] Vancouver Rape Relief has adopted the position that a man's ability to pay for sexual access to other humans often supersedes the right of a woman not to be involved in prostitution.[5] From this perspective, prostitution is a violation of human rights, and women are uniquely vulnerable to this violation. By framing these grievances as rights issues, social movements invite state agencies into the private. Human rights commissions are increasingly having to mediate a broad range of social issues, from sexual reassignment surgery to the provision of adequate food and housing for Aboriginal peoples.

Discussion

The emergence and evolution of the human rights state has run parallel to the development of the social movement society. Consider, for instance, the proliferation of SMOs and the diffusion of social movement activism. The first parliamentary hearings on a bill of rights included only a few civil liberties and labour groups in the 1940s. A small number of SMOs representing churches, women, students, and Jews joined campaigns for human rights legislation and a bill of rights in the 1950s and early 1960s. Little had changed by 1971, when a parliamentary committee again held hearings on a bill of rights. The only difference was a handful of SMOs representing the disabled and ethnic minorities. Even hearings for the federal Human Rights Act in 1977 drew only six SMOs representing women, unions, and lawyers (House of Commons 1976-77a, 1976-77b). By 1981, however, and certainly by the 1990s, the number of SMOs participating in public debates surrounding human rights law had grown exponentially. They were also more diverse: people with disabilities, Aboriginal peoples, women, children, racial minorities, ethnic minorities, prisoners, religions, the poor, sexual minorities, workers, and others formed an expanding policy network of SMOs (J. Kelly 2005; James 2006). As Sally Chivers (2007, 314) suggests, "constitutional politics provided an unparalleled political opportunity to assert the political and social rights of those who had traditionally been marginalized in Canadian society." The human rights state is, in this way, a useful case study of the proliferation and diffusion of social movements.

The proliferation of SMOs has blurred the lines between the state and social movements. The result has been the development of new forms of governance. Human rights commissions are akin to the array of state agencies created in recent decades that provide "new institutional arrangements for social movement influence," which as Johnston points out in the case of the United States Department of Labor or Environmental Protection Agency, "recruit movement leaders as administrators or consultants and engage movement organizations on policy issues, sometimes contracting SMOs to provide services or gather information" (Johnston 2011, 95). The British Columbia Human Rights Commission, for instance, used public funds to help SMOs fulfill its statutory mandate for education. And it is argued that SMOs have been integral to the enforcement and reform of rights law. Another example is the way the human rights state enables SMOs to make new law. The NDP concluded in 1973 that it was politically impossible to include sexual orientation in the Human Rights Code. However, the reasonable cause section allowed the Gay Alliance

Toward Equality to bring a complaint before a board of inquiry in 1975. The complaint had the full support of the Human Rights Branch, which acted as an advocate for the SMO (Ruff 2010). As a result, for the first time in Canadian history, a tribunal ruled that it was illegal to discriminate on the basis of sexual orientation (*Gay Alliance Toward Equality v. Vancouver Sun* [1979], 2 S.C.R. 435). In essence, an SMO and a state agency cooperated to create new law. This was not uncommon: women's rights groups, for instance, often used boards of inquiry to expand the scope of the law to apply to sexual harassment or pregnancy (Clément 2010, 2012, 2014). This extra-legislative process for creating law constitutes a new form of governance.

The professionalization of SMOs and their integration into the human rights state has serious implications for social movements, including the marginalization of grassroots activism. The availability of state funding for SMOs beginning in the 1970s resulted in the proliferation of SMOs with paid staff, boards of directors, offices, legal advisers, and hierarchal structures. Federal and provincial governments established funding programs for women's rights and human rights SMOs, which hired staff to manage and apply for grants (D.E. Moore 1980; Pal 1993; Clément 2008a). As Miriam Smith argues, although state agencies such as human rights commissions may offer institutional recognition, "they may divert SMOs from other types of organizing and other forms of political mobilization ... These strategies of participation are thought to divert the movement from more radical strategies and tactics" (M. Smith 2005a, 130). The Canadian Charter of Rights and Freedoms has encouraged the professionalization of feminist and gay rights organizations, with the effect of redirecting resources away from grassroots activism (D. Smith 1999). In other words, it has depoliticized grassroots mobilization.[6] Unlike in the United States, where the gay and lesbian movement engages in a broad range of activism, the movement in Canada has shifted dramatically since the 1970s towards litigation (M. Smith 2005b, 332). In addition, feminist organizations such as LEAF have become the leading interveners before the Supreme Court of Canada since the Charter was entrenched in 1982 (Manfredi 2004).

The need for trained staff has increased because human rights legislation and the Charter have created opportunities for social movements to use the courts to address an array of grievances. The judicialization of issues such as equal pay requires SMOs with expert knowledge and training, as well as the resources to pursue costly legal battles. The focus on litigation is emblematic of the way SMOs have shifted their focus in recent years towards the state to achieve social change (Manfredi 2004, 15; M. Smith 2005a; Clément 2008a, 160–62). Many activists are concerned that this focus on the law marks "the conservatization of the movement" (M. Smith 2007, 194). In this way, social movements have moved away from disruptive tactics and, as Meyer and Tarrow (1998, 26) suggest, limited their ability "to surprise, disrupt and mobilize." If, as Hank Johnston (2011, 93) claims, "the social movement society may be but the latest stage in the fitful but long-term expansion of how to do politics less violently and with less destabilizing effects on state structures," then the human rights state certainly facilitates that process.

Conclusion

Meyer and Tarrow's definition (1998, 21) of institutionalization described in the Introduction to this volume is consistent with the notion of the human rights state.[7] For example, the largest and most influential women's rights organization in British Columbia, the Vancouver Status of Women, dedicated extensive resources to working within the confines of the human rights state. SMOs that employed the language of human rights focused their energies on the state and embraced state-oriented strategies for social change. SMOs that rejected human rights, such as the Vancouver Women's Caucus or Women Against Pornography, tended to be more decentralized and willing to engage in disruptive tactics such as civil disobedience (Clément 2008b, 2010).[8] The policy networks that have emerged surrounding the human rights state act as a process of inclusion/exclusion that favour SMOs such as the VSW to the detriment of grassroots activism. Activists who "might wish to represent their views to the state through regularized participation in networks of influence in the policy community are simply excluded from doing so because they lack the organizational and financial resources and the experience to deal with government bureaucrats" (M. Smith 2005a, 128). This process has the effect of marginalizing grassroots organizations in favour of professionalized rights-based organizations.[9] Human rights commissions actively encouraged SMOs to mobilize around campaigns for better legislation, which further marginalized grassroots SMOs committed to non-institutional activism or lacking policy expertise (Howe 1991, 793–94; Clément 2008b). As Smith (2013, 224–25) points out, "the women's movement in English-speaking Canada was drawn into the process of Charter-based legal mobilization around human rights claims ... In the years since the Charter's enactment, the women's movement has been drawn into litigation, even as other forms of political mobilization have been relatively weakened." The professionalization of SMOs has historically benefited equality seekers, while issues such as women's economic and political marginalization or subordination in the private sphere has been downplayed because these issues are not within the purview of human rights law. Rather than using rights-based advocacy as a means of achieving transformative social change, SMOs came to have securing legal recognition of equal rights as their objective.

The human rights state thus helps explain the *process* of institutionalization associated with the social movement society. Patrick G. Coy and Timothy Hedeen (2005, 410), using the mediation movement in the United States as a case study, document four steps that lead to co-optation. First, social movements "partly arise in response to a set of grievances or unfulfilled needs that a segment of the population experiences in a shared way" (410). Activists demand access to avenues outside the court system dominated by legal professionals and begin to develop parallel institutions, and elements within the state perceive the need for policy adjustment. Second, "the language and methods of the challenging movement are appropriated, while in the second step the work of movement actors may be appropriated through invitations to participate in policy making" (413). As this process evolves, the dominant norms and values of the state infiltrate the parallel institutions, and movement leaders are brought into the policymaking process. A new state apparatus replaces or infiltrates the parallel institutions and the state provides funding to SMOs, which leads to dependence. In the third stage, "the state and vested interests assimilate both the individuals and goals of the challenging movement, making it hard for the movement to sustain its efforts" (420). In time, movement actors become integrated and committed to the new state apparatus. In the final stage, state agencies transform the original goals of the movement. Bureaucratic interests, such as settling large numbers of cases, become positive outcomes.

There are striking parallels between the human rights state in Canada and the mediation movement. The first anti-discrimination laws were woefully inadequate because they relied on the courts to enforce poorly drafted legislation. SMOs developed strategies for discouraging discrimination, and were largely responsible for enforcing the first anti-discrimination laws. SMOs lobbied for the creation of new institutions that operated outside the courts and focused on conciliation rather than confrontation or punishment. The state responded with the creation of human rights laws and commissions. Human rights commissions mimicked many of the habits of SMOs such as the JLC. In some circumstances, a commission might even employ test cases, such as hiring a black couple and a white couple to test a service provider for discrimination (AG HRB 1977–79). Nonetheless, social movements remained central to the creation, promotion, and enforcement of the law. British Columbia's Human Rights Branch integrated organizations such as the VSW or SWAG into its practices and hired activists as human rights officers. There were clearly inadequacies with the Human Rights Code, as evidenced in the way it allowed for the Socreds' mismanagement. So successfully were many SMOs integrated and committed to this new state apparatus, however, that they fiercely defended the human rights state in 1984. But they failed. The Human Rights Act (1984) created a rigid system with a focus on legal punishment rather than conciliation, which was far from the original goals of the movement that had produced the human rights state. In addition, many activists became concerned with how human rights law reduced discrimination to one factor, such as sex, and failed to account for how individuals experienced discrimination (Duclos 1993; Iyer 1993; Pothier 2001; Réaume 2002). Someone might be discriminated against, not because she was a woman or a person with a disability, but because she was a woman with a disability. In this way, the human rights state diverged from the movement's original goals: it became constrained by the function and content of statutory law rather than addressing the root cause of racial or gender inequality.

The human rights state in Canada is a useful case study of the social movement society: the diffusion and growth of social movement activity; the proliferation of professional SMOs; institutionalization (or co-optation); the engagement of the state and social movements in new spheres of daily life; and social movement activism as a standard repertoire of political participation or policymaking. Social movements have, as Meyer and Tarrow (1998, 4) suggest, become a "perpetual element of modern life."

Notes

1 In addition, refer to media coverage on the following dates in the *Vancouver Sun:* 24, 27, and 29 November 1984, and 12 December 1984.

2 A complete list of all the briefs submitted to the Special Joint Committee on the Constitution in 1981 are available at www.historyofrights.ca/.

3 "Adding gender identity and gender expression to the *Human Rights Act* tells trans people that they can accept themselves and live in dignity free from discrimination and harassment." Egale Canada, 2005. "EGALE and GALE BC celebrate safe schools victory: Final victory for bullied student sends message to schools across Canada." Egale Canada 2011. "About EGALE." Egale Canada 2011. http://www.egale.ca.

4 On the AFN and OCAP, see Assembly of First Nations 2007 and Ontario Coalition
   Against Poverty 2008.
5 On Vancouver Rape Relief, see "Anniversary of the Universal Declaration of Human
   Rights" (Vancouver Rape Relief and Women's Shelter 2002).
6 As Smith (2005a, 348) explains, the Charter "had the effect of centering human
   rights as the dominant frame and ideology of the movement at the expense of
   the liberatory goals of the original gay liberation and lesbian feminist movements, of
   generating a mobilizing structure for lesbian and gay organizing that privileges legal
   networks and litigation-dominated organizations such as Egale, and of furnishing
   the movement with policy resources through legal victory. Without the mobilizing
   structure for litigation and without the pattern of legal victory under the Charter,
   elected politicians would have avoided the hot button of gay rights."
7 Meyer and Tarrow (1998) describe the process of institutionalization as routinization of collective action (challengers and authorities adhere to a common script),
   inclusion and marginalization (granting access to those who adhere to the script,
   and excluding others), and co-optation.
8 There was a correlation between the use of rights discourse to frame an SMO's grievances and its overall strategies for change. While the SWAG, VSW, NDP Women's
   Rights Committee, and others prepared briefs and press releases on everything
   from day care to pornography, Women Against Pornography picketed adult video
   stores and harassed customers as they entered the store.
9 Human rights are only tangibly realized through laws or regulations. Individuals
   and groups can make rights claims and such claims have a powerful moral force, but
   they are not *rights* until recognized by the state. Human rights activists must seek
   out the state to have their rights claims recognized. According to Miriam Smith
   (1999), "rights talk assumes that changing or strengthening the law is in itself a
   means to [achieve] social change and that legal changes are thus the proper goal of
   political struggle and organizing. Rights talk thus defines social and political change
   as legal change."

4

Institutionalization, State Funding, and Advocacy in the Quebec Women's Movement

DOMINIQUE MASSON

Feminist scholars are quick to recognize that the women's movement is more vigorous, stronger, and more densely networked in Quebec than anywhere else in North America. On the organizational plane, the movement currently consists of approximately 300 local groups, affiliated to 17 regional *tables* of women's groups, and about 20 provincial-level associations and *regroupements* – that is, peak organizations loosely coordinating different types of local women's groups. The overwhelming majority of these local, regional, and provincial organizations identify with feminism and see themselves as part of a larger social movement aimed at bringing about change in gender relations. Their action encompasses, in various measures, service provision and popular education, as well as advocacy on behalf of women, the latter being termed *la défense collective des droits* (the collective defence of rights). Local, regional, and provincial women's groups have over time acquired the status of legitimate actors representing women's issues and interests in the policy process. In fact, Quebec women's movement organizations regularly engage, on their own account or as members of coalitions, with various levels of the state, intervening in public policy debates, participating in public consultations, petitioning, pressuring, lobbying, and occasionally taking to the streets. These organizations not only owe their vitality and continued existence to the dedication of their staff, activists, and members but also rely for most of their financial support on a variety of state programs, both provincial and federal.

Almost all women's movement organizations in Quebec are to some extent state-funded, and in the vast majority of cases a more or less substantial proportion of their funding comes in the form of an operational grant (core funding) from provincial sources. A sizable fraction of the movement, particularly local shelters, rape crisis centres, and women's centres and their provincial *regroupements*, have received core funding from the province for three decades or more. In addition, since 2001, a governmental funding policy in support of community action has made core funding for women's organizations the rule rather than the exception, and support for advocacy is an explicit part of the policy's provisions.

This brief portrait of the Quebec women's movement thus seems to lend credence to some of the main tenets of the social movement society (SMS) thesis, especially with regard to the routinized engagement of movement organizations in the conventional tactics of institutional politics (Meyer and Tarrow 1998; Soule and Earl 2005), the formalization and professionalization of movement organizing that sustains these tactics (Meyer and Tarrow 1998; Soule and Earl 2005), and the development of normalized state responses to movement activity (Soule and Earl 2005) that include, according to Howard Ramos and Kathleen Rodgers in the Introduction to this volume, the offer of resources in support of movement organizing and action. Going beyond such a superficial reading of the SMS thesis is necessary, however, if we are to explore its possibilities and limits for analyzing contemporary politics, as this volume attempts to do.

The intellectual project of the SMS thesis is to enable social movement scholars to better "understand the changing relations between contemporary politics and contention" (Meyer and Tarrow 1998, 25). This is an important question; it directs our attention to the ways in which, the extent to which, and the context and conditions in which movement/state relations have been routinized and normalized so that social movements' practices of claims making have become a customary part of contemporary institutional (state) politics. Yet the full exploration of the research program suggested by the SMS thesis is impeded by its reliance on an undertheorized, negative conceptualization of institutionalization processes, as well as by too sharp a distinction between movement politics and state politics, and movements and institutions more generally.

In the SMS thesis, protest and, by extension, social movements themselves become institutionalized when they undergo organizational development (such as formalization), and when they engage with state institutions through the use of less confrontational and more conventional means. This can be seen, for example, in the works of Meyer and Tarrow (1998) and Soule and Earl (2005). In such accounts, institutionalization means acquiring the (necessarily unsavoury) characteristics of formal political institutions, which de-radicalize and eventually tame previously spontaneous, vibrant, and radical movements. Such a conception of institutionalization is in line with the paradigmatic assumptions of early social movement theory (see reviews in Landriscina 2006 and Morgan 2007), in which the progressive character of movements, their capacity for social change, and eventually their very definition have become implicitly equated with specific organizational forms (loose, informal, and based on activists' resources), movement strategies (viewed as mass mobilization and disruptive protest), movement claims (radical and non-negotiable), and relations with states (by definition non-existent or, at best, relying solely on outsider tactics). Deviation from any of these essentialized characteristics invites the negative label of "institutionalization."

Such theorizing has been criticized, however, for being premised on an overly homogeneous and largely idealized vision of movements' history – more precisely for resting on a perception of social movements based on a "disproportionate attention accorded to the struggles of the sixties" (McAdam et al. 2005, 2) or on the characteristics of particular factions within movements of that era – for instance, the New Left or Black Power (Goldstone 2003, 7). In contrast, women's movements, Sawer (2010, 604) suggests, "have been less likely to engage in disruptive or violent action" (see also Kuumba 2001), and institutionalization, she writes, "is part of the way the women's movement has always operated" (602). This is an observation echoed by Dominique Clément in Chapter 3. Negative and deterministic judgments on organizational development and involvement of movement actors in institutional politics, in this sense, appear more normative than analytical; that is, they seem to be linked with specific visions of how social change *should* come about. As well, the marked concern of the SMS thesis for the fading of violent, disruptive forms of protest in movement politics may express an androcentric bias preoccupied with the performance of heroic masculinities in the public sphere. What is lost here is not only an accurate vision of the heterogeneous character of social movement activity, past and present, but the recognition that different organizational forms, strategies, and tactics do different jobs and present different mixes of advantages and inconveniences for movement work (Staggenborg 1988; Riger

1994; Ferree and Martin 1995). To realize its full potential, the SMS thesis needs a revised and more productive understanding of the relationship between movements and states, and between movements and institutions.

In this view, Goldstone (2003), for instance, challenges the too sharp distinction made between movement politics and conventional institutional politics. Not only do "social movements constitute an essential element of normal politics in modern societies," he claims, but most importantly "state institutions ... are interpenetrated by social movements, often developing out of movements, in response to movements, or in close association with movement" (Goldstone 2003, 2). For him, the SMS thesis should be pushed further to show how movement claims shape states, contributing to the democratization of policymaking and to the extension of citizenship rights (2–3). This position accords with current feminist scholarship (see Waylen 1998 or Kantola 2006 for an overview) showing that women's movements have consistently engaged with states from the nineteenth century onward and have been instrumental in shaping state institutions, policies, and programs in various settings, making gains on crucial gender issues ranging from suffrage to married women's right to work, maternity leave, and pay equality to pay equity, the legalization of abortion, anti-violence policies, and the adoption of new normative regimes in international conventions such as the Convention for the Elimination of All Forms of Discrimination Against Women (CEDAW). Many states today manage various policies geared towards or supporting gender equality. These changes were not bestowed on women by benevolent governments. All of them are due to mobilizations that have included unconventional and, more often than not, very conventional forms of interest representation by women's movement actors, in domestic and international political arenas.

Martin's work (2004) is useful for further theorizing the relationship between movements and institutions. Summarizing the classical and contemporary sociological literature on social institutions, she proposes that the latter are constituted by sets of social meanings and recursive human practices that endure over time. More precisely, social institutions are better understood as enduring and patterned "norm-governed social practices" (Tumeola, cited in Martin 2004, 1256). Institutionalization, it follows, can be understood in this light as the outcome of processes through which particular sets of meanings and social practices get inscribed, fixed, and routinized in the life of institutions. Yet institutionalized meanings and practices are not homogeneous or integrated, nor are they ever completely stabilized.

They evolve and change as a result of human agency, tensions and contradictions, social conflict, and innovation (Martin 2004, 1257). Social institutions such as the state can thus be viewed as sites in which social movement actors engage in politico-discursive struggles with the goal of seeing preferred movement meanings and the social practices indexed by these meanings institutionalized in the life and work of target institutions. Conceptualizing institutionalization in this way does not presume the type of tactics (disruptive or not, conventional or unconventional) employed by social movements to reach this goal. It also directs our attention away from the fate of movements towards the unfolding of the political dynamics of the encounter between movements and states in particular contexts, as well as towards their outcomes, understood here as the institutionalization of particular meanings and practices in state institutions and their eventual consequences for the pursuit of movement politics.[1]

Returning to the SMS thesis with such a revised understanding of institutionalization, I propose that social movement societies are characterized (among other things) by the institutionalization of normalized and routinized relations between movements and states regarding the role of movement organizations in the public sphere. The analytical task thus becomes to ask and to understand how such institutionalized relationships between movements and states come about, what their nature is, and how they vary in time and place. To this end, I submit that different political rationalities and their attendant state forms (i.e., state policies and programs) crystallize the institutionalization of different relations between state and civil society, and state and movements – an observation also made by Tina Fetner, Allyson Stokes, and Carrie Sanders in Chapter 2. Adopting a political economy approach suggests that *social liberalism, neoliberalism,* and *contractualism,* as political rationalities, offer a useful theoretical vocabulary for grasping these different relations and understanding the unique character of the Quebec case in the Canadian context.

In this chapter, I use the case of the women's movement as a point of entry into the historical constitution of some of the main features of a "social movement society" in Quebec. These include: the existence of dense and strong networks of formal and professional women's and community organizations that identify with social change; the routine engagement of such organizations in advocacy on the terrain of conventional institutional (state) politics; and the establishment of funding programs and policies that recognize and support the various roles played by these organizations in the public sphere, including those of critique and advocacy. I begin by providing a historical account of the early battles of women's services for funding and recognition to account for the development of provincial funding for women's groups, and to challenge some of the paradigmatic assumptions regarding "institutionalization." Next, I adopt a wider lens to locate the institutionalization of the relations between women's groups and the state within the larger context of the changing political rationalities and state forms through which a loose partnership with the community sector, which would come to be understood in the literature as an intrinsic feature of "the Quebec model" (Jetté 2008, 22), took shape from the end of the 1960s to this day.

Institutionalizing Funding for Women's Groups at MSSS[2]

The idealized portrait of movement organizing that underpins the paradigmatic approach to institutionalization does not correspond to the way the second wave of the women's movement took shape in Quebec. Rather, the beginning of the second wave was characterized by organizational and ideological heterogeneity, as well as by differing orientations towards the state. The Fédération des femmes du Québec (FFQ), for instance, founded in 1966, brought together existing feminine and professional women's associations under a formal, provincial umbrella organization that counted on political pressure and lobbying to obtain legislative reforms to the status of women (Le Collectif Clio 1982, 449–54). From 1970 onward, an array of small feminist organizations began emerging in Montreal, articulating Marxist, socialist, and radical feminist analyses of oppression. Distrustful of a state they saw as inherently capitalist and patriarchal, they favoured consciousness raising, popular education, and feminist cultural production fuelled by activists' resources. The historical record shows that most such organizations were also short-lived (Dumont and Toupin 2003). Activities surrounding the celebration of the International Women's Year in 1975 fostered the dissemination of feminist ideas about women's emancipation throughout the province (Le Collectif Clio 1982, 493) and spurred the creation of women's service groups, notably shelters for battered women, rape crisis centres, and women's centres. Service groups were themselves very heterogeneous in their orientations and organizational forms, and most identified with political projects foregrounding the provision of women-defined, local responses to what were perceived as pressing women's needs for adequate help and for equality of status (Beaudry 1984; Masson 1998).

These local service groups very rapidly sought institutionalized funding from the state as the makeshift combination of volunteer and militant labour, local donations, and short-term funding from governmental employment programs that they relied on was proving both insufficient and too precarious. In 1979, deeming their very survival to be endangered, nineteen shelters founded the Regroupement provincial des maisons d'hébergement; that same year, six rape crisis centres founded the Regroupement québécois des CALACS.[3] The first undertaking of the *regroupements* was to spearhead a collective battle for securing a steady and routine flow of financial resources from the state that would guarantee adequate, recurrent, and stable levels of core funding for all member organizations. Quebec's Ministry of Social Affairs (which would become the Ministry of Health and Social Services in 1985) was their target. Entwined with demands for funding were claims for the recognition of women's service organizations as legitimate service providers and political actors, and for the recognition of the issues, analyses, and solutions they put forward. Also at stake was the protection of the political, programmatic, and administrative autonomy of women's service groups, for which the *regroupements* spelled out their own funding conditions. All these distinct and crucially important meanings they sought to institutionalize – that is, to inscribe or embed in state institutions.

The struggle of women's services for funding and recognition took place from the late 1970s to the end of the 1980s (see Masson 1998, 1999/ 2000 for details) and was mostly fought with conventional means – political lobbying, letters to provincial MNAs, petitions, press releases and campaigns for public opinion, and appeals to insider allies, especially the Conseil du statut de la femme (Status of Women Council) – although demonstrations were occasionally organized. Regarding the issue of funding, the dogged pressure exerted by women's service groups throughout the period resulted in significant gains. The Quebec Ministry of Social Affairs first answered by granting access to a handful, and then to an increased number, of shelters and rape crisis centres to what was initially a small program providing core funding to community organizations (the Programme de soutien aux organismes communautaires, or PSOC). Funding conditions at the PSOC required only that organizations be incorporated as non-profits and provide the ministry with yearly activity reports and financial reports duly adopted by their general assembly of members (Jetté 2008, 197). The ministry also progressively granted funding to the provincial *regroupements* and began funding women's centres. In the last years of the 1980s, it established triennial, renewable, standardized core funding plans for shelters, women's centres, and rape crisis centres.

The inclusion of shelters and rape crisis centres in the consultations leading to the ministry's first policy on violence against women, in 1985, also signalled their recognition as legitimate actors in the policy process. Their participation was instrumental to the inscription, in the language of the policy, of a feminist analysis of violence and of state support for the approaches developed in women's services. Protection of the groups' autonomy was guaranteed by the policy's granting of the status of "autonomous bodies" to community organizations. The delivery of services for abused women was thus to be ensured by parallel networks of state institutions and community organizations, with women's groups retaining full control of their services and programming (Masson 1999/2000, 55). By the end of the 1980s, core funding by the PSOC was understood by women's service groups as supporting, albeit insufficiently, their direct services to women, their activities of prevention and popular education, as well as their involvement in advocacy and coalition building (Masson 1998).

Did the institutionalization of state funding for women's services produce formalization, bureaucratization, professionalization, and depoliticization? Existing scholarship on early women's services, such as the work of Beaudry (1984, 76–91), and my own research on women's service groups in the Saguenay–Lac-Saint-Jean region in the 1980s (Masson 1998) question the premise underlying this paradigmatic line of questioning by suggesting that most women's service groups were *not* politicized from the start.

Initially, the objectives were to help battered women and rape victims and, in women's centres, to provide a space for women to develop personal autonomy. Only a minority of these groups were founded on the basis of radical feminist projects and in Saguenay–Lac-Saint-Jean, identification with feminism was tenuous at the outset. Early women's services seldom developed a critical perspective on organizational models. Incorporating as a non-profit organization, forming a board, and naming officers were both a response to funders' requirements and the standard practice among Quebec's community organizations. Despite the minimal accountability procedures of the PSOC grant, juggling different funding sources made data collection, bookkeeping, and reporting inescapable features of the groups' operations. Yet, the documentary requirements of funders were light compared with those observed elsewhere (see, for instance, Ng 1990), thus helping to keep the development of administrative procedures (i.e., bureaucratization) at a minimum. Finally, women's services were organized as "professional movement organizations" in the sense that they expressed a preference for small-scale organizing relying on the work of paid, permanent staff and the unpaid work of a small number of volunteers and activists, rather than on mass-based mobilizations. It is important to recall that the conventional distrust of professional SMOs by the SMS thesis and much of social movement literature does not take into account the very real possibility that professional activists may further radical causes or use unconventional means. It also typically underestimates the difficulty of constituting and maintaining mass mobilization over time.

Yet, as my research shows, local women's services groups became in many ways increasingly, rather than less, politicized throughout the 1980s as their joining together in the battle for funding created the opportunity to meet with one another, to share, and to refine analyses, modes of functioning, and collective identifications. By the end of the decade, identifying as feminists had become the norm rather than the exception. Rationales for action had moved from helping women and promoting legalistic understandings of equality to struggling against gendered relations of power, male domination, or patriarchy. Explicitly feminist approaches to service work had been developed, and collectively achieved definitions of a feminist identity and orientations to social change in women's shelters, rape crisis centres, and women's centres were institutionalized in the *bases d'unité* (unity platforms) of their *regroupements*. At the *regroupement* of rape crisis centres, for instance, membership was conditional on adopting a radical feminist analysis of violence and the feminist collective as a mode of decision making. Although services and popular education formed the bulk of the action in local women's services, advocacy work, in the form of participation in intra- and inter-movement coalitions and the deployment of a repertoire of pressure and protest, had become infused with a new intensity.

State Funding Then and Now: Institutionalizing State/Movement Relationships in Quebec

Understanding how state funding for women's groups and the recognition of their advocacy role came to be a normal and routine practice of state institutions in Quebec, and understanding the current incarnations of this funding, to which I will turn shortly, cannot be separated from an appreciation of the broader history of the relations between the community sector and the province over the past four decades. The institutionalization of these relations in funding policies and programs helped consolidate a "social movement society" in Quebec. Women's and community movements have been active and significant participants in these processes of institutionalization, resisting certain arrangements and promoting others, with varying results. The twists and turns of this story are themselves intimately linked to the larger picture of the constitution and transformation of the welfare state and of public intervention over that period.

Premised on the role of the state in mitigating social inequality through the development of citizenship rights, social liberalism (see Mahon 2008 or Brodie 2008), as a political rationality, presided over the development and consolidation of postwar liberal welfare states. It also made available a language of social rights, social equality, and redress for injustices that, Brodie (2008) argues, contributed to new forms of political identities and mobilizations. In Canada, social liberalism entailed a relationship with civil society in which the state recognized the latter's role as a space for the political participation and representation of the citizenry (Jenson and Phillips 1996, 112, 116). From the mid-1960s onward, the Citizenship Branch of the Secretary of State of Canada thus implemented funding programs for voluntary organizations that were "couched in terms of citizenship, identity and participation" (Pal 1993, 14). It was in this general political climate that Quebec undertook, in the 1960s, a series of reforms aimed at establishing a modernized and centralized postwar welfare state – what has come to be called "the Quiet Revolution." Left-leaning popular groups *(les groupes populaires)*, citizen's committees, and community organizations representing the interests of the poor and the marginalized were particularly active in this period, launching self-managed social experiments in the form of popular clinics, cooperatives, and community day care. They were also claiming citizens' control over welfare reform as part of a project of establishing social democracy (Hamel 1991; Bélanger and Lévesque 1992). A concern for "citizen participation" on the part of the province arose at this juncture, both as a response to the increase in popular citizen and community movement activity and in keeping with the receptiveness to civil society organizing that characterized the broader political context of the time.

The federal government and the Quebec government thus shared a similar interest in supporting civil society organizations. However, while federal support was framed within a larger project of reinforcing national unity (Pal 1993), provincial support in Quebec was linked to a process of welfare state formation. The modernization of the health and social services sector, a major endeavour that was the object of intense discussions from 1966 to 1971, was the main goal towards which citizen participation was enrolled. The provincial Liberal government attempted to integrate citizen participation in its 1971 reform of health and social services in various ways: (1) by absorbing the popular clinics created by the community sector and transforming them into local state institutions – the *centres locaux de services communautaires* (CLSC); (2) by granting formal representation to "users" and "citizens" on the boards of health and social services institutions; and (3) by providing some subsidies to voluntary and community organizations, initially in an ad hoc manner and then through a small funding program created in 1973 – the Programme de soutien aux organismes privés et bénévoles des services sociaux et de santé (Masson 1998, 83). The failure of state-managed citizen participation in health and social services institutions led the Council of the Family and Social Affairs, which had been mandated to draft a policy regarding community organizations, to suggest in 1976 that citizen participation would be better nurtured outside state institutions, through the development of the community sector (Jetté 2008, 90–102). State funding would enable the Ministry of Social Affairs to benefit from community organizations' capacity for social animation, from their original experiments in service provision, and from their social and political critique to ensure the healthy evolution of state-provided welfare (Jetté 2008, 94–96). For their part, community organizations would see their action, capacity for innovation, and autonomy supported through an operational grant (core funding) (Jetté 2008, 52–53). Elected in 1976, the Parti Québécois government followed suit and enacted these recommendations by creating, in 1977, the Programme de soutien aux organismes communautaires (PSOC). The program institutionalized a relationship between the Ministry of Social Affairs and the community sector founded on the desirability of state support for citizen participation and for innovation in the field of health and social services. Its funding, however, was not a financial priority and the program doled out a mere $1.5 million to about fifty organizations in its first year (Masson 1998, 84). However, budgets were regularly increased over the following years, as a growing number of women's shelters, rape crisis centres, women's centres, and other community organizations successfully pressed the ministry for funding and recognition of the issues they put forward, the needs they articulated, and the services they operated.

The nature of the relationship established between the state and community organizations through the PSOC was, however, very much in flux throughout most of the 1980s, as the economic crisis of the early 1980s and the attendant fiscal crisis prompted the province to search for new avenues to restructure its provision of welfare. Relations between the state and the community sector, which up to then had followed somewhat similar "social liberal" developments in Canada (see Pal 1993, as well as Chapters 3 and 5 in this volume) and in Quebec, would begin to diverge. Newly emerging as a political rationality to guide states through solutions to the crisis, neoliberalism took hold at the federal level with the election of Brian Mulroney's Conservatives in 1985. "Roll-back" neoliberalism, or retrenchment, led the Canadian government to alter significantly its prior relationship with social movement organizations, as it slashed into third-sector funding and further endeavoured to delegitimize women's and other advocacy groups as defending "special interests" far removed from those of the majority of Canadians (Masson 2012). Yet, and despite the election in 1985 of a new Liberal provincial government overtly sympathetic to neoliberal ideas, Quebec went down a different path with experiments that entailed an active recourse to the community sector in the (re)organization of welfare.

One of these experiments was embodied in the 1985 policy on violence against women, the first formal policy to officially recognize the importance of community organizations in ensuring the welfare of Quebec's population. Not only did the policy entrench in its language the autonomous status of community organizations, it also institutionalized a relationship that can best be described as a very loose partnership between state institutions and women's organizations, one in which the latter were understood as working in the public interest alongside of, and independently from, the public sector and with its financial support. The 1980s, however, also featured experiments with contractualism, that is, the integration of community organizations into state-programmed service plans through annual contracts financing only the specific services deemed of interest to the ministry. Such a shift towards contractual relations between state and civil society organizations has been documented in various countries and has been theorized as "roll-out neoliberalism," "inclusive liberalism," or "the social investment perspective" (see Dobrowolsky 2006 and Masson 2012 for more details).

Between 1985 and 1991, these two very different ways of envisioning the role of women's and community organizations in welfare relations – loose partnerships versus contractualization – jostled uneasily as Quebec's Liberals worked towards a new reform of the organization of health and social services. While the budgets and the numbers of funded groups at the PSOC grew at a greater rate (Jetté 2008, 229), uncertainty and unpredictability loomed large regarding the type of relationship to be favoured by the reform. Extensive public consultations were held to which women's and community organizations presented more than 300 briefs. A coalition composed of the three *regroupements* and other provincial women's organizations entered the public debate, articulating claims that were also defended through a wider community sector coalition. Insider allies, including public servants from the PSOC, also intervened. These intense mobilizations eventually yielded major gains. Service contracts were sidelined, respect for the autonomy of state-funded groups was inscribed in Article 335 of the 1991 law reforming health and social services, and representatives of the community sector obtained seats on the boards of the new *régies régionales* (regional agencies) that were to manage the reform.

After 1991, the sheer numbers of groups funded by the province through the PSOC and other smaller programs, as well as the militancy and strength of mobilizations by organizations that increasingly identified as a community *movement* contributed to shift the terrain on which funding for women's and community organizations was negotiated. Looking for ways to formalize the province's relationship with the community sector as whole, and in a gesture that may also have included pre-referendum political calculations, the newly elected Parti Québécois government created in 1995 a Secretariat to Autonomous Community Action (Secrétariat à l'action communautaire autonome, or SACA), to act as a liaison between the government and community groups.[4] A few months later, in June, a large contingent of women's organizations led by the FFQ held the first Bread and Roses March against poverty and violence, in which "a massive coalition of community groups, women's groups, [anti-]poverty groups and students' associations descended on the National Assembly in Quebec" (White 2006, 25). One of the central demands of the Bread and Roses March was "the development of social infrastructures" through public investment in women's and community organizations. In October, the secretariat announced the creation of a special fund in support of community action, part of which was specifically destined to support their defence of social and political rights. The secretariat also had the mandate to develop a governmental policy regarding community action. The more militant sections of the community sector mobilized, and 125 delegates from different domains of activity met in 1996 to create an Advisory Committee to Autonomous Community Action, obtaining official advisory status regarding the elaboration of the policy in 1997. "This committee," White (2008, 24) writes, "collaborated closely with the secretariat and greatly influenced content, even penning some parts of the policy."

Such involvement in and influence on policymaking testifies to the political legitimacy and the political leverage achieved by the community sector as a result of its mobilizations, which also made it into a force to be reckoned with at the very moment when the Parti Québécois government was seeking to establish a "social consensus" in support of its deficit-cutting policies (Laforest and Phillips 2001, 57; Graefe 2003, 11).

The outcome of such a historical conjuncture was the 2001 Policy for the Recognition and Support of Community Action[5] (Gouvernement du Québec 2001), which aimed at harmonizing under a common regulatory framework the various provincial funding programs directed towards the community sector. This policy currently governs funding relations between the province and over 5,000 organizations from the community sector, including women's groups. At its centre is the recognition of the sector's ongoing contribution to Quebec's social development and to the active exercise of citizenship by its population (13–14). While such language may seem to echo the government's earlier interest in "citizen participation," the policy went beyond supporting community organizations as sites for citizens' involvement and social imaginings to recognize their role in political representation, their power of influencing policy, their contribution to the collective defence of rights, and, furthermore, their role of critic, which was to be "recognized and protected, in order to establish the necessary distance between them and the ministries they addressed" (10, 11). Respect for the groups' autonomy was an essential principle of the policy, which reiterated the government's commitment "to ensure the respect of community organizations in the definition of their mission and orientations, their approaches, modes of intervention and functioning" (16).

To support its central tenets, the policy established several mechanisms. Although existing formulas of project funding and service contracts were to remain part of the overall funding scheme, core funding to support salaries and infrastructure costs associated with community organizations' global mission was "to constitute the preponderant portion of the funding granted by the government to the community sector" (25, 27). In turn, this "global mission" was understood as extending from the groups' primary activities – for instance, services to battered women – to "education to the exercise of rights, associational life, activities of concerted action and representation" (28). Recognizing community organizations' "contribution to the vitality of democratic debates" (28), the policy confirmed the continuing existence of a special fund providing core operating monies to community organizations whose primary activity was the collective defence of rights, that is, advocacy

(25). "Supple" accountability requirements, "sensitive to the reality of community organizations" and not placing "an additional burden" on them, were favoured (36). Participatory mechanisms, in the form of an Advisory Committee to Community Action, would ensure the representation of the community sector in the further definition of funding parameters and accountability requirements (42). Finally, the province was to increase its financial support; effectively, since the adoption of the policy, provincial funding to the community sector has almost doubled, from $472 million in 2000–01 to $860 million in 2010–11 (SACAIS 2011, 73).

The progressive features of the 2001 policy attest to the presence and influence of the community sector in the process leading to its elaboration. For this reason, the policy should be analyzed as a co-construction, the result of collaboration between governmental actors and representatives of the community sector, but also the result of conflict. For important compromises were also inscribed in its very structure. First, it was essentially a governance policy, leaving funding in the hands of twenty-two ministries and government agencies. Second, it was a non-prescriptive policy that could not impose its guidelines but could only encourage their adoption. As a result, the funding context post-2001 has been the locus of an uneasy coexistence between different orientations towards the community sector on the part of a fragmented state. The continuing influence of social liberalism as a political rationality is clearly visible in the 2001 policy, as the latter founds its rationale for core funding in the role of autonomous women's and community organizations in the development and exercise of citizenship. It is also clear in the existence of the special fund for organizations whose primary activity is the collective defence of rights. The PSOC, which finances, mostly through core funding, more than 60 percent of the 5,000 community organizations in Quebec and the vast majority of women's groups, similarly aligns with the precepts of the 2001 policy. Yet contractualism represents one-third of all provincial funding (2009–10). It typifies, for instance, funding conditions at Emploi-Québec, where state support is tied to contracts for specific employability services to be provided to targeted populations (see Masson 2012 for details). Finally, the harsh program cuts and delegitimization of activist groups noted at the Ministry of Environment in 2005 (Garon 2008, 28–31) attest to the influence of hardline neoliberalism in some parts of the state. The current situation in Quebec is thus that of a hybrid, complex mix of political rationalities in which social liberalism predominates. Consequently, different types of relations between the province and women's and community organizations coexist, in which loose partnerships marked by dynamics of "conflictual collaboration" (White et al. 2008, 60–69) are preponderant and are characterized by core funding, support for advocacy, and respect for the groups' autonomy. These features are peculiar to the "Quebec model" (Jetté 2008, 339) of state/civil society relations.

The situation in contemporary Quebec stands in sharp contrast to that documented at the federal level and elsewhere in Canada, where contractual relations and the delegitimization of the advocacy role of women's and community organizations have become the norm.[6] Repeated cuts brought on in the 1990s, first by the Chrétien government and expanded more recently by the Harper government to Status of Women Canada, the erasure of women's equality from the latter's mandate in 2006, and the shunning of more advocacy-oriented organizations at the Women's Program can all be analyzed as neoliberal attacks against "the residuals of social liberalism" (Brodie 2008, 157) still inscribed in the discourses and practices of federal institutions. By contrast, and contrary to many other provinces (see Brodie and Bakker 2007, 33, 37–38), successive Quebec governments have maintained to this day a social liberal commitment to women's policy machinery and to broader goals of gender equality for women. Although it may be tempting to attribute the persistence of a more favourable context for women's groups' activity in Quebec to the idea that neither the Liberals nor the Parti Québécois have wished to alienate women as a constituency in the push and pull of sovereigntist politics, there is no strong evidence to support such claim. A more accurate explanation would instead highlight the lesser hold of neoliberal politics in Quebec, as a result of both the success of movement struggles around welfare state restructuring and, from the 1980s onward, the adoption of neocorporatist forms of governance that became one of the hallmarks of the Quebec model in the 1990s. Such governance institutionalized the participation of businesses, unions, and community groups in policymaking (Graefe 2000), thus ruling out the delegitimization of advocacy by the community sector, including women's groups. This continued legitimacy of advocacy – the collective defence of rights – by community organizations and stable, even if insufficient, levels of core funding under conditions that respect the groups' autonomy, have buttressed the capacity of women's movement organizations to pursue their feminist politics through the various strategies and tactics that compose their current repertoire. As well, the continued attachment to the principle of gender equality in both public opinion and political culture in Quebec has been reinforced in recent public debates on "reasonable accommodations" and secularism. Taking centre stage in 2007–08 through the Bouchard-Taylor Commission hearings held under the mandate of the Liberal government, and brought to the forefront again in 2013 by the Parti Québécois's proposal of a "Charter of Values" for Quebec, these debates have elevated gender equality to the status of central marker of Quebec's identity,[7] further entrenching its legitimacy as a basis for political claims making.

Conclusion

In this chapter, I have argued that furthering the intellectual project of the social movement society (SMS) thesis required a revision of paradigmatic understandings of movements' relations with states and, more broadly, of the notion of institutionalization. Echoing Chapters 2 and 8, I also proposed that part of our task as analysts is to understand how SMS comes about – that is, how normalized and routinized relationships between movements and states develop and become entrenched. Adopting a political economy approach, I have taken the Quebec women's movement and its funding by the province as my entry point into the establishment of such relations.

My account shows the historical development in Quebec of provincial funding programs and policies privileging core funding to women's and community organizations, recognizing the groups' autonomy, and supporting their advocacy role, that is, their presence as legitimate critics and political actors in the field of normal politics. These features of the relationship between women's and community movement organizations and the province have almost no equivalent elsewhere in North America (Jetté 2008, 381), if not the world (Dufour, Lachance et al. 2007, 8). Their incremental institutionalization has been, as I have also shown, the result of a dynamic interplay between movements and state, in which movement agency called for state responses that it helped to shape. Significantly, at various junctures Quebec women's and community movement organizations have succeeded in getting movement meanings inscribed (i.e., institutionalized) in funding programs and policies. The relationship between the state and women's and community organizations in Quebec has remained over time broadly aligned with the principles of social liberalism as a political rationality, despite threats from neoliberalism and contractualism. This attests to the influence of struggles waged by movements.

Many, if not most, organizations in the Quebec women's movement are now twenty-five to thirty years old, if not even older, and most have been consistently funded by the province (and occasionally by the federal government) for almost as long. Overall, state funding not only permitted the survival of these groups but also facilitated their development and their resilience over time. It gave them a measure of financial stability that enabled them to build organizational capacity through the hiring of paid staff and the accumulation of experience and political learning, thus providing an enduring organizational infrastructure (see Chapter 1, in this volume) for the pursuit of the missions they defined for themselves. The three hundred or so women's groups in Quebec today strongly identify with feminism and with being part of a movement for change in gender relations. They also engage in a routine manner in a varied repertoire of tactics aimed at bringing about such change, including attempts at making change in and through state institutions by conventional means. Expressions such as "the institutionalization of protest" (Soule and Earl 2005) or "the institutionalization of contentious politics" (Meyer and Tarrow 1998) do little to help us grasp the active efforts of women's organizations to take state institutions to task on their own terrain, and to take state policies and programs, discourses, and practices as objects of dispute, struggle, and contention. As others before me have remarked, social movement theory's paradigmatic view of institutionalization "fails to grapple with the ways activists have tried to embed their values and discourses in existing institutions" (Andrew 2010, 614).

Finally, I suggest that we need theoretical room in social movement studies to understand social movements that have matured and endured, and whose characteristics do not resemble – if they ever did – that of an (idealized) emergence phase. One of these avenues is to go back to sociological conceptualizations of institutions, such as the ones highlighted by Martin (2004), and to also view institutionalization as indexical of processes through which movement discourses, meanings, and practices of contention become recursive and acquire an enduring presence in movement spaces. Such a revised conception of institutionalization would not presume the nature or effects of the meanings that become entrenched, or of the kinds of practices that become recursive, routinized, or even formalized in the course of a movement's life. Indeed, these can encompass, as we have seen here, reliance on professional staff and formal organizations, commitment to feminist and anti-patriarchal politics, and decision making through boards or through feminist collectives. Following this line of thought has already led some scholars, such as Sawer (2010, 603), to argue that women's organizations are, by their very existence, contributing to a process of feminist or women-centred institution building within civil society. Similarly, Andrew (2010, 614) suggests that, to the extent that they have continued to embody and carry forward feminist goals, discourses, and practices, women's movements and their organizations have acquired over time the character of (progressive) social institutions.

Notes

The data presented here have been gathered and analyzed either as part of my dissertation work (Masson 1998) or during the course of my recent research program on "Practices of citizenship and state funding in Quebec women's organizations." I thank the Social Sciences and Humanities Research Council of Canada for supporting both research projects.

1 A similar understanding of social institutions and institutionalization can be found in Mackay, Monro, and Waylen 2009 and Andrew 2010.

2 MSSS: acronym for Ministère de la Santé et des Services Sociaux (Ministry of Health and Social Services).

3 CALACS: acronym for Centres d'aide et de lutte contre les agressions sexuelles (Centres providing help and struggling against sexual assault).

4 Garon, Dufresne, and Guay (2006, 15) mention that the creation of the secretariat was supported by Premier Jacques Parizeau himself and that it was initially attached to the Ministère du Conseil Exécutif, thus underscoring the political importance of the Parti Québécois government's relationship to the community sector during the months that preceded the referendum of 1995.

5 All translations from the 2001 policy are mine.

6 See Dobrowolski 2006 for a general assessment. On the federal level, see Rodgers and Knight 2011; on British Columbia, see Morrow, Hankivsky, and Vascoe 2004; on the situation of Ontario shelters, see Bonisteel and Green 2005; on that of Canadian sexual assault and rape crisis centres, see Beres, Crow, and Gottell 2009.

7 For better and for worse, as gender equality has also been instrumentalized in support of exclusionary politics by proponents in these debates.

PART 2

STATE DYNAMICS AND PROCESSES

5

How the State Shapes Social Movements

An Examination of the Environmental Movement in Canada

CATHERINE CORRIGALL-BROWN AND MABEL HO

There have been many large-scale changes in civil society over the past fifty years. Meyer and Tarrow (1998) argue that we are now living in a social movement society (SMS), where there is more contention than ever before. At the same time, however, movement groups are becoming increasingly professionalized and institutionalized and, as a result, often less disruptive of regular political routines. In essence, this argument focuses on the relationship between the state and social movements and how the former can affect the latter. The social movement society thesis extends classic political process models that also focus on how the state can facilitate, or hinder, social movement activism by creating or reducing opportunities for mobilization and access to political insiders.

This chapter examines how changing government policies for supporting and cooperating with social movements shape the nature and extent of political action within civil society. The Canadian government has a long tradition of funding and cooperating with social movements, although this relationship has changed over time under different federal political leaders. This chapter compares two periods in Canadian politics – the Chrétien/Martin years and the Harper years – in order to assess how these two governments, with their different policies towards social movements, have affected social movement activities in Canada. We examine how government policies in these two periods have increased or decreased opportunities for political activism and how movement organizations have responded to these changing political contexts. We focus, specifically, on how federal support for social movements shape movement decisions about their tactics and targets.

This chapter begins with a historical examination of the relationship between social movements and the state in Canada from the 1960s until today. Next, we examine how changes in the political context in Canada have affected the tactics and targets of two Canadian environmental organizations, World Wildlife Fund and Greenpeace, over a ten-year period (2000–10). Using these data, we examine three major research questions. First, how does the government support and fund social movements in Canada? Second, how has this relationship changed over time? Finally, how do changing government policies and practices of funding and supporting social movements affect what organizations choose to do? We make this comparison by examining whether and how the tactics and targets of two specific movement organizations changed from the Chrétien/Martin period to the Harper period.

The State and Social Movements in Canada

Scholars have long been interested in how elements of the political context, such as government responsiveness to social movements, shape the timing of collective action and the outcomes of movement campaigns (McAdam 1996; McAdam, McCarthy, and Zald 1996; Meyer and Staggenborg 1996; Ramos 2008). Political process theory, in particular, highlights how under ordinary circumstances, challengers (such as social movement groups) are excluded from mainstream decision-making processes. This exclusion is not constant over time. In times of disruption, such as election periods or other times of internal political realignment, social movement activists may have more opportunity to affect government decisions and actions (McAdam 1982). Government leaders can also be more or less responsive to the needs of movements, which can create or limit their opportunities for action and success.

One way that governments can be supportive of social movements is by funding them. However, this is not practised in a uniform way in all countries. For example, France and Germany offer movements considerable funding, whereas Canada and the United Kingdom financially support movements at a lower level, with the United States lagging far behind (Rucht 1996, 1999; Rootes 2003). State funding of social movements can help promote political change by facilitating the development, survival, and resilience of these groups over time (see Chapter 4). In some contexts, however, state funding can compromise real social transformation, leading to co-optation or moderation of social movement groups and causes (Ndegwa 1996; MacDonald 1997; Clarke 1998a, 1998b; Rodgers and Knight 2011). In addition to monetary assistance, governments can support social movements by recognizing their importance, cooperating with them on activities like service provision and consulting with them in policy decisions.

The Canadian federal government has a long history of providing both direct and indirect support for voluntary organizations, including social movements. From around 1900, the federal government has given small grants and other support to charities that serve vulnerable groups through organizations such as orphanages, schools, and group homes. This funding expanded considerably after the Second World War and, over time, the federal government began providing resources to a more diverse range of voluntary and charitable organizations (Pal 1993; Ramos 2004; Clément 2008a; Laforest 2011). In addition to direct funding, the federal government provides indirect financial support for these groups through tax relief for registered charities. Policies for charitable tax exemption were institutionalized in the 1960s and are regulated by the Canada Revenue Agency. This agency determines which organizations qualify for charitable status and monitors the conduct of the registered groups (Laforest 2011).

In this section, we focus on government support for social movements in Canada since the late 1960s. Although the Canadian government had funded and cooperated with social movements well before this time, the end of the 1960s marked an important change in the relationship between the government and such movements. Prime Minister Pierre Elliott Trudeau embraced the role of social movements in helping to create a "just society." This framework understood social movements and community organizations as integral to society as a whole and to alleviating social inequality. Such recognition lent considerable authority and credibility to the work of these groups. Since this time, there have been four key periods in the relationship between social movements and the Canadian state. These periods parallel changes in prime ministership: 1968–83 (roughly coinciding with the Trudeau era, Liberal), 1984–93 (the Mulroney era, Progressive Conservative), 1993–2006 (the Chrétien/Martin era, Liberal), and 2006 to the present (the Harper era, Conservative). While detailed analysis in this chapter focuses on a comparison between the last two periods, we outline the changes that occurred before the election of Jean Chrétien in 1993 in order to give a historical perspective to the relationship between social movements and the state in Canada.

The Trudeau Era (1968–83)

Pierre Elliott Trudeau, Liberal prime minister of Canada from 1968 to 1984 (with a nine-month hiatus in 1979–80), worked actively to strengthen civil society organizations. Trudeau was concerned that Canadian identity was under threat as a result of the national unity crisis that began in the 1960s. He saw civil society organizations that mobilized around various facets of Canadian identity, including organizations that supported official language minority groups, multiculturalism, and women, as a way to strengthen the Canadian state (Pal 1993). During this period, the federal government provided substantial funding, including core funding, to many social movement groups in Canada in order to help them promote and pursue their causes at the federal level (Comeau and Santin 1990; Fleras and Elliott 1992). Through this funding, the government conferred legitimacy on these groups as mobilizers of collective action, and political advocacy was considered an important component of their activities. The favourable social and political environment not only "fostered the growth of the voluntary sector by facilitating the organization of various groups, but also made the sector more dependent on the federal government for core funding" (Laforest 2011, 28).

The decade of the 1970s was a period of growth and prosperity for social justice groups in Canada that focused on a range of issues. As noted in the Introduction to this volume, many important organizations, such as the Gay Alliance Toward Equality, the Congress of Aboriginal Peoples, and Greenpeace, were founded during this period. Among these groups, the women's movement was particularly well supported and funded by the federal government. The National Action Committee (NAC) on the Status of Women, Canada's largest women's organization, began relying on federal funding in 1972 and, by the mid-1980s, was obtaining at least two-thirds of its annual budget from federal sources (Bashevkin 1996). Surprisingly, the fact that Canadian women's groups relied so heavily on federal funding did not lead to co-optation and routinization, as we might expect from social movement society theory. Instead, this funding fostered more radicalization by women's groups in Canada than occurred in other countries, such as the United States. Without the need to attract and retain support from philanthropic foundations and individual members, Canadian women's groups could be more contentious and critical (Vickers, Rankin, and Appelle 1993).

Among First Nations organizations in Canada, however, reliance on government funds came at the cost of competition within the movement over a limited pool of resources. For instance, Tennant's study (1990, 173) of British Columbia Aboriginal organizations found that "separate and massive" funding largely inhibited the creation of a broad-based movement in that province because of competition between groups. Thus, reliance on government funding allocated to specific status groups led to divisions among Aboriginals and presented a major obstacle to pan-Aboriginal mobilization or identity formation (Ramos 2006).

Government funding during this period had a variety of sometimes contradictory effects on social movement activism in Canada. Government funding and recognition helped establish organizations and was associated with increased protest among some groups, as seen by the women's movement in Canada. At the same time, federal funds sometimes hindered mobilization because of competition that emerged among organizations, as illustrated by the First Nations organizations in Canada. While some groups benefited from government support, others did not, and this discrepancy created tensions within certain movement sectors.

The Mulroney Era (1984–93)

Brian Mulroney, Progressive Conservative prime minister from 1984 to 1993, had a very different relationship with social movement organizations. This is partly because he did not see social movement organizations, particularly the more politically active ones, as critical actors in Canadian politics. As a result, the federal government began cutting funding and support to these groups in the late 1980s, began reducing their opportunities for participation in the policy process, and openly attacked the legitimacy of advocacy organizations.

Mulroney also weakened government's existing relationships with SMOs by expanding the range of groups that could compete for funding, particularly by incorporating groups on the political right. For example, NAC's status as the voice of English Canadian women was challenged when a conservative women's organization, REAL Women (Realistic, Equal, Active for Life) began to contest their funding in the late 1980s (Bashevkin 1996, 2009). The funding of this conservative group served the political function of weakening the leftist women's movement in Canada.

From the perspective of moderates, federal funding cuts to women's groups resulted from NAC's rejection of a lobbyist orientation and its adoption of an aggressive protest stance. This shift led "the federal government to lose patience with being insulted" (Bashevkin 1996, 237). In many ways, this historical shift mirrors Meyer and Tarrow's social movement society thesis (1998) and is also an example of reduced political opportunities for some groups. While groups still had access to government officials and bureaucrats during this period, such access was now predicated on a less contentious and more institutionalized set of tactics and interests on the part of social movement organizations.

The Chrétien (1993–2003) and Martin (2003–06) Era

When Jean Chrétien, Liberal prime minister from 1993 to 2003, assumed office, he sought to increase the role of voluntary organizations in public policy. The Liberals saw the voluntary sector, including social movements, as a vital component for building the social capital needed to encourage citizen engagement (Phillips 2001). There was also a realization that the government increasingly needed the voluntary sector to deliver services (M. Smith 2005a). Essentially, the voluntary sector was seen as an "under-utilized resource" and the government recognized the sector's potential economic contributions (Laforest 2011).

Recognition of voluntary organizations and social movements as a resource for connecting with citizens and delivering services resulted in an important discursive shift in the way the role of these groups was understood. Previously, they were seen to mobilize and represent various segments of the population, particularly groups that were marginalized. Instead, Chrétien saw the voluntary sector as a way to reach the "ordinary citizen" – not the noisy minority or marginalized groups. As Linda Trimble argues, "so-called 'special interests' [were] seen as opposing the claims of the 'ordinary citizen' (i.e., the tax-paying, self-reliant, independent individual). The special claim, need, or interest is a drain on limited state resources, an impediment to a global free market, an excuse for avoiding individual responsibility" (quoted in Laforest 2011, 47). Seeing voluntary organizations as a valuable instrument that the government could use to engage with individual Canadians and to provide services was an important change from the earlier understanding of these groups as having an emancipatory role as agents of social change (Laforest 2011).

The voluntary sector as a whole was reorganized during the late 1990s. An informal network of voluntary sector leaders, the Voluntary Sector Roundtable (VSR), lobbied the federal government for recognition. In response, the Liberals developed the Voluntary Sector Initiative (VSI), a framework policy that reasserted the important role of the sector and committed the government to building a new relationship with voluntary groups (Phillips 2001). This process was clearly oriented towards large national organizations such as hospitals, health charities, and social service agencies, and led to the marginalization of smaller grassroots and urban groups (Laforest and Orsini 2005).

Changes in the funding provided by the Liberal government, which continued the policies of the Mulroney Conservatives, also limited advocacy work on the part of organizations, particularly groups with charitable status (Phillips 2001). In order to retain charitable status, such groups had to limit their advocacy activities to 10 percent of their total expenditures, a rule that remains in place today. Voluntary organizations involved in advocacy quickly came under attack and were derogatorily branded as "special interest groups" (see the Introduction).

The Harper Era (2006 Onward)

The Voluntary Sector Initiative was touted as a positive move by social movement groups, but was never fully realized or implemented by the Liberals. The key issues that prompted its initiation – financing, restrictions on advocacy, guidelines for determining which types of non-profits can be registered as charities, and the stringent reporting and accountability regime surrounding grants and contributions – were not resolved by the Liberals under Jean Chrétien and Paul Martin or the Conservatives under Stephen Harper.

Since the Mulroney years, there has been a general move away from core funding to project-based funding, cuts to the funding of advocacy groups, and the discrediting of "special interest groups." These changes have substantially altered the nature of the relationship between the federal government and social movement organizations. These policies had accumulated over time and, as a result, the voluntary sector was already weakened by the time the Conservatives were elected in 2006. The Harper government instituted a set of cuts to various programs and these cuts focused on eliminating funding to Liberal programs established under the Voluntary Sector Initiative, support for research, and advocacy work (Laforest 2009). The Harper government also allowed funding to for-profit organizations, which further restricted the money available to traditional social movement and charitable organizations.

The more conflictual relationship between the Harper government and social movements has been felt across a variety of movements. The environmental movement, in particular, has been the target of intense scrutiny and control from the Harper government. This movement has seen its funding significantly reduced, particularly funding to large coordinating bodies such as the National Round Table on the Environment and the Economy. There has also been intense government scrutiny of the accounts of some of the largest and most well-established environmental groups in Canada, including the David Suzuki Foundation, Greenpeace, and Tides Canada, and restrictions on access to and content in environmental research (Goldenberg 2012).

In the Harper period, the state in Canada has looked to social movement groups to provide tangible and marketable benefits, such as helping to deliver social services (e.g., women's sexual assault counselling, or assistance to new immigrants) (Laforest and Orsini 2005; see also Chapter 4). These sorts of activities are dependent on the goal, size, professionalization, and institutionalization of the SMO and give movement organizations that are larger and more professionalized increased access to government funding and opportunities to be consulted in the policy processes. In essence, the professionalization and institutionalization that occurs within a social movement society is available and attractive to some groups only. This facilitates the access of large, bureaucratic organizations to resources and decision makers, while smaller groups that are less capable of, or less interested in, professionalizing and institutionalizing forgo such access.

The Case: The Environmental Movement in Canada

The environmental movement is an ideal arena for examining how government support for and funding of social movement organizations shapes the tactics they use and whom they target. Organizations in this movement have been very successful and the movement is increasingly diversified, professionalized, institutionalized, and internationalized (Walker 1991; Princen and Finger 1994; Staggenborg 2008). It has also been effective in putting environmental issues on the political agenda and has led to the creation of government departments and changes in laws and policies (Rucht 1999); it also has broad public support in Canada and internationally (Rohrschneider and Dalton 2002; Chapter 11). Because of its success, the environmental movement has received substantial funding from a variety of sources, although this varies significantly across countries and over time. In Canada, there are now a total of 4,400 environmental organizations that employ 14,900 paid staff, account for 4 percent of all volunteers, and generate $1 billion in revenue each year (Bowen 2006).

In this chapter, we focus on two large environmental groups in Canada, Greenpeace and the World Wildlife Fund, to examine the impacts of regime shift and political context in more detail. Greenpeace is an independent non-governmental organization founded in Vancouver in 1971. Greenpeace aims to protect biodiversity in all its forms; prevent pollution and abuse of the earth's oceans, land, air, and fresh water; end all nuclear threats; and promote peace, global disarmament, and non-violence. Greenpeace Canada has more than 89,000 supporters and a head office in Toronto (www. greenpeace.org/canada/). Internationally, Greenpeace has offices in more than forty countries, with headquarters in Amsterdam (www.greenpeace. org/international/en/).

World Wildlife Fund (WWF) Canada is the Canadian branch of the global conservation organization and was founded in 1967. WWF Canada aims to protect and restore the natural environment ecosystem by conserving the world's biological diversity, ensuring that the use of renewable natural resources is sustainable, and promoting the reduction of pollution and wasteful consumption. WWF Canada has headquarters in Toronto and more than 150,000 members (www.wwf.ca). It is affiliated with a global network of WWF organizations in more than 100 countries and has international offices in Gland, Switzerland (wwf.panda.org).

Greenpeace and WWF are both large, international, professional, federated organizations concerned with protecting the environment. They differ in a number of significant respects, however, including in their selection of tactics and their funding base. Greenpeace was founded on, and built its reputation through, high-risk protest tactics, including sending small boats of activists to stop nuclear testing and whaling (Dale 1996; Harter 2011; Zelko 2013). WWF tends to prefer less contentious tactics and more institutional routes to social change (Train 2003). In addition, WWF has a diverse funding base, receiving money from businesses, governments, foundations, and individual donors, whereas Greenpeace does not accept money from government or business interests. By comparing these two groups and their tactics and targets in the Chrétien/Martin period, where there was relatively more support for their actions, with the Harper period, where this support was more limited, we can assess the effect of government support for social movements on the tactics that they employ.

Data Collection and Methodology

This chapter uses innovative data to examine how funding affects group tactics and targets. Most research on social movements that examines tactical choices uses content analysis of newspaper articles. By coding quotes or text in articles and assessing how journalists describe organizations and their activities, scholars make assertions about the activities and goals of the group (e.g., Ferree 2003; Snow, Vliegenthart, and Corrigall-Brown 2007; see J. Smith et al. 2001 for a discussion of description bias in these media accounts). There is much to be gained from this approach, but it can obscure the tactics and strategies of organizations by filtering their messages through the eyes of journalists, editors, and others. In this analysis, we code press releases, which are documents created by the organizations themselves. By examining the documents that organizations create, in which they can present their complete frames and outline their tactics and strategies in detail, we are better able to assess how group activities and frames have changed in response to different political contexts.

For this analysis, we collected, coded, and analyzed two main types of documents from the period 2000–10. This time frame captures two different periods in Canadian federal politics: a Liberal period of government before 2006 and a Conservative period after 2006. The leaders and parties in these two periods had different attitudes towards social movement organizations, and examining press releases over these ten years enabled us to compare how government support for SMOs shape their activities. We coded the press releases from Greenpeace and WWF Canada that are available on the groups' websites. We selected every third press release, yielding a total of 359 press releases coded, 205 and 154 press releases for Greenpeace and WWF Canada, respectively. We used this data to see the tactics used by each group over time, and the targets of each group's actions. These data enabled us to examine changes in the tactical choices of each group over time.

We used the press releases to code elements of the tactical choices of the social movement groups. In each press release, we coded the number of mentions of government, the tactics the group used, whether the group called the public to action, whether the group described research in the press release, and whether they mentioned coalition work with other social movement organizations.

Analysis

Figure 5.1 depicts the percentage of press releases per year that mention the government, by group. In essence, this figure demonstrates the extent to which these groups were discursively engaging with the government, both critically and constructively, during this time period. It is clear that this engagement ebbed and flowed over time. Both groups had periods in which they discussed government actions and inactions extensively in their press

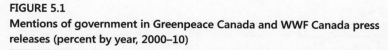

FIGURE 5.1
Mentions of government in Greenpeace Canada and WWF Canada press releases (percent by year, 2000–10)

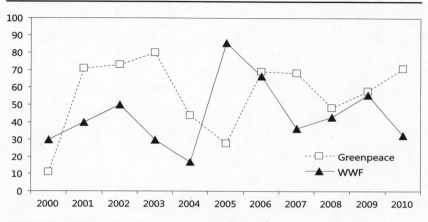

releases (in 88 percent of the WWF Canada releases in 2005 and 80 percent of the Greenpeace releases in 2003), and periods in which they engaged little with government actions in their releases (16 percent for WWF Canada in 2004 and 10 percent for Greenpeace in 2000).

Both groups seem responsive to the electoral cycle in their engagement with government actions – discussing these actions (or inactions) more immediately before elections and declining in their discussion of government actions after elections have been concluded. However, the level of engagement with government policy, and discussion of that policy in press releases, did not differ substantively in the Conservative era after 2006 from the earlier Liberal era.

Figures 5.2 and 5.3 show the tactical choices of WWF Canada and Greenpeace over time. Each figure displays the percentage of press releases each year that (1) proposed a contentious tactic (such as a protest, demonstration, or march); (2) called on the public to engage in some type of action; (3) used research; and (4) discussed formal coalitions with other social movements.

WWF Canada increased its use of contentious tactics over the period from 2000 to 2010. Whereas it never discussed contentious tactics in press releases from 2000 to 2004, it began calling for such tactics in 2005,

FIGURE 5.2
Tactics employed by WWF Canada (percent by year, 2000–10

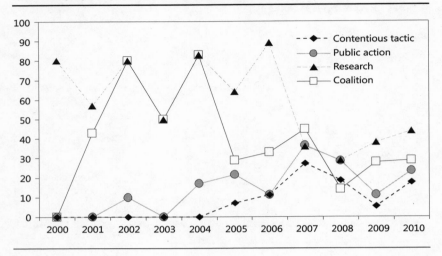

FIGURE 5.3
Tactics employed by Greenpeace Canada (percent by year, 2000–10)

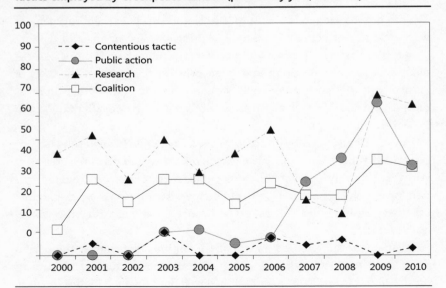

in 6 percent of press releases, rising to 28 percent in 2007 and declining slightly since then. There was also an increase over time in calls for the public to engage in activities on behalf of the group. Although there is a general increase, it was also responsive to the electoral cycle. It increased before elections (2002 and 2005), dipped in election years (2003 and 2006), and rebounded to higher levels after elections (2004 and 2007).

Research activity was quite prominent in the WWF Canada press releases (50–90 percent of press releases) until the election of Stephen Harper, when it declined sharply to around 30–43 percent. Coalitions were also used relatively frequently prior to Harper's election (50–80 percent of press releases). However, this declined to 13 percent in 2008 and climbed back to only around 30 percent in 2009 and 2010.

Greenpeace was quite consistent in its use of contentious tactics, which hovered around 5–10 percent of press releases throughout the period. At the same time, its propensity for calling on the public to engage in action increased. This was not done from 2000 to 2002, reached around 20 percent of press releases from 2003 to 2006, and then increased sharply to a high of 68 percent of press releases in 2009 (declining slightly after that time). It is important to note that although Greenpeace is known for its contentious tactics, such tactics are only one of the things that it publicizes in its press releases. Even when these actions are discussed, they are more often described (such as the unfurling of a sign on Parliament Hill, or boats of activists engaging in civil disobedience) and not used to call the public to action. While Greenpeace is associated with contentious tactics, these tactics are often carried out by a small group of activists (Dale 1996).

Greenpeace used research in 35–55 percent of its press releases prior to Harper's election in 2006. This number declined sharply after his election, to 21 percent and 18 per cent in 2007 and 2008, respectively. There was a resurgence in research activity in 2009 and 2010, with mentions in around 70 percent and 67 percent of press releases, respectively. Coalition work by Greenpeace has been slowly increasing over time and does not seem to be responsive to changes in prime minister.

Comparing the activities of WWF Canada and Greenpeace, we can see their responses to different political climates converging and diverging over time. Both have increased their calls to the public over time, and have grown sharply in their propensity to involve the public in their work since Harper took office in 2006. Both groups also declined in their research activity with the election of Harper, but have rebounded since then.

The groups differed, however, in their use of contentious tactics and co-alitions over time. Whereas WWF Canada increased its use of contentious tactics, something that it never described in its press releases before 2004, Greenpeace did not significantly alter its use of these tactics over time. In addition, WWF Canada reduced its coalition work over the 2000–10 period, whereas Greenpeace increased its use of this tactic during the same period.

The use of coalition tactics has declined for WWF Canada but increased for Greenpeace over time. Coalitions can add credibility to a group by expanding the perceived constituency for which the group is seen to speak. They also carry risks, however, such as tying a group to allies that might be perceived as tainted or contentious (G. Murphy 2005). In an era when the environmental movement is under much scrutiny and is subject to intense criticism from the government, as is the case post-2006 in Canada, the different strategies adopted by the two groups could be the result of their different identities. When the government has a particularly negative relationship with the environmental movement as a whole, groups that are out of favour, such as Greenpeace, may be strategic to cooperate with other organizations. On the other hand, groups such as WWF Canada, which are seen by the government as less contentious and therefore less problematic, may feel it wiser to work alone instead of risk being tainted by allies that are seen as "radical." The contrasting strategies of the two groups highlight the varied terrain that organizations face when interacting with government.

Discussion and Conclusion

This chapter brings together an examination of the historical relationship between the state and social movements in Canada over the past half-century and a systematic and detailed analysis of the changing tactics and targets of two large environmental groups in Canada from 2000 to 2010. The first part of this chapter examines the historical relationships between social movements and the state in Canada and answers our first two major research questions: what is the relationship between the state and social movements in Canada, and how has this relationship changed over time?

There has been a widespread transformation in the relationship between social movement organizations and the government of Canada over the past half-century. Many of the features of the modern social movement society that Meyer and Tarrow (1998) propose are evident in this historical period in Canada. For example, the boundaries between conventional and unconventional activities have become increasingly blurred for Canadian social movements. The Canadian government has encouraged, and rewarded to some extent, this shift towards the incorporation of institutional activities by social movements. While Trudeau in the 1970s saw social movements as important players because of how they advocated for marginalized groups and provided services for groups in need, later federal governments, culminating in the Harper government after 2006, now see them as either a nuisance or, in a more market-based way, as a service delivery mechanism. Social movements are encouraged to specialize in non-contentious activities, which can overlap with the activities of other actors, such as charities or political parties. Groups that continue to engage in advocacy or other more contentious or critical activities have been less likely to receive either funding or privileges such as charitable status that can facilitate fundraising. These changes in the relationship between the state and social movements in Canada have benefited larger, more professional and bureaucratic organizations that are more able to fulfill certain requirements, such as increased budget reporting and calculable results, and are more able to engage in fundraising activities.

The second part of the analysis is a more in-depth examination of how government engages with social movement organizations and how they affect the targets and tactics used by social movement groups. This portion of the analysis addresses our third major research question, on how changes in government support for social movements affected their tactics and frames. Through systematic content coding of press releases from Greenpeace and WWF Canada, we are able to assess the extent to which the political context in Canada shapes the activities of social movements. We examine these groups from 2000 to 2010 in order to compare two different periods in Canadian politics.

As discussed earlier, the Chrétien/Martin period was characterized by a generally more positive relationship between the state and social movements. Voluntary groups were seen as a way to increase social capital and reach "ordinary" citizens. They were also recognized as an important mechanism of service delivery and as economic contributors. The Liberal governments in this period were, at least rhetorically, committed to building relationships with social movement groups. It is important to note, however, that the state still imposed new and greater restrictions on the actions of these groups during this period, including a limit on advocacy work and increased reporting and accountability measures, which many groups found cumbersome.

The Harper government has been generally less supportive of social movement activities. Since Harper became prime minister in 2006, there have been severe cuts in funding to social movements. Beyond simple funding cuts, there is also a generally more conflictual relationship between the state and social movements. Many movements, particularly the environmental movement, have experienced intense scrutiny and criticism of their work. While it is a vast oversimplification to suggest that the Liberal period was completely supportive of social movements and the Conservative period has been totally restrictive, the shift from the Liberal governments of Jean Chrétien and Paul Martin to the Conservative government of Stephen Harper represented an important change in the relationship between movements and the state in Canada.

By comparing the framing of WWF Canada and Greenpeace across these two periods, Liberal and Conservative, we can see that the groups responded in similar ways to the changing political context and that their tactical choices were affected by changes in government. Both groups have increased calls to the public over time. Both groups had higher levels of research activity before Harper came to power, experienced a sharp decline in research activity afterwards, and are now increasingly reporting research findings. This is not surprising given the often hostile attitudes of the Conservative government to the research activities of environmental groups (Mancini 2013).

The two groups differ, however, in their use of coalitions over time. Coalitions are a fairly traditional tactic, and it is interesting that Greenpeace, usually considered a more contentious group, is electing to use this tactic more often. This could reflect the highly strained relationship between Greenpeace and the Harper government (Goldenberg 2012), which could be pushing Greenpeace to find allies. As WWF Canada's relationship with the government is less strained, it may be less in need of allies.

It is clear that the relationship between the state and social movements has undergone widespread change over the past fifty years. These shifts have affected all social movement groups to some extent. Groups sometimes react in similar ways but this is not always the case. For example, while both WWF Canada and Greenpeace have increased calls to the public to engage in action as well as increased their use of research, they have diverged in their use of coalition tactics in reaction to the Harper government.

Future work should extend these analyses by examining a wider range of groups. For example, smaller grassroots groups are differentially able to take advantage of some of the changes occurring in the relationship between the state and social movements in Canada. Many changes in the funding and support of social movement organizations in Canada have been directed towards large, professionalized organizations, such as the groups examined in this analysis. Future research should assess how smaller, more grassroots groups have experienced these changes. In addition, movements that are based on identities, such as the women's movement and gay and lesbian rights, First Nations, or other civil rights groups, might experience these changes in very different ways because of their different focuses. In addition, examining these relationships in other countries would make possible a comparative assessment of the role of national context on these processes and offer a comparison of social movement societies.

6

Immigrant Collective Mobilization and Socio-economic Integration in Canada

PHILIPPE COUTON

Immigrants have become both the targets of and participants in some of the most significant social and political movements in Western countries in recent decades. Anti-immigrant far-right parties and movements, urban riots, human rights organizations, and anti-discrimination movements, just to take a few examples, all share a direct and visceral connection to immigration. Starkly contrasting discursive and ideological positions have emerged in countries on both sides of the Atlantic to frame immigration, from overt xenophobia to staunch anti-racism to free-movement transnational cosmopolitanism. This is an observation echoed by David Meyer and Amanda Pullum in Chapter 1. If we are increasingly living in social movement societies, then immigrants, diasporas, refugees, and the constellation of ethnic and cultural groups they produce are central dimensions of this emergent social reality.

But immigrants also offer a strong reminder that mobilization does not necessarily mean protest or some other form of overt social and political contention. Despite the often rancorous and violent nature of immigration debates, most immigrants mobilize their collective resources in often surprisingly diverse and powerful ways outside dominant institutions, but not primarily for contentious purposes. Immigrants in Canada and other host societies have long organized their own collective social, cultural, and economic lives, anchored by a range of social and political structures, contributing along the way to the emergence of some of the most vibrant urban cultures throughout the world and spearheading numerous social movements (Wiseman 2007). In this respect, they are not markedly different from, and often overlap with, other important social movements, including in particular organized labour, women's movements, and the human rights movement. With human mobility reaching unprecedented levels, immigrant/diasporic collective organizing and mobilizing is becoming far more significant than ever before (Cordero-Guzmán 2005). For this reason, if a social movement society exists, immigrant mobilization must be considered.

Immigrant-origin ethnic groups have been playing a broad range of increasingly significant social, economic, and political roles throughout the world, but with markedly different consequences for the members of those groups. While in some cases strong ethno-immigrant communities act as powerful agents of socio-economic mobility and integration, in others they mostly isolate newcomers from the mainstream and constrain their economic achievements. This is a crucial issue in Canada, where immigration and multiculturalism continue to be of high importance and the success of newcomers is a source of concern, for both immigrants and policymakers, particularly since some immigrant groups experience more difficulties than others.

The unevenness of the socio-economic integration of Canada's immigrants is not a new phenomenon, but it has become more pronounced in recent decades. The general medium- to long-term trend has been marked by impressive gains by nearly all ethno-immigrant groups in terms of educational and occupational achievements, particularly when compared with the heavily ascriptive socio-economic hierarchy that prevailed in Canada well into the 1950s and '60s (Herberg 1990). Marked inequalities persist, however, particularly in terms of income, as a number of recent studies have shown (cf. Galabuzi 2006). Some of this persistent inequality is due to the discriminatory treatment suffered by a number of minority groups, especially affecting those who belong to multiple and overlapping vulnerable groups (immigrant visible-minority women in particular; see Chui and Maheux 2011).

But some of this inequality is also the result of the interaction between host society and immigrant social structuring. Recent immigrants vary greatly in how they organize their communal lives after migration and in the degree of their collective mobilization. This is of no surprise to social movement researchers. For instance, McCarthy and Zald (1977) recognized that organizations are an essential facilitator of both social movement and main-stream politics. They offer the sites where networks are formed and are the seeds for both contests for power and resistance to it. This is in line with the social movement society (SMS) thesis, which argues that there is in-creasing overlap between social movement organizations and the tactics of NGOs, advocacy groups, and other types of organizations and institu-tions (Caren, Ghoshal, and Ribas 2011). Organizations can be particularly important for what Steil and Vasi (2014) call "insider tactics," which work within existing social and political systems rather than outside of them as protest tactics typically do. Communal organizations are particularly im-portant for immigrants, who are often left out of mainstream social and political channels, and would have only limited opportunities for political engagement without structures that specifically represent their group (Steil and Vasi 2014, 1113). As a result, in order to understand the unequal relations among immigrant groups and the dominant population, it is im-portant to understand their organizations as places where the collective re-sources of ethno-immigrant communities are pooled. Those looking at the plight of immigrants in Europe have seen the link to (social movement) or-ganizations as important (see Floris 2013 and Nicholls 2013), and the same is also recognized in North America (see Tarrow 2005; Steil and Vasi 2014).

In this chapter, two ethno-immigrant communities that head the list of collective organizing in Canada, Koreans and Ukrainians (see Table 6.1), are examined in order to understand the role of immigrant organizing in the SMS. Both are well known to researchers in North America. They differ in many important ways from each other. One is a recent immigrant com-munity consisting mostly of first- and second-generation individuals, iden-tified as a "visible minority." The other is one of Canada's oldest, most established, and still highly mobilized European-origin ethnic communities, and is still experiencing significant new immigration to this day. What they have in common is a high density of well-structured organizations and net-works and distinctive mobilization strategies. Koreans have long been noted in many studies for their entrepreneurship and numerous, interlinked com-munal organizations (Light and Bonacich 1988; Yu and Murray 2007), and Ukrainians are one of the world's important, well-organized diasporas (Satzewich 2002; Satzewich, Isajiw, and Duvalko 2006).

Ukrainians and Koreans also present us with two important pathways to integration that may result in markedly different outcomes for the individ-uals who benefit from them. We know, for instance, that dense networks and strong communal organizations can have mixed social, economic, and

TABLE 6.1

Charitable organizations and other characteristics of selected ethno-immigrant groups (2006 census and Canada Revenue Agency data)

Community	Group size	% Foreign-born	Median individual income $	% Self-employed	% Unemployed	Number of organizations	Per 1,000 capita organizations	Average spending per organization $
Korean	116,718	84.7	9,000	17.4	4.5	245	2.10	221,489
Ukrainian	294,624	14.8	28,000	10.2	3.3	559	1.90	1,261,622
Chinese	1,133,069	77.9	15,000	7.3	5.3	371	0.33	2,910,475
Filipino	310,754	77.5	23,000	2.7	3.8	35	0.11	163,905
Lebanese	83,571	56.6	15,000	7.8	5.9	14	0.17	104,979
Portuguese	251,082	60.9	25,000	5.1	3.3	27	0.11	486,847
Italian	731,938	40.6	28,000	6.8	3.4	50	0.07	403,884
Russian	80,796	53.0	19,000	10.2	5.8	44	0.54	597,906

Note: Columns 1 to 5, 2006 Public Use Microdata File Census data; columns 6 to 8, 2007 Canada Revenue Agency charity data (reflects 2006 fiscal year). "Group size" refers to single answer to census ethnicity question; "foreign-born" includes all members of the group born outside of Canada, whether they are immigrants or non-permanent residents. Percent self-employed for entire Canadian population = 7.2; percent unemployed = 5.1.

political consequences. Considerable evidence indicates that the social capital produced by immigrants is a powerful economic tool that eases labour market entry (see Couton 2011 for more details on that literature). But this entry effect often comes at a price: the jobs provided tend to be enclave-oriented, at a lower wage level, and with fewer prospects for mobility and a siloed political power. This is certainly true for Koreans, for whom dense organizing facilitates access to financing, information, and other support for small business formation (typically in family-operated retail). This provides an effective way to secure employment (as evidenced by the very low unemployment rate of the community), often for a whole family. But the work is hard, the hours are long, and the monetary reward is often modest and the ability to influence the mainstream political sphere is tenuous. The Ukrainian example is less obvious, with multiple generations present, lower numbers entering the country currently, and less evidence of widespread small-scale entrepreneurship. Strong networks and organizations may be a mixed blessing in some social and political areas for this community. Institutional elites within the community, for instance, tend to become entrenched and somewhat inflexible when dealing with new immigrants. Ukrainian Canadians, however, seem to have found an equilibrium between strong ethnic solidarity and mainstream social, economic, and political success. They are one of Canada's most successful ethno-immigrant groups, and their dense networks have clearly been an asset in attaining this enviable position.

The effect of immigrant collective organizing is also part of the now-classic debate on immigrant entrepreneurship (Waldinger 1994). Recent research has amply confirmed the link between social capital/social networks and immigrant entrepreneurship in a number of countries, periods, and settings (Salaff et al. 2003). Furthermore, social capital and immigrant entrepreneurship/enclave formation are mutually reinforcing. Enclave businesses benefit from networks and non-economic organizations to become established (religious organizations, for instance), and later become part of those networks, transcending their initial economic objectives and reinforcing the ethnic economy and in turn their political standing.

On several levels, migration theory overlaps with, and in some cases becomes indistinguishable from, social movement theory – a point that is missed by both literatures and is central to social movement societies. Communal structuring and mobilization are the frequent result of hardship and discrimination. Breton (2003) calls this phenomenon "defensive structuring," a term coined by Siegel (1970), which has also been applied to other, non-ethnic communities. Ethno-immigrant communities mobilize collective resources in an effort to resist societal forces that limit their opportunities or repress their social and political aspirations. Migration and the mobilization of ethno-immigrant communities, however, are thought to result from two conceptually opposite forces. Neoclassical models, on the one hand, expect inequality within and between countries to disappear in the medium to long term as a result of "factor price equalization," a major dimension of which is labour reallocation. As De Haas (2010) puts it, in the neoclassical model, migration is simply the optimal spatial reallocation of those factors and should contribute towards the spread of economic development. Political economy and state-centric models point out, on the other hand, that states and other political forces not only interfere with this resource allocation model but often completely control it, creating many of the subsequent social and political issues related to immigration.

The two perspectives lead to two very different expectations. One projects that immigrants will be distributed relatively smoothly and uniformly according to economic needs (e.g., skills, other forms of human capital), eventually blending with receiving cultures and populations. The other foresees that immigrants are profoundly affected by political processes and decisions that shape their identities, opportunities, and strategies. If mobilization is in part a response to grievances, as Gamson, Fireman, and Rytina (1982) note, then one would expect it to be far more common under the second scenario, with immigrants encountering significant constraints and obstacles to their successful socio-economic integration.

The evidence is of course overwhelming that the vast majority of migrants live in a world described by the second theoretical perspective. Their very migration is often the direct result of state policies and political processes, and, as social movement political opportunity theorists note (cf. Meyer and Minkoff 2004), their communal organizing and collective mobilization are deeply affected by these forces. North African immigrants in France (Sayad 2006), Turks in Germany, Mexicans in the United States (Massey 2009), to take just a few notable examples, have all been profoundly affected by receiving and sending states' histories, cultures, and policies. Canada is no different in this respect, and there is evidence that the current policy environment may reinforce some of the effects of the relationship between low-level, enclave-centred employment and community organizing. Canadian immigration policies have been very strongly based on skill selectivity but without the expected result of smooth, individualistic economic integration, and many new immigrants end up working beneath their education and skill levels.

The enclave effect may also be more than just economic. The insular organizations of the enclave, including ethnic businesses, churches, and associations, have been noted for their cultural and political conservatism, often by younger members of those very communities (Li 2007, 104, 113). Enclavic conservatism can usually be attributed to a "don't rock the boat" attitude, resulting from long-standing, often brutally racist and exclusionary treatment by mainstream society. Such experiences have meant that much organizing occurs through business associations, which in turn influence cultural activism, media campaigns, protest politics, and electoral and party politics by a wide range of immigrant groups.

The types of collective strategies devised by immigrants to address the difficulties most of them face when adapting to a new society do vary greatly, however, as already noted. It is important to know the consequences of these varying strategies, the reasons why some immigrants use them more than others, and the ways in which these strategies may be inflected by policy choices. A good place to start, therefore, is to analyze the most clearly defined of these collective models, through the Korean and Ukrainian experiences, in order to understand their core features and whether they may be applied by other immigrant groups.

The purpose of this chapter is therefore to identify, describe, and analyze forms of communal immigrant mobilization in order to understand how they contribute to social and economic integration and in turn political engagement. Original statistical evidence gathered by the author from Canada Revenue Agency administrative files, data from the latest available census (2006), and several other data sets, in combination with secondary sources, documentary evidence, and other sources of information are used to explore the immigrant communities' mobilization.

My research seeks to document the magnitude and consequence of communal mobilization and its effect on various indicators of socio-economic achievement. Unlike a narrowly specified hypothesis, the empirical analysis is guided by a general expectation that strong immigrant collective mobilization is not linearly related to socio-economic achievement but is conditioned by a number of other factors. Compared to more established ethno-immigrant communities, collective organizing is expected to be much more of a defensive strategy for recent immigrants facing an often difficult labour market and an unwelcoming social environment. The chapter first turns to the Korean community in Canada to document the main aspects of its collective organizing and their consequences. This is followed by a presentation of the organizational pattern evident in the Ukrainian community and a general discussion of the implications of these findings.

The Korean Case

Canada is home to a very large section of the global Korean diaspora. There are between 200,000 and 300,000 Koreans in Canada, according to various estimates, most of whom have arrived over the last twenty years (Lindsay 2007). Korean migration and travel to Canada increased rapidly during the 1990s and has remained high since then. Several reasons have been cited for this increase, including a growing reluctance to migrate to the United States, a more open Canadian immigration policy, and, until recently, a favourable exchange rate against the Canadian currency (Han and Ibbott 2005).

Canada's Korean-origin population has become renowned for its very high level of self-employment and familial working arrangements, made possible by its tightly knit networks and institutions:

> In 2001, 31% of employed people of Korean origin worked for themselves, compared with 12% of all labour force participants in Canada. Those of Korean origin also make up a disproportionate share of all unpaid family workers in Canada. Indeed, 2% of all workers in Canada designated as unpaid family employees in 2001 were of Korean origin, whereas those of Korean origin made up only 0.3% of the total Canadian workforce. (Lindsay 2007, 15).

Despite, or perhaps because of, this high level of self and family employment, the average income of Koreans is considerably lower than that of the general population, and a much larger proportion of the Korean population falls below the low income cutoff (see Lindsay 2007 for details).

Korean entrepreneurship in Canada is therefore not a path to successful economic integration but very much a defensive strategy. Furthermore, it is reinforced by and translated into a range of mobilization strategies, including demonstrations, political activism, and awareness raising. A good example of the type of mobilization deployed by Koreans is OKBA, the Ontario Korean Businessmen's Association, which represents about 2,500 businesses in Ontario and has been one of the most vocal and visible community organizations in the province for many years. The association has issued a large number of press releases, sent delegations to Parliament, and organized several large-scale demonstrations in Ottawa, Toronto, and beyond. All of these activities have centred on core concerns of Korean small-scale retailers: illegal tobacco sales, in-store safety, the cost of insurance, and so on. OKBA is probably the single most vocal advocate for convenience store owners, the niche business where Koreans have been particularly successful. By its own estimates, it represents a sizable part of the convenience store sector in Ontario: its members make up 27 percent of all independent convenience stores in the province, with combined sales of $2 billion (Kim 2010).

OKBA has issued at least three press releases on the specific topic of the illegal tobacco trade, which it argues is both costing the livelihood of some of its members and causing far broader damage to Ontario, encouraging organized crime and circumventing the age restriction and other policies designed to curb tobacco use. Koreans in British Columbia have also been successful at organizing their community's business sector, publishing, for instance, two different business directories that advertise Korean businesses (as well as several non-Korean mainstream businesses, including large banks, legal services, etc.) to Koreans. The *Korea Times Vancouver* and the Korean Businessmen's Co-op Association of British Columbia (KBCABC, www.kbcabc.com) publish their respective directories, allowing the community to support its own businesses and to organize its economic activities. In British Columbia, just as in Ontario, some of these Korean organizations have spearheaded mobilization in defence of the material and political interests of small businesses. KBCABC president Harry Hur, for instance, has taken clear and very public positions against what he has described as the unfair business practices of large tobacco companies and against the Harmonized Sales Tax in British Columbia (NDP Caucus 2010; Baron 2011), which was ultimately defeated.

OKBA and KBCABC are both dual-purpose, enclave economy organizations that provide group-buying (wholesale) services to their members, along with other business services, and the advocacy and mobilization described above. Their primary purpose is not protest, but the significant resources they control, and the large networked, organized memberships can be readily mobilized both through mainstream and contentious channels to defend a communal or a broader cause. This type of organizing can only strengthen the enclave niche business so many Korean immigrants in Canada favour. Because they are primarily business organizations, and because they identify Koreans primarily as small business operators, these organizations tend to entrench the position of their members and the outside perceptions of the Korean community.

Local business organizations also have links with the larger Canada Korea Business Association (https://ckba.org/), whose main purpose is to encourage business relations between the two parties but which also organizes events and provides funding for various other Korea-oriented events and organizations. The CKBA is in turn linked to the government of Korea, in particular KOTRA (Korea Trade-Investment Promotion Agency), the Korean government agency in charge of encouraging trade and investment by Koreans and in Korea. KOTRA, established in 162 countries, prides itself on having played a central role in the emergence of Korea as a major economic power, through "economic diplomacy" and other investment promotion activities (KOTRA 2012). In that sense, the strong, well-organized Korean community in Canada is an important dimension of the global economic policy framework deployed by the home country. This should help the community transcend its fairly narrow economic base, but may also further embed Korean entrepreneurs in the ethnic sub-economy by forging links and supply chains primarily with the home country.

This focus on small-scale family business has come at the expense of other forms of organizing. As the Korean Canadian Women's Association (KCWA) noted recently:

> Until now, the Korean community in Toronto has not had many opportunities of professional job fairs and career connections through the community's own network in comparison to other bigger ethnic communities such as the Chinese and the Indian community. (KCWA newsletter, May 2011, 9; http://www.kcwa.net).

Korean women may be right to complain. The community's preference for family businesses is partly responsible for the fact that Korean women have one of the lowest employment rates among visible-minority women in Canada, well below that of European-origin women (Chui and Maheux 2011, 27). Traditional gendered divisions are also reinforced within the ethnic church, which acts as a cornerstone organization of the Korean community. The leadership role men play in the economic sphere is reflected in their equally dominant role in church activities. In most Korean ethnic churches, organized activities go far beyond religious services and other spiritual functions. They provide leisure, social, and material activities, all of which are made possible by women, who do the frequently arduous work of cooking, cleaning, and organizing. Most are aware that the division of labour is unbalanced, and that these conditions are not reflective of the social mainstream (Chung 2008, 73–78).

Evidence even suggests that Korean ethnic churches in Canada are more conservative than their counterparts in South Korea:

> It was mentioned by Participant A that when she was in Korea, she was taught to respect women's rights and fought for equality. Interestingly, she points out that the Korean church in Canada, which might be expected to have been influenced by the western culture, is actually more conservative than churches in South Korea. She explained why she thought women had more power in churches in Korea. (Chung 2008)

The increased traditionalism of immigrant organizations compared with homeland counterparts is not unusual. It is frequently the result of the relative isolation of the community, and, in this case, can also be attributed to the reinforcement of gendered roles by business and occupational practices. Many feminists have criticized what they see as an often overlooked form of patriarchal domination, left undiscussed in the name of cultural difference (Bannerji 2000; Cha 2009). But Korean women themselves are combating gender inequality within their own community, by creating their own spaces and networks, and by renegotiating domestic and family responsibilities (Cha 2009).

This and other evidence points to a highly mobilized but narrowly focused, defensively structured community. This strategy has not been without rewards. Korean immigrants occupy an important socio-economic sector, are a visible and vocal section of the Canadian population, and are building a future for their children. The community also enjoys a low unemployment rate, confirming the hardworking reputation of its members (see Table 6.1). By many economic and non-economic measures, Koreans form a very successful, tightly knit community. However, their position is also the result of unintentional policy consequences, including non-recognition of skills and a limited willingness on the part of various levels of government to recognize the collective choices of the community (Cha 2009).

This mixed picture is confirmed by broader studies in Canada and beyond. Recent research on the Koreans in Canada presents a contrasting picture that includes high levels of acculturative stress and family tensions but also communal resilience and solidarity (Noh, Kim, and Noh 2012). Noh and Avison (1996) report that ethnic support networks are important coping resources for Korean immigrants experiencing psychological distress, and are more generally an effective stress suppressor. This is all the more important since the same study also finds that support from mainstream sources have no effect on the stressors associated with mental health problems. The support offered by the larger community may even be perceived as threatening or controlling (Noh and Avison 1996, 203), while the assistance offered by co-ethnic community members often overlaps with friendship, family, and neighbourhood networks. Distinctions between business, religious, welfare, and social (in the sense of providing opportunities for group activities) associations and organizations are therefore often blurred. They may all provide a wide variety of overlapping forms of support, from setting up a small business to alleviating psychological distress.

Clearly, then, ethnic entrepreneurship is far from being simply an economic activity. It has far-reaching social and political consequences, which were particularly evident for Koreans in the United States in the 1980s and 1990s (Min 1998, 2008). The tensions between Korean small business owners and African Americans are well known, and were the cause of conflicts escalating to full-fledged riots in the early 1990s. Koreans had found a successful niche as "ghetto grocers," a business few were willing to enter. But this also caused resentment from chiefly African American neighbours and problems with suppliers and even government authorities. Yet these tensions were also surprisingly rapidly resolved, largely as the result of organizational activity by greengrocers of Korean origin, who addressed public perceptions of the problems, raised funds, and demonstrated, relying on powerful "reactive solidarity."

Korean immigrant entrepreneurship in Canada may be changing and is increasingly reaching into new and promising areas. Evidence is mounting that Koreans are expanding their business operations into sectors well beyond small-scale, low-income retail and services. The most striking of these trends is the rapid increase and growing significance of international education, where entire economic sectors are emerging in order to serve Korean international students coming to Canada. Most of these businesses have deep roots in existing and now well-established Korean networks, particularly in and around Vancouver (Kwak and Hiebert 2010). Evidence points to an incubation effect of the existing enclave economy so well developed by Koreans in Canada:

> Korean ESL school coordinators often find their work through social networks, and many Korean education agency owners learn how to establish

and maintain their businesses from other Korean business owners. Considering the degree of clustering and the incubation effect, this small part of the Korean-led economy can be regarded as a form of an ethnic niche economy. (Kwak and Hiebert 2010, 145)

The proliferation of communal institutions may also have advantages beyond the mixed economic success noted above. For instance, Yu and Murray (2007) note that Koreans in Vancouver have the highest number of media outlets per capita, much higher than more established ethno-immigrant communities such as the Chinese or South Asian communities. This proliferation is a clear sign of communal vitality, but also of divisions, poor coordination, and instability (many of these media outlets are small and short-lived). The community's organizational profile is also marked by a strong religious focus and, more important, the relative lack of other types of organizations, especially compared with Ukrainians, as Table 6.2 shows.

The contrasting pictures of Korean Canadian community life described above leaves many questions unanswered. The main one is whether the group's most salient feature – institutional proliferation and its complex linkages with communal mobilization, entrepreneurship, enclave-centred business practices, and ethno-religious structures – is the main reason for the generally modest socio-economic level and political standing of its members. This is an implicitly comparative question about whether other communities experiencing similar conditions have similar outcomes? Direct comparisons are always difficult, but Ukrainian Canadians offer the next best thing – a revealing contrast. As will become evident below, the consequences of immigrant organizing are far more complex than the defensive structuring evidenced above.

The Ukrainian Case

Canada's Ukrainian immigrants and their descendants are in a very different situation from Korean immigrants. The Ukrainian Canadian community is mostly Canadian-born (1,205,050 people identified themselves as Ukrainian in the 2006 Census, with the vast majority second or third generation). It is a community that has experienced several significant migration waves over the course of the past century, most recently following Ukraine's difficult post-independence period. This has enabled the community to form what is perhaps the strongest ethno-immigrant network of organizations and institutions in Canada, including schools, cultural organizations, educational structures at all levels, and religious institutions across the country

TABLE 6.2

Types of charitable organizations in selected ethnic groups, 2012*

Type of charity		Chinese	Filipino	Lebanese	Korean	Ukrainian	Portuguese	Italian	Russian	Other	Total
Welfare	N	19	2	5	1	28	4	12	2	18,055	18,128
	%	5.2	5.7	35.7	0.4	5.2	16.0	24.0	4.5	21.8	21.5
Health	N	13	0	0	1	0	0	0	0	5,740	5,754
	%	3.5	0.0	0.0	0.4	0.0	0.0	0.0	0.0	6.9	6.8
Education	N	57	0	6	23	70	1	12	3	13,481	13,653
	%	15.5	0.0	42.9	9.7	12.9	4.0	24.0	6.8	16.3	16.2
Religion	N	242	26	1	200	413	19	16	37	29,779	30,733
	%	65.8	74.3	7.1	84.0	76.3	76.0	32.0	84.1	36.0	36.5
Community	N	19	6	1	6	30	1	8	2	12,966	13,039
	%	5.2	17.1	7.1	2.5	5.5	4.0	16.0	4.5	15.7	15.5
Other	N	18	1	1	7	0	0	2	0	2,808	2,837
	%	4.9	2.9	7.1	2.9	0.0	0.0	4.0	0.0	3.4	3.4
Total	N	368	35	14	238	541	25	50	44	82,829	84,144
	%	100.00	100.00	100.00	100.00	100.00	100.00	100.00	100.00	100.00	100.00

* Differences between the column totals and the column contents are due to errors associated with rounding and weighting.

(Baczynskyj 2009; Couton 2011). Despite marked differences with Korean newcomers, Ukrainians share a propensity for strong communal organizations and well-organized ethno-cultural networks. These social structures have served them well during their long presence in Canada and continue to provide assistance to new immigrants. Over 3,000 Ukrainian immigrants came to Canada in 2010 alone, and between 2,000 and 3,000 have settled in the country yearly during the last decade. Recent Ukrainian immigrants are therefore numerically not far behind Koreans (see CIC 2011) in recent, strictly numerical terms.

Historically, Ukrainians are one of Canada's greatest collective success stories. Most of the early immigrants, and many in the successive waves, had low skills and education, worked in low-paying occupations, and stood near the bottom of Canada's socio-economic hierarchy as late as the 1950s despite a decades-long presence in Canada. Ukrainians also formed a well-organized group, in part because of the practice of block settlement – the migration and settlement of entire communities – usually in the Western provinces. This had the effect of strengthening communal solidarity, but also of limiting mobility, the classic enclavic quandary. Yet by the 1980s Ukrainians had made some of the most impressive gains of any ethno-immigrant community in the country, with 32 percent having obtained some post-secondary education in 1981, up from only 3 percent in 1951 (Herberg 1990). Ukrainians had also risen near the top of the socio-economic ranking as measured by two other key dimensions – occupational achievement and income – and continue to do well today, as Table 6.1 shows. Much of this mobility was the result of the profound changes that Canadian society experienced during the intervening decades, and of the equally profound changes in immigration and integration policies. But the depth of the Ukrainian communal solidarity, involving a broad range of structures – including churches, political parties, schools, and media – and spanning the entire political spectrum (see Hinther and Mochoruk 2011), was also a key factor.

As Loewen and Friesen (2009, 64) showed in a sweeping historical study of immigrants in Canada's Prairie provinces, Ukrainians leveraged their strong sense of communal identity to climb the socio-economic ladder:

> The avenue to middle class respectability through the employment of ethnic symbols was most boldly taken by the larger groups. Ukrainians in places such as Saskatoon bore their ethnic badge proudly. But it was a particular kind of ethnic exhibition that was accompanied by signs of assimilation.

Their research further shows that Ukrainian identity was maintained and reconstructed in a broad range of organizations and institutions, spanning classes and neighbourhoods and playing a multitude of roles. This was no simple ethnic maintenance, in other words, but a complex process of "ethnic reinvention" that saw Ukrainians shift their attention from homeland politics and ethnic-boundary maintenance to a strong, dynamic, locally anchored ethnicity aimed at securing a place in Canada's evolving social structure for the second and third generations (Loewen and Friesen 2009, 64).

An important dimension of this ethnically anchored mobility was the strong presence of women in many of the key institutions of the community. Some of the roles women played were, as might be expected, traditional and tied to gendered expectations, not unlike many contemporary immigrants. But many also played a central role in a range of political movements, including a number of radical factions. They also initiated the creation of what would become key cultural institutions and promoted the advancement of education and economic mobility for women (Swyripa 1993).

Ukrainians are proud of their history in Canada, and celebrate the rich institutional life that has supported their community. Ukrainian Canadian Congress president Paul Grod summarized this attitude recently, during one of the events marking the 120th anniversary of the Ukrainian presence in Canada:

> They experienced extreme physical hardship settling the prairies, discrimination and later internment as enemy aliens. In spite of all these barriers, Ukrainian Canadians were instrumental in building a strong Canadian nation and as a result we are proud to consider ourselves its founding peoples. Four successive waves of immigrants built the Ukrainian Canadian community which we enjoy today – cultural centers, churches, schools, retirement and nursing facilities – a community that cares for its people from cradle to grave. Today, many other Ethnocultural communities look with admiration at our community. We are recognized as one of the top 2 most influential ethnocultural communities in Canada. What is more telling of our success, Canada today considers itself the most Ukrainian country outside of Ukraine. (UCC 2012).

A few recent studies have documented the social and economic achievements of recent Ukrainian immigrants to Canada (Isajiw, Satzewich, and Duvalko 2002; Pivnenko and DeVoretz 2003). Pivnenko and DeVoretz (2003) label recent Ukrainian immigrants as "overachievers." Their earnings are higher than those of other immigrants and their economic integration is much faster. Pivnenko and DeVoretz (2003, 20) attribute their relative earnings advantage to "greater official language abilities, a more favourable occupational distribution, and greater education," but say nothing about the social structures available to Ukrainian newcomers. According to Isajiw, Satzewich, and Duvalko (2002), recent immigrants from Ukraine have only limited ties with the existing Ukrainian community, choosing to participate in mainstream institutions and networks instead.

Could this mean that Ukrainians are simply allocating their labour successfully, unwittingly following economic modelling? Other evidence points to a slightly different reality. Since 1991, a relatively small but increasing number of immigrants have been arriving from newly independent Ukraine, what some have called the fourth wave of immigration. Many of them are deeply attached to their ancestry and culture, as Isajiw, Satzewich, and Duvalko (2002) report, despite frictions with existing Ukrainian Canadian institutions. For instance, a recent study in Saskatchewan indicates that the strong Ukrainian presence there is a powerful draw for many Ukrainian immigrants (Kostiyuk 2007). Furthermore, the Ukrainian Canadian Congress was active in attracting immigrants to Canada and helping them adapt to their new environment. This fourth wave of Ukrainian immigration has flocked to churches and other key Ukrainian institutions (Isajiw 2010). Some of the tensions between established Ukrainians and the new arrivals can be almost entirely attributed to political differences:

> Many informants disagreed with the politicized notion of Ukrainian that characterizes the Ukrainian community and resented having to choose "sides" between a Russian-Soviet identity and Ukrainian nationalist identity in order to be accepted. For its part, the organized community and the schools which represent it, may feel that the rejection of Russian language use, the role of aggressor played by Russia and the Soviet Union in Ukrainian history and centre to right politics are non-negotiable elements which identify Ukrainians in Toronto. (Baczynskyj 2009, 107)

The intensity of the debates between the different groups of ethnic Ukrainians is in itself testimony to the strength of the community. The proliferation of organizations and institutions has fuelled an intense political debate, further intensified by Ukraine's tumultuous transition to independence. The broad solidarity that emerged during the Orange Revolution of 2004 further confirms that Ukrainians from various generations feel a strong sense of solidarity despite differences. The tensions and frictions, moreover, have certainly not prevented recently arrived Ukrainians from succeeding economically. Rather than using their communal institutions for a purely defensive economic strategy, Ukrainians have been engaging in vital social and political debates, channelled by high-level organizations, including research chairs, national federations, and international umbrella organizations. Factionalism has also been an integral part of the history of Ukrainians in Canada. The tension between nationalists and communists was a defining characteristic of the early history of Ukrainians in Canada, and continued to be felt late in the twentieth century (Swyripa 1999). These political tensions were partly the cause of the high degree of communal organizing within the community. Political rivalries prompted factions to create their own newspapers, community organizations, and associations.

The contemporary overall institutional profile of Ukrainian Canadians is also very diverse, as Table 6.2 shows, and their presence at all levels of the cultural, political, and social mainstream is well established throughout Canada, especially in their historical areas of settlement in Western provinces. There are also very few signs of narrow occupational concentration, the result of a long-standing presence in Canada as well as the breadth of the community's organizations. Defensive structuring was certainly an important aspect of Ukrainian community life during some of its history, but the depth and breadth of services, activities, and opportunities offered by Ukrainian communal organizations today clearly show that this is no longer the case and that they are politically more mainstream than their Korean counterparts. Having played a major role in one of Canada's defining policies – multiculturalism – during its inception, having seen members of its community elected at all levels of the political structure, and having secured a permanent presence in all manner of key social and cultural institutions, Ukrainians are an integral part of the dominant Canadian society.

Implications

The observed differences between the Korean and Ukrainian trajectories raise a number of questions. The first is of course whether these can be said to constitute "models" of immigrant social, economic, and political mobilization. Koreans and Ukrainians may simply be idiosyncratic examples, interesting in their own right but not particularly instructive or relevant for other immigrants. There is some reason to believe, however, that they may represent a fairly stark dichotomous set of possibilities. For example, Fairlie and colleagues (2010) report that most Asian-owned businesses in Canada earn quite a bit less than the national average, seemingly confirming that self-employment may be a defensive strategy in a difficult labour market for many recent immigrant communities. There is also ample evidence that entire industries are becoming economic enclaves for underemployed immigrants. These ethnic businesses are not thriving enterprises but small-scale, family-owned, likely enclavic retail or food-serving operations. Involvement in the ethnic economy may also hamper interaction with the wider society. Immigrants who work chiefly within their own ethno-cultural community are much less likely to be involved in social activities and politics outside of their group (Fong and Ooka 2002).

If this form of enclavic defensive mobilization with all its attendant problems is a trend, and there are many indications that it is, many immigrants are therefore opting to mobilize their collective resources in order to build organizations and institutions, outside of the state, that protect them from mainstream economic and social life. As Howard Ramos and Kathleen Rodgers note in the Introduction to this volume, this might be a sign of social movement societies in the plural sense, with multiple political spheres rather than an overarching polity engaged by all. This is not a new phenomenon, of course, and many immigrants have resorted to this strategy, often to their long-term advantage, as seen with Ukrainian Canadians.

The Ukrainian model, of a large, well-organized group able to maintain a strong presence at all levels of Canadian social, cultural, economic, and political life, and thereby providing direct and indirect support to the newcomers who continue to arrive, is likely becoming more difficult to achieve for many more recently arrived immigrant communities. Ukrainians have been able to build a strikingly influential political presence in Canada, from the days of emergent organized labour, to the advent of multiculturalism, to recent debates about post-Soviet Europe, despite a tumultuous history and tensions with both the homeland and Canadian society. And this influence extends much further than Canada. With Ukraine experiencing a difficult democratic transition, the global Ukrainian diaspora is poised to play a key role in that political process. The cultural, linguistic, and political skills of this diaspora are essential to this influence, which has been strongly pro-democratic and staunchly opposed to some of the authoritarianism of Ukrainian political forces, particularly Viktor Yanukovych's recent erratic decisions (Motyl 2011). This is in line with Tarrow's observation (2005) that diasporas play increasingly important roles in transnational politics and activism.

The Korean Canadian and Ukrainian Canadian examples also suggest a broader conclusion about the evolution of political contention in Canadian society. The creation and maintenance of communal, frequently diasporic, complex, multi-role social and political structures by populations of immigrant origin is increasingly easier, for a number of well-known reasons, such as better communications, travel, and pluralistic normative systems, chiefly. This also propels ethno-immigrant communities to the heart of what defines a social movement society – the spread of mobilization and collective claim making across political spheres. But for most immigrants, their contention only rarely translates into overt protest. It can take that form, of course, and countless immigrant groups, large and small, from Tamils to Syrians to Congolese, have taken to Canadian streets recently. But the bulk of immigrant mobilization, like that of other groups, takes on more mundane and less visible forms, such as resource pooling, event organizing, network formation, religio-spiritual activities, letter writing, lobbying, or press releases. Whether or not this will usher in a new era of widespread diasporic, organized social and political mobilization remains to be seen, but elements of such a trend are already present.

7

Uncooperative Movements, Militarized Policing, and the Social Movement Society

LESLEY WOOD

As earlier chapters in this volume show, the social movement society (SMS) thesis argued that protest was increasingly institutionalized and professionalized (Meyer and Tarrow 1998). According to the thesis, those who remained outside of the institutionalized arrangements were marginalized and sometimes repressed (Meyer and Tarrow 1998). In the original collection of works on the SMS thesis, McCarthy and McPhail (1998) noted that alongside changes to social movements, the policing of protest had become institutionalized, less violent, and more dependent on negotiation and communication with protesters. Marching, rallying, and petitioning had become routine for a wide range of interest groups – and organized in consultation with cooperative police forces.

However, when the cycle of protest associated with the global justice movement emerged and accelerated, an increasing proportion of protesters stopped collaborating with the police. They attempted to disrupt the operations of their targets and achieve their goals through direct action. These actions were hampered by police using militarized tactics, including the less lethal weapons of pepper spray, projectiles, and Tasers, riot control units, barricades, and intensive surveillance. Examining the policing of protest events since 1995, it becomes clear that while most police continue to prefer cooperative relationships with protesters, those who refuse to cooperate, or who are expected not to cooperate, with the police are attracting an increasingly militarized response. It appears that the social movement society has inadvertently resulted in militarized policing strategies against its most contentious protesters. The dual strategy of protest policing has become modular and spread, with consequences for contentious politics in general, and for democracy in particular. The spread of the social movement society, although increasing the normalization of protest politics, has limited the space for dissent for those unwilling or unable to cooperate with state authorities.

The Emergence of Negotiated Management

The professionalized coordination between police and protesters described as negotiated management, liaison policing, or "public order management systems" (POMS) emerged out of the waves of protests of the 1960s and 1970s. The policing of protest in that era was characterized by images of police violence against protesters, with tear gas, truncheons, and the infiltration and disruption of the FBI's Counter Intelligence Program, COINTELPRO (Skolnick 1969; Davenport and Eads 2001). During that period, police responses to protest were characterized by what has been called an "escalated force" strategy, which attempted to respond to lawbreaking as criminal action, using the full scope of law enforcement techniques (J.D. McCarthy and McPhail 1998; McPhail, Schweingruber, and McCarthy 1998). Although it led to large numbers of arrest and much anger, the strategy did not effectively establish order and was seen as accelerating urban unrest and rioting, and as violating civil liberties. As McCarthy and McPhail (1998) note, controversy over this strategy led to federal studies, public outrage, and legal challenges. In their wake, the new strategy emerged, with its public order management systems, and spread during the 1970s and 1980s to police forces around the United States and beyond.

McPhail, Schweingruber, and McCarthy (1998) list five key dimensions of the POMS approach as follows:

1. Policing is centrally concerned with protecting the rights of demonstrators to protest.
2. It is recognized that community disruption is an inevitable by-product of protest, and the police mainly attempt to limit the extent of the disturbance.
3. Negotiation between police and protesters is emphasized before and during a protest, recognizing that this will limit conflict.

4. Arrests are rarely made by police, and when they are made, they are selective, orderly, and often planned in advance through negotiation, and often take place only after several warnings. Only protesters who break the law are arrested.
5. Force is used only as a last resort to protect the safety of persons or property.

This model was intended to make protest less disruptive and more predictable by establishing and maintaining clear lines of communication between police and protesters. These systems were characterized by the negotiation between affected parties, by planning on the part of authorities, and by encouragement of planning on the part of protesters (J.D. McCarthy and McPhail 1998, 91). By the late 1980s, large-scale protests in the United States over nuclear weapons, abortion, gay and lesbian rights, peace, AIDS, human rights, and labour were widespread, organized by formal, professional organizations. These organizers often attempted to influence state policy through large, permitted marches and rallies, combined with civil disobedience actions that were often prearranged with police. This style of institutionalized, normalized protest was part of what Meyer and Tarrow (1998) dubbed a "social movement society," discussed elsewhere in this volume. Tilly, Tarrow, and others have argued that this corresponded with democratization – a way to do politics by "other means," as authorities increasingly saw social movements as legitimate expressions of interest and identity (Tarrow 2011; Tilly and Wood 2012). The police used negotiated management with protesters most of the time, and even those protesters who refused to cooperate were dealt with in a more professionalized and restrained manner than previously (J.D. McCarthy and McPhail 1998, 103).[1]

Although demonstrations that police perceived as threatening continued to be policed aggressively, police across the United States, Canada, and elsewhere adopted the POMS or negotiated management strategy for the majority of demonstrations (Soule and Davenport 2009). McCarthy and McPhail (1998) use DiMaggio and Powell (1983) to explain the diffusion of the model, arguing that its acceptance was a result of macro-social processes that are more or less external to the police organizations: coercive constraints on the organization, normative constraints on the organization, and mimetic processes where one organization copies others (J.D. McCarthy and McPhail, 104). All three of these forces facilitated the diffusion of POMS to officers in the United States, along with federal programs that offered important incentives. The spread of a similar model was observed in Canada (de Lint and Hall 2009), in the United Kingdom (Waddington 1994), and in continental Europe (della Porta and Reiter 1998; della Porta, Peterson, and Reiter 2006). While this model of negotiation, permits, and planning limited the costs of protesting and facilitated large-scale actions, observers noted that it also made social movement protest less threatening and newsworthy, limiting the leverage of the less powerful (J.D. McCarthy and McPhail 1998; de Lint and Hall 2009; Earl 2011).

The Challenge to Negotiated Management

When the global justice wave of protest began to emerge in 1998, increasing numbers of protesters refused to negotiate with the police or obtain permits. In North America, some of these protesters cited Ward Churchill's writings on *Pacifism as Pathology* (1986) or interpreted the history of the Black Panther Party to argue that prearranging arrests with the police in an orderly fashion was a losing strategy, one that constrained the leverage and threat of the challengers, limited media coverage, and didn't represent the crisis at hand. In the United States, this attitude was nurtured in the forest defence, radical environmental, animal rights, and anarchist movements of the early 1990s. In Canada, police use of pepper spray at the APEC protests of 1997 underscored the ongoing threat the police represented (Ericson and Doyle 1999). This trajectory became publicly visible at the Seattle protests in 1999, when increasing numbers of protesters stepped outside established protocols of negotiation with the police and successfully disrupted both the World Trade Organization (WTO) summit and the city at large.

This confrontation was seen as a policing disaster and launched a new period of re-evaluation and training (M. King and Waddington 2005; PERF 2011). Federal programs were established by the Department of Justice in the United States to develop and train police forces in dealing with disruptive protest (Beasley, Graham, and Holmberg 2000). As Noakes and Gillham (2007) report, in the year following the WTO protests in Seattle, US police forces invested heavily in new riot gear and sent representatives to seminars sponsored by the International Association of Chiefs of Police and the US Department of Justice designed to provide public safety agencies with the skills, knowledge, strategies, and tactics necessary "to control a new breed of protester" (Beasley, Graham, and Holmberg 2000). Equivalents were set up in Canada and Europe. Although the new approach was framed as supplementing negotiated management when protesters refused to communicate with police, it began to appear with increasing frequency, after being evaluated as a successful, feasible, and appropriate response to protest.

The components of this strategy included pre-emptive arrests; the increasing use of less lethal technologies – pepper spray, tear gas, projectiles, and increasingly Tasers; barricades and walls that limit the mobility of protesters; intelligence gathering on protesters' strategy and tactics – electronic and otherwise; and riot control or specially trained units. Since 1999, these practices have spread to new sites and contexts, along with increasingly modular understandings of when, where, and how to use them.

Homeland Security

This model of protest policing that combined negotiated management and militarization used intelligence gathering to determine which trajectory a police operation would take. It spread widely after the attacks of 9/11 and the waning of the global justice movement in the United States and, to a lesser extent, Canada. Protesters who didn't cooperate faced an increasingly militarized state and police forces able to justify more militarized and expensive policing strategies, ones that increased their surveillance and disruption of movements in the name of security and fighting terrorism. During this period, the police experimented with militarized tactics against a wider variety of protesters, in a wider variety of contexts. This became apparent at the 2003 protests against the Free Trade Area of the Americas meeting in Miami, where policing was "characterized by the creation of no protest zones, heavy use of less-lethal weaponry, surveillance of protest organizations, negative advance publicity by city officials of protest groups, preemptive arrests, preventative detentions and extensive restrictions on protest timing and locations" (Vitale 2007, 406). This "Miami model" was not used everywhere. Whether police implemented a militarized model or used negotiated management or some mix of the two depended on changes to the field of policing, police knowledge, and interactions in the local political context.

The Emergence and Diffusion of a Dual Model

In the dual model of protest policing that emerged, those who negotiate and communicate clearly with police are treated to a "soft hat" strategy most of the time, whereas those who refuse to do so, or those who appear to become "unpredictable" and therefore threatening, face a more militarized "hard hat" or "riot control" strategy.

Della Porta, Peterson, and Reiter argue that policing of counter-summits in the global justice movement involved a mix of negotiations and coercive force, construction of no-go areas, increasing intolerance for minor violations, and massive use of intelligence and legal repression. Mike King and David Waddington found that the policing of "national" protest events in Canada during the mid-1990s had gelled into a recognizable two-pronged model characterized by conciliatory and consultative processes on the one hand and an increasingly militarized and potentially overtly offensive and escalatory public order strategy on the other. John Noakes, Brian Klocke, and Patrick F. Gillham (2005) argue that at protests in post-9/11 Washington, the Metropolitan Police Department of the District of Columbia (MPDC) tightly controlled the space in which transgressive groups like the Anti-Capitalist Convergence (ACC) demonstrated, but were much more lenient with contained groups.

Supporting the SMS argument, negotiated management remains the preferred policing strategy for the vast majority of protests in Canada and the United States. It is preferred because it is understood to be the "best practice" for professionalized forces, limits costs, and has fewer potential risks. Hall and deLint (2003) analyzed interviews with Canadian officers and found that the police continue to see that the "best way" to maintain order is to limit the show and use of force while relying on negotiation and persuasion to resolve conflicts.

If we look at newspaper coverage of protest events before and after the Seattle protests in 1999, it is clear that the dual strategy is a consistent feature in different cities. Examining a catalogue of protest events from Toronto, Montreal, New York City, and Washington, DC, I found that 85 percent of the 2,257 protest events identified during the 1995–2005 period in the four cities unfolded without arrest, and less than 1 percent involved the use of militarized tactics such as pepper spray or riot control units. According to this evidence, there is little sign of a wholehearted turn towards militarized tactics. However, the 15 percent of these protest events in which police arrested protesters show that not all police/protester conversations end with cooperation. This proportion varies from city to city: 21 percent of protest events in the catalogue in New York City involved arrests, but only 9 percent of the protest events in Montreal. As Chapters 4 and 8 show, there are clear local differences in the pattern of interaction between police and protesters. But overall it is clear that police rely on negotiated management for the vast majority of events but shift to a militarized approach for a significant and visible minority. As de Lint and Hall (2009) show, "in contexts where the police perceive a threat to public interest or safety, in particular when groups refuse to play by the rules of the game, police thinking shifts markedly to the view that extraordinary force is necessary and justified both to prevent and control public disorder." As time has passed, more and more police agencies have used this dual model, incorporating not only a shared set of tactics or practices but also rules around the reasons or triggers for shifting from negotiated management to militarized tactics. In order to understand the logic of police decision makers, we must look more closely at the processes that underlie the transformation of police knowledge and strategy.

Police Knowledge

In their landmark work on protest policing, della Porta, Fillieule, and Reiter (1998) emphasize how police knowledge affects police strategy. In order to understand police knowledge, they note, we need to understand how the context or field of policing is changing, and how knowledge in one site is affected by actions, interactions, and knowledge in other sites. As Pierre Bourdieu (1990) explains in *The Logic of Practice*, the strategy of actors comes from the interaction between lived experience and internalized rules and the structure of the field. Police strategy is shaped by the interaction between the experiences of police and their internalized understandings of the role, relationship with, and understanding of protesters. By looking at how these interactions unfold as police struggle among themselves and with other actors over symbolic, economic, and political capital, often in the currencies of legitimacy and autonomy, one can better understand the rise and wane of particular practices and the shift toward a dual model of protest policing.

For example, when the Royal Canadian Mounted Police (RCMP) used pepper spray against global justice protesters at the APEC summit in Vancouver in 1997, this strategy was challenged as illegitimate by opposition party politicians, human rights lawyers, NGOs, and protesters. A federal inquiry into the policing of the event was launched. In turn, the RCMP defended its strategy and legitimacy using the frameworks of its field and attempted to translate these frameworks for a broader audience. Even though it could be argued that the incident cost political capital in the larger political field, the force was able to maintain and possibly even increase its status in the field of protest policing, where it was portrayed as both a victim in larger political struggles and a leader in terms of policing strategy. The RCMP's explanation of its strategy and its reception facilitated ongoing police use of pepper spray. But the numbers and media coverage can tell us only a limited amount. Instead, we must track such struggles over each of the tactics by looking at debates themselves, and the explanations that the police offer to different audiences about their reasons for turning to pepper spray. As should be clear, the diffusion of practices among police forces is affected by local interactions with protesters, among police, and with other actors, including political authorities, private industry, and the media.

Each choice is partly a struggle over forms of capital – to be seen as right, good, modern, and effective among their peers, before the budget committee, in the media, in city council, in training institutes, and elsewhere is a goal of police leaders. Each of these interactions and performances is interpreted through "categories of perception and assessment." Such categories are "organizing principles of action" that allow the social agent to display their value and effectiveness (Bourdieu 1990, 13).

Such processes underlie the diffusion and incorporation of the technologies and strategies as well as the categories of perception and assessment that help police decide when it is appropriate to shift from negotiated management to militarized policing. Although structural boundaries of race, class, age, gender, and so on offer widely shared categories that the police often use to evaluate protester behaviour, they also draw on shared definitions of threat and risk. Both the "broken windows" and "intelligence-led policing" frameworks have been major influences on police strategy over the same period.

The broken windows framework was made famous by New York City's Police Department (NYPD), which was heralded as "cleaning up" that city in the late 1980s and early 1990s. Alex Vitale (2008) argues that the NYPD brought this model into protest policing, where broken windows became transformed into a "command-and-control" strategy that involved full enforcement of the law in order for the police to exert control over the streets and spaces of the city. This approach prioritized establishing and defending the appearance of order in order to maintain order. Most of the time, this involved "soft hat" policing and attempts at negotiation, but it also involved the use of barricades and permits to maintain control, shifting to mass arrests, riot gear, and more significant barricading when protesters were perceived as potentially disorderly. As Vitale reports, in New York City a refusal to communicate and cooperate is seen as a trigger for arrests and escalation.

The second major influence on police evaluations of protester behaviour is intelligence-led policing. This framework is part of a wider neoliberal emphasis on limiting risk and increasing the predictability of social life. It attempts to evaluate risk through the collection of information and the pre-emptive channelling or controlling of behaviour. Intelligence-led policing frameworks migrated to Canada and the United States from the United Kingdom in the context of post-9/11 fears over terrorism (Sullivan and Hendriks 2009; Earl 2011; K. Williams 2011). Unlike the broken windows model, which emphasizes situational threats that protesters pose in the moment as triggers for militarized policing, intelligence-led policing uses intelligence to identify potential threats in advance of events, encouraging pre-emptive policing and disruption of those potential threats. As Kristian Williams (2011) points out, the goal of intelligence-led policing is to understand threats in order to prepare for them, and sometimes to neutralize them. Similarly, Noakes and Gillham (2006) argue that there is now an attempt to "manage the risks of crime through the strategic control of suspect populations deemed to be a greater potential threat to social order" through what they call the "new penology."

In this approach, protesters are evaluated in terms of the potential threat they present to public order. In this framework, protest activities are grouped with terrorism as points on a spectrum of "threat" or "risk." As Newman and Clarke (2008) urge in their Department of Justice publication *Policing Terrorism: An Executive's Guide*, police chiefs must "think of terrorism as a crime" and "[not] waste time on motives." They are instead encouraged to assess risk and threat and to gather intelligence.

As de Lint and Hall (2009) note, within this framework, protesters who don't negotiate in advance or those who refuse to negotiate are seen as threats. Reluctance or refusal to cooperate signals risk and the possibility of threat, and can justify the decision to move beyond existing negotiated management practices. Indeed, Vitale (2007) argues that non-cooperation is the main reason forces turn to militarized tactics. A refusal to work with police liaisons can be interpreted as "non-compliance," which has led to incidents of "over-policing." Indeed, in 2003 the Police Review Commission asked the Berkeley Police Department in California to establish a category of "non-cooperative/non-violent" in an attempt to ensure that batons and less lethal weapons weren't used against non-violent protesters deemed "uncooperative" (Police Review Commission 2003).

If protesters are deemed "uncooperative" because they don't negotiate with police in advance, then police face the challenge of determining how to respond. This classification may trigger a shift to militarized policing automatically or trigger further attempts to evaluate who is a threat using past experience or experts from within or outside of policing institutions.

Patrick Rafail's analysis (2010) of police behaviour in Canada confirms that protesters lacking in "preparation" are more likely to be arrested. He examined city-level protest policing of 1,152 demonstrations that occurred between 1998 and 2004 in Montreal, Toronto, and Vancouver. The clearest and most consistent finding is that when protesters didn't "pre-mobilize," police were more likely to arrest. Pre-mobilization is measured by the presence of placards; dissemination of informational material to bystanders; having a speaker to address the crowd; uniformity in the attire of the participants; a media liaison; and transportation used to bring the demonstrators to and from the protest site. Pre-mobilization is of course much more likely to correspond with negotiated management, with its greater predictability. Rafail (2010) also finds that police are more likely to arrest participants in groups that are seen as unprofessional, unpredictable, and unwilling to negotiate – such as anarchists or youthful protesters. The most obvious trigger for escalation is the presence of the anarchist "black bloc" – a protester strategy clearly associated with defiance of police orders.

Evidence of this understanding can be found in the Ontario Provincial Police training for front-line officers assigned to the 2010 G-20 protests in Toronto. One PowerPoint slide used in the training noted that there were protesters and there were anarchists. According to the briefing, anarchists are willing to use a lawless action to achieve their goal of abolishing the government. "Some, not all anarchists will wear all black clothing or carry them in a bag ... Safety equipment is often worn to protect them from *lawful removal by police* [emphasis in original]. To help with articulation if there are to be protests, please go home or at your work station and Google Black Bloc. Look at their behaviors and clothing." As part of the training, officers also watched videos of past protest events. Such training sessions encourage standardized, militarized responses to triggers like the presence of anarchists or a refusal to negotiate, as distinct from the behaviour of activists at any particular protest event. It certifies and disseminates a particular understanding of what a "threat" looks like and what will trigger a militarized police strategy.

Diffusing the Triggers for a Militarized Response

The spread and successful incorporation of this dual model with its rules for escalation is not automatic but is dependent on local political conditions.

"Diffusion ... [is] *defined as the acceptance of some specific item, over time, by adopting units – individuals, groups, communities –* that are linked both to external channels of communication and to each other by means of both a structure of social relations and a system of values, or culture" (E. Katz 1968; emphasis added). Incorporating the dual model into a police agency involves the diffusion of both the militarized tactics and technologies and the rules for using them. Past research on diffusion suggests that three conditions underlie the successful incorporation of a new tactic or strategy. The first is a perceived crisis in the status quo; the second is access to expert knowledge about alternatives. In the case of protest policing, such access is rapidly increased when there is a high-profile event with outside involvement, new leadership, or increased participation in policing conferences. A third condition is that potential adopters must see themselves and their context as similar in some way to previous users of a practice – they "attribute similarity."

Perceiving crises, accessing information, and attributing similarity are social, interactive processes among individuals and organizations with different roles, interests, identities, and histories. They also involve interpretive processes where individuals and organizations consider and reflect on their past, present, and future strategies and identities and those of other practitioners.

If the diffusion of new practices or frameworks is understood to be both interactive and interpretive, it becomes clear that understanding the increasing use of militarized tactics and the spread of a dual strategy go beyond simple imitation or evolution. The perception of a crisis and a desire for a different strategy occur when police opinion leaders interpret the possibilities offered by other police strategies as preferable to the status quo. Such reflection most likely takes place when either an extraordinary event, such as a political convention or summit, is announced or when a new wave of protest, such as Occupy, is understood to present new challenges for protest policing. At such points, police turn to available sources of information.

Police have had increasing access to information about new technologies including militarized tactics in recent years because of changes to the structure of the field of policing. These include the increasing role of extra-local policing networks such as the International Association of Chiefs of Police (IACP) and the Police Executive Research Forum (PERF), as well as policing research and training bodies. These networks have created new forums and ways for policing leaders to access information and deliberate about practices and strategy. At the same time, the increasing saturation and speed of media has given police greater awareness of the optics of their practices and a wariness about rejecting the best practices that other police forces are adopting (della Porta, Fillieule, and Reiter 1998; G. Marx 1998). Both integration and the use of electronic media are helping to disseminate the expectation that protesters who refuse to cooperate with police signal potential threat and should trigger for militarized tactics.

As this model has spread to new forces and contexts, local challenges to the definition of "threatening protesters" become less visible. Later adopters have become more confident about the appropriateness of the model and spend less time adapting the strategy to their local context. This modularity increases the likelihood that police will make errors in its application.

As the model is now read by many police forces, a lack of negotiation or the presence of known anarchists in an organizing body should trigger a militarized strategy. On the surface, this criterion makes some sense. However, and especially during periods of greater mobilization and its associated coalition building, the presence of uncooperative protesters may correspond with a broader range of protesters with diverse tactics. If police decide to use a militarized strategy with barricading or kettling techniques, a riot control unit, and less lethal weapons in this context, they may limit disruption and win public applause, or they may end up arresting a wide array of participants, diminish trust with future activists, and invite public condemnation, as they did at the Toronto G-20 protests of 2010, Montreal's student protests of 2012, or Occupy Wall Street in 2011–12.

Waves of Protest and the Dual Model

Whereas the negotiated management model emerged, consolidated, and spread during a period of movement decline, the dual model emerged during a period of movement emergence, with its militancy and experimentation. Police experimented with and established the strategy through the rise and fall of the global justice movement. It lasted into the new wave of protest associated with the Occupy movement and the provincial wave of protest of the student strikes in Quebec.

The framing of "uncooperative protesters" as a trigger for militarization has changed the landscape for social movements and other challengers in Canada and the United States. The use of militarized tactics against a wide range of protesters has diminished trust between increasing numbers of

FIGURE 7.1
Cycle of distrust and militarization

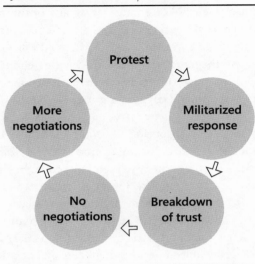

protesters and the police, and the state more generally. As this cycle of distrust converges with an accelerating wave of protest, the space for tolerated social movement activity narrows (Figure 7.1).

The increasing diffusion of this dual model has meant growing numbers of incidents where militarized repressive tactics are used against diverse crowds, including those who had previously coordinated with the police (Figure 7.2). This can lead to increased solidarity between conventional and transgressive protesters. We need only look at the policing of the explicitly non-violent Occupy movement for examples. When the NYPD deputy inspector pepper-sprayed young women within a fenced-in area at Occupy Wall Street, the public and the media went wild, and participation in and the militancy of the movement rapidly increased. Similarly, when a campus police officer pepper-sprayed students associated with the Occupy movement at the University of California at Davis campus, trust in the police declined, limiting the likelihood of future cooperation and coordination between protesters and police. As it stands, within a context of escalating mobilization, the dual model and its militarization is not dividing and conquering different types of protesters but rather building solidarity between previously cooperative and uncooperative protesters, increasing the militancy of the movement.

FIGURE 7.2
Process of escalation of policing

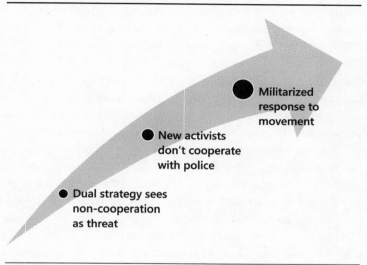

Militarized
response to
movement

New activists
don't cooperate
with police

Dual strategy sees
non-cooperation
as threat

By 2012, it appeared that the dual strategy of protest policing with its trigger of non-cooperation had consolidated and diffused widely. It is a strategy that was developed with the goal of limiting risk and threat. However, the risk of the strategy itself is that it is difficult to implement without controversy, especially during an accelerating wave of protest, when diverse and new participants are protesting and the media and the larger community are attentive and more sympathetic. In societies that have legal rights to freedom of assembly, association, and expression, police cannot easily mandate protesters' communication and joint planning.

Experienced protesters who in the past may have cooperated with the police are increasingly likely to have ties to those who have faced pepper spray, riot control units, and barricades, reducing trust with the police and legitimizing non-cooperation. In addition, images and reports of police repression that are rapidly shared with new protesters make these "newbies" less likely to trust police as facilitators of social movement activity. Indeed, in recent years, inexperienced activists often assume that they will be arrested, pepper-sprayed, or beaten by police – partly as a result of seeing such images. This lack of trust puts police in a difficult position. If protesters don't cooperate and police overenforce, they face increased resistance and militancy. If protesters don't cooperate and police are seen to underenforce, and property destruction or disruption ensues, the police may face political heat and public scorn.

The normalized repression of uncooperative protesters shows us how the social movement society shrinks the space for those unwilling to "play the game." The institutionalization of social movement activity may weaken the boundaries between social movements and electoral politics and incorporate a wider set of political actors. However, the rules by which these challengers must play are strict. In the social movement society, the policing of protest may become more routine and communicative and less violent. It is clear, however, that over the past fifteen years, those outside of this arrangement are increasingly punished. In response, the police have drawn from the best practices within their professional, globalizing networks and have established that those who reject a model of negotiation and cooperation pose a threat; as a result, a militarized response is appropriate. Such responses, when accelerated by the waves of protest associated with the global justice and Occupy movements, have diminished the trust many protesters have in police, increasing the likelihood that clashes between police and protesters will continue at large-scale protests in the foreseeable future.

Note
1 This is contested by some researchers who note the emergence of SWAT (Special Weapons and Tactics) teams during this period (Kraska and Kappeler 1997).

PART 3

HOW PEOPLE PARTICIPATE

8

Social Movement Communities in the Movement Society

SUZANNE STAGGENBORG

In the first edition of *Power in Movement* (1994), Sidney Tarrow asked in his concluding chapter whether a "social movement society" was emerging. David Meyer and Sidney Tarrow later edited *The Social Movement Society* (1998), arguing that, since the cycle of protest of the 1960s, movements have become more frequent and protest tactics more widely diffused than in previous decades; at the same time, protest is becoming more institutionalized. This is an important idea – that protest tactics have spread to more groups in society, and that protest has become a regular way of doing political business. It suggests that there are ways for movements to mobilize fairly rapidly when grievances are framed cleverly because models of collective action are everywhere and protest has become institutionalized. Thus, when the editors of *Adbusters*, the Canadian anti-consumerist publication, called in 2011 for Americans to occupy Wall Street in the wake of the Arab Spring and other large protests around the world, a visible movement was quickly born. Of course, this movement didn't come out of nowhere; social movement scholars know that movements build on pre-existing networks and organizations, collective identity, and collective action frames.

In this chapter, I argue that we need to go beyond documenting levels of protest, types of actors involved in protest, and forms of protest in order to assess the value of the social movement society (SMS) thesis. This type of work is important, but it doesn't get at the underlying mechanisms and processes (McAdam, Tarrow, and Tilly 2001) that allow for the development of a social movement society. My argument is that *social movement communities* are the basis for the social movement society; we need to look at how these communities are expanded and how they support a social movement society (or why they fail to do so). I begin with a look at some of the empirical findings associated with the SMS thesis, followed by a discussion of the concept of a social movement community (SMC) and how the latter is important to understanding the former. I then employ these concepts in discussing two cases that I have studied: the World March of Women (WMW) in Montreal and the Pittsburgh G-20 protests. I conclude with a discussion of the theoretical implications of my analysis for the idea of a social movement society.

The Social Movement Society Thesis

Meyer and Tarrow (1998, 4) proposed three hypotheses regarding the idea of a movement society: (1) social protest is now a constant, rather than sporadic, feature of modern life; (2) protests occur more frequently and are used by more diverse actors to advance more diverse claims than ever before; and (3) movements are becoming more professionalized and institutionalized. Beyond the articles in their edited volume, which address these hypotheses using empirical data on various countries, the importance of the thesis is demonstrated by ongoing work that attempts to evaluate the SMS argument (Rucht and Neidhardt 2002; McAdam et al. 2005; Soule and Earl 2005; J.D. McCarthy, Rafail, and Gromis 2013). Soule and Earl (2005, 346) summarize the key arguments of the SMS thesis as "the over time expansion of protest, the over time diffusion of protest, the over time institutionalization of protest, and the over time institutionalization of state responses."

The empirical evidence for the SMS thesis is mixed, but suggests that there is something important to the idea. Regarding the expansion of protest, event data coded by Rucht and colleagues from newspaper accounts in West Germany shows an upward trend in the number of protest events in the 1980s (Rucht 1998). Based on the World Values Survey, McCarthy and colleagues (2013) note that protest participation also appears to have increased in a number of other European countries, making the SMS thesis plausible for European societies. Data for the United States tell a different story, however. Soule and Earl (2005) use event data coded from the *New York Times* between 1960 and 1986 to show that the number of protests in the United States declined over time, although the size of events increased.

They also found fewer organizations involved in more recent protest events, but suggest that this might mean a consolidation of the social movement sector, with fewer but larger social movement organizations (SMOs) mobilizing larger events and more people. (And, of course, the *New York Times* is less likely to mention smaller organizations than larger ones.) McCarthy and colleagues (2013) extend Soule and Earl's analysis to 2006, and find little support for the SMS thesis in the United States. They analyze protest events in New York City from 1960 to 2006 and find a decline in overall protest since the 1960s. In contrast to Soule and Earl, they found a steady decline in the presence of SMOs until the mid-1990s, when they detected an increase in SMOs, providing some support for the SMS thesis. Insofar as SMOs play an important role in maintaining an SMS, this provides support for the argument of David Meyer and Amanda Pullum in Chapter 1 about the role of professionalization; although SMOs are not necessarily professionalized, those that make the *New York Times* generally are.

Regarding the diffusion of protest to new constituencies, Rucht (1998) found a rising number of claims in West Germany in the 1980s; more protestors were making more claims than ever before, going beyond the claims associated with national movements such as the women's movement and peace movement to a variety of different issue areas. Using data on Chicago, McAdam and colleagues (2005) found that protest had shifted markedly since 1970; while much of the protest activity in 1970 was urban- and/or campus-based, and often involved disadvantaged minorities, after 1980 public protest was more likely suburban and often initiated by advantaged groups. Based on event data across the United States, Soule and Earl (2005) did not find an expansion in the number of claims made, but rather a decline in the number of new claims over time; nor did they find more new organizations and groups involved in protest. But they did find some upswing in conservative or right-wing claims in the mid-1980s. Looking at student protests across the United States, McCarthy and colleagues (2013) found a decline in student involvement in protest, both at the high school and college levels, suggesting that new generations have not taken up protest tactics and contradicting the SMS thesis. They do note the rise of the Tea Party movement as an indication that more conservatives are adopting protest tactics, in line with SMS expectations. Meyer and Pullum (Chapter 1) emphasize the organizational structures and resources underpinning the Tea Party as an example of current movement mobilization.

With regard to the institutionalization of protest and state responses to protest, there are also mixed findings. One argument is that less contentious forms of protest (e.g., petitioning) have increased in frequency, whereas more contentious forms (e.g., blockades, building takeovers) have not; as protest spreads to more constituencies, it may be becoming more moderate. Looking at West Germany, Rucht (1998) actually found that collective protests there became more radical through the 1980s. Although only a small proportion of protestors participated in violent events, the number of events involving violence and property damage increased in these years. In Chicago, however, McAdam and colleagues (2005) found that protest changed from being more disruptive and public in 1970 to being more peaceful, routine, and local in nature after 1980. Based on data across the United States up to 1986, Soule and Earl (2005) also found support for the idea that tactics have become more moderate. McCarthy and colleagues (2013) found an overall decline in use of violence by protesters in New York City, but found that the use of civil disobedience was quite high in recent decades.

As for responses to protest by police, American scholars have noted the routinization of police/protester relations following the 1960s, as a "negotiated management" style of policing came to replace the "escalated force" style of the 1960s (J.D. McCarthy and McPhail 1998, 96). McCarthy and McPhail (1998, 109) found that the vast majority of protests have become much more orderly and routinized since the 1960s, and they conclude that "protest has been incorporated as a normal part of the political process." Studying policing in France and Italy, della Porta, Fillieule, and Reiter (1998) also found that, in general, police handling of protest had come to rely more on "persuasive strategies" than on repression. However, they caution that the way in which the authorities, including both political authorities and police, "perceive protest groups dramatically affects the treatment they give those groups"; protesters such as foreigners, immigrants, young people, or extreme leftists are still likely to encounter repressive police tactics in some situations (della Porta, Fillieule, and Reiter 1998, 119).

In the aftermath of the 1999 Seattle protests and the 2001 terrorist attacks on the United States, scholars have noted a new phase in policing response aimed at achieving "strategic incapacitation" of escalating protests (Gillham and Noakes 2007). In New York City, McCarthy and colleagues (2013) find, contrary to SMS expectations, that use of force by police has increased in recent decades. Lesley Wood argues in Chapter 7 that a dual strategy of policing has emerged, with militarized tactics used against protesters who refuse to negotiate with police. This finding has mixed implications for the SMS thesis; Wood notes decreased "space for the social movement society" accompanying the militarization of policing, but also that repression may increase solidarity and militancy among protesters, which could lead to expanded protests.

Social Movement Communities in Movement Societies

These inconsistent findings on the empirical predictions of the social movement society thesis suggest that we need to pay attention to historical changes and local/national contexts. As Howard Ramos and Kathleen Rodgers suggest in the Introduction to this volume, it makes sense to talk about *social movement societies* rather than a single global SMS when we take into account the varying conditions that give rise to ongoing movement campaigns. I argue that we should look at the organizational structures and ideological and cultural bases that sustain movement societies and at how these vary in strength over time and place. This approach is also evident in other chapters in this volume: Dominique Masson (Chapter 4) links government funding to the institutionalization of women's organizations in Quebec, which support a social movement society there. Tina Fetner, Allyson Stokes, and Carrie Sanders (Chapter 2) document the community development and institution building that have supported the religious right in Canada and the United States. Dominique Clément (Chapter 3) shows how social movements created a human rights state that facilitates the diffusion of protest in Canada. In Chapter 10, Jim Conley provides a way of thinking about how cultural contexts affect movement societies by focusing on the conventions and justifications available to potential collective actors.

The concept of a social movement community is useful for analyzing the cultural and organizational bases of movement societies because it enables us to think about the diverse elements of movements, including movement organizations, movements within institutions, networks of groups and individuals, cultural groups, and meeting places within communities. In examining these diverse elements of movement communities, we can look at how movements become institutionalized, how ideologies spread, how particular cultural conventions support movements, how protest tactics get diffused, and how collective action campaigns are launched. In other words, we can examine how movement communities create the conditions for a social movement society; variations in movement communities can help to explain differences in social movement societies. As movement societies are established, movement campaigns in turn affect movement communities by building networks and identities among participants.

Although the concept of a social movement community is often applied to the local level (e.g., Staggenborg 1998), where there is a spatial element to community and where activists from different groups are likely to interact physically, it might also be applied to regional, national, and international levels. To employ the concept of movement community to study extra-local movements, we need to think about how activists are connected to one another and how they develop a collective identity as part of an "imagined community" (B. Anderson 1991), if not a face-to-face community (Aunio and Staggenborg 2011). Websites and other information and communications technologies (ICTs) are obviously important to national and international movement communities such as the Occupy movement, but there are also other ways in which networks and collective identity get developed and maintained, such as campaigns that bring people together to protest in places like Ottawa and Washington and connections made through institutionalized venues such as meetings sponsored by the United Nations.

Within global movements, Aunio and Staggenborg (2011) conceive of three different types of movement communities, which may interact and overlap in a global movement society. *Professional communities* consist of professional activists, frequently associated with NGOs, who often interact with one another at international conferences such as the UN-sponsored conferences on climate change and women's rights. These activists use expert knowledge to collect and disseminate information on behalf of "principled ideas" (Keck and Sikkink 1998), typically engaging in what McAdam, Tarrow, and Tilly (2001, 7–8) call *contained* as opposed to *transgressive* contention. They have insider status within institutionalized policy circles, as they contribute their expertise to international institutions and movements. Professional activists often share information and remain in touch with one another between conferences and other events where they meet; through these exchanges, they maintain a collective identity and can be mobilized into movement campaigns.

Grassroots communities consist of activists who are more likely to engage in transgressive contention, employing direct action tactics and pressuring institutions from the outside. They may employ the resources of professionals and provide them with activist energy during international campaigns and events, but grassroots activists are likely to return to their local movement communities after such actions (Tarrow 2005). *Conscience communities* consist of members of the public who share the values of the movement and occasionally become involved in limited ways in movement actions; they have been transformed from "bystander publics" with minimal concern for movement aims (Turner 1970, 152) into constituents who have adopted some elements of movement ideology and identity. The mass media and ICTs are important in spreading movement ideas to conscience communities, which may participate in transnational movements through means such as cyberprotest, online petitions, and conscientious consumerism.

All of these different types of communities are important to transnational movements, and all of them must continually imagine themselves to be part of a shared collective identity. Insofar as there is a global social movement society, these communities are regularly engaged in transnational campaigns – that is, movement communities support the ongoing campaigns characteristic of a movement society; collective campaigns then strengthen the three types of movement communities, perpetuating the global movement society. Important research questions include the ways in which these different communities support ongoing campaigns; how protest is spread to more diverse sets of actors; and how institutionalized or professionalized communities interact with grassroots and conscience communities.

Insofar as a movement society exists, it must support at least periodic movement campaigns; collective action is used routinely by a diverse range of actors in an SMS. Social movement communities, whether local or extra-local, are important in launching movement campaigns, and it is during the course of campaigns – locally, nationally, or internationally – that the structures of movement communities and the connections of groups within and across movement communities become visible. A lack of network connections or centralization may lead to failure to mobilize or to a preference for certain strategies within campaigns. Movement campaigns also have important influences on the structures of movement communities – they often build organizations, create coalitions, and develop networks. This can occur within the movement community, across movement communities (e.g., women and labour); and across levels (e.g., local and international). Movement campaigns affect subsequent campaigns through their influence on political opportunities, models of "contentious performances," and networks (Tilly 2008a; Staggenborg and Lecomte 2009; V. Taylor et al. 2009). This approach contributes to dynamic analyses of social movement interactions and to an understanding of the mechanisms and processes affecting movement mobilization and strategy (McAdam, Tarrow, and Tilly 2001).

In the following sections, I look at two different movement campaigns and the social movement communities that supported them: the 2000 World March of Women in Montreal, which was part of a larger international campaign, and the 2009 protests against the G-20 Summit in

Pittsburgh, which might be considered part of a broader global justice movement. My discussion of these two campaigns is aimed at demonstrating, first, the importance of movement community structures for collective campaigns and, second, how variations in the structures of SMCs can help to explain local, regional, and national differences in social movement societies.

The World March of Women

The international women's movement dates back to the nineteenth century (Rupp 1997) but has expanded greatly in recent decades. An organizational infrastructure for the global women's movement was created as the United Nations, responding to pressure from women's groups, established offices to deal with women's issues and declared 1975 International Women's Year. Beginning with the first official UN women's conference in Mexico City in 1975, the United Nations has sponsored a series of world conferences on women, including the Fourth World Conference on Women, held in Beijing in 1995. The United Nations has provided resources for an international network of women to meet and plan for the conferences and follow-up actions. Many professional activists are part of this international women's movement community, including NGO staff members, UN personnel, and feminists from government delegations (Antrobus 2004). With the expansion of international women's networks, the movement addressed more and more issues relevant to women around the world, and grassroots activists also became connected to the international women's movement. One of the concerns that helped to create unity among women in many different countries was "violence against women," a category that included such issues as rape and domestic violence, female genital mutilation, sexual abuse, and forced prostitution (Keck and Sikkink 1998). This expanded international women's movement community is now one element of a global social movement society.

The history of the WMW illustrates the importance of local movement communities in supporting collective action campaigns and in expanding social movement societies, both locally and internationally. The Fédération des femmes du Québec (FFQ), a long-standing feminist organization founded in 1966 in Quebec, was responsible for initiating the WMW. Remarkably, the WMW spread across the globe as marches were held in over 160 countries in October 2000, and it continued as an international organization that held events around the world again in 2005 and 2010

(Dufour and Giraud 2007a, 2007b). The FFQ was able to play this role in expanding the international women's movement because it had expanded its own mobilizing activities and organizational agenda in Quebec in the early 1990s.

This expansion was a result of both political opportunity and leadership that took advantage of that opportunity through framing and collective action strategies. The FFQ began to enlarge its mobilizing activities and organizational agenda in the early 1990s, under the leadership of then vice president and later president Françoise David (interview with Françoise David in Rebick 2005, 246–50). The FFQ had both individual and group members, but until that point it was mostly individuals who participated in the organization. David argued that member groups needed to be engaged and that the issue of poverty, given Quebec's unemployment rate of 14 percent at the time, would mobilize many new activists. She guessed correctly that, by framing poverty as a women's issue, the FFQ would be able to enlist community groups concerned about poverty and to mobilize more people to participate in the women's movement. Inspired by the American civil rights movement, David proposed a Quebec Women's March Against Poverty, which the FFQ organized in 1995. Known as the Bread and Roses March, it took place over ten days, with some 800 marchers making their way through sixty cities and villages in the province to the capital of Quebec City. The campaign received broad support from conscience communities in Quebec, and some 20,000 supporters participated by waving bread, roses, and purple ribbons as the marchers passed by. It also won concrete victories from the Quebec government, consciously exploiting the new Parti Québécois government's need for women's votes in the upcoming referendum on sovereignty (interview with Françoise David in Rebick 2005, 247). Most importantly for the social movement society in Quebec, the 1995 march enlarged the constituency of the women's movement through the issue of poverty and created new movement community bonds that would support the larger, more international WMW campaign.

The 1995 campaign not only enlarged the organizational infrastructure of the FFQ and the Quebec women's movement community, but also strengthened collective identity among feminists, expanded support among the population, and prompted local feminists to address new global issues. The professional movement community was important in this, as international development groups with connections to the FFQ had invited eighteen women from countries such as Cameroon, Nicaragua, and the

Philippines to join the marchers. FFQ leaders interested in the idea of a worldwide march discussed it with these women, who provided encouragement (interview with Diane Matte in Rebick 2005, 250). Their participation, together with strong support from a conscience community, led FFQ leaders to imagine an international community of women and a worldwide campaign. The UN World Women's Conference in Beijing, which was held soon after the Bread and Roses March in 1995, provided an organizational opportunity. Fresh from their successful campaign, FFQ leaders travelled to Beijing and gave a workshop on the Bread and Roses March that was greeted with much enthusiasm by participants (Rebick 2005, 245). This effort sparked the formation of an international coalition led by the FFQ, with representatives from more than fifteen countries that subsequently organized a WMW. The Quebec women's movement community reached out to other communities through international networks; through the input of local and international communities, it was decided that the WMW would adopt the two issues of poverty and violence against women as the overriding themes of the campaign because these were seen as "the two issues that affect women most in their daily lives" (interview with Diane Matte in Rebick 2005, 251).

In Montreal, the FFQ helped to organize a WMW coalition that attracted participants through various mobilizing structures in the movement community, including women's centres, community organizations, and union women's committees. As Dominique Masson shows in Chapter 4, these organizational bases were institutionalized; unions were strong in Quebec and women's organizations and community centres received government funding to serve their constituents. There were also existing networks among groups and individuals, some created by the 1995 Bread and Roses March and others forged or strengthened by the new WMW campaign. As a result of each campaign, more individuals were drawn into participation in women's movement organizations, thereby fortifying the structures of the movement community (Staggenborg and Lecomte 2009). Significantly, these organizational structures were ideologically flexible and willing to move into new issue territory; for example, the unions in Quebec were already active on issues beyond traditional labour issues and could easily be brought into the WMW campaign.

The WMW campaign resulted in an ongoing organization that connected feminists around the world. The organization is a decentralized "global network that organizes worldwide mobilizations every five or six years" (Dufour and Giraud 2007b, 1156). In 2005, the WMW relayed a

Global Charter for Humanity around the world, and in 2010 another campaign of international actions was organized. In an international study of the WMW, Dufour and Giraud (2007a) show that women who participated in both the 2000 and 2005 marches created a unified and lasting collective identity through sustained transnational activism. They did so by building on local movement communities, which were then strengthened through the campaigns. To develop an international movement community, the WMW organization increasingly aligned itself with the global justice movement and moved away from the UN process, using the strategy of the Global Charter as a means of engaging grassroots activists and creating "a space of discourse" and a "women of the world" collective identity (Dufour and Giraud 2007a, 312–13). Thus, the WMW was able to mobilize grassroots and conscience communities, deliberately expanding beyond the professional communities of the main transnational women's networks (Dufour and Giraud 2007a, 314). Coordinating committees have been founded in various countries, and new ties have been forged among national groups (Dufour and Giraud 2007b, 1160–61). In Quebec, some 15,000 women gathered in Quebec City on 17 May 2005 to welcome the charter, "based in large part upon the activists' capacity to reactivate networks that supported the 2000 mobilizations and on the fact that the women's movement was deeply rooted in the various regions of Quebec" (Dufour and Giraud 2007a, 317).

The case of the WMW shows the importance of movement communities, from the local to the international level, in building social movement societies at different levels. Movement communities are often decentralized, and they may encompass a wide variety of individuals and groups; over time, they may shrink or expand, and they may experience scale shift. Through the creation of networks and collective identity, local, national, and international movement communities can be connected. The expansion of movement communities requires mobilizing structures, effective frames, and campaigns that engage new groups, generate public support, and spread collective identity. Where SMCs are strong and there are ongoing campaigns, we are likely to see a stronger and more extensive social movement society. In the case of the 2000 WMW in Montreal, organizations in the movement community, such as women's centres and union women's committees, served as mobilizing structures for the campaign, demonstrating the causal connection between movement communities and the ongoing collective action characteristic of a movement society. Once such a campaign is launched, it will likely lead to further campaigns, in part due to its influence on networks in movement communities (Tilly 2008a).

The Pittsburgh Protests against the G-20

On 28 May 2009, the White House announced that Pittsburgh would be the site of the G-20 meetings on 24–25 September 2009. The immediate response of local activists suggests the presence of a vital local movement community, though not a completely unified one. Various groups began at once to organize a wide range of activities before and during the G-20 Summit, most of which were routinized and legal, in line with the SMS thesis, but some of which were illegal and/or confrontational direct action tactics. The People's Summit consisted of two full days and an evening of speakers and workshops on a wide range of issues such as poverty, racism, war, human rights, and the environment beginning the weekend before the G-20 Summit. Two large-scale marches were held, one unpermitted march called the People's Uprising on the first day of the G-20 Summit, and a permitted one called the People's March on the second day of the Summit. Other activities during the week included a March for Jobs and a tent city organized by a national organization called Bail Out the People; a rally and march by an interfaith group calling itself the G-6 Billion; a Women's Tent City put together by the local chapters of Code Pink, the Women's International League for Peace and Freedom (WILPF), and others; another tent city set up by a coalition called the Three Rivers Climate Convergence to emphasize climate justice and sustainable living; poetry readings by a group called Poets on the Loose; a two-day International Peace, Justice and Empowerment Summit; People's Voices, a forum with finance ministers from Argentina, Brazil, South Africa, and India; and a rally and concert around the theme of clean energy jobs. Several international organizations also made appearances during the G-20 week. Most dramatically, Greenpeace climbers scaled Pittsburgh's West End Bridge to hang a large banner calling attention to climate change, resulting in their arrests and much media attention, and Oxfam also garnered media attention with a demonstration employing large cutouts of G-20 leaders.

To assess the strength of the SMS that produced these activities, we need to look at the nature of the local movement community and its connections to national and international activists. Among the many movement organizations in Pittsburgh that became active in the protests or provided activists were "anti-authoritarian" (anarchist and other) groups, anti-war and women's peace groups, environmental organizations, racial and economic justice organizations, unions, and civil liberties groups. There were two main centres of organization for the G-20 protests: a loose coalition of local anti-authoritarians called the Pittsburgh G-20 Resistance Project (PGRP) and an alliance of groups and individuals loosely associated with the Thomas Merton Center (TMC), a peace and justice movement centre. There were connections among these two centres of activity in that a few activists participated in both alliances and there were prior network connections among the groups and individuals.

Many activists in the movement community were connected through the TMC, which was founded in 1972 by anti–Vietnam War activists as a peace and justice centre dedicated to principles of non-violence. Thus, there was an established movement centre in Pittsburgh, although the TMC suffered from resource shortages and did not receive government funding like many women's and community centres in Quebec. At the time of the G-20 protests, however, the TMC was providing meeting space and other resources to some twenty-five organizing campaigns and projects, and also had a list of "friends and affiliates" of the TMC that included a broad range of groups. In the months leading up to the G-20 Summit, the TMC hosted eight public meetings of activists that were intended to create some co-ordination of efforts and information sharing among the different groups organizing protests of the G-20. One of the most active projects of the TMC was its Anti-War Committee (AWC), formed in January 2003 to oppose the US invasion of Iraq. The AWC planned and staged large, permitted anti-war protests in Pittsburgh in 2003 and in subsequent years on the anniversary of the invasion of Iraq. When the White House announced the Pittsburgh G-20 meetings, the AWC decided immediately to use its experience to organize a large permitted march against the G-20, enlisting help through the TMC-sponsored alliance.

Thus, in line with the SMS thesis, the Pittsburgh movement community had a history of engaging in institutionalized protests sanctioned by the city permit process. During the months leading up to the G-20, however, the AWC and other groups were forced to wage a major battle over permits, which the city withheld on the grounds that this was a federally controlled national security event. Permits for most events were obtained only after protesters filed suit with the aid of local civil liberties lawyers. Meanwhile, the PGRP organized its more contentious People's Uprising without permits and with a greater degree of disruption. The police, for their part, departed significantly from the "negotiated management" style and amassed a huge police force with outside reinforcements for the G-20. In line with the dual policing strategy noted by Lesley Wood in Chapter 7, the police aimed militarized tactics largely at unpermitted demonstrations, using tear gas, rubber bullets, and new technology such as the Long Range Acoustic Device

(LRAD) to battle protesters. Although few arrests were made during the organized protests, police lines confronted protesters at the People's Uprising and the police arrested nearly 200 protesters and bystanders, including students, mostly on the grounds of failure to disperse on the evening of 25 September at the University of Pittsburgh. Following the G-20 Summit, students and activists who had been arrested banded together in a police accountability campaign and, with the help of civil liberties lawyers, filed a class action lawsuit. A protracted investigation of police conduct as well as lawsuits against the city of Pittsburgh resulted.

For the most part, the Pittsburgh G-20 protests were planned by the local grassroots movement community, with little connection to professional communities. Greenpeace and Oxfam staged their dramatic protests without involving local activists, but some national and international groups worked with local groups to add to the locally organized protests. Bail Out the People sent members to Pittsburgh who attended the public planning meetings in the months before the summit. These activists moved into a black community during the summer and worked with the Monumental Baptist Church to organize a March for Jobs, invoking the memory of Martin Luther King Jr. and bringing unemployed people to Pittsburgh from across the country. Members of Avaaz, an Internet-based international group concerned with a range of progressive issues, also attended the public planning meetings. Participants in the "Avaaz action factory," who travel around to assist protests, worked with the Three Rivers Climate Convergence and provided resources to it. Several environmental organizations from across the country were in touch with activists in the Three Rivers Climate Convergence and also provided some resources. Other national and international groups that came to Pittsburgh and attended some of the planning meetings included Health Gap, a group concerned with AIDS and health care, and the Seeds of Peace Collective, which provides hot meals and medical support to protesters.

Pittsburgh anarchists were part of a national network of anarchists, and one important local group, the Pittsburgh Organizing Group (POG), was a member of the Northeast Anarchist Network (NEAN) and worked with both NEAN and the Midwest Action Network to plan and participate in actions to disrupt the Republican National Convention (RNC) in St. Paul, Minnesota, in 2008. During the summer before the G-20 protests, anarchists from Pittsburgh travelled to a number of cities to report on plans for the upcoming protests and to urge people to travel to Pittsburgh for the summit. The TMC's Anti-War Committee was also connected to national networks, such as the National Assembly to End the Iraq and Afghanistan Wars, and solicited endorsements from national groups for the G-20 protests. Following the Pittsburgh protests, anti-war activists became involved in providing advice and planning for the G-8 protests in Chicago in 2012.

Connections to organizations outside Pittsburgh, as well as networks within the local movement community, helped to shape the nature of the organizing and protests in the city. Because members of POG had experienced the demonizing of anarchists at the RNC demonstrations, they were determined to reach out to the local community and the mainstream media to explain who they were and why they were protesting the G-20. In addition to talking to the press, PGRP activists also attempted to connect with a potential conscience community by going door to door in many neighbourhoods distributing a newsprint broadsheet that explained without jargon why demonstrators were protesting the G-20. Although it is difficult to assess the outcome of this community outreach effort, there is evidence in local newspaper coverage that the media strategy was at least partially successful (Kutz-Flamenbaum, Staggenborg, and Duncan 2012). And after the arrests of many bystanders near the University of Pittsburgh, separate from the organized demonstrations, the conscience community appeared to grow, as many students and members of the public criticized the police actions and supported the protests. Following the G-20 Summit, the police accountability effort expanded as G-20 arrestees joined members of the African American community in the Justice for Jordan Miles campaign to protest the beating by police in January 2010 of an unarmed black teenager.

Networks in the local movement community were also strengthened in other ways during the G-20 campaign. Although they were connected to one another, members of the PGRP and the TMC-based alliance were in some ways separate movement communities within Pittsburgh, and they needed to find ways to cooperate during the G-20 protests. This was accomplished in part through their collaboration in producing a statement of respect for diversity within the movement, known as the Pittsburgh Principles, which helped to avert conflict among local groups. This collaboration originated early in the planning for the G-20 protests when activists from the PGRP approached members of the AWC, whom they knew through the Thomas Merton Center and from past collective campaigns such as the anti–Iraq War protests. National networks and experiences, particularly of anarchists, provided a model for the Pittsburgh Principles, which were essentially an agreement not to criticize one another publicly and to avoid interference with one another's events. The Pittsburgh Principles were inspired by similar principles adopted by activists in St. Paul, Minnesota, on the occasion of protests at the site of the Republican National Convention in 2008. Activists familiar with the St. Paul Principles were also aware of conflicts that had occurred at global justice demonstrations, particularly between anarchists and other protesters. They wanted to avoid such conflicts in Pittsburgh and, owing in part to the Pittsburgh Principles, did so successfully.

Mobilization of the Pittsburgh G-20 protests relied on the organizational infrastructure of the local movement community, which supports the Pittsburgh social movement society. Although organizations form and decline, and some become dormant after periods of activity, progressive movement activity since the protest cycle of the 1960s has been continuous in Pittsburgh. While many participants trace their activism to the Vietnam War era, younger activists, including college students, have also joined their ranks, making for a multigenerational movement community. Although the Thomas Merton Center is a movement centre for some activists, it does not encompass all groups in the community and it lacks sufficient resources. Progressive or leftist activists in Pittsburgh share some ideological positions, but there are also areas of disagreement. Some issue areas lacked effective organizations and leadership. These features of the general movement community help to explain the ability of specific communities (e.g., anarchists, peace activists) to mobilize, and they also affect the ability of different groups to work together. Thus, there was a fair amount of duplication of efforts in the G-20 protests organized by local activists. Resource shortages, organizational problems, and battles with the city also contributed to problems with some efforts, such as the Three Rivers Climate Convergence, which ended up consisting of a few tents in a public park that were confiscated by police. National and particularly international organizations also seemed to lack significant connections with local groups, limiting the support they provided; local initiatives might have benefited from better connections between professional and grassroots movement communities.

Conclusion

The social movement society thesis is provocative, but the mixed evidence for its predictions suggests that we should think more about the conditions that give rise to movement societies. Variations over time and place are important, and we need to explain how and why social movement societies are present in some cities and nations at some times but not others. In an SMS, collective campaigns are ongoing and spread to new groups. It is useful to look at local collective action campaigns, to see how they emerge and how the structures of movement communities support campaigns and get developed in the wake of campaigns. It is also important to look at the connections between local movement communities and campaigns and national and international ones – how grassroots, professional, and conscience communities come together to support a global movement society (Aunio and Staggenborg 2011). The two cases detailed above help to illustrate this research agenda.

The WMW case provides some clues as to how a social movement society is formed and expanded. In Quebec, where many movements thrive, protest is institutionalized in mobilizing structures such as unions and community organizations. Before the mid-1990s, the women's movement was fairly well established in Quebec, but not well connected to national and international communities. It took political opportunity, economic grievances, and leadership to spread movement concerns to new constituents. By framing poverty as a women's issue, taking advantage of the PQ's political situation, recognizing economic grievances, and using the well-established march tactic, the organizers of the Bread and Roses March helped to spread feminist claims to new grassroots groups and conscience constituents. The success of the WMW also depended on professional communities at the international level, and mobilizing structures such as the UN-sponsored meetings, to further diffuse claims and expand issues, addressing concerns about both poverty and violence against women shared by many women around the world. By bringing together multiple types of communities and employing the march tactic often associated with the civil rights movement, the campaign helped to expand the international women's movement, creating a new ongoing international women's movement organization. It is this type of organizing and collective action that expands social movement societies at local, national, and international levels.

The Pittsburgh G-20 protests were also mobilized through the structures of the local movement community. Long-standing mobilizing structures and connections among activists allowed for quick organization of fairly extensive protests, although weaknesses in the resource base and decentralization of the community also led to difficulties in pulling off some strategies and duplication of efforts. Connections to national and international groups were generally weak, and local groups did not receive a great deal of aid from extra-local groups, but the protests helped to create some bonds. During the G-20 protests, both institutionalized and less routine, more contentious tactics were on display. The impact of the civil rights movement and the long-established march tactic was as obvious in Pittsburgh as in Quebec. Groups such as the AWC assumed they would seek permits, while anti-authoritarians assumed they would not do so. Yet police actions affected everyone, shaking up the routine assumptions of many activists, leading to ongoing actions and possibly expanding the local conscience community. Most importantly, the G-20 protests created connections and strengthened collective identities that would carry over into subsequent campaigns, such as the Occupy Pittsburgh offshoot of Occupy Wall Street.

The ongoing protests and expanded movement constituencies that define a social movement society rely on the structures of local social movement communities – and on the multiple communities that allow for scale shift to the national and international levels. These movement community structures support collective campaigns, which in turn affect movement communities. (Generally, we would expect movement campaigns to strengthen networks and organizations in movement communities, but a conflictual campaign might also weaken community bonds.) We can expect variations in movement societies across time and place, depending on the structures of movement communities and on the history of campaigns in local areas. Montreal and Pittsburgh provide two examples of fairly well developed movement communities that also differ in many ways, and we can see changes in both local communities as a result of campaigns such as the WMW and G-20 protests. Other locales may lack the characteristics of a movement society because of the weakness of their movement communities and a lack of collective campaigns.

9

No to Protests, Yes to Festivals

How the Creative Class Organizes
in the Social Movement Society

JUDITH TAYLOR

On a hazy, cool summer morning in 2009, my family got together with old friends and their three young daughters in their backyard for weekend brunch. They live in a neighbourhood called the Junction, in Toronto's west end, on a street with modest row houses and young families. As our children scrambled after one another, ducking bees and jumping off our friends' tidy tool shed, they told us the news. An infrequently used train track just several feet from their house was going to be mobilized for a diesel commuter train line, and some 400 trains would be expected to rumble past their house each day, with serious implications – in terms of noise, toxicity, and vibration – for their neighbourhood and several others along the train corridor. The train was planned for the Pan American Games in Toronto in 2015.

Immediately I suggested, "You should call the newspapers and have them do a story on your family and the impact of breathing in diesel fuel and the noise and vibration!" – but I slowed as I saw the looks on their faces. My partner said, "Forgive Judy, she's American, they all prostitute their lives for politics." When I followed by saying that they could join a fledgling organization working to electrify the line rather than use diesel, called the Clean Train Coalition (CTC), they nodded. Some of their friends and neighbours were involved, but they hadn't yet plunged in. They'd never joined a political organization, attended a political rally, or written an angry letter to a city councillor.

This chapter is about the schism between my academic expectation of activism and my friends' lived hesitancy. Put differently, this chapter looks at bridging research on civic and political engagement with the social movement society (SMS) thesis of constant and institutionalized protest. The former illustrates political reticence, while the latter postulates the ubiquity of political engagement. How do we make sense of these seemingly disparate truths? The case has been made that scholars have portrayed activism to be far more reflexive and commonplace than it actually is (McAdam and Boudet 2012). Others have demonstrated that while activism might be more pervasive, general civic participation has been steadily declining (Putnam 2000; the Introduction to this volume). And research on appetite for political deliberation and participation is similarly discouraging, illustrating that while people appear to want to express their desires and concerns in public, their tools of expression, analysis, and imagination fail them (Eliasoph 1998). How can everyday political appetite be so minimal but social movements be constantly mobilized? Of course, culture is not internally consistent (R.H. Williams 2004, 101), but this inconsistency is worthy of more attention than it has received.

The SMS thesis offered by Meyer and Tarrow (1998) gets a lot of things right. Protest is a regular feature of contemporary life; social movements are institutionalized and social movement actors are often professional movement employees; movements share tactics, adapting as they notice the success of some approaches and the failure of others; protesters and the state are reliably cooperative with one another in the theatre of social change making; and the shape collective action will take is reliable and demographically diffuse. That said, this kind of analysis renders people (on whom mobilization is dependent) a tad mechanical. One can imagine a sea of wind-up robots habitually marching, participating in sit-ins in university administrative offices, dutifully drawing protest signs, and collecting their cheques at the end of every month.

It used to be a sociological given that participating in protest was preceded by a set of social psychological processes, in which individuals would develop an understanding of society and power that was personally challenging, painful, and empowering. Developing political consciousness has been understood to be a pretty big deal by scholars of social movements. Political commitment was thought to be the product of intense debate, review of one's childhood and assumptions about justice, and confrontation of personal prejudices (Mansbridge and Morris 2001; B. Thompson 2001; Hercus

2005). In short, becoming an activist was thought to be a good deal of work. The development of conviction about and commitment to things not as they are is the ballast that enables people to confront the state, demand attention from fellow citizens, and abandon once-prioritized activities in favour of organizing.

Once in movements, another phase of difficult learning and emotion ensues, as people come to understand what active others think of them, and the extent to which they may be found useful or possessing leadership qualities (Morris and Staggenborg 2007). Certain tasks are humiliating, such as being turned away from politicians' doors, picketing in the rain as motorists honk with disrespect, or flubbing a media opportunity. Dealing with personality conflicts, differences in strategic approaches, concerns about inclusion and exclusion, and being viewed by one's neighbours as an agitator can also be quite draining.

But perhaps this is no longer the case. Does the institutionalization of protest mean there is less stigma attached to being an activist, that activism is something to which people must no longer acclimatize through complex emotional and social reckoning? Is political engagement so normalized that the psychological hoops activists used to have to jump through to develop and express dissent no longer exist? Is protest just one of many worthwhile options in a day – grocery shopping, doing laundry, attending a rally, going for a swim? Is being part of a movement society the ultimate cognitive shortcut through all that we used to understand as emotional work?

Drawing on an ethnographic case of community engagement – specifically, interviews and two years of participant observation notes with the Clean Train Coalition, I seek to connect these seemingly disparate ways in which we consider mobilization and political engagement, generating hypotheses about the social psychology of political action and the effect of social movements on political engagement.[1] It would be reasonable to conclude that the structural, organizational, and cultural predispositions to activism would filter down to the community level, making activism easier to engage in than it once was. On the other hand, it may be the case that civic activism is *not* just one among many professional options, like being a teacher or lawyer, and that people know as much. They know it involves, sooner or later, uncomfortable engagements with difficult questions about the distribution of power and privilege in society. Such engagements can disrupt the perceptions of themselves that they have taken for granted, and how they imagine others perceive them.

CTC participants are people who are generally sympathetic to progressive social movements – largely but not exclusively white, well educated, lower middle class, and interested in urban vitality – but the majority were not politically active prior to the diesel train announcement.[2] These are Richard Florida's "creative class" (2004) – historians, musicians, Web builders, graphic artists, non-profit directors, teachers, clothing designers. They are not "everyman" (Eliasoph 1998), nor are they upper middle-class executives and middle managers (Lamont 1992). The creative class, lying somewhere between these more economically specified categories, has been credited with a host of social and performative goods that are linked with spectacular economic health and revitalization. Displacing traditional movement understandings of how society is improved, Florida's central thesis is that this population, imbued with creative talent, technological sophistication, and tolerance for diversity, will through its production and consumption, make life better in the cities where they reside.

The "creative class" designation has been cogently critiqued for its amorphousness (Kraetke 2010; L. Reese, Faist, and Sands 2010) and for displacing traditional understandings of injustice and class inequality (Ponzini and Rossi 2010). This is not the first theory to displace the significance of social class, even as a central mechanism for why and how people organize (Beuchler 2000), but this case illustrates that displacing or misplacing class can be very consequential for the character of mobilization. Inhabiting the creative class designation, either volitionally or through attribution, produces considerable anxiety (R. Gill and Pratt 2008). Gill and Pratt argue the anxieties of the creative class derive from having to earn middle-class salaries yet work as independent contractors in the labour force, with little stability and assurance and the constant requirement to acquire new skills.

It can also be said that the anxiety of members of the creative class results from living with conditions of *both* embourgeoisement and proletarianization, accruing cultural capital for their skills, knowledge, and interests while earning modest and precarious incomes that threaten their middle-class maintenance or aspirations, with little sign of organizing against this trend (but see Abrahamian 2012). Creative class members have urban tastes and sensibilities (Woldoff 2011) but persistently lower income and employment status than fellow university graduates in other sectors (Abreu et al. 2012). To locate this conundrum more specifically in the community I studied, members may be quoted in the newspaper but they live by the train tracks. This mix produces what R. Gill and Pratt (2008, 14) call an "attitudinal mindset that is a blend of bohemianism and entrepreneurialism." While this mixed sensibility and its attendant anxiety might be useful for organizing a neighbourhood farmers' market, how is it for opposing a government decision? If we are a social movement society, how do creative entrepreneurial people capitalize on the supposed social acceptability of resistance to create better conditions for themselves and society more generally?

Analyses of interview transcripts and meeting notes indicate two divergent types of participants: labour left and creative class. Labour left participants tended to be slightly older, had participated in social justice movements and initiatives prior to this one, and had some prior experience with trade unionism. Creative class participants tended to be first-time homeowners, in their thirties and early forties, and supportive of, but inexperienced with, social justice movements, but still civically engaged in community projects such as farmers' markets, parks, and creating or preserving city bicycle lanes. These groups did work effectively together, despite divergent understandings of the problem and themselves, different tactical orientations, and different affective or emotional registers. They were also very aware of their differences and saw these differences as significant. As one labour left participant said, "It's about how you view politics, power, and the world." Because the CTC campaign was initiated and influenced most centrally by creative class people, I focus more on their orientation here, but use the labour left orientation as a clarifying contrast.

This campaign was influenced by participants' cultural adherences (Polletta 2012) and life course experiences (J. Taylor 2007), not simply resource or strategic constraints or repertoires. As a city, Toronto has had one of the strongest cultures of labour organizing, with unions, social movements, and liberal and left political parties working closely on campaigns. In the early 2000s, however, people from NGOs and the non-profit sector began to organize themselves in the city not as social activists but as *social entrepreneurs*. Social entrepreneurs have a social *mission* but not social movement, funded through social financing. This approach focuses not on oppositional consciousness but on partnering with governments and corporations and enabling cooperation among NGOs by housing them in large, loosely organized cooperative working spaces, to enable them to become "a catalyst for social change." The Centre for Social Innovation (CSI), founded in 2004 and now with three compounds in Toronto's downtown core, has come to represent the creative class approach to change making.

The CEO of the centre, Tonya Surman, has a biographical note on the centre website (http://socialinnovation.ca) that projects social activism as fun and well meaning (but non-confrontational), and a morally traditional preoccupation that is good for children and engaged in by women who profess to value mothering more than professional engagement. Protest is "raising a ruckus" rather than disrupting commercial infringement on human dignity, and even her political commitment is self-caricatured as hyperbolic. The causes or outcomes of injustice are not named; rather, activism is rendered an amorphous good time for spirited people, almost like an advertisement for a summer camp – "creativity, connectedness, and fun." The creative class approach to activism is collective but the behaviour lacks any contention – it's a big street party or a community garden. Enemies, targets, analyses of power, and contention are entirely absent. In the metaphor of biology, adrenaline is the old movement juice, endorphins the new.

Such an approach envisages transforming the old-school strident social activists into effectual, cooperative social entrepreneurs, capable, unlike their predecessors, of working in partnership with power holders. It is a politic oriented to collaboration, optimism, and compromise, and explicitly averse to naming causes, problems, and inequities but promising to innovatively and effectively modify them. The centre both reflects and transmits with considerable influence an approach to social change making that resonates with the disposition of the creative class, as I will show in the next section. These are broad strokes, with particular attention to the thoughts, decisions, and actions of people who fit into the creative class designation, because they are the largest group in the CTC and the most consequential for it strategically and tactically.

Strategic Orientation

Strategy is the central overarching approach a movement takes, and strategic orientations are the worldviews and commitments that animate both; that is, they share the tactics that people use to make change. Consistent with Richard Florida's portrayal (2004) of the creative class, participants in the CTC are by any measure, talented, positive, productive, and generous people who rely on creative work for their livelihood and choose to live in dynamic urban neighbourhoods. Through interviews and observation of tactics, I gleaned that their central orientation to social change is *belief in the power of truth and information*. For them, carefully researched facts, if communicated clearly and effectively to decision makers, enable the best decisions and the most just outcomes. Participants found shortsighted, and what many termed "unintelligent" decisions made seemingly without the benefit of research and analysis, to be the most troubling, saying, for example: "If the government can't find the extra amount of money to electrify this, don't do the project. Don't build it wrong." Building something wrong – spending money for a short-term event and with long-term environmental hazard, having more environmentally sound technologies and not making use of them – was portrayed as nonsensical and unethical.

Creative-class change makers are also not afraid of delving deeply into "high investment" subject matter, such as government adjudication processes, medical research, science, and transportation. They are deeply comparative in their analyses, reaching globally for best and worst practices. The outcome of research and analysis, they believe, should be positive solutions that benefit the greatest number of people. Solutions should be based on knowledge and compromise of interested parties. They are not oppositional, they are collaborative, and if things do not work as they hoped, they tend to find fault in their own approach and try to learn from mistakes. One respondent who frequently published op-ed pieces put it this way:

> For me, I just think knowledge is power. The research is going to save you. If you put something out for public consumption and you are incorrect, they got you, they can say you don't know what you are talking about. Has a railway ever converted from steam to electric? Um, how about the Pennsylvania Railroad! So for me it's, "Don't screw around with us, we can get or have the information."

Interviewees also were eager to connect across a broad number of political, civic, and urban issues. One participant talked to me about research he conducted on the preponderance of asthma in populations in the vicinity of train tracks. Others had extremely technical knowledge of the effect of particulates on lungs. Still others had extensive interest in trains, focusing on the development and evolution of electric trains in Europe, and suggesting how to make trains that traverse through neighbourhoods useful to those inhabitants along the rails, or discussing the merits of light rail versus underground subways.

Participants also bridled at platitudes they found empty. One frequently mentioned in interviews was the idea put forward by cabinet ministers that Toronto had to have an air-rail link to look like a "world class city" for the Pan Am Games. They objected to the use of similar concepts such as "global contender" and "globally competitive" because they felt these were placeholders used to make policy decisions that were not transparent and based on research, dumbing down public education and engagement, and substituting for evidence and a more complex presentation of possibilities.

Participants in the CTC believe that the city and public resources are for everyone, and do not like calling attention to their individual needs. They also do not locate themselves as classed actors, privileged or marginalized. They eschew "Not in My Backyard" (NIMBY) politics as politically unwise and genuinely unrepresentative of their ethos and impulses, unlike their US counterparts (Eliasoph 1998). They believe that, as city dwellers, they should absorb a fair amount of chaos in exchange for the convenience and amenities urban life affords. When one participant, known to be a thoughtful conciliator, was asked whether he thought CTC participants would have mobilized against a parole office in the neighbourhood, he said:

> No. Because we would say that is OK. We are all about social cohesion. We
> have an ethic about including those who have less. Health effects we could
> get behind, because everyone stood to lose, it was something everyone
> shared, and it was the true story.

They appreciate class-diverse neighbourhoods, making sure they patronize both a new hipster coffee place, the sign of gentrification, and the family-owned hardware store on their corner that has been there for several decades. One interviewee spoke of gentrification in her neighbourhood, pointing out that not all changes have occurred because more financially secure people with different consumer habits have arrived. "Oh, the porn store is gone, but that's the Internet's fault." Florida's use of the word "tolerance" is key here – they enjoy multiculturalism and class diversity, but they are more likely to sensitively coexist with neighbours different from themselves than befriend them.

Participants did not offer personal information or engage in "identity deployments," such as mother, homeowner, or taxpayer, in interviews or the campaign. Almost all preferred talking about public health, neighbourhoods, or the construction of urban space. They often responded derisively to interview questions that asked them to think in more individual, less public-minded ways. I interviewed a soft-spoken father of two who had never been part of a political campaign before working on development of the initial CTC website (www.cleantrain.ca). Towards the end of our interview, I suggested that it was interesting no one spoke to me about concerns for the value of their house or mobilized their identities as homeowners. His immediate answer surprised me. "That's disgusting! To say something like that. Pretty repulsive. This is so much bigger than that."

Personal gain and loss did not figure prominently in participants' public political rhetoric. One mother of two small boys framed it differently for me, but only at the end of our interview, as I was leaving the house. "Look, it's painful. I want my brother and his wife to move in to our neighbourhood. I love our neighbourhood and I want them to be close to us. And now I feel they would not want to move here, because of the train. That hurts." Social ties and networks, and community pride, came up in interviews, not personal monetary gain and loss. This aversion to expressing material concern, even of a modest kind, was notable.

While supportive of progressive politics, they did not themselves feel oppositional towards government and corporations. One early CTC participant and organizer said:

> There is a strong desire to try to shed the old Left analysis of power – us and them, and labour and owners, and really just try to be solution oriented. Like, how do we co-create solutions to make our communities better?

Many participants expressed empathy for those in government, saying that big decisions like transportation involve tremendously challenging considerations, particularly in an era of fiscal cutbacks. In fact, many discussed the problems in ways that sounded more as though they saw themselves as stewards of their community than individual citizens with expectations. For example, one participant explained his involvement in opposing the diesel train lines this way:

> I was concerned about safety because those tracks, people just casually walk across them. People with school kids are going to get their lunches at Weston Road and so I called, and they said they would put in pedestrian bridges. But then I started talking with more neighbours and the business owners and we realized this was a really bad idea because it would separate the residential community from the business community and you will have a boarded up – like a U.S. city – in the middle of Toronto.

A number of participants had high expectations of themselves in terms of the kind of citizenship they would exercise – raising questions carefully, conducting research, rationally expressing concerns, meeting with and listening to government representatives, voting. This labour and composure was not discussed as necessary in lieu of responsible government, but complementary to it. Prior to their CTC involvement, most participants (though fewer after it) believed that their local and provincial representatives aimed to act in the best interests of citizens, and were largely accountable to them. A committed father in his thirties explained:

> We have a lot of credibility. We could actually impact this decision-making and have a positive outcome where the planet gets changed, instead of ... positioning ourselves against the government.

The overarching strategy of the CTC was to gain *credibility* in the eyes of government, newspapers, and informed fellow citizens. Being found credible, in their minds, advances the likelihood of winning the campaign. In essence, they perform a diligence of research, thinking, consultation, and communication that they expect to see from government, aiming to win by using their skills and attending to the problem as measured non-partisans. Rather than targeting the government from below, they saw their efforts as shared management of a problem. This strategic orientation suggests that the SMS thesis of widespread familiarity and comfort with contention may be grossly overstated. Conciliation, not contention, best describes the campaign.

Tactical Mapping

Tactics come from a larger routinized set of possibilities, but movement actors still meaningfully select, avoid, and create them in adherence to the image they would like to project, and the approach they believe will be most successful. In the case of the CTC, the goal was to mobilize – without the trappings of a social movement. Most participants favoured the tone of a professional citizens' association rather than a protest group. This makes sense because the great majority of CTC participants in 2009 had almost no prior experience with activism, a fact most emphatically offered in interviews. Here is one characteristic admission: "I was never an activist. I never previously held a placard. I have never protested anything. I have never not eaten for anything. I have never not slept for anything. I have never locked myself to anything, and yeah, I have never marched in anything." Accompanying such admissions was often an implicit assessment that such actions stood outside definitions of productive citizenship, and that civil disobedience and direct action were radical and unseemly. Initial participants who had activist orientations were discouraged from participating or were asked to conform to the subtler approach.

Information gathering and messaging were key tactics used by the group to gain legitimacy and credibility in their effort to oppose the diesel trains. The CTC began with a query on a neighbourhood listserv, meetings around a kitchen table, and the development of a name and logo. Many described the process as beginning with significant amounts of information gathering, sense making, and then more information gathering. Participants wanted to make sure they knew everything that the province was planning to properly think through the implications. Said an early joiner: "We invited someone from Metrolinx.[3] We took lots of notes. We shared the notes amongst ourselves. We circulated the notes to our email list in the neighbourhood." Many described concentric circles of amassing, communicating, and refining knowledge about the trains. Participants were initially consumed with grasping the situation and figuring out how to communicate the findings in the most clear and accurate ways possible. Another participant summarized: "This was fought at a very detailed level." Participants debated names – *Green Train* or *Clean Train* – but came to agreement fairly quickly, and a graphic designer in the group made a logo that everyone quickly adopted. They also used initial meetings to reach consensus on the tone of the campaign. One participant summarized this decision as follows:

> There was an early decision that we were going to be very positive with the messaging, that it wasn't going to be "No, no, no, no." It was going to be, "Yes, let's make things greener, let's make them cleaner, let's make them electric," and that we were really not going to be particularly antagonistic but our motto was really going to be we want to work with the government of Ontario to make this the best possible project and legacy, and really ensure the money is well spent.

Participants felt that the messaging had to be constructive and positive, expanding the nature and work of community associations not only to flag problems but also to collaborate in finding solutions. Many were very energized and attracted by the prospect of using their skills to benefit their community and be part of a "legacy" (a word many used), and did not simply want to oppose a bad plan. They were keen to use personal skills for the cause and to project competency.

In addition to looking professional, being affectively conciliatory, and having ample information, CTC members also invested in technology. Participants met for a broad strategic planning meeting, working on "branding" the campaign, building a website and mailing list, and using a Web-based project management tool, "Basecamp," to set up different working groups, such as media, op-ed and letter campaigns, research, outreach and membership, and other key tasks. They were struck by their initial success in generating a letter-writing campaign, publishing editorials, and gaining recognition.

The problem with technological investment was that some members were tasked with updating websites, and, lacking any real dedicated staff, there was no way to respond to the hundreds of e-mails that poured in. Offers of volunteer help went unanswered, and Web architects received feedback from fellow organizers and the general public that was often hard to stomach, ranging from criticisms of colour and style to snide comments such as "you chose to live by the tracks, it's your problem." In addition, most campaign communication was conducted online rather than in person, to which some participants attributed unnecessarily caustic exchanges between organizers. Finally, events advertised on the Web without face-to-face contacts on the ground did not bring in new participants, illustrating that technology facilitates but cannot easily replace traditional face-to-face community organizing (Stoecker 2002).

Networking and making alliances were also a central tactic. Participants obtained meetings with the public transportation office responsible for carrying out the expansion, Metrolinx, and attended any public meetings Metrolinx hosted. They reached out to environmental NGOs, real estate agencies and condominium developers, journalists, train buffs, and school boards. They raised monies to commission experts to write evaluative reports, and asked others to speak at community meetings. To reach a broader base of potential allies, they positioned themselves as constituents rather than particular party adherents. A long-time CTCer offered, "The community doesn't give a damn if you're Liberal, NDP, Green, or Conservative. They're concerned about the trains." They also never wanted to paint a party as the enemy, reasoning that doing so would make it difficult for a party to retract initial positions and develop new ones. Many took pride in the fact that the campaign would talk across parties; a minority found the approach politically naïve but did not initially break ranks to oppose it.

CTC also organized musical events and park gatherings as a key tactic, choosing to bring people together with banners and T-shirts rather than protest signs. The most galvanizing event, called "the Human Train," involved bringing the variously affected communities along the tracks together by walking through one another's neighbourhoods, culminating in a rally at a large park with speakers and musical acts. The event, which drew over a thousand participants and received considerable positive media coverage, was also carefully managed for tone. An organizer sympathetic to this gentle approach admitted: "We couldn't call it a demonstration, we couldn't call it a protest, it was a parade. It was a walk, it was maybe a march." Such events were tactical culminations, in which organizers publicized facts about diesel pollution while promoting positive alternatives (electric trains). They exhibited the effects of their hard work in making allies by having speakers such as Toronto's chief medical officer and a trustee from the Toronto school board. They made use of their connections to the arts and their emphasis on positive tone by having high-profile musicians perform. They used the website and listserv to publicize these events and reach wider audiences.

Similar events included the "Clean Air for Little Lungs Stroller Parade" at Queen's Park (the seat of the provincial government), which included a health advisory team staffed by grassroots members of the CTC, and featured a song written for the event called "Go Electric," which became a galvanizing tool at subsequent rallies for activists opposing the diesel train. Such songs exemplify the kind of creative, original, positive, grassroots, and highly professional and polished initiatives that people who comprise the creative class can and did produce. Interestingly, however, participants discussed music not as a social movement tool they had seen used effectively elsewhere but as a means of keeping the messaging upbeat and attractive, and as reflective of the skills found within creative class neighbourhoods. Holding a parade rather than a protest also indicates deep ambivalence towards confrontation. Participants enacted "gentle activism" (Coombs 2012) or "contention in disguise,"[4] suggesting that activism is not as accessible as the SMS thesis suggests.

Organizers developed crucial networks of alliance across the city with politicians, ousting some and electing others more sympathetic to their cause. They worked effectively with toxicologists, professors, engineers, and other professionals to communicate about the dangers of diesel fuel emission; they also maintained a core group of active volunteers and organizers who, through debates and disagreements, disappointments and burnout, kept momentum. Nonetheless, the following year Metrolinx voted in camera to purchase eighteen two-car diesel trains from Sumitomo Corporation, arguing that they could not electrify by the 2015 Pan Am Games (Grant and Buchanan 2010). It was a major blow to CTC architects and participants, causing them to reflect on what they had learned and what they might have done differently. Interestingly, almost no one referenced movements they knew about and wanted to emulate, nor did they conclude that it might have been wise to pay more attention to similar kinds of community mobilizations. This kind of disconnect raises questions about the extent to which ours is, in fact, a movement society. Meyer and Tarrow (1998) assert that movements are learning from one another and becoming more effective as a consequence, but this action was relatively disconnected from previous and contemporaneous campaigns.

Post-Campaign Reflection

CTC participants' reflections on what they had learned were strikingly coherent. They professed to have a better understanding of how government, class and privilege, and power, operate. Most remained proud of the campaign, did not regret their involvement, and opted to keep working to oppose the diesel trains. Those members of the CTC who had prior activist experience and did not subscribe to its overall approach felt vindicated. Their most central claims were that there is little correlation between being right and winning, that political power does not inhere in average middle-class people, and that building a diverse base of opposition is as important tactically as meeting individually with powerful people.

One of the central realizations CTC participants cited was the idea that government is persuaded by power, and not, as they had assumed, by knowledge. A particularly committed CTCer confessed: "We tried logic, and morality, and all these other kinds of arguments, and none of them work. I guess we just didn't know how to go about making politicians feel that they better do the right thing." While some blamed their disappointment on the Liberal party and the premier who had authorized the trains, others determined that all politicians were dishonest and motivated principally by the desire to maintain power. Many expressed the genuine pain they experienced being ignored, surveilled, hoodwinked, lied to, and placated with promises to look into greener solutions that did not materialize. One participant admitted his belief that government staff were lurking on the CTC listserv:

> I cannot tell you how many times, three days before our press release, they would produce literature, and leaflet with the message that pollution is not an issue, telling people frankly what they wanted to hear. I did see that they had money, political power, staff, and that this issue was far bigger than us.

Like others, this participant had previously believed that citizens had more democratic possibilities for reaching out meaningfully to politicians and working with them, and had difficulty coping with the incredulity he felt in the aftermath of the campaign. This disappointment was often paired with realizations, equally painful, about class status, cultural capital, and social influence. Countless interviews included the sentiment "It wouldn't be happening if we were Rosedale," one of Canada's oldest and wealthiest neighbourhoods. Many participants concluded that they had overestimated their own social capital and underestimated the salience of old-fashioned capital: money. They identified how the absence of wealth hurt them in three ways. First, the provincial government made plans to run toxic commuter and air link trains through their neighbourhoods because they were considered unimportant. Second, their efforts to mobilize were curtailed by lack of financial resources to hire organizers and public relations firms and celebrities who could publicize their cause. Third, because they were not considered well-to-do citizens, government agencies and representatives ignored their campaigns. One participant summed up what he felt to be his naïveté this way:

> Another problem for us was resources. We had no big donors! We were creative industry types, not deep pockets. We were all new at this, all idealism. We wanted to be smart, have conversations.

Acknowledging the way in which people have come to adopt the creative class designation, this participant illustrates the difference between, on the one hand, being in an occupational niche that is credited with making cities vibrant, and, on the other hand, having political power. One of the few participants with prior activist experience, a long-time labour organizer, summed up the problem slightly differently: "They are professional class people who moved into a working class neighbourhood and got treated like working class people, and did not like it." While he had pushed CTC members to pay more attention to building a base and mobilizing neighbourhoods much more comprehensively, he acknowledged that meeting with cabinet ministers feels more important than pounding the pavement.

Community organizing is politically powerful but also painful, as individuals narrated more personally the risks and stakes of the trains instead of promoting positive solutions and citing academic research and policy-speak. One mother of two small children said as much: "Canvassing door to door was stressful. Talking to people was stressful. I like organizing, I know how to make an event successful, but canvassing was too much. It was the first time I was personally connected." In many ways, canvassing was unattractive because it did not seem time-efficient (in contrast to an e-blast or a website), was considered a tool for the disenfranchised, and was emotionally arduous. In addition, as this last quote reflects, it was difficult to talk about one's own neighbourhood and health while staying positive and upbeat.

Members also began to muse about how their strategic adherence to gaining credibility, with all the associations of white, upper-middle-class professionalism, also prevented them from attracting a more racially and class-diverse base, as well as a politically diverse one with people more keen to practise direct action. Another CTCer committed to only positive messaging mused: "It's 20/20 hindsight, but it wouldn't have hurt to just encourage [more confrontational constituents] on the side and say, hey, that's great, go ahead, let us know if you want anything." Because the CTC wanted political action against the trains to be streamlined and affectively positive, its members discouraged new constellations of people with different understandings of effective mobilization from acting independently. Running such a tight campaign may have alienated and prevented more diverse political mobilization that could have added political pressure and made the CTC appear more attractive as a negotiating partner by comparison. A more seasoned activist confessed to watching from the sidelines because CTC participants were not interested in experienced activists if they didn't have the right pedigree or affect. She said it was painful to watch them, but her conclusion was hopeful: "A whole new layer of people learned that governments can do what they like and that we need to learn together about how we fight this and go forward." To her, middle-class people had entitlement but didn't necessarily know how to organize an opposition.

Conclusion

In this chapter, I have analyzed the strategic orientation, tactical repertoire, and post-campaign reflections of one creative class community that mobilized for change. Reifying this population and its political approaches is not useful, given its diversity – creative class members have different economic resources and can work at cross-purposes (Catungal, Leslie, and Hii 2009). That said, people self-identify as creative class members, and social policymakers and urban planners have credited this group with being agentic and consequential, producing "wealth creation, urban regeneration, and social cohesion," among other things (R. Gill and Pratt 2008). It is worth attending to how they mobilize when things don't go their way.

This population, which plainly has a fair amount of resources and capacity, found activism on its own behalf very challenging even though it was extremely committed, hardworking, and impactful. At the outset of this chapter, I discuss the particular anxiety of class dislocation and ideation that can be read in its organizing tactics and understandings of what should and did happen. Lacking either working class consciousness or resources (such as unions), or the cultural heft of the managerial and professional classes, creative class folks occupy a limbo that makes political action complicated. Yes, they mobilized, but with considerable trepidation and without an apparent accrual of political consciousness born of interest or observation. From this we might conclude that we cannot count rallies and claim to know we understand much about mobilization.

And so, whether protest is now convention, as the SMS thesis asserts, is perhaps less interesting than what people are organizing for, how they are doing it, and how they make sense of what they've done. It could be that people are mobilizing more, but that they are doing so with wildly divergent levels of conviction, purpose, or efficacy. In essence, the SMS thesis tells us little about why political engagement and consciousness are lagging, and can obscure this fact.

In their SMS thesis, Meyer and Tarrow (1998, 14) call everyday people rising up and then returning to their normal lives to make sense of what they've done "romantic" – but it still very much exists. When movement scholars accept a set of assumptions about the ubiquity of mobilization, a crucial amount of nuance is lost, to the detriment of our understanding of political consciousness, political subjectivities, and change making. As this case suggests, in an era when activism is presented as fashionable, there are well-educated, politically progressive, middle-class people who will not use the words *protest* and *march,* who believe that citizens are unwise to critique their governments without offering positive conciliatory solutions, and who think that discussing power and naming capitalism make one a militant. The civic fictions that governments compassionately incorporate citizens' concerns when they are rationally conveyed, or that citizens can collaborate with government to build society, are still deeply held beliefs that are disrupted by civic injustice. The expected social contract is still being expected, and broken, and it still elicits shock, anger, and a host of difficult emotions in people. The basic lesson of progressive social movements – that government and corporations will, for economic expediency, sell out people and what matters deeply to them – continues to be learned anew by people, arduously and unwittingly, even if marches are regularly booked with the city and everyone knows how to rally.

Notes

This chapter is dedicated to the CTC participants whose civic engagement was and is extraordinarily generous to fellow citizens, and whose legacy is yet to be determined.

1 A research associate, Jennifer Cyper, participated in the CTC as an activist, and collected field notes for this project from 2009 to 2011. I also draw on twenty interviews we conducted with CTC activists. All names of participants have been omitted.

2 I resemble CTC participants politically and demographically, sharing their worldviews, tactical inclinations, and disappointments.

3 Metrolinx is a provincial agency created to improve transportation in the Greater Toronto and Hamilton area.

4 Thanks to Kathleen Rodgers for this phrase.

10
Justification and Critique in the Social Movement Society

JIM CONLEY

In 1762, from his residence near Geneva, Voltaire undertook to clear the name of Jean Calas, a Huguenot who was accused of murdering his son for apostasy. Condemned by a tribunal in Toulouse, Calas was broken on the wheel and executed. Challenging the verdict, Voltaire opened the secret *Ancien Régime* judicial proceedings to public scrutiny and public judgment. In 1765, the conviction was overturned and the remaining members of the Calas family were rehabilitated (Gay 1965; Claverie 1994).

Over a century later, in his famous open letter of 1898, *J'accuse*, Émile Zola denounced the French military's injustice and anti-Semitism in condemning Alfred Dreyfus to life imprisonment for allegedly supplying military secrets to Germany. Zola's intervention, which led to his conviction for libel and flight to England, was a prominent part of the mobilization of republican France against monarchist and Catholic reaction that eventually secured the exoneration of Dreyfus (Cobban 1965; Fournier 2007).

Nearly a century after Dreyfus, Robert Latimer, a Saskatchewan farmer, was convicted for the second-degree murder of his severely mentally and physically disabled daughter, Tracy, who according to her family was in constant pain. He was sentenced to a year in jail on the recommendation of the trial jury, but the mandatory sentence of life imprisonment was imposed on appeal. Supporters mobilized to shorten the sentence, starting a petition, mounting a yellow-ribbon campaign, and holding rallies and vigils. The campaign failed, and Latimer served time until he became eligible for parole (CBC News 2010).

In 2007, a newly arrived Polish immigrant who expected to meet his mother at Vancouver International Airport was left to wander the arrivals area for ten hours. Unable to speak English and given no help by airport personnel, an increasingly distraught Robert Dziekanski died after being repeatedly tasered by four RCMP officers. The police claimed that the victim was dangerous and threatening, but the court-ordered release and subsequent broadcast of a bystander's video discredited their account, producing widespread moral outrage and anger. A provincial commission of inquiry concluded that the police actions were unjustified, and the officers who testified at the inquiry were charged with perjury (Milbrandt 2012).

These four episodes provide a historical and social context to the routinization, diffusion to new actors and issues, and institutionalization of protest that Meyer and Tarrow (1998) characterized as the social movement society (SMS), and they draw attention to the key place of claims of injustice in contentious social movement societies.

In this chapter, I draw on developments in political and cultural sociology in France (Boltanski and Thévenot 2006) and North America (Lamont and Thévenot 2000a) to propose an alternative to frame analyses of injustice claims and to argue that scandals and affairs developed as standardized social forms along with the social movement in what can be called critical or contentious societies. I also argue that new digital media, in conjunction with the mainstream mass media, provide increased opportunities for publicizing injustices that can lead to scandals, affairs, and social movements. In this context, and with these tools, social movement scholars can better grasp the distinctiveness of the social movement society.

In each of the four episodes outlined above, the legitimacy of state actions against individual persons was challenged, claims of injustice were made, and moral outrage was aroused. Claims of injustice are a familiar feature of many, although not all, social movements (Benford and Snow 2000), and these four examples raise the question of how such claims involving singular individuals or events do or do not become broader public issues. Within the framing approach that dominates studies of social movements, injustice claims are often understood using the concept of injustice frames (Gamson, Fireman, and Rytina 1982; Gamson 1992, 1995). Frame analysis, however, focuses on the strategic deployment of categories rather than on the dialogue of critique and justification of situated actions. In the first part of this chapter, I show how the pragmatic sociology of critique developed by Luc

Boltanski and Laurent Thévenot (2006) provides insights into the complex and often messy process by which people evaluate events in ways that may lead to the emergence of scandals, affairs, and social movements..

Scandals, Affairs, and Social Movements as Social Forms

The four episodes outlined above are instances of scandals and affairs that, like the social movements they exist beside and resemble, are standardized social forms that have existed for over two centuries. A scandal involves widespread public indignation against a real or apparent transgression; an affair results when a defence of the alleged transgressor challenges either the procedures leading to the accusation or the transgressive character of the offence. In the Calas, Dreyfus, and Dziekanski cases, the denouncers attempted to lift the veil of state secrecy and challenge the official version of events; in the Latimer case, supporters attempted to redefine its criminal nature. The affair as a social form originated in the last half of the eighteenth century (Boltanski and Claverie 2007; Kalifa 2007), around the same time as the social movement repertoire (Tilly 2006b; Tilly and Wood 2012). Both affairs and social movements became associated with political democratization in relatively stable parliamentary or presidential forms. In contrast to the prior more direct and immediate repertoire of contention, both forms targeted authorities indirectly, by publicizing a cause and appealing to both authorities and public opinion (Tilly 2008a). They did so in different ways: affairs with a grammar of impartiality, generality, and indignation (Boltanski 1999); social movements with performances displaying worthiness, unity, numbers, and commitment (Tilly and Wood 2012). Affairs have sometimes provided occasions for mobilizations and campaigns using the social movement repertoire (as in both the Dreyfus and Latimer affairs), but not always. Also like social movements, affairs have often depended on entrepreneurs like Voltaire or Zola, who use their renown to draw attention to the injustice.[1]

Like sexual, political, financial, and artistic scandals (Adut 2008) and conventional protest in the SMS, there is a risk that a proliferation of affairs will become "politics as usual," lacking the capacity to polarize and disrupt, and reducing their political effectiveness. The Latimer case illustrates this, and exemplifies the frequency, small size, and short duration of many mobilizations in the SMS (McAdam et al. 2005). The SMS is in this respect part of a broader critical or contentious society in which public claims of injustice and wrong proliferate (Tilly and Tarrow 2006). The Dziekanski case, in which a bystander's video created the affair, raises the issue (addressed by Meyer and Pullum in Chapter 1) of the emerging role of digital media for contemporary social movement societies. To illustrate the digitally mediated formulation of injustice claims that may lead to scandals, affairs, and social movements, this chapter examines an additional example in detail. A street dispute in Toronto's Kensington Market shows the role of a repertoire of evaluation in the development of injustice claims from a singular event, and sheds light on the significance of both digital and conventional mass media for making and diffusing contentious claims that may or, as in this case, may not generate sustained collective action.

From Framing Injustice to Justification and Critique

As in movements themselves, concepts of justice and injustice have long been prominent in scholarship exploring what Barrington Moore (1978) aptly called the social bases of obedience and revolt. Moore sought to develop an anthropology of potentially universal conceptions of justice and injustice. In contrast, Charles Tilly left room for more historical variability when he argued that a population's repertoire of contention is in part shaped by its prevailing "standards of rights and justice" (Tilly 1978, 156). But it was William Gamson's injustice frame concept that came to dominate social movement scholarship. As one of three movement-framing tasks (along with agency and identity), an injustice frame is charged with the job of defining a situation as morally objectionable, attributing responsibility to actors (or, less easily, to social structures), and arousing moral indignation in a "hot," emotionally charged cognition (Gamson, Fireman, and Rytina 1982; Gamson 1992, 1995).

Despite promising beginnings in an innovative social psychological experiment that demonstrated a series of "divesting" acts by which participants who were not social movement activists came to rebel against "unjust authority" (Gamson et al. 1982), the concept of frame came to hide what participants were doing under the formula of "*adopting* an injustice frame." The research of Gamson and his colleagues showed that for such rebellion to occur, participants had to work to interpret disquieting or upsetting features of the situation, question elements of the taken-for-granted principles of justice at work in the encounter, make these doubts public to the group, and denounce the procedures as unjust. Unfortunately, the tentative, uncertain, and exploratory process of arriving at a judgment of injustice came to be replaced by a "frame" ready to be taken off the shelf, "adopted" and applied to the situation like a template. While rightly emphasizing the possibility of different assessments, the notion of adopting a frame ignores ways in which the properties of situated events both enable and constrain dialogic processes of justification and critique.

The replacement of dynamic interactional processes by static frames has been one of the many critiques of the abundant framing literature initiated by David Snow (Snow et al. 1986; Snow and Benford 1988, 1992). Four major criticisms are relevant for the purposes of this chapter. First, an overly strategic focus on the deliberate framing activities of movement elites striving to mobilize participants for collective action led the approach to neglect the meaning work performed by ordinary actors (Benford 1997; Masson 1997; Steinberg 1998, 1999; R.H. Williams and Kubal 1999). Second, it has been prone to oversimplification, ignoring the multiple frames that actors bring to situations, and the multivocality and multiple layers of meanings that escape the intentions of speakers (Benford 1997; Steinberg 1998, 1999; Benford and Snow 2000; P.E. Oliver and Johnston 2000). Third, frames have been reified, as meanings created in social relations come to be treated as real and independent of the interpretations and constructions of actors in events, situations, and interactions (Steinberg 1998, 1999; Mische 2003; Hoffbauer and Ramos 2014). Fourth, at the same time that it has ignored the relational processes involved in framing injustice, the framing literature has worked with an overly open-ended conception of the cultural resources from which frames, especially injustice frames, are constructed. While benefiting from the move away from values and interests as explanations of action, the notions of a toolkit of "symbols, stories, rituals, and world views" (Swidler 1986, 273) or of "stories, myths and folk tales" (Snow and Benford 1988) have failed to provide an analytical framework for understanding how injustice claims are formulated, and contributed to a laundry list of descriptive frames. Master frames (Snow and Benford 1992; Carroll and Ratner 1996) suffer from the same flaws as ordinary frames, and so have not filled the void.

It did not have to be this way. In their initial discussion of the "legitimating frames" against which injustice frames are constructed, Gamson and colleagues (1982, 123) write of injustice frames as interpretations that "the shared moral principles" of participants are being violated. Rather than exploring these shared principles of justice, however, the issue was dropped. The gap has subsequently been noted, but not filled. For example, Gamson (1988, 220) himself characterized as "much too vague" his own itemization of "the meaning systems that are culturally available for talking, writing, and thinking about political objects: the myths and metaphors, the language and idea elements, the frames, ideologies, values and condensing symbols."

While maintaining that broader political cultures contain themes and counter-themes in dialectical counterpoint (see also Ferree et al. 2002), he leaves the content of these themes and counter-themes open, and the conceptions of the broader cultural framework for the creation of injustice frames undeveloped.

There is an alternative. The pragmatic sociology of justification and critique can supply the pieces missing from the framing literature by emphasizing dynamic processes rather than static frames, ordinary actors in addition to movement elites, and a complex repertoire of evaluation based in institutionalized political traditions rather than ad hoc frames. Starting from the capacity of ordinary people to engage in moral judgments, the approach developed by Luc Boltanski and Laurent Thévenot in *On Justification* (2006 [1991]) provides a historically grounded theoretical model of conventions used in justification and critique, and of the often messy and uncertain process in which these conventions are used to make judgments of justice and injustice, and to denounce the latter. Frame analysis does not need to be abandoned, but it can be improved by being located within the broader framework provided by this pragmatist sociology.

In the next section, I summarize the main arguments of the pragmatic sociology of critique, and then analyze a small dispute on the streets of Toronto to illustrate the contribution of this approach.

The Pragmatic Sociology of Justification and Critique

In recently translated work that is only beginning to receive attention in anglophone North America (Lamont 2012, 208), Luc Boltanski and Laurent Thévenot (2006 [1991]) established a program of research into how ordinary people justify and criticize social arrangements. The work that has come to be known as the pragmatic sociology of critique rests on two foundations: a model of a plurality of "orders of worth" based on "higher common principles" of the common good in Western political traditions, and a specification of the social processes of qualification, "rising in generality," and "reality tests" through which social actors engage in the justification and critique of actions, actors, and objects in situations of dispute. The pragmatic sociology of critique fills the gaps identified in the framing literature by providing a developed model of the cultural resources upon which actors draw in making judgments of justice and injustice, and by considering how they do so in given situations. That is, they outline the pragmatics of justification and critique.

Boltanski and Thévenot are not the only scholars to consider how, "as controversies unfold over time, people are forced to think about their moral intuitions in order to develop explicit positions" (Jasper 1992, 339). Jasper examined the use of "god terms" in instrumental and moralist rhetorics, and Steinberg (1999, 2002) performed a dialogic analysis of "speech genres" and "discursive fields" in the "talk and back talk of collective action" of nineteenth-century English weavers. But Jasper and Steinberg both remained immersed in the rhetoric of the conflicts they studied, and, like Gamson, they did not model the broader cultural resources used by participants. Rhys Williams (1995) has linked social movement frames to broader cultural patterns in covenant, contract, and stewardship models of the public good in the United States, and characterized the external cultural environment of movements as "boundaries governing what can and cannot be [intelligibly and legitimately] expressed publicly" (R.H. Williams 2004, 102). Unlike these alternatives to framing, Boltanski and Thévenot model both a repertoire of evaluation having public legitimacy in Western societies and its pragmatic use in situations that demand justification (Lamont and Thévenot 2000b). They argue that the tension between notions of human equality rooted in the Western political tradition and the inequalities resulting from requirements of social order has led to the development of six conventional justifications for the latter. These are institutionalized to various degrees as orders of worth[2] that are available for actors in complex modern societies to draw on in disputes, for both justification and critique.

Boltanski and Thévenot (2006) identified six orders of worth – inspired, domestic, fame, civic, market, and industrial – and two have been proposed subsequently – connectionist or network, and green. Inspired worth comes from non-conformity, creativity, emotion, and authenticity independent of public recognition or ties to a community. In contrast, domestic worth derives from upholding traditions, trustworthiness based on personal reputation and character, and loyalty to people and places. Fame or renown depends on the mediated approval and esteem of an anonymous public (not specific, co-present domestic others). Civic worth invokes solidarity and equality between citizens concerned with the common good in a rule-governed world of public spaces. Market worth values the private pursuit of private interests, in which the common good is served by free competition for commodities (as in Adam Smith's invisible hand), and worth derives from purchasing power. Industrial worth comes from functional efficiency, expertise, long-range planning, measurement, and science. Network or "connectionist" worth is based on extending networks and connections by actively developing innovative projects (Boltanski and Chiapello 2005). Green or environmental worth emphasizes uncertainty and prudence (Latour 1998) or sustainability, interdependence, stewardship, and the singularity and uniqueness of beings in nature (Thévenot, Moody, and Lafaye 2000, 256–63).

The worth of acts, persons, and objects is ranked in different, often incompatible ways in each order, and there is no overarching principle to adjudicate between them. In contrast to unspecified themes and counter-themes, or legitimating and injustice frames, this model proposes that there is a repertoire of evaluation – a limited plurality of conventional orders of worth – by which social arrangements (of authority, the division of labour, or distribution) can be justified or criticized. The model of orders of worth enables us to see how people perform pragmatic operations of justification and critique in situations where actors attempt to resolve controversies without resorting to force. For Boltanski and Thévenot, this can range from mundane daily life to more formal or politicized disputes. How does this happen?

Justifications and critiques are applied in practice in reality tests,[3] in which judgments are made about the relative worthiness of the beings (whether humans or things) involved in the dispute according to the criteria of an order of worth. Tests first of all involve an operation of qualification or an answer to the question of what order of worth should be applied to the situation. Qualification invokes a "higher common principle" as a convention of equivalency that makes it possible to compare beings and rank their worthiness. Should actors, actions, policies, or institutions be evaluated in terms of authenticity, fame, loyalty, efficiency, or some other convention of equivalence? Specially formulated tests (such as elections, art auctions, performance reviews) are typically set up to prioritize one order of worth, but as we shall see, ordinary situations are often ambiguous, and participants or observers must first make qualifying judgments.

The judgments of worth made in tests can be criticized in two ways. On the one hand, the implementation of the test may be attacked for allowing forms of worth outside the one being tested to be transported into the situation, such as judgments of industrial safety being corrupted by market considerations. In such "corrective" critiques (Boltanski and Chiapello 2005), purification of the test through the removal of irrelevant criteria is sought. On the other hand, more radical critiques seek not to reform a given test but rather to substitute a test from a different order of worth, i.e., a different principle of justification. For example, a radical critic might denounce both market value and industrial safety in assessing a resource project, and argue that ecological sustainability or the protection of unique species and habitats is the appropriate test.

There are consequently two types of dispute: one concerning the qualification of objects and persons in situations, or what standards of evaluation are applicable; the other concerning whether those standards have been properly applied. Although compromises between orders of worth are possible and frequent (Thévenot 2006; Boltanski and Thévenot 2006), the orders of worth provide incompatible modes of justification, each supported by different conceptions of the common good. How do these play out in ordinary disputes?

In disputes, participants "rise in generality" from the specifics of the situation to the higher common principles of orders of worth. The central claim is articulated by Laurent Thévenot (2006, 204) thus: "Ordinary disputes are, on the occasion of increases in generality in disagreements, moments when public qualifications are used to critique and to justify." Why? Once a dispute becomes public and agreement is not reached, participants who seek a resolution without resorting to violence are pushed to provide justifications that can be generalized, rather than depending on the specifics of the situation (on which a private agreement might be based). Observers rise in generality when they consider the actants in the situation as "tokens" of "types"; that is, as representing a class of persons or objects that are equivalent in the specified way, and therefore comparable. In so doing, they are enlarging the scope of the dispute from the contingencies of the particular, local situation to something more far-reaching in significance. As Adut (2008) has shown in the case of scandals, publicization is key: once a dispute has become public, participants are compelled to provide reasons that will be tested according to the standards of one or more orders of worth.

Despite its fleeting character, a minor altercation in Toronto in 2006 can tell us something about how participants in, or in this case observers of, mundane disputes engage in justification and critique. "Ordinary disputes raise the same kind of issues [of the common good and orders of worth] when the level of generality in the cognitive treatment of people rises. At such moments, public qualifications are used to criticize and justify, and those qualifications fit into constructions of the common good" (Thévenot 2007, 415). I will first illustrate the rise in generality from details of the situation to the higher common principles of several polities (showing the operation of reason-giving using conventions).

An Incident

Near the end of January 2006, the *Toronto Star* (Powell 2006) and CBC News (2006a)[4] reported on the controversy aroused by an incident in Toronto's Kensington Market, a several-block area of small shops and restaurants. Photographs of a brief altercation between the driver of a car and a cyclist/pedestrian were posted on a local blog, and a vociferous debate (a "flame war," in Internet parlance) immediately erupted.

The incident began when the driver tossed a hamburger and its wrapping onto the street. A bike courier who was walking her bike on the sidewalk picked it up, opened the car door, and "returned" it to him. The driver then left his car, threw coffee at her, and grabbed her by the helmet. In the ensuing scuffle, the courier's bike lock key scratched his car. A passing photographer chanced to document what happened next (Citynoise 2006). The driver grabbed and upset the courier's bike, knocking her down. He then stamped on her rear wheel, and the two scuffled until passersby subdued him. The police arrived, but no charges were laid.

Boltanski and Thévenot's model at first appears to have little relevance to this dispute. Their model is intended to address only regimes of justification, that is, situations where actions and decisions need to be publicly justified or legitimized because there has been some form of disruption, critique, or dispute. Justification constitutes a reflexive break in action, which cannot go on all the time or life would grind to a halt. As observers from Goffman (1971) to Tilly (2006a, 2008b) have noted, much of the time disruptions in the course of action are repaired, reflected upon, ignored, tolerated, or locally accommodated without rising in generality to public justifications and critiques. The model is thus not intended to apply to an incident like the Kensington Market altercation, in which an act of violence precluded the interruption in the course of action required for justification and critique (Boltanski 1990; Boltanski and Thévenot 1999, 2006). In contrast to the limited comparisons or equivalences in a test within an order of worth, violence removes limits on the resources opposed parties may bring to the dispute.

The missing delay can be recovered after the fact, in moments of reflection, when parties to or observers of the interaction consider what happened and draw on the higher common principles of an order of worth to qualify or find equivalences between the persons and objects involved and to judge their worth (Wagner 1999). Such cognitive and evaluative judgments were found on the CBC News website, which solicited and then published twenty-six signed letters commenting on the episode (CBC News

2006b; subsequent references to letters all refer to this source). Thanks to the photographs posted on the citynoise.org website and their subsequent dissemination by news media, a private confrontation that would have been visible to only the few bystanders on the street became public, and therefore subject to the pragmatic imperative of justification. The latter will be explored first, followed by an examination of the parts played by digital and mass media.

The letters published by CBC News aim at both generality and the capacities of the actors through justifications and critiques of the driver and the cyclist. Judgments are addressed to one or more of three actions, which thereby take on the quality of tests: the driver's initial act of throwing the hamburger on the road, the cyclist's act of opening the car door and "returning" it, and the driver's subsequent assault on the cyclist.

As we will see, the letter writers rise in generality from the contingent particularities of the situation to raise issues of the common good, representative of a class of events. That is, the actor or object becomes qualified not as a singular individual but as a token of a class or category (the operation of qualification); the actions likewise are not considered in their particularity but as having more general significance. In contrast to the framing literature, which treats meaning as cognitive interpretations, the participants are understood to be making evaluative judgments in which acts are regarded in terms of what they reveal about the capacities of the actor rather than in terms of their effects on the world (Boltanski 1990).

The letter writers are uncertain about what conventions to apply to the dispute, and are faced with an initial task of qualification. By focusing on different actions, they are deciding which objects are relevant or essential to the situation, and which are contingent. They apply different orders of worth to actions and objects in the situation, and rather than betraying confusion or inconsistency, this mixture of arguments is an indication that the situation itself is ambiguous and uncertain: it can be looked at from a variety of social worlds and it is not clear what "test" should be applied. In any case, only six writers invoked more than two orders of worth, an equal number offered critiques or justifications that stayed within one world, and the majority referred to only two. Civic and domestic, and to a lesser extent industrial, qualifications predominate, while fame, inspired, and market evaluations rarely appear. As this incident is just illustrative, I will examine only the first three.

Civic justifications refer to the common good in terms of the solidarity of an anonymous and general public good, represented by legitimate authorities. In this case, civic legitimacy takes the "republican" form of soli-darity found in France, rather than the liberal "equal rights" form common in the United States (Thévenot, Moody, and Lafaye 2000, 246; Thévenot and Lamont 2000, 310–11). In the letters posted on the CBC News website, civic justifications for the courier are combined with critiques. On the one hand, she is qualified as a worthy being in the civic world: "a good citizen" (John R. Paterson, Victoria, BC) doing her "civic duty" and having "a civic conscience" (Robert Holmes, Dundas, ON). On the other hand, she is criti-cized for impulsively acting on her own rather than involving the proper authorities by taking the licence number of the vehicle, rounding up wit-nesses, and reporting the offence: "Far better to keep a cool head and report the matter to police" (Darrell Noakes, Saskatoon). Recognizing that the police are unlikely to act – "There is little enforcement of litter laws" – another provided a more nuanced justification of the courier's act: "Even if she did go too far ... at least she did not simply do nothing like happens all too often" (Ian McTavish, Canoe, BC). None of the observers directly qualify the driver in terms of civic worth, but there are implicit attributions of civic unworthiness in praise for the courier and the implication that the driver is a proper object of police action, the kind "we should all stand against" (Dr. André M., Ottawa). It is rather from the domestic order of worth that the driver is most vehemently criticized.

In the domestic world, protection and support, trustworthiness, per-sonal character, loyalty, good manners and propriety, and attachment to place are valued attributes. Although the courier is criticized for lack of courtesy, the driver is harshly denounced by several letter writers invoking a domestic order of worth. He is one of the "too many people [who] have no respect for others" and are "inconsiderate jerks" (Mark Harvey, Winnipeg), or "lazy, thoughtless, witless, stupid slobs" (Tony Hamill, Toronto). Not only is he an unworthy human in the domestic order, the driver is also dis-qualified as a non-domestic animal – "a litter bug" (Howard Pearcey, n.p.) or "pig" (Tony Hamill, Toronto) – and the object he discarded is qualified as disgusting, polluting "matter out of place" in a proper household (Douglas 2005). One writer even qualifies the street as a domestic space: "I look at the street as an extension of my living space and for someone to throw garbage on it is like throwing it through my living room window" (D. Hemm, n.p.). The level of generality raised by this writer is notable: he refers not to the particular street in Kensington Market or his own street, but to "the street" in general. Finally, the driver is criticized for violating a patriarchal domestic hierarchy of protection and support in this rhetorical question:

"OK here we have a guy, throws out trash on the street, throws coffee on a woman, attacks a woman and we are asking who is in the right?" (Randall Holder, n.p.).

In the industrial world, the common good is served by efficiency, predictability, reliability, and the contribution of persons and things to the satisfaction of social or organizational needs. Breakdowns, accidents, and disruptions indicate lack of worth in this world. Justification and critique from the industrial world appear in the letters first as critiques of the driver's littering as a threat to safety because it creates hazards that cyclists must dodge. It is generalized to an attitude that makes cyclists vulnerable to the dangers posed by a motor vehicle, qualified by one writer as "a weapon more deadly than any firearm" (Darrell Noakes, Saskatoon) and which, according to another, "seems to give the occupants a sense of being removed from what happens around them" (Louise Lafond, Hamilton, ON). The courier's actions are also criticized for potentially causing a traffic accident and for endangering herself, showing that what would be valued in an inspired world – taking a risk, or authentically expressing one's emotions – is disqualified in an industrial world as dangerous and disruptive.

This brief analysis of the Kensington Market incident illustrates three of the principles elaborated by Boltanski and Thévenot that stand in contrast to the implicit assumptions of the social movement framing literature. The first is that ordinary people are not just a passive audience for the framing activities of movements and media, but exercise a capacity to make cognitive and moral judgments about justice and worthiness in situations of discord.

Second, it shows that in making those judgments in the context of disputes, they do not simply apply a cognitive frame. Instead they actively draw upon and qualify the social and material features of the situation, and rise from those particulars to more general judgments in which the details of the situation become representative of a broader class of events or processes.

Third, and most important, in making those judgments ordinary observers make use of a repertoire of evaluation, that is, a plurality of orders of worth. In contrast to the ad hoc and vague formulations of cultural resources in the framing literature, Boltanski and Thévenot's model specifies a limited number of conventions that can be found in use by both ordinary people and social movement activists (Moody and Thévenot 2000; Thévenot, Moody, and Lafaye 2000). Although there are advantages to an inductive approach favoured by the framing literature, it has led to the proliferation of specific frames rather than accumulation of knowledge about processes. By focusing on tests within orders of worth, and the corrective and radical critiques brought to bear on them, the model advocated here replaces blunt metaphors like "framing contests" (Zald 1996; Benford and Snow 2000) with a more nuanced framework for understanding "meaning work" in social movements. Nor is the alternative proposed here static, as the model is open to exploring the conditions for the development of new orders of worth such as the network or connectionist worth and the green or environmental ones discussed earlier. One scuffle does not a sociology make, but it does suggest a way to open up the black boxes of frame analysis and lead it in productive new directions.

Social Movement Society: A Critical Society?

Considered as part of the sequence of affairs with which this chapter began, the Kensington Market incident also serves to illustrate some of the changes highlighted in the SMS thesis (Meyer and Tarrow 1998). What has changed from the Calas affair in the eighteenth century to Dreyfus in the nineteenth, Latimer in the twentieth, and Kensington and Dziekanski in the twenty-first?

First, the figures responsible for publicizing the issues or denouncing them as injustices became less prominent. Voltaire was already a famous *philosophe* and satirist when he undertook the defence of Calas (Gay 1965); likewise, although literary naturalism was becoming passé, Zola's fame had already been established when he denounced the injustice done to Dreyfus. As with Dreyfus, it was originally Latimer's family, as well as friends and neighbours, who came to his defence, but the case was eventually brought to nationwide attention by Allan Blakeney, head of the Canadian Civil Liberties Association and former premier of Saskatchewan. In the Kensington Market and Dziekanski cases, in contrast, it was neither the more or less domestic networks that intervened on behalf of Dreyfus (prior to Zola) and Latimer, nor the publicity provided by fame (Voltaire, Zola, Blakeney). Instead, it was unconnected and previously unknown bystanders who publicized the events. Despite the continuing role of celebrities in social movements (Meyer and Gamson 1995), less *fame* is needed to create an affair and arouse public outrage and debate over injustices.

A second dimension of differences between the five episodes explains the declining importance of fame revealed by the last two cases. Constructing the first two affairs was costly. It required the rhetorical and literary abilities of Voltaire and Zola, the "immense labour" of the former in gathering reports and activating his networks to exonerate Calas (Claverie 1994), and in the Dreyfus affair the deployment by both sides of a mass of evidence, expertise (e.g., handwriting analysts), and publications (Loué 2007). In contrast, the apparently authoritative evidence (Milbrandt 2012) of a bystander's photographs and a video recording were enough to constitute the Kensington Market and Dziekanski affairs, respectively. Most important, the fragmentary visual evidence provided by the bystanders was both produced and disseminated easily and at low cost through a blog and through the mainstream mass media.

Unlike studies that examine how existing activists use low-cost digital technologies to mobilize, communicate, coordinate, create imagined communities, build decentralized networks, make contentious claims, diffuse tactical repertoires, and develop new media to avoid traditional mass media gatekeepers (e.g., Ayres 1999; Juris 2005; Garrett 2006; Maratea 2008; Earl and Kimport 2009; Brym et al. 2014), this chapter has followed Gamson's pioneering work by going back a step to examine the effect of digital technologies on the formulation of injustice claims in the absence of social movement activists.

The Kensington Market and Dziekanski affairs were not the e-movements, e-mobilizations, or e-tactics described by Earl and Kimport (2011), but they took advantage of the same affordances of digital technologies as those forms of action, with similar implications. An anonymous bystander with a camera can easily become a whistleblower whose images may be picked up by mainstream media competing for audience share in a fragmented multimedia universe. People may or may not be mobilized or compelled to act, or even called upon to act, but the issue or injustice rapidly becomes public knowledge. To return to Gamson's early language, "encounters with unjust authority" that might otherwise be known only by individuals who are physically co-present, or tied to them, are rapidly transformed, at low cost, into public spectacles of mediated "distant suffering" (Boltanski 1999). The resource requirements for this "pre-movement" aspect of mobilization for collective action – publicizing an injustice – have declined precipitously. This has implications for new forms of claims making, the role of social movement organizations in them, and the kinds of claims that are made. This chapter has examined the changing conditions for one mechanism involved in the scale shift (McAdam, Tarrow, and Tilly 2001) from a local dispute to a public issue from which movements as sustained claims making can emerge. The usual focus on activists misses this by looking at collective action only after it has developed. It misses the communities and history from which movements emerge (as examined by Fetner, Stokes, and Sanders in Chapter 2 and by Staggenborg in Chapter 8).

The declining resource requirements for publicizing injustices also have methodological implications. The proliferation of websites, blogs, and forums makes accessible to researchers some of the messy and ephemeral processes in which people – whether movement entrepreneurs, activists, or publics – work to understand and form judgments about contentious or problematic events. These are not the only places to access them, and they have limitations, but because, like the incident I have described, they are often ephemeral and may not give rise to collective action in the form of protests, campaigns, or social movements, it is only occasionally and sporadically that researchers (like Taylor in Chapter 9) find themselves in a position to investigate these processes "live" and "in person" from the start. This does not mean that the analysis of texts on the Web should replace other forms of research, or that frames and strategic framing ought to be abandoned. Concepts of frames and framing have done useful work for our understanding of social movements and there is no reason that they should cease to be productive. But the theoretical resources and research topics explored here can provide additional insights into contentious collective action in social movement societies. The model of orders of worth provides a coherent way of conceiving the cultural resources that social actors draw on in making claims of justice and injustice. It is plural, and open to further development in line with social changes, but it is not so open-ended as to lead to the descriptive laundry list to which the framing literature has been prone. Unlike proposals to restore ideologies to pride of place, these orders of worth are not just ideas and beliefs (P.E. Oliver and Johnston 2000), but are rooted in social and material arrangements. That is, to a greater or lesser degree (varying historically and between societies), they are institutionalized in modern, complex Western societies (and other societies too, most likely in different ways that need to be explored).

This chapter has tried to show that scandals and affairs can be considered components of the repertoire of contention of modern complex societies, which can be characterized as "critical societies" (Boltanski 1990; Boltanski and Chiapello 2005; Boltanski and Claverie 2007). On the one hand, they contain a repertoire of evaluation on the basis of which social actors criticize and justify social arrangements: plural orders of worth, including but not limited to the domestic, fame, inspired, civic, industrial, and market worlds. On the other hand, such societies contain a repertoire of contention through which social actors pursue their critiques: plural social forms, including scandals and affairs in addition to the hybrid (Sampson et al. 2005), conventional, and transgressive (Tilly 2006b) forms of the social movement repertoire.

Notes

My thanks to the editors of this volume, Howard Ramos and Kathleen Rogers, and to three anonymous reviewers, for their useful comments on earlier drafts of this chapter. I am also grateful to the participants in the social movement society workshop, especially Suzanne Staggenborg, for their encouragement.

1 For full discussions of scandals and affairs from which my understandings are derived, see Boltanski 1990, 255-65 and 1999, 55-61; Boltanski 2004, 389-90n38; Boltanski and Claverie 2007; and Adut 2008.

2 The French word employed by Boltanski and Thévenot is *grandeur*, which connotes size and height as well as "greatness." Thévenot (2004, 12) has endorsed "worth" as an imperfect but adequate translation.

3 The French term *épreuve* also connotes "trial" and "proof," ideas that are only partly conveyed by the English term "test." "Reality test" is the best translation (see Boltanski and Thévenot 1999, 367).

4 Canadian Broadcasting Corporation (CBC), Canada's national publicly funded Internet, radio, and television network.

11

The Concept of Social Movement and Its Relationship to the Social Movement Society

An Empirical Investigation

DAVID B. TINDALL AND JOANNA L. ROBINSON

In this chapter, we assert that an empirical extrapolation of the social movement society (SMS) thesis is that we should observe relatively widespread membership in social movements. At the very least, we should expect to find that most people who belong to organizations that are normally associated with social movements should be potentially classified as being part of a given social movement. While we argue that this is a potential inference from the SMS thesis, we are skeptical of such a conjecture. In contrast, we are somewhat more pessimistic about the SMS thesis as it applies to mass participation in movements. In this chapter, we review and consider several different conceptualizations of social movements to evaluate the SMS thesis. We do so by drawing upon social survey data from a nationwide probability sample and provide a quantitative analysis.

Since the 1950s and 1960s, social movements and their tactics – including protests, petitions, and boycotts – have increasingly been recognized as a legitimate form of political action across Western democratic societies (Tarrow 1998). Social movement scholars have pointed to the increase in protest, coupled with the widespread acceptance of protest as a form of political action, as evidence of the emergence of a social movement society (Meyer and Tarrow 1998; Rucht 1998). They argue that the dramatic social and cultural changes over the last forty years, including increased levels of education, the emergence of mass media, and the rise of post-materialist values, has resulted in the diffusion and institutionalization of protest across the United States and other Western liberal democracies (Inglehart 1990; Meyer and Tarrow 1998; Inglehart and Catterberg 2002).

As others have noted in this volume, Meyer and Tarrow (1998) proposed the concept of the "movement society" and pointed to three trends that characterize it:

1. Since the 1960s, protest has gone from an irregular occurrence to a perpetual and pervasive element of social and political life.
2. Protest has diffused across time and space, becoming a political strategy used by a wide range of social actors across political divides and social milieus. New information technology and the mass media have made it easier for contention to be mounted and have created solidarity across social groups and territories.
3. With the professionalization of movement organizations and actors, movement tactics and repertoires, including protest, have become a routine and institutionalized form of political action. Movements have become professionalized, while at the same time, states have recognized the legitimacy of protest and have responded with increased professionalization rather than violence.

While studies engaging the SMS thesis thus far (e.g., Tarrow 1998; Rucht 1998; Soule and Earl 2005; Dobson 2011) have made an important contribution towards understanding the diffusion of protest over the last forty years, or individual involvement in organizations (Corrigall-Brown 2012), few have engaged the debate over how to conceptualize social movements themselves in the SMS. Conceptual classification, and participation, in a social movement is often arbitrarily defined by membership in a particular type of organization, attendance at a protest event, or participation in a movement-related activity. While some studies show that individuals with higher levels of organizational membership are more likely to be involved in protest activities (McAdam 1982; Schussman and Soule 2005), other scholars challenge the use of individual characteristics, such as attendance at a protest event, as indicators or measures of an SMS and stress the importance of examining how individual traits of movement actors combine and influence the structural patterns of social movements (Diani 1992; Diani and Bison 2004).

Conceptualizing movements as aggregates of discrete units ignores the collective processes and structures that shape social movements, including individual and organizational networks. Diani (1992), for example, argues that what makes social movements distinct from other forms of collective action are the connections that occur between independent sites, events, and actors that link them together into a collective experience, with shared identities and goals across time and space. He defines social movements as "networks of informal interactions between a plurality of individuals, groups and/or organizations, engaged in political or cultural conflicts, on the basis of shared collective identities" (Diani 1992, 1). Subsequently, Diani and Bison (2004) argued that social movement scholars should recognize social movements as a specific mode of coordination of collective action – distinct from other episodes of collective action, including discrete protest events promoted by one-off coalitions, or specific organizations devoted to a cause but disconnected from the broader organizational field address-ing similar issues. These individual events should be considered measures of social movements only if there is evidence of their connectedness to each other.

In distinguishing between organizations, coalitions, consensus move-ments, and social movements, Diani and Bison (2004, 283) defined social movement processes as

> instances of collective action with clear conflictual orientations to specific social and political opponents, conducted in the context of dense inter-organizational networking, by actors linked by solidarities and shared iden-tities that precede and survive any specific coalitions and campaigns.

Recently, Diani (2012, 106) further refined aspects of his conceptualiza-tion of social movements as:

> the intersection of dense networks of informal interorganizational exchan-ges and processes of boundary definition that operate at the level of broad collectivities rather than specific groups/organizations, through dense interpersonal networks and multiple affiliations.

Following from the conceptual work of Diani (2012; 2013; Diani and Bison 2004), in this chapter we argue that examining social movements as social networks involving shared identities and actions – linked together across time and space – is a better way of examining the SMS thesis than focusing upon individual characteristics or discrete protest events (see also

Chapters 8 and 13 for similar critiques). Using data from a national survey of members of environmental organizations in Canada, we empirically assess the implications of Diani's definition of social movement for understanding the breadth of "social movements," and to what extent Canada is a "social movement society."

We adopt an approximate version of Diani's definition (Diani and Bison 2004) operationalized at the micro level, and examine the extent to which members of environmental organizations can be classified as part of the environmental movement (on conceptual and empirical grounds).

The preceding should be qualified by emphasizing that this scheme is inspired by Mario Diani's body of conceptualization work, but our operationalization is not a strict translation of Diani's ideas, as his framework focuses on the meso level of analysis. Diani's framework does not explicitly make assertions about expectations at the micro level of analysis, but we assert that it is also useful to speculate on the degree of movement membership and movement participation among individuals.

The Importance of the Environmental Movement

Examining the environmental movement is useful for measuring the SMS thesis because it is one of the largest and most influential movements of the late twentieth and early twenty-first centuries. Various commentators in the social movement literature have described the environmental movement as an exemplar of so-called "new social movements" (Dryzek et al. 2003; Harter 2011). Other scholars have noted the importance of the environmental movement more generally in contemporary Western society, especially in relation to current crises such as global warming (Gould, Schnaiberg, and Weinberg 1996; Brulle 2000; Pellow 2007). Since the 1960s, the environmental movement has been successful in shifting social consciousness and shaping policy outcomes (Rose 2000; M. Smith 2005a). Dryzek and colleagues (2003) contend that in terms of numbers and policy influence, it has had a larger impact than most (and possibly all) other movements. The environmental movement is present in all developed countries and most developing countries, and is diverse across membership base, issue focus, and responses to state structures. Indeed, Castells (2004) has described the environmental movement as one of the most important social movements of the twentieth century.

To elaborate on a few of these points, it can be noted that the environmental movement is diverse and professionalized, has a large membership base, and, unlike many other social movements, has demonstrated the ability to mobilize a wide range of constituents and resources over a sustained period of time (Brulle 2000). The mainstream environmental movement has become institutionalized; it is part of the decision-making process and has helped define the social and political agenda when it comes to environmental protection and regulation (Rose 2000; Obach 2004; Roberts et al. 2005; M. Smith 2005a). More recently, some scholars have argued that the environmental movement is entering a period of transformation and revitalization, as organizations and actors recognize the need to build bridges with other movements in order to extend their influence and remain relevant (Obach 2004; R. Gottlieb 2005). Further, in the context of Canadian society and politics, many scholars have suggested that the environmental movement is one of the most important in the country (R. Murphy 2006; Stoddart and Tindall 2010; Stoddart 2012). In many ways the environmental movement is the ideal case for evaluating the SMS thesis.

Research Questions

Based on our intersecting interests in conceptual definitions of social movements, the SMS thesis, the role of social networks in social movements, and the environmental movement in particular, the three questions that guide our analysis are:

- How widespread is participation in social movement activities among environmental non-governmental organization (ENGO) members/supporters in Canada?
- What proportion of ENGO members/supporters in Canada can be classified as members of the environmental movement (as conceptually defined)?
- What proportion of ENGO members/supporters are environmental movement members (as conceptually defined) who participate in environmental movement activities?

Relatedly, several hypotheses correspond to these questions and also guide the analysis. Our central hypothesis is:

H1: A relatively small proportion of ENGO members will be empirically classified as (environmental) social movement members (<50 percent).

We have two lines of reasoning for offering this hypothesis. First, many analyses of social movements use nominal operationalizations for classifying people into movements, such as organization membership. Our classification scheme, by contrast, is based upon a more rigorous conceptual framework and entails other criteria than mere SMO membership. Relatedly, we expect that a certain proportion of nominal ENGO members will be "filtered out" from being classified as movement members when these criteria are considered. Our second line of reasoning is based on our past empirical research. We have conducted a number of earlier surveys of ENGO members (see Tindall 2002, 2004; Robinson et al. 2007) and have observed that involvement in social movements is substantially lower than is commonly assumed by looking at ENGO memberships.

Based on these two lines of argument, we would expect movement membership to be substantially lower than 50 percent of ENGO members. However, because it is difficult to suggest a specific threshold based on theoretical grounds, we offer <50 percent as a relatively liberal prediction as this would indicate that a majority of organization members are not in fact movement members, and it is a number that is meaningful in terms of familiar discourse (e.g., a minority).

As a result, the general hypothesis can be extended to make more specific predictions about participation in social movement activities:

H2a: A relatively small proportion of ENGO members will be classified as environmental social movement members who participate in social movement activities (<50 percent).

H2b: A relatively small proportion of ENGO members will be classified as environmental social movement members who participate in institutionally oriented social movement activities (<50 percent).

The logic here is similar to that described above, with the additional caveat that we expect the proportion of ENGO members who are also movement members and who participate in social movement activities to be even lower than the proportion of ENGO members who belong to the movement.

Again, for lack of a theoretical rationale to give a specific number, we have provided the prediction that <50 percent of ENGO members will be movement members who participate in these various activities. Some might contend that the criteria outlined in these expectations are narrow. We would counter such a critique by noting that based on logical criteria and past empirical research, we would actually expect the proportions to be far below 50 percent, and thus we offer broad definitions to see how an alternative understanding of movement participation affects understanding of the SMS argument.

Methods

The data for this study were collected, with assistance from the environmental organizations listed below, using a mailed self-administered questionnaire distributed to a stratified systematic sample (with a random start) of environmental organization members across Canada. The data were collected between June and November 2007. The main national and large regional organizations in Canada participated in this survey. The participating environmental groups included: the Canadian Wildlife Federation, the David Suzuki Foundation, Équiterre, Greenpeace of Canada, the Sierra Legal Defence Fund (now known as Ecojustice Canada), the Sierra Club of Canada, the Sierra Youth Coalition, the Wilderness Committee (formerly known as the Western Canada Wilderness Committee), and the World Wildlife Fund of Canada.

The sample for this survey was 1,227, which represents a 32.3 percent response rate. (The response rate is based on 1,227 returned questionnaires divided by 3,799, which is the number of questionnaires sent to valid addresses.[1]) The response rates for the surveys were relatively low in absolute terms, although not necessarily in comparative terms (see Muller and Opp 1986; Opp 1986; Tindall 2002). Indeed, they are typical of those found in similar studies.

The questionnaires were distributed to the ENGO respondents between June 2007 and November 2007. The questionnaires were provided in English or in French depending upon database records maintained by the ENGOs regarding their members (the questionnaires were provided in French for organizations where there were substantial numbers of known francophone members; otherwise the questionnaires were provided in English). There were 1,227 completed questionnaires. The margin of error for the survey is ±2.8 at the 95 percent confidence level.

The sample was stratified by the different organizations, and in some instances, where there were substantial numbers of both francophone and anglophone members, by language group. The general procedures involved the researchers sending questionnaire packages and reminder postcards to the ENGOs. The ENGOs were given instructions on how to draw a systematic sample with a random start from their membership/supporter lists in order to print labels for the questionnaire packages and reminder postcards. In general, the ENGOs affixed address labels to the prestamped questionnaire packages and reminder postcards.[2] They then distributed the questionnaire packages (on behalf of the researchers), and subsequently (about two weeks later) mailed the reminder postcards. Through this procedure, they were able to protect the confidentiality of their membership lists.

There is no evidence of substantial sampling bias related to non-response. Based on typical patterns of non-response bias (Dillman et al. 2002), we might expect people with more available time, or those who feel more strongly about the issues covered in the questionnaire, to be more likely to respond.[3] On the other hand, an analysis of key variables such as level of participation in movement activities reveals a roughly normal distribution. Most people participated in activities to a relatively moderate extent, with fewer people either being relatively highly active or having relatively low levels of activity. It is certainly not the case that the sample was made up of respondents who were mostly highly active or mostly inactive.

The individual cases were weighted in proportion to the relative size of the respective ENGO for the total population of ENGOs (based on these nine organizations.) Values for ENGO size were based on the number of members/supporters of each organization provided in annual reports from the organizations at the time of the study, and from information provided in interviews with representatives of each organization. (In some of the tables reported in the chapter, there are small differences between totals and the contents of the tables because of rounding errors associated with weighting.) Our measures included:

Identification with the Environmental Movement. Respondents were asked: "For the following statements please indicate whether you: 5. completely agree, 4. mostly agree, 3. partly agree/disagree, 2. mostly disagree or 1. completely disagree: You identify yourself as a member of the environmental movement."

Range of Ties. Respondents were provided with a list of environmental organizations, and were asked: (1) whether they had an acquaintance who was a member of the group, and (2) had a close friend or relative who was a member of the group. If the answer to either of these questions was yes, then a tie to the group was coded as existing (tie = 1, no tie = 0). Range of ties was then calculated by summing across the groups.

Activism Ever. Respondents were asked whether they had ever participated in a set of activities, and if so, how often they participated (never, occasionally, or frequently) in various activities.

Activism Past Year. Respondents were also asked whether they had participated in any of the activities in the past year, using the above response categories.

Two-Criteria Definition of Environmental Movement Membership. We constructed two versions of our movement membership classification scheme, one based on two criteria and the other based on three. The two-criteria definition of movement membership was based on range of ties and level of environmental movement identification. To be classified as a member of the movement, respondents had to be *tied to at least two organizations* (e.g., have a social network tie to at least one person in two different organizations). This idea is extrapolated from Diani's conceptual definition. Normally there needs to be more than one organization in order to talk about the existence of a movement. Translating this insight to the individual level, a person needs to be tied to at least two organizations to be considered structurally part of the movement.

We use a sliding threshold for identification to indicate membership. For those respondents with at least two ties, "partly agree" (coded 3) was the criterion for the "weak definition," "mostly agree" (coded 4) was the criterion for the "medium definition," "completely agree" (coded 5) was the criterion for the "strong definition."

We considered this categorization scheme to be somewhat more liberal than the three-criteria definition, but we explored the latter because we wanted to be able to assess a definition that is independent of "participation" in order to avoid criticisms of tautology for certain analyses where we examine participation.

Three-Criteria Definition of Environmental Movement Membership. The three-criteria definition of movement membership is based on range of ties, level of environmental movement identification, and level of participation in select activities. To be classified as a member of the movement, respondents had to be *tied to at least two organizations.*

Also, to be classified as a member of the movement (using the weak definition), respondents had to participate (Ever) in two or more of the following six activities (drawn from Table 11.3):

c. Volunteered for an environmental organization
e. Written and sent a letter, fax, or e-mail to a newspaper about an environmental issue
i. Signed a petition about an environmental issue
j. Attended a community meeting about an environmental issue
k. Attended a rally or protest demonstration about an environmental issue
r. Worked to elect someone because of their views on the environment.

To be classified as a member of the movement using the medium three-criteria definition, respondents had to be tied to at least two different ENGOs, at least mostly identify with the movement, and participate at least occasionally in at least two of the above six activities. To be classified as a member of the movement using the strong three-criteria definition, respondents had to be tied to at least two different ENGOs, completely identify with the movement, and participate frequently in at least two of the above six activities.

Let us now turn to an examination of these measures and, more specifically, test the SMS thesis by looking at participation in activism, followed by alternative definitions of membership, and, finally, test how these definitions of membership are associated with participation.

Results

We begin by introducing the participants to the survey, looking at a number of descriptive statistics of their participation in environmental politics. Table 11.1 shows frequencies, percentages, and other descriptive statistics for agreement with the following statement: "*You* identify yourself as a member of the environmental movement."

Over half (56.2 percent) of the sample "mostly agree" or "completely agree" that they are members of the movement. If one adds the category "Partly agree/disagree," then 81.8 percent of respondents at least partly agree that they are members of the movement. This finding initially casts some doubt on our main hypothesis, as a majority of respondents at least partly agree that they identify as members of the movement.

We examine this further in Table 11.2, which provides descriptive statistics for the distribution of the number of different ENGOs that respondents had ties to.

As can be seen, a majority of respondents did not have ties to any ENGO (55.4 percent). Another 27.1 percent had a tie to only a single group. Thus, 82.5 per cent of respondents had one or fewer ties to ENGOs. Given that

TABLE 11.1
Frequencies for identification with the environmental movement

	f	%
1. Completely disagree	57	4.9
2. Mostly disagree	153	13.3
3. Partly agree/disagree	296	25.6
4. Mostly agree	396	34.2
5. Completely agree	255	22.0
Total	1,157	100.0
Mean	3.55	
Mode	4	
Standard deviation	1.12	

TABLE 11.2
Frequencies for range of ENGO ties (weighted by ENGO)*

	f	%
0	680	55.4
1	333	27.1
2	90	7.3
3	45	3.6
4	36	2.9
5	20	1.6
6	6	0.5
7	9	0.7
8	1	0.1
9	5	0.4
10	2	0.1
11	1	0.1
12	0	0.0
13	1	0.1
Total	1,227	100.0
Mean	0.88	
Mode	0	
Standard deviation	1.50	

* Differences between the column totals and the column contents are due to errors associated with rounding and weighting.

one aspect of our criteria for movement membership is that people have social network ties to at least two organizations, this finding is more in line with our main hypothesis.

Table 11.3 shows percentages and other descriptive statistics for participation in various types of environmental movement activities in the past year. Donating money was the most common activity, followed by being a member of an ENGO and by boycotting a product or company. Generally, respondents were more likely to participate in activities with lower costs in time (such as signing a petition) than activities that entail higher costs (such as serving on an advisory board). Somewhat noteworthy is the fact that there were no activities that a majority of respondents frequently participated in. Conversely, a majority of respondents had never participated in thirteen of these twenty activities (if we include "Other").

Table 11.4 contains a summary of results that provide a first test of the

TABLE 11.3

Percentage of participation in various types of activism (past year) (weighted by ENGO)*

Activities	Never (1)	Occasionally (2)	Frequently (3)	Mean	SD	Valid N
a. Been a member of an environmental organization	28.1	36.4	35.6	2.08	.79	1,136
b. Donated money to an environmental organization, other than purchasing a membership	14.8	53.1	32.2	2.17	.66	1,163
c. Volunteered for an environmental organization	78.6	16.5	4.9	1.26	.54	1,135
d. Written and sent a letter, fax, or e-mail to a government official regarding an environmental issue	61.1	33.3	5.6	1.45	.60	1,139

▶

Activities	Never (1)	Occasionally (2)	Frequently (3)	Mean	SD	Valid N
e. Written and sent a letter, fax, or e-mail to a newspaper about an environmental issue	83.0	15.6	1.4	1.18	.42	1,127
f. Written and sent a letter, fax, or e-mail to a company/ corporation about an environmental issue	82.0	16.1	1.9	1.20	.45	1,135
g. Written and sent a letter, fax, or e-mail to another organization regarding an environmental issue	82.7	15.1	2.3	1.20	.45	1,130
h. Telephoned a government, company, or other organizational official regarding an environmental issue	88.7	10.7	0.6	1.12	.34	1,136
i. Signed a petition about an environmental issue	37.8	47.4	14.8	1.77	.69	1,142
j. Attended a community meeting about an environmental issue	67.0	29.9	3.1	1.36	.54	1,138
k. Attended a rally or protest demonstration about an environmental issue	86.2	12.6	1.2	1.15	.39	1,129
l. Participated in an information campaign for the general public about an environmental issue	78.5	19.5	2.1	1.24	.47	1,129

▶

Activities	Never (1)	Occasionally (2)	Frequently (3)	Mean	SD	Valid N
m. Made a presentation to a public body about an environmental issue	93.1	5.9	1.0	1.08	.30	1,129
n. Given a lecture on an environmental issue to a school group or voluntary organization	93.1	5.7	1.2	1.08	.31	1,133
o. Served as a representative on an advisory board formed around an environmental issue	92.0	6.8	1.2	1.09	.33	1,121
p. Purchased a book, T-shirt, poster, mug or other merchandise from an environmental organization	36.4	52.4	11.1	1.75	.64	1,144
q. Boycotted a product or company because of environmental concern	30.0	45.8	24.2	1.94	.73	1,129
r. Worked to elect someone because of their views on the environment	72.5	23.5	4.0	1.31	.54	1,136
s. Voted for someone because of their environmental views	49.7	33.3	16.9	1.67	.75	1,153
t. Any other activities (that you have done to help conserve the environment?)	48.7	33.4	18.0	1.69	.76	524

* Differences between the row totals and the row contents are due to errors associated with rounding and weighting.

TABLE 11.4
Two-criteria definition (identification and ties) of environmental movement membership

	Two-criteria definition					
	Weak *Ties ≥ 2* *Identification ≥ 3*		Medium *Ties ≥ 2* *Identification ≥ 4*		Strong *Ties ≥ 2* *Identification ≥ 5*	
	f	%	f	%	f	%
Non-members	1,048	85.4	1,072	87.4	1,173	95.6
Members	179	14.6	155	12.6	54	4.4
Total	1,227	100.0	1,227	100.0	1,227	100.0

main hypothesis that only a minority of ENGO members can be classified as members of the environmental movement. This table provides three versions of the two-criteria definition based on the number of organizations a respondent was tied to and on his or her level of identification. These definitions are more liberal than the three-criteria definition we report in Table 11.5. We will discuss the implications of this below.

TABLE 11.5
Three-criteria definition (identification, ties, and participation) of environmental movement membership

	Three-criteria definition					
	Weak *Ties ≥ 2* *Identification ≥ 3* *Participates* *occasionally ≥ 2*		Medium *Ties ≥ 2* *Identification ≥ 4* *Participates* *occasionally ≥ 2*		Strong *Ties ≥ 2* *Identification ≥ 5* *Participates* *frequently ≥ 2*	
	f	%	f	%	f	%
Non-members	1,079	87.9	1,098	89.5	1,207	98.4
Members	148	12.1	129	10.5	20	1.6
Total	1,227	100.0	1,227	100.0	1,227	100.0

Movement Membership: Two-Criteria Definition

The weak two-criteria definition defines as a member of the movement someone who is tied to at least two ENGOs and at least "partly agrees" with the statement that he or she is a member of the environmental movement. Using this definition, only 14.6 percent of respondents could be classified as a member of the movement. This is statistically significant ($t = 35.15, p < .001$).[4]

The medium two-criteria definition defines as a member of the movement someone who is tied to at least two ENGOs and at least "mostly agrees" with the statement that he or she is a member of the environmental movement. Using this definition, only 12.6 percent of respondents could be classified as a member of the movement. This is statistically significant ($t = 39.47, p < .001$).

The strong two-criteria definition defines as a member of the movement someone who is tied to at least two ENGOs and "completely agrees" with the statement that he or she is a member of the environmental movement. Using this definition, only 4.4 percent of respondents could be classified as a member of the movement. This is statistically significant ($t = 78.05, p < .001$).

Thus, based on the theoretical criteria we presented earlier, even using the most liberal definition of movement membership, only 14.6 percent of ENGO members are classified as members of the environmental movement. These findings provide substantial support for the hypothesis that only a minority of ENGO members actually belong to the environmental movement in a conceptual sense.

In Table 11.5 we undertake a full examination of our main hypothesis by using our three-criteria definition: in addition to the criterion that people have ties to people in at least two organizations, and the varying levels of identification with the movement criterion, we also include the criterion that respondents have participated (to varying degrees) in at least two of six key activities.

Based on the weak three-criteria definition, 12.1 percent of respondents are members of the movement. This is statistically significant ($t = 40.75, p < .001$). Based on the medium definition, 10.5 percent of respondents are members of the movement. This is also statistically significant ($t = 44.97, p < .001$). Based on the strong definition, only 1.6 percent of respondents are members of the movement. This is also statistically significant ($t = 133.51, p < .001$).

So here, even using the least restrictive definition (that people partly identify with the movement, have ties to people in at least two organizations, and participate at least occasionally in two activities), only 12.1 percent of respondents can be classified as members of the movement. This provides strong support for our assertion that only a minority of ENGO members can be classified as being part of the movement.

Participation by Membership

In Tables 11.6 and 11.7, we explore participation further, and examine the percentage of people who participated in various activities in the past year who are classified as part of the movement based on the two-criteria definition (in Table 11.6) and the three-criteria definition (in Table 11.7).

TABLE 11.6

Percentage of ENGO members who are movement members (two-criteria definition) and who participate in various social movement activities (past year) (weighted by ENGO)

Activities	Two-criteria definition		
	Weak	Medium	Strong
a. Been a member of an environmental organization	14.3	12.3	4.6
b. Donated money to an environmental organization, other than purchasing a membership	12.9	11.2	3.9
c. Volunteered for an environmental organization	6.9	6.3	2.0
d. Written and sent a letter, fax, or e-mail to a government official regarding an environmental issue	9.9	9.0	4.0
e. Written and sent a letter, fax, or e-mail to a newspaper about an environmental issue	5.9	5.4	2.6
f. Written and sent a letter, fax, or e-mail to a company/corporation about an environmental issue	5.6	4.8	2.2
g. Written and sent a letter, fax, or e-mail to another organization regarding an environmental issue	5.1	4.8	2.1
h. Telephoned a government, company, or other organizational official regarding an environmental issue	3.7	3.4	1.5
i. Signed a petition about an environmental issue	12.4	10.7	4.3

▶

Activities	Two-criteria definition		
	Weak	Medium	Strong
j. Attended a community meeting about an environmental issue	7.3	6.8	2.6
k. Attended a rally or protest demonstration about an environmental issue	4.8	4.4	1.8
l. Participated in an information campaign for the general public about an environmental issue	6.2	6.0	2.3
m. Made a presentation to a public body about an environmental issue	3.2	2.9	1.1
n. Given a lecture on an environmental issue to a school group or voluntary organization	2.6	2.5	1.0
o. Served as a representative on an advisory board formed around an environmental issue	4.2	3.9	1.2
p. Purchased a book, T-shirt, poster, mug or other merchandise from an environmental organization	10.0	8.8	3.7
q. Boycotted a product or company because of environmental concern	12.7	11.1	4.6
r. Worked to elect someone because of their views on the environment	5.4	5.0	2.2
s. Voted for someone because of their environmental views	8.5	7.2	3.3
t. Any other activities (that you have done to help conserve the environment?)	6.3	5.7	2.7

TABLE 11.7

Percentage of ENGO members who are movement members (three-criteria definition) and who participate in various social movement activities (past year) (weighted by ENGO)

Activities	Three-criteria definition		
	Weak	Medium	Strong
a. Been a member of an environmental organization	11.8	10.3	1.8
b. Donated money to an environmental organization, other than purchasing a membership	11.1	9.7	1.5

▶

| | Three-criteria definition | | |
Activities	Weak	Medium	Strong
c. Volunteered for an environmental organization	6.9	6.2	1.4
d. Written and sent a letter, fax, or e-mail to a government official regarding an environmental issue	8.7	8.0	1.4
e. Written and sent a letter, fax, or e-mail to a newspaper about an environmental issue	5.6	5.3	1.1
f. Written and sent a letter, fax, or e-mail to a company/corporation about an environmental issue	5.3	4.6	1.1
g. Written and sent a letter, fax, or e-mail to another organization regarding an environmental issue	5.0	4.8	1.1
h. Telephoned a government, company, or other organizational official regarding an environmental issue	3.5	3.2	1.0
i. Signed a petition about an environmental issue	10.7	9.4	1.5
j. Attended a community meeting about an environmental issue	6.9	6.4	1.5
k. Attended a rally or protest demonstration about an environmental issue	4.6	4.2	1.1
l. Participated in an information campaign for the general public about an environmental issue	6.0	5.7	1.3
m. Made a presentation to a public body about an environmental issue	3.0	2.8	0.8
n. Given a lecture on an environmental issue to a school group or voluntary organization	2.3	2.1	0.5
o. Served as a representative on an advisory board formed around an environmental issue	4.2	3.9	0.8
p. Purchased a book, T-shirt, poster, mug or other merchandise from an environmental organization	8.3	7.4	1.3
q. Boycotted a product or company because of environmental concern	10.6	9.4	1.6
r. Worked to elect someone because of their views on the environment	5.1	4.7	1.2
s. Voted for someone because of their environmental views	7.7	5.7	1.2
t. Any other activities (that you have done to help conserve the environment?)	5.3	4.8	1.2

We consider results for both of these definitions because examining results based on the three-criteria definition alone might seem tautological as participation is included in the three-criteria definition. Table 11.6 reveals that even using the most liberal definition, only a small proportion of respondents can be classified at members of the movement who participated in select activities in the past year. Using the *weak two-criteria definition*, for five of the twenty items the percentages of respondents who could be classified as being members and participating in these activities were in the teens. For all other items using this definition, only single-digit percentages of respondents could be classified as members who participated in select activities.

Even smaller percentages of respondents could be classified as members of the movement who participated in select activities using the other definitions in Table 11.6 and Table 11.7. More specifically, when we consider "institutionally oriented" activities, only a very small proportion of respondents were members of the movement who have participated in such activities. For instance, between 3.2 percent and 0.8 percent of respondents had made a presentation to a public body about an environmental issue in the past year. Between 2.6 percent and 0.5 percent of respondents had given a lecture on an environmental issue to a school group or voluntary organization in the past year. Finally, between 4.2 percent and 0.8 percent of respondents had served as a representative on an advisory board formed around an environmental issue in the past year.

In sum, using even the most liberal version of the sliding criteria we offer here, only a small minority of ENGO members can be classified conceptually as being members of the environmental movement. Further, even smaller numbers of ENGO members can be classified as movement members who participate in select activities such as institutionally oriented ones.

Conclusion

The findings reported in this chapter dovetail with some previous observations in the social movement literature that are skeptical of certain parts of the social movement society thesis (Soule and Earl 2005; Caren, Ghoshal, and Ribas 2011; Corrigall-Brown 2012). The results show that looking beyond protest and formal memberships is a worthwhile test of the SMS argument. The data presented here provide strong support for our contention that only a minority of environmental organization members can conceptually be considered active members of the environmental movement. With regard to the SMS thesis and the suggestion that we might expect to find widespread participation in social movements, we can say that when we employ a definition of environmental social movement membership that is based on *network ties, identification, and participation,* only a very small proportion of ENGO members are members of the environmental movement who participate in select movement activities.[5] Of course, we are looking at only one movement and it is possible that if we were to include multiple movements, the percentage of people who could conceptually be classified as movement members and movement participants would increase. We believe we have shown that further examination across other organizations and movements is warranted.

In some ways, our findings run counter to the SMS thesis. While social movement repertoires may have become institutionalized in some ways, only a small minority of people can be classified as belonging to social movements; more specifically, only a small minority of environmental organization members can be classified as belonging to the environmental movement. All of this said, mass involvement in social movements is not always the key factor in their success. An example of this can be seen in the campaign to stop clearcut logging of old-growth rainforests in British Columbia. In the early 1990s, there was a good deal of protest about such logging. While some initiatives were taken in response to these protests, by the mid-1990s environmental protests in the province were largely ignored by the provincial government. However, once environmental social movement leaders began a market campaign, travelling to Europe and the United States and persuading governments and corporate customers for BC forest products to boycott products from old-growth forests, the provincial government and, more notably, forest companies operating domestically took notice and began doing things differently. Among other things, this pressure appears to have led to a trend of forest companies seeking forest certification, which was based on meeting environmental and social standards. Thus, it was ultimately a strategy of elite movement actors – rather than mass protest by rank-and-file members – that made a difference. (See Berman and Leiren-Young 2011.)

The results reported in this chapter may help to explain the disconnect between self-reported concern about environmental issues and relative lack of behavioural action on the part of individuals. With regard to a semi-related topic, in recent years there has been a debate about "the death of environmentalism" (Shellenberger and Nordhaus 2004). In particular, it has been argued that as environmental organizations have become increasingly formalized and reliant on foundations for funding, grassroots involvement in them has declined. Our results suggest that this interpretation may, in part, be a consequence of conflating membership in an environmental organization with membership in the environmental movement. It seems to be the case that most environmental organization members are not very centrally engaged in the movement. But perhaps it is unrealistic, in the first place, to assume that all or most environmental organization members are therefore "members" of the movement.

Notes

This research project was supported through several research grants from the Social Sciences and Humanities Research Council of Canada. We would like to thank Andrea Rivers, Josh Tindall, and Noelani Dubeta for their assistance with this chapter. We would also like to thank Mark Stoddart, Todd Malinick, and Andrea Streilein for their assistance with the research. Finally, we would like to thank Mario Diani for his helpful feedback on an earlier version of the chapter. Please send correspondence to D.B. Tindall.

1 We originally distributed 3,918 questionnaire packages, but 120 of them were returned because they had incorrect addresses (and related issues). In calculating the response rate, we excluded these 120 invalid addresses.

2 One organization provided the researchers with the labels for the packages and reminder postcards, and the researchers mailed these directly to the respondents.

3 One of our main claims in this chapter is that relatively few people who belong to environmental organizations can be classified as members of the movement. If there is sampling bias associated with interest in the topic of this study, this would mean that we have likely overestimated the number of people in the movement. If this was true, it would mean that we are being relatively conservative in our claims, and in fact an even lower proportion of ENGO members belong to the movement than we report here – thus providing even stronger support for our hypotheses.

4 In the interest of being systematic in our analysis, and in order to provide technical tests of the hypotheses, we have calculated tests of significance. To do this, we compare the observed frequency of movement members with the criterion of 50 percent as stated in the main hypothesis. All of the tests are highly statistically significant. However, it is usually the case that what is of substantive interest is not statistical significance per se but the direction and magnitude of the effect. Here there are relatively large effects. The proportion of the sample who can be classified as being a member of the movement using our criteria is substantially lower than 50 percent, and thus clearly a minority.

5 Relatedly, the scale of social movement membership is sometimes exaggerated. For example, McAdam (1989) discusses the stereotype of people who were radical social movement participants in the 1960s, who then sold out and became materialists who bought BMWs and became stockbrokers twenty years later. McAdam argues that this stereotype does not stand up under empirical scrutiny. While many people may have either participated in cultural events of the 1960s or been supportive of

social movements, only a small percentage of the general public were actually members of the movement, and these social movement participants tend to have a high level of continuity in terms of their involvement in movement activities and organization over time (although they may move from one movement to another).

PART 4

KNOWLEDGE AND CULTURE

12

Alternative Policy Groups and Global Civil Society
Networks and Discourses of Counter-Hegemony

WILLIAM K. CARROLL

A decade and a half ago, Meyer and Tarrow (1998, 4) posited that in advanced democracies, the increasing frequency and recurrence of protest, the expanding range of protest constituencies and their claims, and the increasingly professionalized, institutionalized, and conventional character of protest were giving rise to the "social movement society" (SMS). Although the thesis was presented at the level of individual nation-states of the North, in the ensuing years the rise of "alter-globalization" politics and the burgeoning literature on "global civil society" has raised the question of what happens to the SMS model when we scale up to a transnational level. More recently, Tarrow (2011) has suggested that the growth of global movements and of global civil society imparts a new meaning to the term "movement society," distinct from the image of routinization and institutionalization that was central to his and Meyer's original formulation. However, the implications of global movements for the SMS remain unclear.

In this chapter, I consider this issue from the perspective of one emergent component of global civil society: *transnational alternative policy groups* (TAPGs), which in recent decades have generated knowledge for alter-globalization politics or the "globalization from below" movement. TAPGs are think tanks of a different sort from the mainstream and conservative policy groups that inform political and corporate elites. Within a neo-Gramscian understanding of social movements as potential agencies of counter-hegemony, of radical transformation (Maney, Woehrle, and Coy 2005; Carroll and Ratner 2010), as pursued here, TAPGs appear as "collective intellectuals" whose agency may facilitate connections and convergences among movements, transecting national borders and posing democratic alternatives to neoliberal globalization. This chapter gives a comparative overview of sixteen TAPGs located in both the North and South, the political projects they construct discursively, and the networks through which they exert political and cultural influence, in dialogue with subaltern classes and democratic movements. In the conclusion, I address some of the challenges TAPGs face as actors on the contested terrain of global civil society, and some of the implications for the social movement society.

Global civil society can be defined as "the realm of non-coercive collective action around shared interests and values that operates beyond the boundaries of nation states" (Glasius, Kaldor, and Anheier 2006, v). It is a field of contention, distinct from the global economy and the inter-state system yet internally related to both. Reflecting the superior material and cultural resources of a dominant class, this terrain has long been dominated by a cosmopolitan bourgeoisie (Van der Pijl 1998). Such hegemonic policy groups as the Mont Pèlerin Society and the Trilateral Commission have been the object of extensive research, underscoring their importance as *sites of conventional knowledge production and mobilization* (KPM), sometimes known as "policy-planning" (Domhoff 2006). By the twentieth century's closing decades, a new breed of "advocacy think tanks" (Abelson 1995) was actively shaping the neoliberal project of market-centred society (Stone 2000; Macartney 2008). Widely implemented in the 1980s and 1990s as the political complement to economic globalization, neoliberalism tended to increase economic disparities and to degrade public goods (Teeple 2000; Harvey 2005) while thinning the social basis for political consent and expanding the range of disaffected social interests (Cox 1987; S.R. Gill 1995). By the mid-1990s, neoliberal policies had provoked a variegated grassroots politics of "alter-globalization" – resisting the "corporate agenda" but also putting forward democratic alternatives (Carroll 2003; J. Smith 2008; Stephen 2009; Coburn 2010). Transnational movement organizations such as Friends of the Earth International (established in 1971), La Via Campesina (established in 1993), and Our World Is Not for Sale (established ca. 2001) developed along with a transnational public sphere in and around the World Social Forum (WSF, established in 2001) (Fraser 2005).[1] All this seems to project some of the SMS tendencies identified within liberal democracies by Meyer and Tarrow in 1998 (and by others as early as the 1970s; see the Introduction to this volume) onto a global plane. Indeed, the substantive content of "global civil society" very much represents SMS tendencies towards institutionalization, professionalization, and permanent mobilization of movements – mostly in the form of non-governmental organizations (NGOs) that interact both with the WSF and with International Governmental Organizations (IGOs) and national states, blending insider approaches such as lobbying with outsider approaches such as protests and grassroots campaigns. In other respects, however, TAPGs, and the alter-globalization movement politics in which they are embedded, raise questions for the SMS thesis, as we shall see in the concluding section of this chapter.

Meanwhile, transnational social movements themselves face major challenges as collective actors within global civil society. A key challenge is that of framing a politics of alter-globalization that inspires activists and movement sympathizers to look beyond national theatres of contention and siloed, single issues. This requires the production and mobilization of counter-hegemonic knowledge: knowledge that critiques dominant political-economic practices and relations while promoting alternative strategies and visions that, as taken up in practice, might foster a cathartic shift from the episodic, fragmented resistances typical of subalternity to a shared ethico-political project that can become "a source of new initiatives" (Gramsci 1971, 367). Activist groups themselves generate such knowledge, through what Eyerman and Jamison (1991, 55) call their "cognitive praxis" (see also Chapter 14). However, a primary focus on protest means that their limited resources tend to be channelled into campaigns, protests and direct action, lobbying, and other immediate forms of collective action. In contrast, although they are aligned with transnational movement organizations (Carroll and Sapinski 2013), the groups investigated in this research focus their efforts not on collective action in the immediate sense but on the production and mobilization of alternative knowledge – a crucial resource for building the counter-publics that vitalize alter-globalization politics. These groups have sought to provide intellectual leadership for transnational movements and have come to occupy a unique niche within global justice politics. In the perspective of the SMS model, such intellectual leadership might be seen as contributing to the institutional durability of transnational movements, and thus to a transnational SMS.

As the imagery of "from below" and "from above" suggests, globalization is a complex, multifaceted phenomenon. Operating on many scales, it is the emergent product of various practices and processes involving flows of goods, services, ideas, technologies, cultural forms, and people (Kellner 2002). My focus here is specifically on *transnational* alternative policy groups. TAPGs are transnational in a double sense: they produce and mobilize knowledge about issues that transcend national borders, for constituencies in global civil society who cut across national borders. These groups engage in practices of alter-globalization by addressing political, economic, and cultural issues that cut across national borders and by operating in social spaces that also cut across borders. Their work is significantly transnational in both content and form.

TAPGs are the counter-hegemonic response to transnational hegemonic initiatives such as the Trilateral Commission, Bilderberg conferences, and the World Business Council for Sustainable Development (see Carroll 2010b; Richardson, Kakabadse, and Kakabadse 2011). Schematically, we can conceptualize think tanks of the left and right as sites of KPM embedded in opposing historical blocs or "global networks" (J. Smith 2008). Each organization develops and deploys knowledge, in conjunction with aligned movements and organizations, with the strategic intent to make its bloc more coherent and effective. Concretely, this entails quite different practices of knowledge production and mobilization. Neoliberal think tanks, generally committed to capitalism and hierarchy as principles of economic and political organization, fit easily into existing elite structures. Their messages, strategically focused on well-formed policy networks, are routinely conveyed by corporate media that share the same worldviews and values (Hackett and Zhao 1999). TAPGs, on the other hand, as collective intellectuals of an incipient global left, face the challenge of reaching a massive, diverse potential constituency, of creating new political methodologies that go against the grain in giving shape to emergent oppositional practices, and of participating in the *transformation rather than replication* of identities, social relations, and institutions (cf. Carroll 2007).

From the perspective of a social movement society, such centres of alternative knowledge production and mobilization furnish infrastructures, within alter-globalization politics, for sustained and ongoing movement activity. They might be seen as agencies and sites for institutionalizing movement activism, and with it a social movement society, on a global scale. By the same token, however, certain features of these groups, and of the transnational movements they support, might be seen as challenging the scenario of a social movement society, whether as originally formulated or in the current restatement (see Chapter 1).

A Preliminary Judgment Sample

The research program presented in this chapter is still in its early stages. My analysis here centres upon sixteen major TAPGs. Each satisfies three criteria that operationalize the concept of TAPG as a distinct agency of KPM, including: (1) the group's core function is *production and mobilization of knowledge*, including research, that challenges existing political-economic hegemonies and that presents alternatives, creates new paradigms, and so on; (2) a significant part of that KPM deals with *transnational issues* and speaks to *transnational counter-publics;* (3) the group engages a wide range of issues and is thus not specialized in just one domain (such as water, trade, or capital/labour relations).

These TAPGs were sampled from a larger set of eighty-four international organizations engaged in research and knowledge production, and the sample was stratified to include representation of major regions of the global North and South. The eighty-four were compiled from my own knowledge of the field plus a number of keyword searches in the online version of the *Yearbook of International Organizations,* which is the main source of information for this study. The sixteen selected organizations met the three specified selection criteria particularly well, compared with the other organizations, and that is why they are the focus of the sample of analysis. For instance, Amnesty International produces knowledge for social change but it is primarily a social movement organization (SMO) engaged in ongoing, information-rich political campaigns. Much the same holds for Friends of the Earth International, the world's largest network of grassroots environmentalist groups, which produces and mobilizes alternative knowledge in various forms but is focused on political action. University of Sussex–based Institute of Development Studies produces knowledge that occasionally challenges existing political-economic hegemonies and presents alternatives, but more typically holds fast to the political mainstream. Montreal-based Centre for Research on Globalization serves more as a website for alternative journalism than as a centre for research. Moscow-based Institute for Global Research and Social Movements orients itself primarily to activists based in Russia and only incidentally to other audiences. Vermont-based Global Justice Ecology Project takes up global ecological issues with a focus on forestry and climate change, for a largely American activist community. These kinds of groups can be thought of as "near-TAPGs." Admittedly, the line between them and the sixteen groups I have selected for close examination is somewhat blurry.

Table 12.1 offers a temporally sequenced list of the sixteen TAPGs. Four groups were formed in the mid-1970s, at the culmination of the 1960s protest wave and as the crisis of the postwar era set in. After 1976 there was a near-hiatus of a dozen years, during which just two TAPGs were established, both in 1984. In the past two decades or so, and particularly from the mid-1990s to 2005, TAPGs proliferated, as an intellectual aspect of the gathering global democracy movement but also as critical responses to the crises and contradictions of neoliberal globalization.

TABLE 12.1
Sixteen key transnational alternative policy groups

Established	Name	Acronym	On WSF IC
1974	Transnational Institute (Amsterdam)	TNI	Yes
1975	Third World Forum (Dakar)	TWF	*
1976	Centre de recherche et d'information pour le developpement (Paris)	CRID	Yes
1976	Tricontinental Centre (Louvain-la-Neuve, Belgium)	CETRI	Yes
1984	Development Alternatives with Women for a New Era (Manila)	DAWN	Yes
1984	Third World Network (Penang)	TWN	Yes
1989	Third World Institute (Montevideo)	ITeM	Yes
1990	Rosa Luxemburg Foundation (Berlin)	RosaLux	No
1994	International Forum on Globalization (San Francisco)	IFG	Yes
1995	Focus on the Global South (Bangkok)	Focus	Yes
1995	Z Communications (Woods Hole, MA)	ZCom	Yes
1997	Network Institute for Global Democratization (Helsinki)	NIGD	Yes
1998	People's Plan Study Group (Tokyo)	PPSG	No
2001	Centre for Civil Society (Durban)	CCS	No
2005	Alternatives International (Montreal)	Alter-Inter	Yes
2005	India Institute for Critical Action: Centre in Movement (New Delhi)	CACIM	No

* Participates on the WSFIC (World Social Forum International Council) through the World Forum for Alternatives, a joint venture with CETRI.

In this series, we can see that continental Western Europe has held the largest clutch of groups (five of sixteen). North America – heavily over-represented as a favoured site for hegemonic think tanks[2] – is comparatively underrepresented in the world of TAPGs. Perhaps this reflects, among other things, the relatively disorganized state of left politics in North America. Despite my purposive selection strategy in composing the sample, left think tanks of the South (comprising seven of the sixteen) are vastly underrepresented relative to the distribution of world population – the legacy of the material and cognitive injustices of colonialism and imperialism (de Sousa Santos 2006) is also evident in the overall distribution of international NGOs, which heavily favours the global North (Beckfield 2003). The *regionalized* character of counter-hegemonic KPM is expressed not only in the location of TAPGs but also in the scope of their work. Some groups (e.g., TNI, IFG, NIGD, RosaLux, and ZCom) aspire to a fully global purview. That all of them are based in Europe and North America suggests a continuing strain, within the world system's North Atlantic heartland, of cosmopolitan universalism in the framing of counter-hegemony. On the other hand, a number of mostly Southern-based TAPGs focus their efforts on issues and publics that are transnational yet also regional. For instance, CCS trains its efforts to a considerable degree on southern Africa; Focus has an Asian focus (as does PPSG); DAWN, TWN, ITeM, and TWF all take the global South as the target for their KPM.

The sixteen TAPGs are also diverse in political priorities, including the extent to which they focus their efforts on *prefigurative* KPM: cognitive praxis that takes up alternative futures, as distinct from critiquing existing reality. Groups such as TWN, CETRI, and ITeM focus on critique of current political-economic conditions; others consciously strive to construct counter-hegemonic projects that prefigure actual alternatives to neoliberal capitalism, as in TNI's New Politics initiative, Focus's "deglobalization" paradigm, IFG's post-capitalism project, and ZCom's "participatory economics" program. In prefigurative KPM, the point is not simply to critique mainstream policy or to offer policy alternatives designed to be implemented within existing institutional arrangements. Rather, prefigurative KPM consciously cultivates and promulgates radical alternatives that set in motion processes of transformation rather than replication. To accomplish this, alternative policy groups need to be in close dialogue with the social movements whose collective agency can drive transformative change; indeed, much of the work of counter-hegemonic KPM involves just such a dialogue – well exemplified by the extensive movement partnerships of groups like DAWN, TNI, and CCS.[3] In much the same way that participatory action research, as a methodology, subverts the distinction between knowledge production and social change (Reason 2011), in prefigurative KPM the line between research and political action blurs, as functions of the think tank merge with those of the social movement organization.

Importantly, these TAPGs are not all of a piece in their political projects. Focus places the "paradigm of deglobalization" at the centre of its social vision; other groups, such as NIGD (also IFG), hew more closely to a vision of democratic globalization, explicitly contrasted with neoliberal globalization. TWN trumpets Third World resurgence, reminiscent of the 1970s movement for a "new international economic order" that was choked by the rise of transnational neoliberalism (Bair 2009). Despite this diversity, some overarching points of convergence can be discerned, suggesting a master frame that informs the practice of these groups: (1) the critique of neoliberalism – of the class power and disparities it reinforces and the problematic implications of endless, unregulated accumulation by dispossession; (2) the importance of social justice and ecological sustainability as paramount values – a nascent social vision of global justice and sustainable human development (Magdoff and Foster 2011); (3) the belief that such an alternative future can be achieved only through grassroots democratic movements; (4) the ethical and strategic importance of North-South solidarity; and (5) the value of critical analysis that can inform effective and appropriate strategies for creating change. These elements of a master frame help specify the *content* of counter-hegemonic knowledge, as produced and mobilized by transnational alternative policy groups.

The Social Space of TAPGs

To gain a more systematic understanding of TAPGs as agents of alternative KPM, I examined websites for content pertaining to three issues: (1) framing the political project, (2) TAPG organizational form, and (3) location in the world system. Websites give us only one view of the life of a group, yet for TAPGs they are key vehicles of knowledge mobilization. Indeed, the increasing use of the Internet means that many TAPGs devote considerable resources to their online presence; thus, much can be learned from studying the texts and visuals that comprise each group's website. All sixteen TAPGs maintain websites with extensive pages, and make varying use of Web 2.0 interactivity. My comparative reading of the sixteen websites suggested five characterizations, documented in Table 12.2, that position TAPGs vis-à-vis each other in what we can think of as a social space.

Each characterization was coded as a binary, with "1" indicating the presence of the leading distinction (as shown in Table 12.2) and "0" its absence. Clearly, these categorizations oversimplify a complex reality. We know, for instance, that all groups engage in prefigurative KPM to some extent and offer some sort of critical ecological analysis. For some groups, however, these or other aspects of KPM are especially central, whereas for others they are much less so; it is a matter of predominance in the life of each group.

Figure 12.1 is the result of a multidimensional unfolding algorithm[4] that places the sixteen TAPGs into a two-dimensional space, according to our five characterizations. Both the groups and the attributes are represented as points. The proximities and distances in this joint space are optimized to reflect similarities and differences among the TAPGs on the five criteria.[5] Thus, groups that are positioned close to each other have a very similar profile across the attributes. The joint plot is simply of heuristic value in summarizing similarities and differences among the sixteen groups. What the

TABLE 12.2
TAPGs categorized by frames, organizational forms, and position

Characterization	Description
Framing issues	*How each group defines its alternative politics*
Prefiguration	Explicit emphasis in KPM is on envisaging and building post-capitalist alternatives, versus a concentration on critique and resistance to current hegemonies.
Ecology	Explicit emphasis in KPM is on critical analysis of the ecological crisis and possible remedies, versus more generic reference to ecological issues (as in support for "sustainable ways of life").
Organizational issues	*Group structure and membership*
Network	The group exists mostly as a network (typically with a small paid staff that coordinates things), versus a formal organization (with branches perhaps in other countries) whose staff produces and mobilizes knowledge.
International	Active or core participants are based in many countries, versus participants based predominantly in a single country.
Positional criterion	*Location of headquarters within the global order*
South	The group is headquartered in the South, versus in the North.

FIGURE 12.1
Joint space of sixteen TAPGs and five characterizations

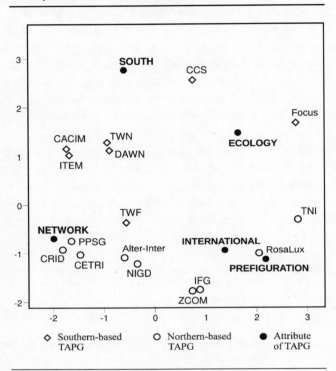

social space shows is how counter-hegemonic KPM is differentiated according to the discursive, organizational, and positional (North-South) characteristics of transnational alternative policy groups.

The space is partially structured by a North-South distinction that runs
roughly from top to bottom, with the Southern-based TAPGs gravitating
towards the top. Four groups whose KPM emphasizes post-capitalist alternatives (PREFIGURATION) are headquartered in the global North; we
see in the diagram that they tend to have substantially international core
memberships (INTERNATIONAL). TNI, IFG, RosaLux, and ZCom instan-
tiate these TAPGs of the North; their projects are explicitly post-capitalist
and their active constituencies are transnational. Compared with some of
their Southern counterparts, whose work often centres on urgent critiques
of and resistance to neoliberalism's new imperialism (Harvey 2003), these
groups have charted and made reasoned arguments for radical futures.

That said, two Southern-based groups (Focus and TWF) do offer prefigurative visions and both have international memberships – suggesting that there is a tendency for groups whose practices are more internationalized to frame their KPM in a prefigurative way, perhaps because their approach to alternatives is not so bound within national borders and the policy options of national states. A diverse array of TAPGs, based in both North and South, gives ecology pride of place in their critical analyses, including TNI, ZCom, and IFG in the North and Focus, CCS, DAWN, and TWN in the South. These TAPGs take up the ecological crisis as a salient theme and combine it with a critical analysis of neoliberal capitalism and its unfolding economic crisis.

A final distinction that organizes the social space of TAPGs contrasts networks with more formal organizations. As Jackie Smith (2008, 124) has found, a trend since the 1970s has been for transnational movement organizations to adopt more networked, coalitional structures. Indeed, eleven TAPGs are organized as networks, and two – the Third World Network (TWN) and the Network Institute for Global Democratization (NIGD) – call attention to this in their very names. Whereas TWF, ZCom, and IFG combine network organization with a strong prefigurative program of KPM, other networked TAPGs de-emphasize the construction of prefigurative visions in favour of the construction of *open spaces* for dialogue. CACIM, for instance, has been organized as a network and features among its initiatives an "open space process" to "critically explore and interrogate the concept and dynamics of open space even as we use such spaces to explore and advance thinking and action."[6] In contrast, Berlin-based RosaLux provides the best example of a highly organized global think tank of the left with a clear vision for post-capitalism and a commitment to theorizing and building alternative structures in the here and now. Affiliated since 1996 with Germany's Left Party, RosaLux comprises a global brain trust of democratic socialism, with offices on five continents.

The diversity of political frames, organizational forms, and spatial locations in this social space points to a larger reality. Taken as a whole, the sixteen TAPGs comprise a spatialized organizational field that takes in rhizomic "open spaces" for dialogical engagement (e.g., CACIM) as well as more arborescent groups (e.g., RosaLux), which may have greater capacity to articulate and advocate prefigurative alternatives (Evans 2008; Carroll 2010a). In much the same way that, for the right, an organizationally diverse array of policy groups creates a rich discursive field that "offers possibilities for nuanced debate and diverse action repertoires, all within the perimeters of permissible neoliberal discourse" (Carroll and Shaw 2001, 211), the set of TAPGs seems to offer a diversity of sites, North and South, for constructing counter-hegemonic alternatives, a cognitive praxis that requires both open spaces and more strategically oriented organizations engaged in prefigurative KPM and collective will formation. But that very diversity also points to the difficulty in combining both aspects of counter-hegemonic politics – the rhizomic and the arborescent – in a single place, a classic conundrum that has beset many left parties as well as, more recently, the World Social Forum, with its perennial debates over its identity as "open space" or "movement of movement" (de Sousa Santos 2008; Worth and Buckley 2009).

Networks of Transnational Policy Groups

In the study of hegemonic policy groups, sociologists have employed network analysis to map the relations that link such groups to each other and to corporate elites (Carroll 2010b, 226–27). By pulling top corporate directors onto their boards, the World Business Council for Sustainable Development, the Trilateral Commission, and other transnational policy groups play especially integrative roles, linking business leaders to leaders and intellectuals from other fields and creating a unified voice within a discursive field enriched by the diverse transnational initiatives of the policy groups. Networks have also been shown to be both prerequisites for and emergent elements of social movements (Diani 2011; see also Chapter 11); hence, a conception of transnational counter-hegemony as a "historical bloc" of aligned socio-political forces directs our attention to the activist networks that TAPGs help sustain and enrich (J. Smith 2008).

The network of TAPGs needs to be approached as a formation that is both multi-tiered (existing both at the level of individual activist-intellectuals and at the level of groups and organizations) and multiplex in the nature of its social relations (consisting in various kinds of ties). In Figure 12.2, we see the inter-organizational relations as of summer 2011, with Southern-based TAPGs shown in grey and Northern-based TAPGs shown in black. Organization-to-organization ties, which may range from active collaboration in ongoing projects to indicating an affinity through a website link, have been gleaned both from listings in the *Yearbook of International Organizations (YIO)*, a well-established source of information on the organizations of global civil society (H. Katz 2006; J. Smith 2008), and from TAPG websites. The depth and strength of these can be difficult to assess from the information at hand, and the mapping is almost certainly incomplete, since websites (and *YIO* listings) vary in the extent to which they report partners.[7]

FIGURE 12.2

Ties among sixteen TAPGs

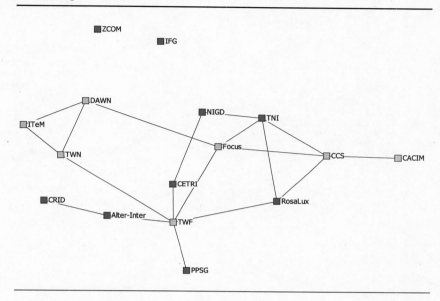

Although fourteen of the sixteen groups form a weakly connected component, the sociogram shows that Northern-based TAPGs tend not to engage in extensive inter-organizational networking. The two US-based groups, ZCom and IFG, are isolates, and Tokyo-based PPSG is brought into the network only by TWF's nomination. Moreover, Northern-based TAPGs active in the network tend to link up with other Northern-based groups, a finding consistent with Beckfield's observation (2003) that core-based international NGOs (INGOs) are far more central in the global polity than INGOs based outside the core.

If inter-organizational relations show some evidence of North-South cleavage, the direct participation of 11 of our 16 groups on the International Council (IC) of the Word Social Forum mitigates this disjuncture (see Figure 12.3). The IC is the World Social Forum's planning group, and has representation from 129 organizations.[8] For TAPGs, it is clearly the great attractor – a key site for dialogue and collaboration across groups, and thus for the formation of subaltern counter-publics. Adding membership ties to the WSF IC (the round node) pulls all 16 TAPGs into a connected configuration, corroborating findings from surveys of activists in attendance

FIGURE 12.3
Ties among sixteen TAPGs and the World Social Forum International Council

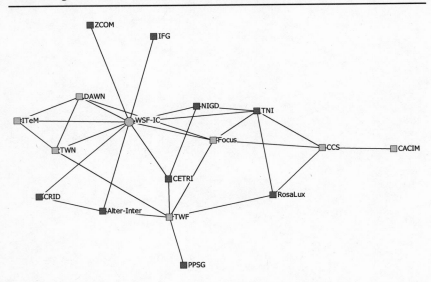

about the integrative importance of the WSF for the global left (E. Reese et al. 2008).

As a multi-tiered formation, the network of TAPGs is constituted both by the relations among groups and by cross-memberships and other practices of activist-intellectuals that traverse group boundaries.

Figure 12.4 adds to our earlier sociogram the activists closely associated with any of the sixteen TAPGs, as triangular nodes, showing ties created by overlapping group memberships – when an activist plays a central role in two (or more) groups. Although such cross-membership is rather common in the directorates of the transnational capitalist class (Carroll 2010b), it is rare in this alter-globalization network. Among core activists, most groups have no overlapping memberships with other groups; individuals with cross-memberships number just five. These activists knit six of the sixteen TAPGs into a connected network, but compared to tightly knit corporate-elite networks, the sparseness is striking, though not surprising. In class terms, it of course reflects massive resource disparities, but also the difference between a hierarchically organized minority and a largely disorganized majority whose structures are more horizontal. The former is inherently easier to pull together via ties among the relative few at the top; the

FIGURE 12.4

Inter-organizational and interpersonal ties among sixteen TAPGs

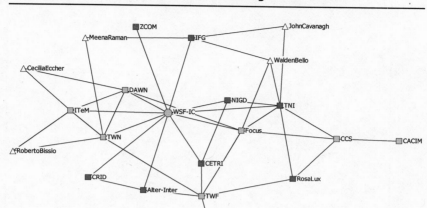

latter – what de Sousa Santos (2008) has termed "a global left" – inheres in a multitude of loosely organized social circles, a rhizomic form that minimizes the likelihood of very many overlapping memberships. Indeed, the IFG and TNI are both loci of overlapping memberships in great part due to the high-profile "fellows" (Walden Bello being a prime example) who compose their boards, an arrangement that formally resembles elite organizations of the transnational capitalist class.

The global network of TAPGs is still more than a set of cross-memberships and organizational linkages, however; it is continually instantiated through the practices of activist-intellectuals as they cooperate and collaborate. Consider as an example the thirty-eight "Assemblies of Convergence" on major cross-cutting themes that comprised the final day of the 2011 World Social Forum. Each assembly was organized by multiple sponsoring groups. The point of these assemblies was to go beyond "open space" discussions and to formulate strategies and action plans for creating change. Seven of our sixteen TAPGs co-organized a total of nine assemblies, as depicted in Figure 12.5, where the lines link organizations to the WSF assemblies they co-organized. In this sociogram, TAPGs are shown as black squares, other co-organizers of assemblies are shown as grey squares, and the assemblies are shown as white circles. Montreal-based

FIGURE 12.5
Assemblies of Convergence co-organized by seven TAPGs at the World Social Forum, 2011

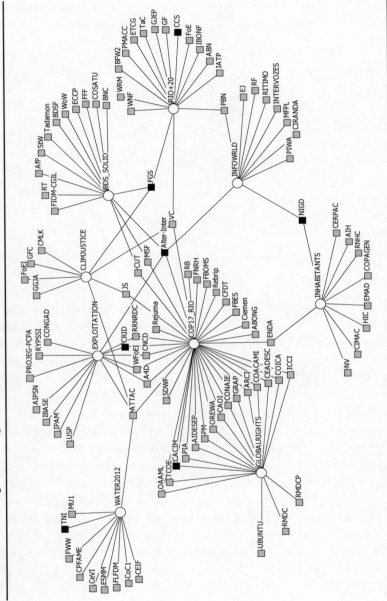

Alternatives International, itself a coalition of seven groups, co-organized four assemblies; Focus co-organized three; CACIM, CRID, and NIGD co-organized two each; and TNI and CCS each co-organized one. Here we can discern the facilitative role that several TAPGs played, spanning political domains – as in CACIM's co-sponsorship of the assemblies on the Global Network for Collective Rights of the Peoples ("GLOBALRIGHTS" in the sociogram) and the Road Map of Struggles: Cop 17, Rio + 20 and After ("COP17_RIO" in the sociogram). Equally, it is clear that at the WSF, TAPGs were joined by many movement groups playing similarly facilitative roles – Paris-based ATTAC, São Paulo–based Via Campesina, Amsterdam-based Friends of the Earth International, Manila-based Jubilee South, and Oxford, UK–based Pambazuka News, to cite a few key ones in the network. At the WSF, TAPGs collaborate with a diverse set of movement groups and NGOs, creating a horizontally networked counter-public and thereby extending an aspect of the social movement society onto a transnational plane.

A particularly important instance of this phenomenon, which I take to be integral to the formation of a transnational counter-hegemonic bloc, has been ZCom's "Zspace" site, an online "community of people committed to social change" who number in the thousands, participate in a host of virtual forums, and share commentaries and various forms of art. Earlier, we saw that ZCom does not appear to have inter-organizational ties to other TAPGs, nor are its key protagonists (a small collective that includes Lydia Sargent and Michael Albert) active in other TAPGs. In the network of inter-organizational relations, ZCom is effectively an isolate, although it does participate on the WSF International Council. However, if we consider the network of Zspace authors and the TAPGs in which they are active, as in Figure 12.6, we find extensive participation in this transnational counter-public – from TNI and RosaLux as well as CCS, Focus, and IFG.

As a site for producing and mobilizing counter-hegemonic knowledge, Zspace pulls together the work of activist-intellectuals from eleven of our sixteen TAPGs (including ZCom itself), linking up such high-profile contributors as Vandana Shiva, Patrick Bond, Samir Amin, Hilary Wainwright, Susan George, Gregory Wilpert, Jai Sen, and the ubiquitous Walden Bello.[9] The example of ZCom shows that TAPGs positioned on the margins of the global network according to one criterion may be well connected according to another. The niches TAPGs have come to occupy within the organizational field of alter-globalization entail specific practices of knowledge production and mobilization, creating a variety of ties that position each TAPG within the wider field of global civil society.

FIGURE 12.6

The network of ZCom contributors active in TAPGs, Fall 2011

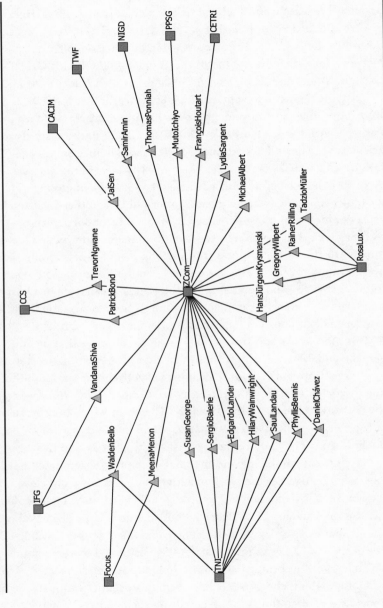

Conclusion

These preliminary findings point towards a nascent historical bloc, a transnational network of counter-publics organically articulated to a range of movements opposing neoliberal globalization (if not capitalism). As producers of alternative knowledge, TAPGs occupy a complex social space that is differentiated by varying political projects, organizational forms, and locations in the global system. However much it is overshadowed by the far more extensive and established bloc that sustains capitalist hegemony, the fledgling formation of such a transnational counter-hegemonic bloc is important not only for its transformative political potential but for the implications it carries vis-à-vis the SMS model.

If we consider the main hypotheses advanced by Meyer and Tarrow (1998, 4) – on the increasing frequency and recurrence of protest, the expanding range of protest constituencies and their claims, and the increasingly professionalized, institutionalized, and conventional character of protest within advanced democracies – a focus on TAPGs as collective intellectuals for transnational activism supports some of these assertions but raises questions about others. In TAPGs we find an expanding collection of relatively durable transnational organizations that employ sophisticated skill sets in producing and mobilizing knowledge for a range of activist movements and counter-publics that has definitely expanded since the rise of alter-globalization politics in the 1990s. TAPGs offer cognitive resources for transnational social movements and for global civil society; indeed, they seem to provide a political-cultural infrastructure for the social movement society at a transnational level. Two aspects of this analysis complicate our understanding of the SMS model, however.

First, the approach taken here steps away from the tendency to centre the analysis on (nation) states (Magnusson 1997, 102–5) – the society in the SMS model. Transnational alternative policy groups do not confine their activities and associated networks within the borders of states, nor do they primarily address governments. They do not fit *within* social movement societies as conventionally understood; instead, they operate across and even beyond them in prefiguring a world beyond the normalized capitalist democracies that the SMS thesis takes for granted (for similar critiques, see also Chapters 8, 13, and 14). In pointing *beyond*, spatially and temporally, they also point up the provincialism in the SMS model as an account of the normalization of movement politics within the United States, in a specific era.[10]

There is a paradox at work here, between the transnational and the national, which merits further investigation. The focus of TAPGs on global civil society may free them in some measure from narrowly state-centred thinking and action, yet the persistence of what Nancy Fraser (2005) terms the Westphalian inter-state system reproduces the position of national states as the apparent seats of political power. In practice, much of the movement activism that TAPGs inform and support is carried out by nationally based SMOs whose limited resources are often focused within and upon those states. As they operate in transnational spaces, TAPGs face the challenge of establishing the relevance of their analyses and initiatives to local, on-the-ground movement actors, through tangible, dialogical collaborations. Master frames of global justice may resonate only weakly with local issues (Snow and Benford 1992); to put the matter pragmatically, their relevancies need to be demonstrated. As Karl Marx (1844) observed, theory, including the critical discourses that TAPGs produce and circulate, "becomes a *material force* as soon as it has gripped the *masses*" (emphasis in original). The corollary is that political ideas that remain detached from practice are little more than what Gramsci called "castles in the air" (quoted in Germino 1990, 19).

In field work underway at several of the groups featured here, I am exploring the tensions between the transnational framing work of TAPGs and the national theatres of contention within which many SMOs associated with them function. Interviews have revealed that as an alternative to embedding KPM at local/national levels of movement formation, some TAPGs engage with UN institutions and other organizations of "global governance." For instance, three of our TAPGs have been core participants in the Civil Society Reflection Group on Global Development Perspectives, which produced the report *No Future without Justice* as a special issue of *Development Dialogue* in June 2012. Widely distributed at UN-sponsored forums, the report called for a revival of the principles and values of the Rio Declaration on Environment and Development and the UN Millennium Declaration. This approach to mobilizing alternative knowledge resembles the scenario of the SMS model, but in a global field where TAPGs and other collective actors engage with intergovernmental organizations, holding them and national states to account. Such a scaling-up of the SMS to the global level contains all the possibilities of routinization and institutionalization in the original SMS thesis, along with the structural bias, noted earlier, that tends to reproduce a core/periphery divide within global civil society.

Second, although TAPGs can be seen, in accordance with the SMS model, as *professionalized* in their activism, their professionalism does not lead in any simple sense towards conventionality. As we have seen, they are not exclusively, or even primarily, focused on the "politics of demand" (Day 2005), whether through protest or lobbying. Instead, TAPGs show commitments to the generative politics of prefiguration – that is, constructing alternative knowledges, practices, and policies outside of the dominant political-economic paradigm. The pull of statist politics and engagement with intergovernmental organizations may be strong for some TAPGs, but the trajectory does not appear to be towards co-optation and interest-group competition for positional goods. Rather, these groups seem to be engaged, along with various movement organizations, in a more transformative praxis. TAPGs do, as in the SMS model, provide durable organizational loci for cognitive praxis, but their projects appear to point not to institutional capture and normalization but to generative politics that, in a transnational context, aims to transcend the institutional structure of capitalist modernity. This prospect, telegraphed in the World Social Forum's slogan "Another world is possible," is quite distinct from the scenario of institutionalization within national social movement societies.

In short, the example of TAPGs as collective intellectuals for transnational social movements invites us to rethink the Weberian narrative in the SMS thesis, in which professionalization carries with it tendencies towards institutionalization, co-optation, and even perhaps oligarchy. With their emphasis upon the production of knowledge that critiques, empowers, promotes democratic participation, and prefigures another world, TAPGs may be seen as sites for *a counter-hegemonic form of post-elite professionalization*. As cognitive agencies for alter-globalization, TAPGs point up the limits of the social movement society, a formulation that was developed within liberal social movement theory and focused exclusively on advanced capitalist democracy (specifically the United States), before the emergence of globalization-from-below as a visible phenomenon with the 1999 "Battle in Seattle" (Bornstein 2009). It should not be assumed that the emergence of durable organizations and practices of transnational counter-hegemony portends an eventual process of co-optation, institutionalization, and integration into hegemonic structures. The narrative remains to be written; hence, the prospect of system-transforming change should not be closed off analytically.

In these ways, the study of TAPGs as sites of alternative knowledge production and mobilization in global civil society complicates the original

SMS formulation and opens onto a broader conceptualization of movements in the early twenty-first century and what may be at stake for them and for us.

Notes

This chapter draws upon two previously published articles (Carroll 2013, 2014). The research has been supported by a grant from the Social Sciences and Humanities Research Council of Canada.

1 For readers interested in more detailed accounts, the information-rich websites of these and other transnational activist organizations are worth consulting. See, consecutively, http://www.foei.org/, http://viacampesina.org/en/, http://www.ourworld isnotforsale.org/, and http://www.forumsocialmundial.org.br/.

2 Of the 400-odd free market think tanks that make up the global network supported by the Atlas Economic Research Foundation, 177 are based in the United States and Canada and 85 are based in Europe (http://www.atlasnetwork.org/partners/global -directory).

3 For RosaLux, the dialogue of prefiguration includes interlocutors in movements as well as activists within Germany's Left Party, for which it serves as an intellectual centre. Other TAPGs operate at a distance from formal political parties.

4 Namely, prefscal, accessed within the Statistical Package for the Social Sciences (SPSS). Often used in the analysis of individual preferences, multidimensional unfolding treats the rows and columns of a n*m matrix as two classes of objects (here, TAPGs and their attributes) and fits them into a space of reduced dimensionality in which objects with similar profiles are proximate to each other.

5 For clarity's sake, in a few cases I have slightly shifted the position of groups.

6 http://cacim.net/twiki/tiki-index.php?page=Overview.

7 These inter-organizational relations are directed lines: a given nomination by one TAPG may or may not be reciprocated by the other.

8 A full list of International Council members is available at http://www.forumsocial mundial.org.br/main.php?id_menu=3_2_1&cd_language=2.

9 Since data were collected for this chapter, ZCom has integrated Zspace into a broader initiative: the IOPS Project. IOPS (International Organization for a Participatory Society) is taking shape as "a revolutionary organization that aims to win a better world through flexibly exploring and advocating long term vision, building the seeds of the future in the present, empowering the lives of its members, organizing in an internally classless and self-managing way, and winning improvements, now, in current society even as we constantly seek a new society for the future" (http://www.iopsociety.org/).

10 As Michael Burawoy (2009, 37) has observed, "U.S. sociologists [are] accustomed to thinking of their sociology as universal, but from outside the United States our sociology can look quite provincial, expressing the peculiarities of our exotic society."

13

Wilderness Revisited

Canadian Environmental Movements and the Eco-Politics of Special Places

MARK C.J. STODDART

The social movement society perspective typically judges success on the ability of movements to translate their claims into changes to law or policy. This framework is less attentive to the ways in which movements shape culture (see Chapters 12 and 14). While the desire to effect change within economic or political structures drives a great deal of social movement activity, this does not exhaust the reasons that social movements emerge, mobilize, and make claims to the public. While more difficult to measure, many (if not most) social movements also seek to transform cultural values, beliefs, and collective identities (Giugni 1998; Rochon 1998; Castells 2004). The social movement society is characterized by the increased professionalization of social movements, or by the use of social movement tactics by an increasingly broad range of actors (see the Introduction and Chapter 1). As Corrigall-Brown's work (2012) demonstrates, an emphasis on highly professionalized and institutionalized movements deflects attention from much of the everyday activism that goes on in the social movement society. Similarly, it is worth examining the cultural work of social movements and how this contributes to social change.

Research in a range of fields – including history, sociology, political science, environmental studies, and geography – demonstrates that discourses of wilderness have been well used to convey claims about the importance of nature (e.g., see Wilson 1998; Nash 2001; Magnusson and Shaw 2002; Reed

2003; Cormier and Tindall 2005; Schrepfer 2005; Barman 2007; Cronin 2011). Images of wilderness are a standard part of the cultural toolkit environmental movements use to provoke a shift in public understandings of environment/society interaction. While the wilderness ideal is not the sole property of environmental movements, it has been repeatedly used by environmentalists, particularly as they have argued for the protection of special or threatened places from extractive development (i.e., forestry or mining) or industrialization. This chapter approaches environmentalists' cultural work by examining how ideas of wilderness are used in conflicts over ski resort development at Jumbo Pass, British Columbia, and over off-highway vehicle (OHV) use in the Tobeatic Wilderness Area, Nova Scotia.

If built, the Jumbo Glacier Resort will be the only year-round ski resort in North America. Conflict over the development has been going on for over twenty years, involving resort developers, environmental organizations, and a succession of New Democratic Party (NDP) and Liberal provincial governments. Major points of conflict include the desire for local community control over new development and potential impacts on local wildlife, particularly grizzly bear populations. The provincial government approved the resort in March 2012 and subsequently passed legislation allowing for the creation of a Mountain Resort Municipality at Jumbo. After twenty years of conflict, this was a major turning point, which sparked a new wave of opposition by environmental movements and the Ktunaxa First Nation.

The Tobeatic Wilderness Area is home to old-growth forests (which are rare in Nova Scotia) and endangered wildlife. It has long been a popular destination for canoeing, hunting, and fishing, with professional outfitters operating in the area as tourist guides. The Tobeatic was protected through a Protected Areas Management Plan in 2006. In the years leading up to this, environmental groups and recreational associations mobilized to exclude OHV use in the area. OHV use was targeted because it risks damage to soil and vegetation, it contributes to air and water pollution, and its noise pollution may disrupt local wildlife.

As observed in Chapter 5, different groups within the same social movement "specialize" in terms of the tactics they use and the identity they present to the public, and have different capacities to benefit from the changes that characterize social movement societies. Both Chapters 5 and 11 focus on well-established, large environmental organizations in their analysis. By contrast, the cases examined here are regional conflicts located in rural areas and largely driven by local organizations. Admittedly, they may lack the drama and spectacle of national movements or mass protest. However, as McAdam and Boudet (2012) note, the disproportionate focus of social movement scholars on national and transnational – and typically urban – movements has created a "stylized view" of social movements that does not reflect the local activism that constitutes most social movement activity. This paired case study, which is grounded in local and rural activism, helps correct this stylized view and also offers broader theoretical insights. In particular, by linking textual analysis and interviews with core activists, we gain a better understanding of the tensions and incongruities

self-presentation, media representa-
ts' understanding of their issues.
is analysis is how the Tobeatic and
andscapes in environmental organiz-
age. This question provides an entry
eraction with wilderness that are val-
Drawing on interviews with environ-
s, the second question concerns how
f wilderness in relation to their cam-
Tobeatic. This enables us to examine
wilderness offer a framework for an
sses some of the shortcomings inher-

Canadian environmental conflict in order to highlight the importance of the cultural dimensions of the social movement society. Although effecting social change within political and economic structures is important to most social movements, movements are also concerned with altering the dominant norms and values of the broader society in which they operate (Giugni 1998; Rochon 1998). A cross-national comparison of the trajectory of environmentalism illustrates how environmental movements assume different cultural forms as they emerge within different political contexts and evolve over time. Through their analysis of Sweden, Denmark, and the Netherlands, Jamison and colleagues (1990, 8) distinguish between movements that have more of a "success orientation," or focus on "the achievement of specific aims," and those that have more of a "value orientation," or focus on "the expression of specific values and the following of a way of life." Among contemporary environmental movements, those oriented around 100-mile diets, green consumerism, or voluntary simplicity are examples of value-oriented forms of environmentalism that seek to provoke cultural change by asking individuals to shift their worldview and behaviour in relation to the environment.

The success of social movements is often measured by changes to policy, but other key outcomes are cultural shifts in collective identity and social values. As Castells (2004) argues, environmentalism and feminism are exemplars of social movements that have had profound cultural influence over the past several decades. Whether or not people adopt "social movement identities" by self-identifying as environmentalists or feminists, many of the beliefs and norms that originated within these movements about the equality of women or the status of the environment have filtered out from social movements and have become ingrained within broader societies.

The protection of wilderness, understood as untouched land where the "absence of men [sic] and the presence of wild animals is assumed" has long been a key component of North American environmentalism (Nash 2001, 3). In environmental thought, wilderness is often idealized as someplace free from the degradations of industrial society. It offers a refuge from the rationalized rhythms and routines of modernity (Plumwood 1998; Cannavo 2007). During the late nineteenth and early twentieth century, this idea of wilderness was embodied by the project of creating national parks and promoting nature-oriented tourism (Jasen 1995; MacEachern 2001; Dawson 2004; Cronin 2011). Environmental organizations throughout Canada routinely draw on symbols of wilderness, including large animals, uninhabited mountains, or giant trees, in campaigns to protect places defined as ecologically unique, special, or particularly well suited to outdoor recreation (Cormier and Tindall 2005; Mortimer-Sandilands 2009; Vander Kloet 2009).

The wilderness ideal resonates with many Canadians. In a 2008 survey, for example, "wilderness" was among the top ten symbols that define Canada (Ipsos 2008). Despite the cultural resonance of wilderness, however, the limitations of the wilderness ideal are well rehearsed by environmental sociologists, historians, and geographers. An emphasis on wilderness led many Canadian environmental organizations to be slow to recognize and mobilize against other environmental harms, such as urban air and water pollution (Wilson 1998). In the United States, environmental justice activists and scholars have been critical of large, wilderness-focused environmental organizations, charging them with neglecting the disproportionate burden of ecological degradation and risk placed on working class and ethnic minority communities (Agyeman, Bullard, and Evans 2003; Mohai, Pellow, and Roberts 2009). Despite its success as a cultural frame and mobilization tool, the wilderness ideal impacts the environmental movement by narrowing its range of potential supporters and by limiting its ability to do movement bridging with social justice organizations (Haluza-DeLay and Fernhout 2011).

Other environmental scholars argue that wilderness is a cultural construction that often obscures long histories of Aboriginal inhabitation of "untouched" wilderness landscapes, or ignores the forced removal of inhabitants from protected wilderness areas (Willems-Braun 1996–97; MacEachern 2001; Laudati 2010). For these authors, the wilderness ideal reinforces an ecologically problematic culture/nature binary. Even as the focus is on the protection of "untouched" nature in demarcated protected zones (national or provincial parks), the normal operation of capitalist resource extraction and pollution proceeds apace beyond the boundaries of wilderness areas (Cronon 1995; Luke 1997; Cannavo 2007). To adopt a term from Bruno Latour, the cultural construct of wilderness that is central to much environmental politics works to "purify" connections between social systems and nature, thereby defining them as disconnected systems (Latour 1993).

The social movement society perspective emphasizes the institutionalization and diffusion of social movement forms, tactical repertoires, and modes of social interaction. Research carried out using this framework conceptualizes movement success primarily in terms of policy change. However, this perspective downplays the significant cultural work that social movements engage in and neglects the push for cultural change that is a component of many activists' desire for social change. Other chapters in this volume discuss the use of digital media by the Occupy Movement (Chapter 1), the use of broadcast media by evangelical Christianity (Chapter 2), and the use of "duelling websites" and "duelling media campaigns" in conflicts over the Alberta oil sands (Chapter 14). The present analysis examines the cultural work of environmental movements mobilized against the Jumbo Glacier Resort ski development in British Columbia and off-highway vehicle use in Nova Scotia. Two questions guide the analysis. First, how is the wilderness ideal used in environmental organization websites and mass media coverage of these two environmental movement conflicts at Jumbo Pass and the Tobeatic Wilderness? Second, how are the special places that are the objects of environmental mobilization understood and interpreted by core environmental activists? There certainly has been "trouble with wilderness" (Cronon 1995), in terms of what this cultural framework blocks out from environmental politics. However, an analysis that links textual analysis to interviews with core activists suggests a more complex model for an ecopolitics of wilderness protection. In sketching out the possibilities for a more nuanced vision for wilderness-oriented environmentalism, this analysis demonstrates the value of broadening the social movement society perspective so that it is more attentive to the cultural work of social movements.

Methodology

The social movement society perspective has paid relatively little attention to the cultural work done by social movements. This gap is addressed here through an analysis of the cultural meanings attached to the objects of environmental claims in conflicts over Jumbo Pass and the Tobeatic Wilderness. This analysis draws on a textual analysis of mass media coverage and environmental organization websites, as well as semi-structured interviews with core members of environmental organizations.

The Factiva online database was used to sample articles from the *Globe and Mail* and the *National Post*, Canada's two leading national newspapers. A keyword search of the terms "Jumbo Pass," "Jumbo Glacier," and "Jumbo Resort" produced a sample of twenty-five articles about Jumbo Pass (sixteen from the *Globe and Mail* and nine from the *National Post*), published between 1983 and 2009. Almost all were published after 2003. A similar keyword search for the term "Tobeatic" produced a sample of only nine articles (eight from the *Globe and Mail* and one from the *National Post*), published between 1992 and 2005, indicating that this issue rarely received national media coverage. Factiva was also used to sample articles on Jumbo Pass from the *Vancouver Sun*, the larger of two British Columbia newspapers with province-wide distribution. Ten articles were found and they were published between 2002 and 2005. A Factiva keyword search of the Halifax *Chronicle-Herald*, the major daily newspaper of Nova Scotia, produced a sample of eighty-eight articles on the Tobeatic Wilderness, published between 1999 and 2009.

A sampling frame for environmental organization websites was constructed from all of the organizations cited in the media coverage. Using an approach that might be termed "Internet ethnography," detailed notes were written on all of the organization websites that had relevant content

(Hewson 2008; Hine 2008). Google searching was used to locate websites for these organizations, resulting in a sample of four websites related to Jumbo Pass and eight related to the Tobeatic.

Representatives of the environmental organizations cited in the media coverage were contacted by mail and e-mail and asked to participate in the interview phase of the research. Between March and May 2010, semi-structured interviews were carried out with five Jumbo Pass activists and three Tobeatic activists. While this is a small sample, all of the interviewees are core activists who dedicate a significant amount of time and effort to these campaigns, rather than rank-and-file members, whose participation tends to be limited to financial donations or occasional participation (Stoddart and Tindall 2010).

The newspaper articles, website notes, and interview transcripts were imported to NVivo software for qualitative analysis, where they were manually coded and analyzed. Top-level coding categories focused on areas such as political interaction and environmental governance, news sources, outdoor recreation and the environment, protest tactics, and representations of nature. Each top-level coding category was subdivided into more precise categories. Coding was carried out separately for the different data sources (mass media texts, websites, interviews) and cases (Jumbo Pass and the Tobeatic), and results were integrated analytically using a series of qualitative comparison tables.

The mass media analysis involved analyzing themes and news sources as "discourse networks," which adopt the tools of social network analysis to map links among elements of discourse, or between discourses and social actors (Mohr 1998). News sources, identified by organizational affiliation, make up one mode of network data and are represented by square nodes. Discursive themes, represented by circular nodes, make up the second mode of network data (see Figures 13.1 and 13.2). Node size reflects the centrality of sources and themes within media coverage of the Jumbo Pass and Tobeatic conflicts. Ties between nodes show that a theme has been used by a news source, while tie thickness reflects how often each news source uses a particular theme.

The first question that guides this analysis is: How are the Tobeatic and Jumbo Pass defined as wilderness landscapes in environmental organization websites and mass media coverage? These environmental conflicts are engaged through an analysis of environmentalist-produced web content and coverage from key national and provincial newspapers, as well as through interviews with core members of key organizations involved in these two conflicts. The second guiding question is: How do activists interpret the meaning of wilderness in relation to their campaigns to protect Jumbo Pass and the Tobeatic? This question is engaged through interviews with core members of key organizations involved in these two conflicts. This multiple-method approach goes beyond an analysis of mediated discourses about ecopolitics to gain insight into environmentalists' interpretations of the places that are the objects of their claims. This combination of approaches enables us to grasp the complexities of the cultural work done by social movements, which has been underexamined in the social movement society literature.

Images of Wilderness in Environmentalist Websites

Environmental organization websites provide an entry point for examining how Jumbo Pass and the Tobeatic are represented as objects of environmentalist mobilization. Much of the claims making related to Jumbo Pass focuses on calls for local decision making and frames the development as a breach of local democracy. At the same time, Jumbo Pass is defined as home to grizzly bears, and much of the focus of the websites is on the need to protect these large animals and their environments from human intrusion. While grizzlies serve as iconic figures of mountain wilderness, environmental organization websites also argue that the ski resort will negatively impact other species, including mountain caribou, mountain goat, wolverine, bull trout, cutthroat trout, and lynx. While hiking, backcountry skiing, and heli-skiing appear as appropriate modes of interaction with the Jumbo Pass landscape, this wilderness and wildlife environment requires protection from the permanent infrastructure of ski resort development.

Environmental organization websites also define the Tobeatic as wilderness. The importance of the Tobeatic is asserted with reference to its size (it is said to be Nova Scotia's largest wilderness area) and with reference to its role as endangered wildlife habitat. Non-motorized recreation, including hiking and canoeing, is defined as an appropriate mode of interaction with this landscape. OHV use is deemed an ecologically illegitimate form of recreation, due to air, water, and noise pollution, as well as soil damage in forests and wetlands. During the campaign to protect the Tobeatic, activists also mobilized against a proposed quartz mine. Although the mine would have been located outside the boundaries of the Tobeatic, it was seen as a risk to the wilderness values of the Tobeatic because of its impacts on adjacent waterways.

Images of Wilderness in Mass Media Coverage

Both the Jumbo Pass and Tobeatic landscapes are defined as wilderness and wildlife landscapes in environmental organization websites. Environment-alists make claims on behalf of wildlife and wilderness values in opposition to ski resort development and OHV use, which are defined as ecologically illegitimate modes of outdoor recreation. Turning to provincial and national news coverage of these conflicts allows us to gauge how successful environmentalists were at conveying these cultural symbols within the mass-mediated public sphere. Figures 13.1 and 13.2 are two-mode social network diagrams that map connections between news sources and key discursive themes within the news coverage of these conflicts. These figures provide an overview of which social actors and which discourses have most success-fully entered media portrayals of these environmental conflicts.

As Figure 13.1 illustrates, the Jumbo Pass conflict is largely defined by three key groups of actors: environmentalists, the ski industry (primarily the Jumbo Glacier Resort developer), and the British Columbia provincial Liberal government. The main themes linked to environmentalists are the negative environmental impacts of the resort, local decision making, grizzly bear impacts, and characterizations of Jumbo Pass as wilderness. As Figure 13.2 illustrates, the Tobeatic conflict is dominated by two key groups of

FIGURE 13.1

News sources (by organizational affiliation) and key themes, Jumbo Pass

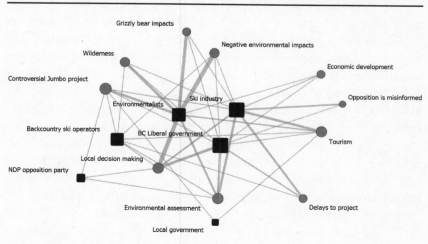

FIGURE 13.2
News sources (by organizational affiliation) and key themes,
Tobeatic Wilderness

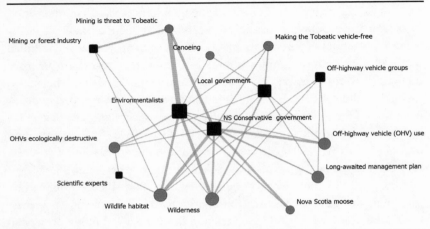

actors: environmentalists and the Nova Scotia provincial Conservative government. The main themes linked to environmentalists are characterizations of the Tobeatic as wilderness and wildlife habitat, the environmental risks of a proposed (and defeated) quartz mine outside the boundaries of the Tobeatic, and the negative impacts of OHV use.

Environmentalists successfully access the media as key news sources. Stories in national and provincial news outlets circulate environmentalists' claims, which characterize the Jumbo Pass and Tobeatic landscapes as wilderness and wildlife landscapes that require protection from ecologically inappropriate recreational use. In both cases, media coverage echoes environmental organization web content. In media coverage of the Jumbo Pass conflict, the discourse of Jumbo Pass as wilderness is countered by a discourse of Jumbo as an ideal ski hill, articulated by resort proponents and supporters. The idea of Jumbo Pass as wilderness is further disturbed by a counter-discourse of Jumbo Pass as not-wilderness because there is a history of logging in the area. Whereas the wilderness character of Jumbo Pass is sometimes contested in media coverage, the construction of the Tobeatic as a wilderness place is not disputed by environmentalist opponents.

Environmentalist opponents, including ski resort developers and OHV users' groups, gain access to the media. However, they are less central to media discourse networks than environmentalist sources, and their claims are less central than claims about wilderness and wildlife values. Environmentalists' cultural interpretations of contested environments, as articulated through organization-produced websites, are diffused to bystander publics through provincial and national media. As such, both cases represent successful environmental movement outcomes.

The successful diffusion of movement claims through the media obscures other ways of making sense of Jumbo Pass and the Tobeatic. First Nations groups (Mi'kmaq in Nova Scotia, and Ktunaxa and Sinixt in British Columbia) have interests in land use decision making, yet are marginal to media constructions of these places as pristine or untouched environments.[1] Also, although focusing narrowly on Jumbo Pass and the Tobeatic and calling for their protection makes sense strategically, the emphasis on wilderness protection brackets out questions about appropriate and inappropriate modes of recreation and tourism development outside these special places.

Finally, small-scale forms of recreation, such as canoeing, hiking, or backcountry skiing, are valued as ecologically acceptable modes of interacting with wilderness environments. Adopting a narrow focus on what happens inside the boundaries of these special places distracts our attention from the intimate connections between these modes of outdoor recreation and broader networks of car and airplane travel that link local wilderness environments to nearby cities and towns, and outward from there to global tourism networks (Sheller and Urry 2004). The environmental impacts of these transportation and tourism networks are not immediately apparent within the Tobeatic or Jumbo Pass. However, they involve their own ecologically harmful "withdrawals," such as use of fossil fuels and other resources for cars, planes, and their associated infrastructure, as well as "additions," such as greenhouse gas emissions and air pollution (Schnaiberg and Gould 2000). As such, the separation between valued and contested modes of outdoor recreation masks an "ecological irony," in Szerszynski's sense (2007) of the gap between professed ecological values and engagement in ecologically harmful behaviour.

Activists' Interview Talk: Towards a Different Politics of Special Places

In this section, I turn to core activists' interpretations of the places that are the objects of their claims. Interviews with core activists add a layer of complexity to our understanding of the cultural work done by environmental movements. Activists' interpretations of Jumbo Pass and the Tobeatic suggest a more nuanced model of an ecopolitics of special places, which addresses some of the limitations of the wilderness ideal that circulates through environmental organization websites and the mass media.

Jumbo Pass as Wilderness

Core activists involved in the Jumbo Pass conflict distance themselves from the notion of Jumbo-as-wilderness that circulates in the mass media and is often reinforced by the imagery of environmental organization websites. Instead, core activists articulate a definition of the Jumbo Pass landscape that is distinct from popular understandings of wilderness as untouched and uninhabited. As one respondent notes, this mythological view of wilderness is untenable in contemporary societies.

> I mean, is there any place on this planet that is truly pristine? You know, this kind of discourse is an attempt on the part of the supporters of the resort to marginalize the opposition to Jumbo as coming from a strictly environmental standpoint. We have been very explicit, I have said in probably three dozen media interviews ... the Jumbo valley is not pristine. It's had logging, it's had mining, it has a heli-ski operation, it has guide outfitting, it has hiking [but] it works for grizzly bears, it works for people, it works for a local economy at a small scale. It is a very, very unusual picture of sustainability ... The place has seen logging and mining ... there's lots of negative environmental impact that is, has occurred in the Jumbo Valley. That does not de facto mean that this place is not worth protecting. (Jumbo Pass interview no. 3)

This model of wilderness is more nuanced than representations of Jumbo Pass found in mass media coverage of the conflict. Activist definitions of wilderness also indicate a tension between environmental organization websites' reliance on wilderness imagery to claim that Jumbo Pass is worth protecting and core activists' more complex interpretations of this place.

The value of the Jumbo Pass landscape is defined primarily in terms of animal habitat, with particular reference to grizzly bears and caribou. These are large animals that have difficulty cohabiting with humans in towns or cities and that may be displaced by large-scale resource extraction. For example, one participant distinguishes the "wildness" of Jumbo Pass from notions of untouched wilderness as follows:

> Of course it has been logged and there have been forest fires through it and it has been mined, but guess what, there has been no permanent settlement

up there of any kind. And there are, on occasion, there are still caribou going though ... There certainly are grizzly bear, there's wildlife of every kind
and so it may not be wilderness, we've never said it was wilderness that I'm
aware of ... I'll tell you this, I once was up there sitting as the sun went down
on a June evening and as I was watching those grizzlies ... and I was sitting
there watching as the sun went down thinking, if I don't get out of here I'll
be dead by morning because I can't live overnight and those bears will just
go carry on munching their glacier lilies. (Jumbo Pass interview no. 1)

Participants criticize government grizzly bear studies that supported the
environmental assessment approval for the project and cite studies by bear
biologists and experts that argue that the resort development will displace
the local bear population. Participants also criticize the notion of grizzly
impact mitigation used by developers, which assumes that the bears would
simply move into adjacent valleys, because this would displace current
small-scale recreational users from these areas as well.

The wildness of Jumbo Pass is also defined in terms of its distance from
the nearest towns, absence of permanent infrastructure, and lack of services in the area. Jumbo Pass is also defined as a recreational space for hiking
and cross-country and backcountry skiing. Humans are part of the Jumbo
Pass landscape and their use of the space is valued, provided they come as
visitors rather than as permanent residents. For example:

There is some heli-skiing up there. We'd never be able to get that out, but
heli-skiing is far, far less intrusive than a resort that's going to have accommodation for seven thousand people. So we don't want motorized traffic
up there, off-road traffic I'm speaking of. (Jumbo interview no. 2)

Often, participants argue that the real estate development and road building
associated with the ski resort are the most problematic aspects of the resort
proposal, as these will have the most disruptive effects on the local environment. For example:

One of our challenges in communication [about Jumbo Pass] is between
the definite impacts, but somewhat temporary impacts ... of logging and to
a certain point mining as well ... and building a city at the back of the valley.
Real estate never goes away, it never has a little blip and then fades back in
to reclamation by nature ... and you get all sorts of kind of parasitic spin-offs
when there's a major road upgrade and ... every single piece of private land

adjacent to that corridor all of a sudden sees increased development and increased traffic. (Jumbo Pass interview no. 4)

One of the guiding research questions concerns how core activists interpret wilderness in relation to campaigns to protect Jumbo Pass and the Tobeatic Wilderness. Core activists involved in the Jumbo Pass conflict articulate a more complex understanding of wilderness than is circulated in the mass media and environmental organization websites. Core activists assert the value of the existing social-ecological community at Jumbo Pass, which is constituted by hikers, backcountry skiers, grizzly bears, and other animals, which would be put at risk of disruption and profound transformation by the permanent infrastructure of the proposed ski resort and accompanying roadbuilding.

The Tobeatic as Wilderness

Participants involved in the Tobeatic conflict generally describe the area as a wilderness place. When prompted to explain how they understand wilderness in relation to the Tobeatic, which is a region with a history of mining, logging, and hydroelectric development, they articulate what might be termed a relative model of wilderness. The Tobeatic is seen as relatively wild within the social and historical context of Nova Scotia. As participants note, no place in the province meets the romanticized criterion of being untouched by human activity. For example:

> It's as wilderness as you're going to get in Nova Scotia ... much of it has been cut over the last several hundred years by European colonization anyway. Is it wilderness? Well, it's the closest thing in Nova Scotia to wilderness. Now it's not the high Rockies or the Arctic or Labrador, it's not that remote. (Tobeatic Wilderness interview no. 2)

The qualities that make the Tobeatic valuable as wilderness are its size, the presence of fragments of old-growth forests, which are rare in Nova Scotia, its lack of modern roads or infrastructure, and its distance from the closest cities and towns. For example, the same participant tells me:

> I've walked the big island on Sporting Lake and I could not believe from, even after living here for fifteen years ... that there was a place that had a mature Acadian forest like those islands have ... And there are little pockets of old growth, or mature growth, climax growth, red spruce and yellow

birch and maple and hemlock and white pine but, this is the best I've seen in western Nova Scotia. (Tobeatic Wilderness interview no. 2)

Tobeatic participants do not articulate a version of wilderness characterized as nature untouched by human activity. Rather, they understand wilderness as part of a continuum of social-natural environments. This is illustrated by a participant who compares the Tobeatic and Kejimkujik National Park, which is located near the Tobeatic, as follows:

There's never been any kind of attempt to "upgrade" ... the recreation infrastructure [of the Tobeatic], so it's not like [Kejimkujik National Park], where we have wide trails connecting the lakes and big signs and places to rest your canoe and picnic tables at campsites and stuff like that. And most people, myself included, wouldn't want those things [in the Tobeatic] because that would take away from the wildness of it. (Tobeatic Wilderness interview no. 3)

Because Kejimkujik National Park has permanent recreational infrastructure for visitors and tourists, it is viewed as less of a wilderness environment than the Tobeatic.

For activists, OHVs are the main risk to the wilderness value of the Tobeatic. The specific reasons why OHVs are seen as problematic are noise pollution, wildlife disruption, and trail degradation. For example:

When you go on an ATV, first of all, you've got an engine running and you can't hear the beauty, the interaction of the birds, and the wind in the trees and the leaves and everything. And secondly, it scares all the wildlife away. And then they damage all the trails that they're on if they cross them when they're muddy. (Tobeatic Wilderness interview no. 1)

As in the media coverage, Tobeatic activists distance environmentally problematic motorized forms of outdoor recreation from highly valued non-motorized modes of outdoor recreation. The final management plan for the area, implemented in 2006, largely responded to environmentalists' demands to prohibit motorized vehicle use in the Tobeatic. As such, the movement to protect the Tobeatic was successful in terms of policy outcomes.

More recently, the Buy Back Nova Scotia campaign (launched in 2009) has brought together environmentalists and recreational users – including OHV users – to "buy back" forest land owned by the Irving Corporation. In this context, participants framed their discussion of OHVs as a question of where they should or should not ride.

> I think there has to be those [OHV] groups [in the Buy Back Nova Scotia coalition]. I think they will have to accept that there are places they – and I think most of them do – that there are places that they can't go. And that's the way it should be and the Tobeatic is one of those places. But moving forward, if we're talking to one another we should be able to figure out a way that they can maintain a number of their key routes even if there are new areas protected. (Tobeatic Wilderness interview no. 3)

In contrast to assertions that the Tobeatic Wilderness should be kept vehicle-free, discussions about the Buy Back Nova Scotia campaign suggest another interpretation of OHV use. Participants do not define the machines as inherently problematic, but instead suggest that there are ecologically appropriate and inappropriate places for their use.

As in the Jumbo Pass case, environmental organizations that mobilize to protect the Tobeatic draw on symbols of wilderness to represent this place in activist-produced web content. Environmentalist claims on behalf of the Tobeatic are picked up and circulated in the news media, primarily by the provincial Halifax *Chronicle-Herald*. This can be taken as a measure of successful cultural work by environmentalists. In contrast to websites and mass media coverage, however, core activists interpret the Tobeatic using a more nuanced model of wilderness that relies less on idealized images of untouched, uninhabited nature but is more attuned to the social, historical, and ecological context of the campaign to protect this place.

Conclusion

The SMS perspective has primarily focused on the diffusion and institutionalization of social movement tactical repertoires, and on the institutionalization of social movement organizations (see the Introduction to this volume and Chapter 1). However, most social movements are not only interested in political victories but also seek to create broader cultural change (Jamison et al. 1990; Giugni 1998; Rochon 1998; Castells 2004). I have focused on the cultural work done by two environmental movements in their campaigns against ski resort development at Jumbo Pass, British Columbia, and off-highway vehicle use in the Tobeatic Wilderness, Nova Scotia. Through these cases, we see how environmentalist interpretations of nature circulate through environmental organization websites and are diffused through provincial and national news outlets. While social movement constructions of the environment sometimes encounter resistance from movement opponents, the movements to protect Jumbo Pass and the Tobeatic were generally successful at circulating their cultural interpretations through the media into the public sphere. However, interviews with core activists highlight a tension between the model of wilderness articulated by their organizations' websites and mass media coverage on the one hand, and core activists' more complex understandings of the places they seek to protect on the other. The tension between these different understandings of wilderness underscores Jim Conley's caution in Chapter 10 against viewing movement frames as "static" and "ready to be taken off the shelf," and his emphasis on treating the cultural work of social movements as "dynamic interactional processes."

Throughout the history of North American environmentalism, images of untouched wilderness have been used to support claims for the protection of mountain and forest environments. Promoting an idealized notion of wilderness carries unintended consequences, however. Wilderness-oriented environmentalism reinforces nature/society binaries that place a high social value on protected wilderness areas but do little to unsettle the everyday operation of industrial-scale natural resource depletion, or routine air, water, and soil pollution (Cronon 1995; Luke 1997). As environmental movements have successfully raised the cultural value of wilderness places, they have often neglected questions about the misdistribution of environmental "bads," such as exposure to environmental degradation and risk, or of environmental "goods," such as access to natural resources or to high-quality water, air, or recreational environments (Agyeman, Bullard, and Evans 2003; Mohai, Pellow, and Roberts 2009; Park and Pellow 2011).

Bruno Latour's notion of collectives, which are jointly constituted by people, technologies, and nature, is useful for making sense of core activists' talk about the ecopolitics of special places (Latour 2004). Instead of conceiving of the Jumbo Pass and Tobeatic landscapes as wilderness, we might reconceptualize these places as pre-existing collectives of animals that are able to share space with hikers, backcountry skiers, or canoeists, but that risk being pushed out by permanent infrastructure or motorized recreation. The relative interpretation of wilderness articulated by core environmental activists does not seek to "purify" relations between humans and nature to the degree assumed in critiques of wilderness-oriented environmentalism (Latour 1993). While media coverage and activist websites promote a de-humanized and ahistorical image of wilderness, core activists offer another model that resonates with attempts by scholars like Cannavo (2007) or Plumwood (1998) to reconceptualize wilderness without rejecting the idea of leaving room for ecosystems and animals that cannot easily coexist with significant development.

Activists' interview talk suggests that they are well aware that maintaining existing ecological communities at Jumbo Pass and the Tobeatic is deeply intertwined with the "political ecology" of British Columbia and Nova Scotia, wherein attempts to speak on behalf of non-human nature are bound up with politics, economics, and culture (Latour 2004). This model of an ecopolitics of special places is more nuanced than either the model of wilderness protection that circulates through environmental organization websites and mass media coverage of environmental campaigns, or the model of wilderness-oriented environmentalism critiqued by many environmental justice advocates and environmental social scientists. As environmental organizations are successful in their cultural work, they may unwittingly reproduce a problematic notion of wilderness that reinforces nature/culture dualisms, and that is actually at odds with many core activists' personal understanding of ecopolitics. A challenge for many environmental movements, then, is how to mobilize to protect existing social-ecological communities from significant disruption without reifying problematic notions of wilderness as they engage in the necessary cultural work to access the media and reach bystander publics. As the present analysis demonstrates, the ability to articulate a more complex version of social movement issues is often limited by the genre conventions of news media. This key point has theoretical relevance beyond environmentalism, as women's movements, the Occupy movement, the human rights movement, and others examined in this volume also engage the media to communicate with the public and to attempt to influence broader cultural values.

The environmental movements examined here have been successful at translating their interpretations of Jumbo Pass and the Tobeatic into provincial and national news media. However, media coverage of these conflicts reproduces many of the problematic aspects of wilderness-oriented environmentalism, such as downplaying issues of environmental justice and environmental privilege, as well as ignoring the routine ecological degradation occurring outside the boundaries of these contested places. Core activists' interview talk offers a more multifaceted cultural framework for understanding wilderness. Instead of romanticizing ahistorical and unpeopled ideas of wilderness, this framework emphasizes issues of local democracy and questions the type and scale of human engagement with nature in these places. Environmental movements have often been success-ful in promoting cultural change. They may yet play a key role in translating the insider knowledge of core activists into a more reflexive culture of human/nature interaction in social movement societies. Rather than separating wilderness-oriented environmentalism from social justice–oriented environmentalism, the insider knowledge of core activists contains a vision of wilderness that could be part of a more complex ecopolitics of ecological and social sustainability.

Notes

I would like to thank Howard Ramos, Laura McDonald, and Lori-Ann Campbell for their assistance throughout this project. This research was supported by Killam Trusts.

1 Media data collection for this analysis was completed in 2009. Until this time, little coverage was given to Ktunaxa land claims issues. However, recent news media place greater emphasis on the Ktunaxa as a collective actor in the Jumbo conflict.

14

Alberta Internalizing Oil Sands Opposition

A Test of the Social Movement Society Thesis

RANDOLPH HALUZA-DELAY

Assessing claims of a social movement society (SMS) requires examining the non-movement population for the effect of social movement activism. On this front, Alberta is an excellent case study. In particular, the accelerating expansion of the Athabasca oil sands, which provide nearly a quarter of provincial government revenues, has faced extensive opposition. Following from the original (Meyer and Tarrow 1998) and updated (Introduction and Chapter 1, this volume) SMS thesis, three features must be assumed evident if Alberta is considered to operate as an SMS. First, the impact of social movements would be evident in public appropriation of movement repertoires of action, frames, and ideologically attentive understanding(s) of issues. Seeming internalization or habituation of counter-movement framing and repertoires would also be evidence of the appropriation of movement activity, *if* counter-movements engage in movement-like activity. Second, dispositions associated with social movements would also be evident. As Crossley (2003) notes, a sort of "resistance habitus" within movement activists would emerge (Haluza-DeLay 2008) and extend to the wider public. If we assume an SMS, then a generalized resistance, perhaps expressed as cynicism, about corporate or political power would be evident in the general population, as well as a propensity to action in ways pioneered by social movements in the province. Third, "learning" in both process and content occurs in the general population. The SMS thesis proposes a cultural adoption of features associated with a specific social sector. Culture is an assemblage of symbols, knowledge, and behaviours that people use in varying configurations to solve different kinds of problems and meet basic needs. These tools, and the capacity to use them competently, must be acquired, consciously or not, if an SMS truly exists.

Eyerman and Jamison (1991) expand on this last feature through their conceptualization of social movements as cognitive praxis. In particular, movements are successful to the degree that the knowledge they produce is absorbed into the society in which they are active (see also Chapter 12). An example of this can be seen with the civil rights movement, which changed American society by denormalizing racism, promoting rights, and creating new forms of interracial relations. According to Eyerman and Jamison (1991) knowledge produced by social movements consists of at least three types. The first is *instrumental knowledge* and it includes movement-relevant skill development and practices. The second is *organizational knowledge*, which consists of the altered forms of social relations and institutional development that movements propose. The third is *cosmological knowledge*, which includes the basic beliefs and movement-based interpretations of the world. As a result, if Alberta is an SMS, the cognitive praxes of oil sands opposition movements would be absorbed into the Alberta public. The goal of this chapter is to see whether that is in fact the case.

Methodology

My interest in the responses of Albertans to oil sands opposition movements necessitated a methodology – ethnography – that "produces the most direct evidence of action as action unfolds in everyday life" (Lichterman 2002, 121). Auyero and Swistun (2009, 60) declare ethnography well situated to "pierce the screen of discourses" and "capture lived relations and meanings." However, the difficulty in most ethnographic fieldwork is that members' own interpretations are not the totality of the experience of everyday life. Therefore, the approach used in this chapter resembles what Gellert and Shefner (2009) call "structural fieldwork," wherein the researcher combines "deep familiarity with people and locales" and attention to the broader context of the political-economic world system (193). The research began as participant-observation with environmental movement organizations but, guided by an ethnographic imagination, shifted to a broader research question of what might shed light on the relationship between Albertans and the oil sands.

The oil sands have become more than a just vehicle of resource extraction or government revenues in Alberta. They have become a central feature of Albertan culture and a topic of intense consideration by ordinary Albertans. Over the course of five years, I collected data through a variety of methods, including many hours of participant-observation with environmental organizations and local sustainability groups, and informal conversations of Albertans at soccer games, church potlucks, coffee shops, and other public spaces. Like Eliasoph (1999), I was particularly attentive to everyday speech. Eliasoph's ethnographic work on everyday speech and racism unpacked the political culture operative in interpersonal relations with particular attention to the role of "political avoidance" within common conversation on politically charged topics. The same occurs in Alberta regarding the oil sands. I carried a field notebook everywhere. Participant-observation was conducted most intensively between 2008 and 2011, a period that was marked by the most intensive intraprovincial debate over the oil sands. The participant- observation was extended by more formal interviews of key figures and citizens related to the oil sands and oil sands opposition movements. The research program also drew on content analysis of media responses to social movements' actions, discourse analysis of actors' public statements, and focus groups with regular Albertans (Haluza-DeLay and Berezan 2013; Haluza-DeLay, Ferber, and Wiebe-Neufeld 2013; Kowalsky and Haluza-DeLay 2013; Haluza-DeLay 2014; Haluza-DeLay and Carter, forthcoming). Analysis followed conventions associated with both ethnography (Thomas 1993) and discourse analysis (L. King 2007; Snow 2008). For this chapter, the original data were re-examined for features that could characterize an SMS.

The Case of the Oil Sands
Alberta's oil sands are contentious within and outside of the province. They are a mixture of sand, water, clay, and bitumen, which is a very heavy and viscous oil.[1] The product is called "unconventional oil" because of the difficulty of extraction and higher refining needs than lighter "conventional" oil. Oil and gas production, with the oil sands as a substantial portion, is widely considered to be the primary driver of the Alberta economy and increasingly that of the country as a whole (R. Gibbins and Roach 2010). According to the Government of Alberta (GOA), about $4.5 billion in royalties was collected from oil sands projects in 2011–12, marking the third year in a row that oil sands royalty was the top source of Alberta's non-renewable resource revenue.[2] At the same time, according to its calculations, the

Parkland Institute claims that the royalties are excessively low, resulting in a giveaway to the corporate leaseholders because only 10 and 13 percent of profits were returned to citizens in 2009 and 2010, respectively (Campanella 2012; Boychuk 2010). These are far below government targets, which have dropped from 35 percent to the current 20 percent, and are among the lowest returns of any petroleum-producing jurisdiction in the world. The GOA reports that the energy sector overall accounts for 27.6 percent of Alberta's gross domestic product. According to the same GOA factsheet, the oil sands sector also emitted 38.2 percent of total reported emissions in Alberta. The oil sands are the fastest growing source of Canadian emissions, with projected growth in their emissions large enough to cancel out all projected emissions reductions in the rest of the Canadian economy, according to the Pembina Institute (Partington and Demerse 2013).

The Government of Alberta denied, until late 2012, that oil sands production pollutes air or water despite several peer-reviewed published studies (e.g., E.N. Kelly et al. 2009, 2010) showing that it does. Human health effects downstream of the extraction area are also in dispute. There are extensive other environmental, economic, and social costs, according to a wide range of opposition movement organizations, research institutes, and researchers. The "facts," however, are highly contested and journalists (e.g., Nikiforuk 2008; Gailus 2012) and academics (e.g., Davidson and Gismondi 2011) have entered into the discursive "war of positioning" associated with the oil sands – which is itself a debated term. Growth pressure on the regional municipality that includes Fort McMurray, the second fastest-growing city in Canada since the 2006 census, was intense enough that Mayor Melissa Blake asked for a slowdown on permits for new projects. Numerous industry associations, most notably the Canadian Association of Petroleum Producers (CAPP), have vigorously defended the oil sands. At the same time, oil sands opponents have proposed changes to current practices that range from "tweaking" of regulations and practices, known as ecological modernization, to more far-reaching changes, such as creating a "post-carbon" society.

Oil and gas have been central features of Alberta's economy for several decades but this does not mean that there has not been opposition to the energy extraction industry. A poisonous (sour gas) well explosion – the Pembina blowout near Drayton Valley in 1982 – was instrumental in initiating the contemporary Alberta environmental movement as it marked the founding of the Pembina Institute for Appropriate Development. Now known by its shorter name, the Pembina Institute is a unique hybrid of energy consulting firm and environmental non-profit organization. In the 1990s, Wiebo Ludwig gained notoriety as an "eco-saboteur" (Nikiforuk 2002). He was convinced that sour gas drilling was causing severe health complications on the collective farm of the religious group of which he was leader. Ludwig's conviction for several gas facility bombings did little to reduce community conflict over the oil and gas industry. Contemporary oil sands opposition is characterized by similar contentiousness.

Contemporary Social Movement Action Opposing the Oil Sands

Social movement actors involved in opposition to the oil sands today include environmental, labour, Aboriginal, and religious organizations. These organizations and their strategies are described briefly in the following sections, along with the coalition-building and transnational activism that has emerged out of them (for more detail, see Haluza-DeLay and Carter, forthcoming). Counter-responses to activism are mentioned throughout and are further detailed in a later section.

Aboriginal Activism

Aboriginal communities downstream of oil sands developments, or in the path of pipelines to carry product to or away from them, have been long-standing sources of resistance. Of course, they also seek to benefit economically and socially from oil sands extraction but First Nations have protested the environmental health impacts of the projects, their degradation of water and air quality, effects on local fish and game used as food, and limitations on Aboriginal peoples' access to traditional lands caused by the projects. The latter is particularly important and to date no judicial decisions have ruled on the implications for treaty rights of the extensive development around the oil sands.

Both the Athabasca Chipewyan First Nation and the Mikisew Cree First Nation withdrew from the Cumulative Effects Management Association (CEMA) in 2006 and 2007, respectively, in protest against the committee's lack of meaningful progress. Among the reasons stated by the latter was that their membership in CEMA was "often cited and publicly stated by both government and industry as them fulfilling their constitutional duty to consult with the Mikisew Cree" (Mikisew Cree First Nation 2007, 18).

Although industry officials continue to tout the benefits of oil sands development for Aboriginal peoples in the region, First Nations have tried to communicate their concerns more broadly using social justice and treaty rights frames, but to limited acknowledgment in the media or general public attention. In light of the limitations of localized actions and the recalcitrance of both federal and provincial governments on the issue, northern Alberta Aboriginal groups partnered with other movement organizations in taking the fight to Ottawa, corporate offices in the United States and the United Kingdom, and European parliaments. Outside of Canada, the environmental justice frame seems to have played an effective role in mobilizing public opposition to the oil sands.

Environmental Organizations

Numerous environmental non-governmental organizations (ENGOs) are involved in oil sands mobilization. Some are nationally organized (e.g., the Pembina Institute, the Sierra Club of Canada, and Greenpeace), while others are provincial or regional (e.g., the Prairie Chapter of the Sierra Club, the Fort McMurray Environmental Association, and Keepers of the Athabasca). Opposition to the oil sands by ENGOs has escalated in recent years and expanded in both geographic scale and intensity.

Initial strategies by ENGOs attempted to be collaborative, often consisting of recommendations to "tweak" industrial practices or specific projects as well as participation in government-initiated consultation processes. However, several ENGOs followed the two First Nations, noted above, out of CEMA. This withdrawal followed other experiences of government consultation in Alberta on the Boreal Forest Conservation Strategy process in the late 1990s (R.R. Schneider 2002), land use planning (Fluet and Krogman 2009), forest management (Parkins 2006), and industrial development (Masuda, McGee, and Garvin 2008). ENGOs came to believe that meaningful engagement on governmental policy was very limited. ENGO strategy shifted towards court challenges, public awareness campaigns, broad coalitions with other citizen groups, and activism outside the province as a way of putting pressure on internal provincial regulation.

Greenpeace opened an Alberta office led by an Alberta-born activist in 2007 and engaged in direct actions aimed at drawing national and international attention to oil sands operations. One example was Greenpeace's unfurling of a banner at one of Premier Ed Stelmach's fundraising dinners, as seen in Figure 14.1. The premier called Greenpeace an "ecoterrorist" organization (Berry 2010) for these non-violent actions, which raised concerns about the delegitimizing of some forms of citizen action. For the most part, however, these "stunts" appear to have garnered little support among the Alberta populace, although they have contributed to attracting attention to the oil sands as a point of concern.

FIGURE 14.1   A Greenpeace direct action at an Edmonton event with Premier Ed Stelmach. Note the wording on the banner. Photograph by Chris Schwarz, *Edmonton Journal*.

ENGOs have actively partnered with Aboriginal organizations and have been joined by organizations not primarily focused on environmental issues, such as Public Interest Alberta (more known for advocating on social programs), churches, and unions. ENGOs have also drawn on and helped to publicize research and expertise such as academic studies and reports from policy institutes such as the Pembina Institute or the Parkland Institute. Their partnerships (listed in Haluza-DeLay and Carter, forthcoming) also showed that the oil sands were something about which growing numbers of Albertans were concerned.

National ENGOs began pronouncing on the oil sands only in the mid-2000s. Figure 14.2 tabulates references to the terms "oil sands" or "tar sands" in the press releases of the national offices of the Sierra Club. This major player in the national environmental movement did not mention the oil sands issue until 2003. However, according to an interview with a Sierra Club Prairie Chapter director, the Prairie Chapter office had actively campaigned on this issue for a longer period of time. It also more frequently used the term "environmental justice" than the national office, according to

FIGURE 14.2

Number of press releases from the national office of the Sierra Club in which the terms "oil sands" or "tar sands" are mentioned

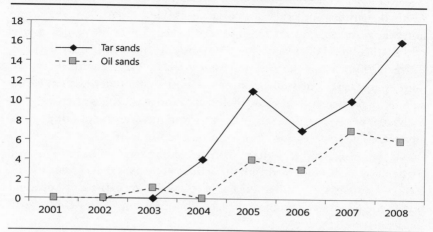

Source: Discursive Opportunities Project, Dr. Howard Ramos, Dalhousie University.

searches in the same database. Canadian environmental groups have not often connected their sustainability frames to social inclusion or justice ones (Haluza-DeLay and Fernhout 2011).

Religiously Based Activism

Religious groups have also been involved in criticism of the oil sands, approaching the issue in a very different way and involving a different constituency than environmental and Aboriginal groups. Two specific insertions of religious actors in the oil sands debate in 2009 drew media attention (D. Gibbins 2010). The ecumenical group KAIROS led a week-long "Delegation to the Alberta Oilsands" with leaders of ten national church denominations. It began in Edmonton and headed north to Fort McMurray and Fort Chipewyan, where it met with industry, government, and Aboriginal leaders. Members of Kairos's Edmonton chapter reported some intra-church discomfort with fellow congregants who are employed in or politically supportive of oil sands development. A similar high-profile and contentious intervention into the oil sands issue occurred earlier in 2009 when the Roman Catholic bishop of the region delivered a carefully researched pastoral letter on the Athabasca oil sands. Bishop Luc Bouchard later reported that few officials actually engaged the substantive issues he raised.

The impact of faith groups is broader than the relatively small proportion of the population that regularly participates in religious services. Religious organizations, when they have been socially active, have long supported Aboriginal groups and other justice concerns (Lind and Mihevc 1994), and in recent years religious groups have revisited environmental issues in light of their theologies of creation-care, stewardship, and eco-justice (e.g., R.S. Gottlieb 2006; Veldman, Szasz, and Haluza-DeLay 2013). For the most part, faith groups carry out study groups, workshops, and other less noticeable actions on particular issues, and these education approaches often focus on individual lifestyle actions rather than socio-structural analysis or political advocacy. The intervention of religious actors in the oil sands debates has raised the profile and legitimacy of criticisms among ordinary Albertans, particularly when combined with the actions of the Aboriginal activists and environmentalists. A result, there has been a widening of the scope of attention to the oil sands as problematic (see Kowalsky and Haluza-DeLay 2013 for details).

Labour Organizations

In recent years, unions and labour federations in Alberta have supported campaigns by environmental and Aboriginal groups and funded the political-economic research of the Parkland Institute. The Alberta Federation of Labour (AFL) partnered with Greenpeace and the Sierra Club in April 2009 to produce the report *Green Jobs: It's Time to Build Alberta's Future* (D. Thompson 2009). At the same time, the AFL developed a report (AFL 2009) and campaign aimed at enhancing job opportunities in the value-added refining of bitumen rather than allowing it to be piped elsewhere.

Limited research has been published on labour organizing in the oil sands. It should not be assumed, however, that workers identify the labour movement as representing their needs. For example, AFL president Gil McGowan was interviewed for an article in an industry magazine that reported on a series of protests about increases in the provincial royalties for oil sands production (Byfield 2007). Employers were able to mobilize workers to oppose such increases. More than 500 workers, for example, rallied before the Alberta legislature in 2007 in one event organized by an energy services company. Far fewer workers attended a quickly organized AFL counter-rally in Fort McMurray the next day in support of royalty rate increases. In this case, industry found social movement tactics useful.

So while labour organizations remain involved, it is unclear to what extent organized labour's activism or policy reports influence the perspectives of individual workers on the oil sands. Furthermore, the labour movement is heterogeneous. Oil sands workers are represented by several unions with dramatically different orientations. Resource issues are often presented in a jobs-versus-the-environment frame. Simon (2003) found that in a British Columbia forestry conflict, the more radical union had more interaction with environmentalists and the moderate one cooperated with the timber companies. Daub (2010) showed that energy workers supported climate policy when framed in ways that provided for a just transition from extraction work that was deleterious to the environment. While labour might broach social justice in the oil sands at times, labour organizations also find themselves in a position in which at least some of their members greatly benefit (or perceive that they do) from oil sands development.

Transnational Activism

Eventually, the struggle against unbridled expansion of Alberta oil sands projects shifted towards transnational arenas amid escalating contestation by governments, industry, and civil society organizations. As political opportunities dwindled even further in Alberta, opposition to the oil sands mobilized elsewhere in Canada, across the North American continent, and worldwide. Transnational advocacy networks (TANs) (Keck and Sikkink 1998) engaged in lobbying of other governments from the municipal to the international level, public education, and investor activism against oil sands–affiliated corporations. Hoffman (2012) describes the oil sands issue as a system with many pieces, any of which could be sites of engagement. The goals of TANs are to segment the system and attack specific pieces. "Dirty Oil" campaigns of various types occurred from 2008, when social movements lobbied the US Conference of Mayors to question cross-border importation of Alberta's unconventional oil. Similar activism occurred in many European countries (Figure 14.3). In response, Canadian oil producers launched a website (www.canadasoilsands.ca, which redirects to the website of the Canadian Association of Petroleum Producers [CAPP], an industry lobby group) to "encourage dialogue" (Cattaneo 2008).

The "AvaTARsands" campaign targeted American citizens and policymakers by drawing parallels between the popular movie *Avatar* and Alberta. A full-page ad was placed in prominent American media in 2010 (see Figure 14.4) and comparisons were again made the following spring, during the Academy Awards season (Mittelstaedt 2010). CAPP even responded with a special section on its website against claims that "Pandora's unobtanium mining is Alberta's tar sands." The attention engendered discussion among

FIGURE 14.3   An anti–tar sands rally in Lisbon, Portugal, in June 2011.
Reproduced with permission from Greg Wagenfuhr.

Albertans as well, demonstrating an increasing acknowledgment among
Albertans that the oil sands were problematic. It was during this time that
we conducted focus groups in three Edmonton churches (Haluza-DeLay,
Ferber, and Wiebe-Neufeld 2013).

Transnational movement organizations have targeted the profits of key
corporations directly. For example, the Rainforest Action Network (RAN)
joined with members of the Lubicon Lake Indian Nation in March 2009 to
lobby the Royal Bank of Canada – the Canadian bank providing the greatest
amount of financing to the oil sands – to withdraw support from oil sands
projects (Barclay 2009). Ethical investors and corporate social responsibility groups produced reports, and questions were raised across several
European countries (Church Investors Group 2008; Crooks 2008). Aboriginal activists, environmentalists, and scientists of international repute presented problems with the oil sands to European audiences. The oil sands
were associated with greenhouse gas emissions, climate change, and global
climate justice. Facing international attention and opposition to Alberta's
unconventional oil production, Alberta and Canadian government officials,

FIGURE 14.4 Advertisement placed in *Variety* magazine comparing the movie *Avatar* to the Alberta oil sands. Reproduced with permission from Corporate Ethics International.

specific corporations, and CAPP responded with extensive public relations campaigns in favour of the oil sands.

Most recently, activists have targeted the web of pipelines that criss-cross the continent, linking them with a range of frames. Approval in the United

States for the Keystone XL pipeline has been stalled from 2011 up to the time of writing. Coastal First Nations and local groups have opposed the Northern Gateway pipeline to the port of Kitimat in British Columbia. At the same time, the energy delivery company Enbridge created and funded an organization – Northern Gateway Alliance – that supported the construction of the pipeline to the Pacific (Hoekstra 2009). In 2012 and 2013, except for these pipeline disputes, little activity occurred within the province of Alberta other than through Aboriginal organizations.

Counter-Response to the Oil Sands Opposition Movements

Transnational organizing drew much government and corporate opposition. As one journalist reported: "The battle line divides two viscerally opposed camps: Those arguing that North America's deepening dependence on Alberta's oil sands industry represents a pragmatic solution to looming energy crises, and those who say relying on oil sands crude marks an irreversible step closer to climate change catastrophe" (Dembecki 2011). Even earlier, a business reporter opined that "Alberta [was] losing the public relations war when it comes to the oil sands" (Yaffe 2008). "Losing the Public Relations War" was also used as a headline for news stories in 2010 and 2012. Provincial and federal governments spent significant amounts defending the oil sands.

Public cynicism grew to the point where even newspaper comics noted the efforts to counter the increasingly negative attention to the oil sands, as seen in Figure 14.5.

A tight coupling of industry and government has evolved, leading to what political scientists Hoberg and Phillips (2011) characterize as "a closed, bipartite policy subsystem where industry has enjoyed a 'policy monopoly.'" Part of their data shows a 97 percent correspondence between provincial and industry actors on policy preferences during a multi-stakeholder consultation process on the oil sands. While their data covered provincial governance, federal Minister of Natural Resources Joe Oliver gained widespread attention drafting an op-ed that called environmentalists "radicals" who do not belong in hearings on economically viable projects (J. Oliver 2012). His op-ed was published five days before the start of a process of hearings into the Northern Gateway pipeline that was to last more than a year. As noted by Ramos and Rodgers in the Introduction to this volume, the spring 2012 federal budget increased funds for the Canada Revenue Agency to audit advocacy by registered charities and since then many environmental charities have been targeted by such audits.

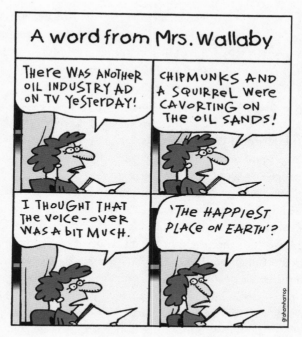

FIGURE 14.5 A comic strip deriding pro–oil sands marketing. *Source:* Graham Harrop, http://www.grahamharrop.com.

The battle over the trajectory of oil sands development has taken place across at least six spheres of engagement:

- *Duelling websites.* CAPP, industry, and GOA-sponsored websites link to each other but not to other organizations like the Pembina Institute.
- *Duelling videos.* Numerous documentaries, mostly negative, about the effects of the oil sands, have been produced, and the Alberta Ministry of Environment and various industry groups have produced shorter public relations videos.
- *Duelling media campaigns.* ENGOs and Aboriginal groups have staged media-friendly and provocative events, while the GOA earmarked $25 million for one public relations campaign on the oil sands alone. CAPP sponsored the "Alberta Is Energy" campaign from 2010 to 2012.
- *Duelling science.* Peer-reviewed and published research critical of the oil sands by scientists such as David Schindler and Kevin Timony was directly attacked by provincial scientists in the Ministry of Environment

and by politicians. Timony won a court case over accusations against his credibility. Government officials touted the Regional Aquatic Monitoring Program (RAMP) as providing better science, although it had failed an independent assessment in 2004 and was denounced by a Royal Society of Canada report in December 2009.

- *Duelling in court.* Environmental and Aboriginal organizations have repeatedly mounted court challenges to compel GOA and federal diligence. The prosecution of Syncrude for the deaths of over 1,600 ducks on a tailings pond began as a private prosecution before being taken over by the Justice Department (Fluker 2010).
- *Duelling ethics.* After detailing many of the issues in the Athabasca oil sands, Bishop Bouchard concluded: "Any one of the above destructive effects provokes moral concern, but it is when the damaging effects are all added together that the moral legitimacy of oil sands production is challenged" (Bouchard 2009, n.p.). Within a year the federal environment minister was calling the oil sands "ethical," following the lead of conservative pundit Ezra Levant's spurious argument (2010) for "Ethical Oil." Levant, it should be noted, referred to Bouchard in just a few pages, supported by merely one footnote. Bouchard declared that no government or corporate actors had approached him on the moral issues that he raised (Warnica 2010; see analysis by Kowalsky and Haluza-DeLay 2013), and despite the title of his book – *Ethical Oil* – Levant addresses Bouchard on only a few factual matters and not the moral questions the bishop raised.

Ultimately, the duelling over the oil sands is cultural politics, which is "an approach that treats culture itself as a site of political struggle, an analytic emphasizing power, process and practice" (D.S. Moore, Kosek, and Pandian 2003, 2). The dominant or hegemonic cultural understanding of Alberta is that of a province rooted in energy production. The common sense notion of Albertan identity is one intimately connected with energy. This is, of course, reinforced by a provincial government that is heavily invested in the oil sands, that devotes extensive money, bureaucracy, and other resources to attract corporate investment, and that staunchly defends and promotes the industry. It is also reinforced by industry efforts that heightened these cultural tendencies. One clear example is the marketing campaign by CAPP that ran from 2010 to 2012. The Alberta Is Energy campaign included radio and TV ads, social media, and a comprehensive website;

surprisingly similar billboards, posters, and public messaging by both provincial government and corporate actors also occurred. As noted by the vice president of communications for another advocacy group aligned with industry, "advocating for the oilsands isn't just about preserving the resource's commercial value ... It speaks to *who Albertans are as a people*" (Yaffe 2008, emphasis added). Radio spots asked Albertans to "start a conversation with your neighbours" about how important energy is for the province. This clear attempt to associate with and reproduce a collective provincial identity reinforces the value of research into the utility of the concept of collective identity in understanding public responses to social movement mobilization (Polletta and Jasper 2001). It also corresponds to the Gramscian version of the hegemonic colonization of the everyday sphere that is civil society and is a litmus test of the presence of an SMS.

What Is the Public Response?

By and large, CAPP was successful in solidifying an identity narrative that *Homo alberticus = Homo energeticus* (Kowalsky and Haluza-DeLay 2013). Furthermore, for the most part, oil sands opposition movements ignored this cultural politics as a terrain of contestation. Their reports on greening the economy had little resonance as a counter-hegemony, and the AvaTarSands and dead ducks campaigns did not present a cogent alternative to the "There Is No Alternative" rhetoric presented by the increasingly tight capital/state partnership.

CAPP's Alberta Is Energy campaign operated amid other assertions that petro-production in general and the oil sands in particular are to be taken as general facts. Public opinion polls have consistently shown some public dissension from this. As early as 2006, 88 percent of a sample of 500 Albertans moderately or strongly agreed that "Protecting the environment is important, even if it means oil sands development occurs more slowly."[3] Public opinion is difficult to track because polls ask different questions and use different sampling strategies. Albertans' support for environmental protection in the oil sands has remained generally strong over the years. Sometimes, but not always, national polls show differences between Albertans and other Canadians. For example, an Angus Reid poll in 2009 showed that while only 29 per cent of Canadians think oil sands production should increase, 62 per cent of Albertans favour the same.[4] More interesting are finer-grained perceptions by Albertans about the oil sands and their province and the extent to which Albertans are taking up movement frames and repertoires.

One feature of public perception in Alberta is that it seems to be characterized by both a critique of the oil sands and a sense of inevitability regarding their exploitation. As a focus group participant reported:

> We do care about the environment. But we can only do what we can do. We can't stop it [oil sands degradation]. What difference could we make? ... there is that helplessness feeling. We don't want our earth to crumble, but with the big item issues can we really do something? It is hard to say, "Yes, you can."

Movements in opposition to the oil sands have thus succeeded in opening opportunities to allow for a public criticism of oil sands (see also Davidson and Gismondi 2011). Their success is also evident in that corporations now publicly communicate their environmentally responsible production. The public critique, however, is countered by the *Homo energeticus* narrative that delegitimizes criticism of something deemed so central to being Albertan. It is also countered by the purported inevitability of petroleum extraction as depicted in Figure 14.6, which shows that one way or another oil will be extracted and exported from Alberta despite domestic and transnational opposition. Seemingly absent is the possibility of a "Plan E" where there is no production of oil to transport.

Another feature of public perception of the oil sands is that Albertans implicate themselves in the problem. Said another focus group participant, "I don't think anyone stands up and says 'Yeah for tar sands.' But, at the end of the day we like to buy our cars. We like our SUVs." Unfortunately, this attitude individualizes what is a genuinely systemic problem and ignores the socio-technical trajectory that has created the contemporary form of petroleum-driven society. Energy use is fundamentally connected to the broader social structure in ways little acknowledged by social scientists (Agustoni and Maretti 2012), much less by the general public. As Jim Conley explores (Chapter 10) and Urry (2008, 343–44) theorizes, "automobility" (or "petromobility") is a social system that revolves around the promotion and expansion of auto and petro industries and cultures. Visible to citizens is car use and not the self-organizing and expanding system of practices and institutionalization related to each. At numerous points during fieldwork, for instance, I overheard the phrase, "Do you drive?" The question is deployed at points of criticism about the oil sands as a means of delegitimizing such criticism by implicating the critic as part of the problem. It is a classic example of "political avoidance" (Eliasoph 1999) and I

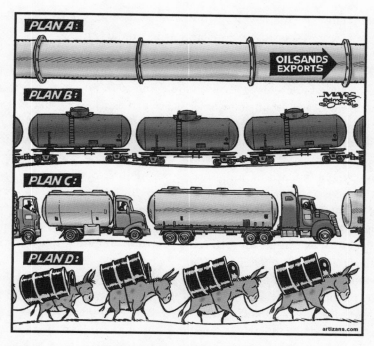

FIGURE 14.6 A comic strip that shows the presumed inevitability of oil sands production. *Source:* Malcolm Mayes, http://www.artizans.com/image/MAY2895/backup-plans-for-oilsands-export-pipeline-color.

noted Albertans increasingly self-censoring themselves as if they were truly complicit in this system. As another focus group participant observed:

> Another feature of public perception by Albertans is lack of awareness of alternatives: To some degree we're stuck. If you want to get out of it you are living a counter-culture life ... We're stuck in the system, and we like the system, even though we hate what it does to the earth.

Another problem faced by oil sands opponents is the struggle to have their framing of issues taken up by media and other publics. While the Pembina Institute has produced numerous reports on diversifying the economy and shifting to green energy, these reports rarely get media coverage and government and industry websites do not link to them as information. The author of *Green Jobs* told me in an interview that it got much better attention outside the province than inside. ENGO framing and reports, Pembina reports, and even the movie *Avatar* – none of these appear to have left Albertans with resources for problem solving on the issue.

Despite many obstacles, a separate study on a local sustainability movement (Haluza-DeLay and Berezan 2013), called permaculture, showed that some of the Edmontonians involved are doing so in response to the criticisms levelled against their own oil sands activism. According to them, they experienced enough negative response to their criticisms that they felt they had to do something to present an alternative environmental praxis. Their response has been to focus on small-scale urban food production, naturalizing urban spaces and private yards, and advocating on issues like food security and transportation alternatives. In some important ways, the result of their criticism of the petro-system has been a strategy of prefiguration of the desired alternative (Maeckelbergh 2011) but it is also a postpolitical turn as it removes intelligent people from more extensive sociopolitical reform (Swyngedouw 2010).

So while a critique of the oil sands status quo seems to have developed in the public, it is unclear just what this critique consists of. Is it the view that the government should do a better job of environmental management? Does it include fundamental questions about the oil sands and petrolifestyles? Can it serve as a more thorough counter-narrative to the hegemony of petro-capitalism?

The tension between environmental values and the existing petroeconomics is evident in other ways. One informant edits a local community newsletter and routinely includes green interests. He says that it is difficult to tell his "green-minded friends" that he works in the oil sands. But he has also written several times that his hope as a forest reclamation specialist is that "forty years from now" the forest will again be a productive ecosystem. Similarly, at a neighbourhood gathering I recorded the following incident:

> The men's consensus: people need to understand how much the Alberta economy relies on the oil and gas industry, especially the indirect benefits. I asked X [a pipeline company professional] about the CAPP ad campaign [Alberta Is Energy]. He was somewhat noncommittal, but thought it ok to remind people [how important oil and gas is to the economy]. He also thought it was necessary to go further though and remind all [of us] of accountability [to the environment]. (Fieldnotes, 11 April 2010)

X wanted to assert environmental stewardship as well as economic development. These diverse views are held in uneasy tension, even by citizens working in the industry. Both of these men participate in churches that have active environmental committees.

Every one of these informants dismisses portions of the anti–oil sands framing and holds to some degree a stereotypical view of "environmentalists." They find themselves in contradictory positions, critical of the problems of the oil sands but uncertain what to do. Many are also politely supportive, or at least not dismissive, of Aboriginal peoples. The oil sands status quo is increasingly developing into a more contentious issue as Albertans struggle with the issues it raises. At the same time, since the socio-structural issues of a petroleum-based society seem so large, citizens remain uncertain about how to live consistent with their felt desires within the conditions of this society.

Conclusion

There is little in the Alberta oil sands opposition story that causes us to think that Alberta illustrates the routinization of an SMS. By most appearances, the movement frame that has been taken up is a generalized criticism of the oil sands, but there is little evidence of incorporation of other frames, repertoires of movement-like action, or a collective ecological identity in contrast to the *Homo energeticus* identity narrative. This is not to mention the lack of other sustained collective action that would characterize social movements. A generalized habitus of resistance as described by Crossley (2003) for movement activists is not evident in Alberta. Being an "environmentalist" is not generally acceptable for most Albertans. We would expect more effect of movements on the populace from the SMS thesis. Social movement action on the oil sands has indeed been sustained, but is less widespread and collective than we would expect if the SMS thesis was applicable in Alberta. Instead, we generally see a polite avoidance of this contentious but very significant subject.

This is not to say there have not been contentious politics in contemporary Alberta. Aboriginal, environmental, labour, and religious groups have all been active in opposition to the oil sands. Each of them has oriented its activism in a different way, so a general assessment of their resonance with the public is worth probing. In many ways, Aboriginal groups present the widest claims because of treaty aspects to the land, but are perceived in the narrowest way. Aboriginal claims making has had far better traction outside the province than within.

Environmental groups have had the most success by problematizing the ecological effects of the oil sands with support from scientific research.

Aboriginal groups have tried to do this with health effects. This strategy is one that the public can understand. However, convinced as they are that the oil sands are an economic driver, the public has not found a resonant alternative in the movement framing. Environmental, labour, and religious groups have all hotly contested the ethical and justice element of the oil sands. In response, oil sands proponents shifted from exclusively emphasizing utilitarian calculation of costs and benefits to Albertans to an argument about the "ethical oil" that is produced in comparison to other petroleum-producing countries – a similar tone to concern over dirty diesel seen in Chapter 9.

Religious groups have engaged select portions of the public on questions of "living faithfully in oil country," the title of an event sponsored by the Social Justice Institute, an organization that originated in the Roman Catholic community in Edmonton. Religious groups are also more heterogeneous than most social movement organizations, which could be positive for dialogue but deleterious for political action because of norms of niceness amid contention and a generally apolitical approach to faith. Like other citizens, members of organized labour are in a conflicted position. Labour has not shown that it can bring its membership to the topic in an effective way. Overall, these results are not what we would expect from the movement-related parts of the SMS thesis.

There has been a vibrant counter-response to the opposition to the oil sands. Compelling evidence exists for shared industry and government interests. This "oil complex" (Watts 2005) has deployed financial resources, international lobbyists, threats of state-sanctioned repression, and widespread marketing campaigns to secure the hegemonic consent of the populace to the oil sands status quo. This capital/state intensity is the most damning argument against Alberta as a social movement society.

In contrast to the projections of the SMS thesis, government has not been polite towards social movement action. There are few to no seats at the table for social movements opposing the oil sands status quo in Alberta. On the contrary, there have been active campaigns to discredit these movements. The duels over environmental science, labelling certain scientists as environmentalists and then castigating environmentalists as "foreign radicals" – these are not what we would expect from the institutionalization parts of the SMS thesis.

Returning to Eyerman and Jamison's (1991) understanding of social movements, we have to conclude that Alberta has not yet, if at all, absorbed much of the cognitive praxis of oil sands opposition. Specifically, the case study shows little uptake in any of the three knowledge types – instrumental, organizational, cosmological – proposed by these scholars. For example, if the oil sands were genuinely internalized as symptoms of an underlying automobility world view (see Chapter 10, as well as Urry 2008) that would require reorganizing transportation options, we could say that some learning from the movement has occurred. However, as with the movement repertoires, movement habitus, or movement frames, or with movement inclusion in policymaking, implementation, or monitoring (on a working partner basis rather than as mongrel watchdog), little tacit social learning from the opposition movements has occurred, contrary to the expectations of the SMS thesis.

The SMS thesis proposes professionalization of social movements and this process is evident among each movement examined. However, it can also be argued that the closure of political opportunities, in contrast to the SMS thesis, has necessitated such a trend. Movement strategies have been forced to change towards "outsider practices" such as court cases, scientific advocacy buttressing claims of health or ecological harm or economic alternatives, technologies of jurisprudence, and sophisticated media counter-responses. Such strategies are probably more effective if done with employed staff with particular skills rather than with volunteer time. In addition, it is telling that as the closing of political opportunities at the provincial and federal government levels have become obvious, social movements have increasingly turned to transnational actions, a strategy appropriate in light of the transnational capitalism that characterizes corporations in the oil sands. The movements against the oil sands have been effective in raising a problematic, but they are still marginal to the main currents of Albertan society and politics. The engagements of civil society organizations appear to have had little effect on environmental governance, and their ways of acting or thinking have not yet presented an adequate alternative to be absorbed by citizens in general or institutions of the non-movement society. There is little sign of a logic of practice consistent with social movement cognitive praxis or resistance habitus. None of our three features of an SMS – public appropriation of movement repertoires, internalization of movement dispositions, and the transaction of movement knowledge in some of the technical, organizational, and cosmological domains – is sufficiently evident in the Alberta public to support claims of the SMS thesis.

Notes

1 http://www.energy.gov.ab.ca/oilsands/793.asp.
2 http://www.energy.alberta.ca/oilsands/791.asp.
3 http://www.pembina.org/pub/1233.
4 http://www.newswire.ca/en/story/411325/new-poll-finds-majority-of-canadians
   -want-fair-global-warming-emissions-cuts-transparency-in-rule-making.

Conclusion

What We Can Say about the Promise
of Social Movement Societies

KATHLEEN RODGERS AND HOWARD RAMOS

In 2011 the Occupy movement became the North American news story of the year. Some argue that it even changed the discourse of the 2012 American election, bringing class back into mainstream politics. International news media attention was also focused on the Arab Spring of 2011 and the mobilizations throughout 2012 that toppled many repressive regimes. This is not to mention how Idle No More arguably brought Indigenous issues to the forefront of mainstream Canadian politics in late 2012 and early 2013. But while these movements were significant, these events are just three examples among a multitude of movements that took shape in North America and elsewhere during the last decade.

Many more movements and campaigns, however, shape contemporary politics but often receive far less attention. Take, for instance, the Feeding My Family campaign during the summer of 2012, which was based in Canada's northern territory of Nunavut. It attracted 20,000 members on its Facebook page, generated widespread protests throughout the region, and ultimately garnered international attention. Its mobilization was a response to comments from the UN Special Rapporteur on the Right to Food that 70 percent of Nunavut households with Inuit preschool children are food-insecure. The movement focused on the issue of food insecurity in Canada's north, grabbing public attention with online photos and protest signs depicting $20 cabbages and $65 chickens. Although this campaign was

small and narrow in its focus and occurred in one of Canada's most economically marginalized and geographically dispersed regions, the success
of its social movement politics was quite unprecedented. One could cite
similar examples from around the world, such as mobilization by Students
for Academic Freedom – a right-of-centre group of students fighting against
perceived academic abuse of conservative ideology, or actions against ur-
anium processing in Toronto's downtown West End, or calls for a Jasmine
Revolution by Chinese activists pursuing a more open society. This is not
to mention the countless local campaigns mobilized to evoke changes in
people's everyday lives. Alongside Occupy, the Arab Spring, or Idle No
More, these movements seem almost insignificant. But in reality they have
been quite influential and are typical of the politics shaping the twenty-first
century.

Recognizing that these types of movements take place alongside Occupy, the Arab Spring, or Idle No More exemplifies the central concern of
this book, that social movements and protest tactics have become "politics
as usual," and are employed by the widest possible range of political actors.
The social movement society (SMS) thesis put forward by Meyer and Tarrow
(1998) provided a framework for understanding this trend and made the
important observation that despite concerns over low voter turnout and
widespread political apathy towards mainstream institutions, the citizenry
of democratic nations have become increasingly likely to act outside them
– adding contentious action to the repertoire of politics.

The goal of this book has thus been to explore the contours of the
SMS argument and to see what the Canadian context can offer as a case
in its analysis. As our introductory chapter indicated, we had good reasons
to assume empirical support for the phenomenon in Canada but also noted
the country as case points towards at least three potential critiques of the
SMS thesis. These included questioning of the *timing* of the emergence
of social movement societies, reconsidering the relationship between
movements and the state or the *political space* where power is contested,
and, relatedly, challenging the notion of social movement society, singular,
versus recognizing that most contemporary states are shaped by multiple
polities and are thus *social movement societies* – plural. In addition, social
movement societies have increasingly faced a growing neoliberal climate. In
the last couple of decades, Canada and most democratic countries have witnessed assaults on labour unions, feminists, environmentalists, and activists
of all varieties. For all of these reasons, we felt that investigating the SMS

thesis would be not only worthwhile but also important for understanding contemporary politics.

The contributors to this volume were asked to critically engage two broad topics: first, whether the SMS thesis remains an appropriate framework for understanding current configurations of state-movement relations; and second, whether social movement scholarship has effectively addressed the dynamics that are said to make up the SMS thesis. They responded to both across four broad sections considering political and historical context, analyzing state dynamics and processes, examining how people participate in social movement societies, and, last, looking at the role knowledge and culture play in contemporary mobilization. In this final chapter, we identify and draw attention to the arguments around which the contributors of this volume have achieved some degree of consensus and to those where they call for greater clarification and elaboration.

We are left with both support for the SMS thesis as well as critiques that demand refinement and elaboration. The idea that social movements in North America are increasingly a routine part of politics and their presence has contributed to institutions, policies, communities, and cultures that facilitate the long-term survival of the movements' goals, as well as that of the movements themselves, is supported by most chapters. The authors, however, have also called for greater specificity of the SMS thesis, and in particular for a re-examination of the historical applications of the argument that explain the conditions and processes through which SMSs emerge, an exploration of what is meant by institutionalization, and a consideration of the implications of political and movement participation that arise as a result of these conditions. Let us elaborate on each in the following sections.

Importance of Subnational and Historical Contexts
Critics of the SMS thesis have argued that in its original formulation the argument lacked historical, cultural, and national specificity. This sentiment is echoed by a number of chapters in this volume. Staggenborg, for example, noted in Chapter 8 that "the social movement society thesis is provocative, but the mixed evidence for its predictions suggests that we should think more about the conditions that give rise to movement societies. Variations over time and place are important, and we need to explain how and why social movement societies are present in some cities and nations at some times but not others." We believe that the focus on the Canadian case has allowed for the consideration of such concerns. While some

contributors examined how state dynamics have presented a wide range of constituencies with opportunities for claims making, several also focused on subnational societies and the social and historical contexts elucidating the processes involved in the formation and operation of social movement societies.

The Idle No More (INM) movement, as an example, is illustrative of how state dynamics and subnational societies define the contours of the SMS argument. Encompassing thousands of participants of diverse Indigenous backgrounds from across Canada, the INM protests of late 2012 and early 2013 justly qualify as a significant instance of Canadian Indigenous mobilization. Because of its unforeseen size, geographic breadth, and durability, the protests fuelled observations about the importance of social media in the facilitation of protest against the ongoing colonization of the country. Scholars certainly agree that technological advancements of the last decade have created new modes of participation, increased the speed of mobilization, and provided reach to a greater number of participants (Earl and Kimport 2011; Castells 2012). But digital media do not create movements. The INM wave of Canadian Indigenous protest is the culmination of long-standing historical grievances resulting from colonization, growing frustration, and the legacy of failed state-Aboriginal negotiations. Contentious forms of political articulation among Indigenous communities are not new and have grown steadily since the late 1960s (Ramos 2006). As the movement progressed, moreover, the importance of different social, cultural, and legal differences among Indigenous peoples were exacerbated. Many activists distanced themselves from established Indigenous organizations, and cleavages emerged among First Nations from different regions. Like most large movements, INM defies simplistic explanations of technological determinism and illustrates the importance of thinking of social movement societies plural rather than singular. Culture, society, and identity are important determinants of contentious action, and subnational and historical contexts must be analyzed if one is to understand contemporary social movement societies.

Several contributors draw attention to the unique dynamics of state support to political challengers in Canada through the funding regimes of the 1960s through the 1990s. The notion of a pure civil society separate from the state is false in the Canadian case because of this relationship (see Pal 1993 for a detailed examination of the role of state funding). Such funding contributed to the growth and institutionalization of a number of movements. However, Masson reminds us that this relationship is not linear. She argues that although the women's movement in Canada enjoyed significant financial support at the federal level, it has been unable to ensure advancements in gender equality, and the endurance of women's organizations has been fragile in the hostile political climate of the 2000s. As she notes in Chapter 4, in Quebec the success of women's groups in taking "state institutions to task on their own terrain, and to take state policies and programs, discourses, and practices as objects of dispute, struggle, and contention" occurred in a dynamic social and historical context in which movement action encouraged the state to support "citizen participation." This "Quebec Model" of state-movement engagement, Masson argues, broadens the understanding of the multitude of roles that institutionalization plays in the life course of social movements.

Other contributors show that there are divergent historical routes to social movement *societies* even within a singular state. This point is made in Chapter 3 by Clément, who argues that lines between the state and social movements can become blurred as social movement societies develop. He illustrates this point by showing the parallel development of the human rights state and social movement societies. Clément argues that activists in British Columbia lobbied for the creation of a policy infrastructure for human rights but also acted as quasi–law enforcement officials as they actively enforced the legislation. The comparative approach taken by Fetner, Stokes, and Sanders in Chapter 2 further elucidates this argument that the nature and timing of specific social movement societies is contingent on context, by demonstrating that even movements with similar ideological platforms are constrained by *pre-existing* institutional infrastructure. Their evidence demonstrates that in the case of the religious right in the United States and in Canada, historical discrepancies between media opportunities resulted in the emergence of two very different national movements. In the United States, religious organizations benefited from unfettered access to radio, whereas their Canadian counterpart "could not harness a similarly broad audience through an infrastructure of media organizations." The authors' argument emphasizes the point that differential state governance of these institutions shaped their utility for religious actors.

Staggenborg, however, argues that beyond the specifics of political regimes, movement societies also rely on local, national, and international social movement communities. In Chapter 8, she refers to the "diverse elements of movements, including movement organizations, movements within institutions, networks of groups and individuals, cultural groups, and meeting places within communities." Carroll echoes this in Chapter 12 by reminding social movement scholars of the interconnectedness of national and subnational actors with transnational ones. Thus, encompassing Fetner, Stokes, and Sanders's use of mobilizing structures and Couton's use of diasporic communities (Chapter 6), Staggenborg and other contributors to this volume recognize the necessity of community structures and subnational contexts for the bursts of movement activity that are characteristic of movement societies.

Despite the significant differences in the nature and trajectory of each movement explored in this book, each chapter demonstrates that social movements have historically responded to state opportunities and have been able to either actively get movement meanings inscribed in the policy infrastructure of the state or take advantage of pre-existing institutional avenues. As a result, activists have been able to promote the long-term durability of movements and their goals. The concern about national, cultural, and historical contingencies, as well as the dynamics of scale, in explaining the existence of social movement societies, represents a call to understand the social processes and mechanisms under which movement societies develop.

Institutionalization Goes Both Ways

Another consensus of this volume concerns the necessity of clarifying the relationship of institutionalization to the dynamics of contemporary social movement activism. To begin with, several scholars in the social movement literature argue that enduring conceptualizations of institutionalization centre on the notion that the penetration of state apparatuses by movements is considered synonymous with co-optation or selling out. In this way, discussions of institutionalization frequently have negative implications that signify an end to active mobilization. But the movements in the Canadian context problematize such a simplistic positioning. Several chapters in this book trace complex pathways between institutionalization and movement mobilization, movement outcomes, and broader cycles of protest.

As a means of rectifying the ambiguity surrounding institutionalization, Meyer and Pullum, in Chapter 1, distinguish between internal and external forms of institutionalization. On the one hand, external institutionalization refers to movement actors who set up "a relationship with authorities that allows the costs of making claims to be reduced, stabilized, and predicted, so that the process of representing a set of concerns or constituents becomes routine." In contrast, internal institutionalization refers to the process whereby organizations establish stability by securing office space, professional staff, and stable financial support. These attributes constitute a measure of success for many movements, but as Meyer and Pullum point out, some movements also actively resist taking on this form so as to avoid co-optation. In this way, institutionalization presents a challenge for activists and scholars alike.

Several contributors took up the challenge, demonstrating how institutionalization is a key mechanism of social movement societies as successful movements penetrate and alter state governance structures, ensuring that their goals become integrated into policy and creating space for themselves as actors in these relationships. Masson, for instance, argues that while institutionalization may be the result of a maturing movement, this does not necessarily indicate its impending death. The same can be seen in Chapter 5, in which Corrigall-Brown and Ho look at the relationship between governing regimes, funding, and environmental activism. In many respects, they show that movements remained independent despite changing regimes and cuts to funding. Couton also illustrates this with the blurring between ethnic business associations and their facilitation of lobbying and protest for Korean and Ukrainian Canadian communities. In this way, contributors complicate earlier interpretations of state-movement relationship. Most notably, rather than viewing institutionalization as the inevitable endpoint of movement mobilization, these processes also create new institutions and communities that subsequent movements can build from for subsequent rounds of mobilization. They also lead to tactical innovation, as seen in how everyday politics is movement politics, as illustrated by Conley in Chapter 10 and Stoddart in Chapter 13.

Fetner, Stokes, and Sanders expand upon these observations by arguing that even the most volatile eruptions of protest can be traced to the long historical development of movements. This is not necessarily a new observation. Scholars of social movements have long observed that social movements do not emerge out of thin air; movements build on pre-existing networks and organizations, collective identity, and collective action frames. As Staggenborg argues, however, it is these networks, or social movement communities, that form the basis for the social movement society. This is shown vividly by Judith Taylor in Chapter 9, in her questioning of the fashionability of protest and how a local group mobilizes against dirty diesel trains in Toronto. Institutionalization and the social movement society create opportunities and constraints that make the contingencies of movement emergence more possible and likely. It is also important, however, to remember that institutionalization works both ways.

Not only do movements get co-opted but institutions can become more contentious. Wood reminds us in Chapter 7 that in social movement societies, it is not only political challengers who become institutionalized but also the rationalities of state authorities. She shows that activists become accustomed to protest zones and the need for permits to protest, but police also recognize the legitimacy of protest and negotiate with activists. Even so, radical action and repression remain, and arguably become, a part of regular politics.

The contemporary context shows that institutionalization of movement politics has meant that Greenpeace has moved from a largely direct action organization in the 1970s to a transnational organization rivalling the brand popularity of many major corporations. At the same time, the Sierra Club, which focused on lobbying and pursuing legislative change, announced in 2012 that it would move away from this and has increasingly accepted direct action politics as part of its repertoire. Likewise, mainstream politicians have been quick to adopt the discourse of Occupy, and many were more than happy to have photo-ops with INM activists. As the contributors have shown, institutionalization sustains movement societies, providing scholars with an understanding of the underlying forces that enable movements to take shape and endure.

How People Act Politically in Social Movement Societies

The contributors also highlighted the importance of unpacking what is meant by political action and participation in social movement societies. As we noted in both the Introduction and earlier in this chapter, democracies around the world are facing less participation in mainstream politics but at the same time more contentious action. A number of contributors have highlighted the contours of this by looking at how people act politically in social movement societies and how they participate in social movements.

As already noted, Staggenborg focused on the importance of communities in creating mobilization and Taylor analyzed how this occurs in the quotidian. Others, such as Jim Conley, extend this insight by offering tools for understanding how situations and grievances escalate from everyday life to public contestation. He does this by introducing new theories of interaction and orders of worth that not only pair well with political action in social movement societies but also help scholars understand how new media can be used to trigger moral judgment and potential action. Participation is also examined in Chapter 11 by Tindall and Robinson, who contest what it means to belong to a social movement altogether.

Using unique data on activist participation and social movement organization membership, Tindall and Robinson question whether being a member of a movement means that one is an activist. Their operationalization of activism through memberships is bound to generate debate, as this shifts understandings of core activists who protest versus those that contribute from afar. It is an extension of insights by resource mobilization theorists that identified chequebook activism decades ago and is an important reminder of the important difference between saying one is political and acting political. A consequence of the normalization of contentious politics is that they are no longer disruptive, and in turn their urgency and efficacy is lost.

Participation is also assessed by Mark Stoddart, who looks at how two local environmental groups mobilized and used the Internet to advocate for environmental justice. He reminds us that much mobilization is missed by the front pages of news media and that activism in movement societies is often unheralded. He likewise reminds scholars that it important not to lose sight of local mechanisms for change, and that most politics are rewarded through committee work, community meetings, and process of deliberation. Social movement societies are those where action need not amount to radical tactics or violence but instead are defined by demands for greater participation.

Political participation is also knowledge and cultural production. Carroll in Chapter 12 and Haluza-DeLay in Chapter 14 show that movement societies are information societies. Their battles are fought not only through the dynamics of state-movement relations but also in the production of counter-hegemonic culture and knowledge. In part, Meyer and Pullum in Chapter 1 also recognize this through the rise of nativist and identity-based conservative politics. A full understanding of social movement societies, however, also demands that scholars look to new outcomes of mobilization, including shifts in social values and the ability to produce new knowledge. Haluza-DeLay shows that the failure of the environmental movement in Alberta is linked to its inability to contest the predominance of the oil economy and resource economy that has defined the province and increasingly the country. He recognizes that until social and cultural values are changed, environmentalists will never taste true success. Carroll engages similar ideas by looking at the importance of transnational alternative policy groups in current social movement action. He shows that their production of knowledge extends across transnational borders, but also highlights how social movement societies still remain defined by North-South global inequalities.

As many of the contributors illustrate, to truly understand social movement societies means that one must reinvestigate what it means to participate in politics – both mainstream and contentious. As Meyer and Pullum
note, the rise of digital media has changed the landscape of mobilization
and was not fully considered when he and others began contemplating the
SMS thesis. Because of this, not only are protests diffusing to new constituencies but they are also tied to calls for deliberative democracy. Occupy,
the student protests in Quebec (the Maple Spring), Feeding My Family, and
INM are all actions against the so-called democratic deficit. They are movements that typify the cycle of mobilization of the early twenty-first century
and extend social movement societies beyond well-established and well-
funded professional organizations to unaligned citizens who have not previously engaged in lobbying or policymaking – not to mention protest. In the
context of social movement societies, this places a greater emphasis on understanding how activists and politicians conceive of political participation.

New Dilemmas and New Directions
It is clear from all of the contributions to this volume, however, that despite
the promise of increased avenues for deliberation, social movement societies have also created new dilemmas for activists. Meyer and Pullum raised
this question in Chapter 1 when they considered how the increased appeal
of social movement activism both broadens and cheapens public discourse:
"When social movement activism becomes widely diffused, used by the advantaged as well as the excluded, it may be that viable paths towards influence for the excluded have become even harder to find and follow." In other
words, it is possible that with increased activity and use of social movement
forms, movements are achieving fewer goals and having less impact than in
earlier periods. Have social movement tactics become "cheapened" by their
average appeal, or have they become the vehicle for democratic reform?

The different chapters offer some potential insights on the answer to that
question. By considering social movement societies, plural, as many of the
contributors have done, we get a greater sense of the fields of political struggles. Deliberative processes rarely occur in macro contexts, and most grievances, struggles for power, and politics occur at subnational and prefigurative
levels. The contributors have shown that the SMS thesis can be used to
better understand recent demands to "go local" and to adopt greater participation and governance by everyday people. The full engagement of the SMS
thesis, however, demands that scholars shift their lenses of interest from the
large-scale acts of contention that garner widespread news media attention

and focus instead on the mundane politics that shape social and historical contexts and in turn social movement societies.

The mechanisms and outcomes of institutionalization, moreover, are questioned by the different contributors. They show that institutionalization does not only mean co-optation but can also mean facilitation. They show, moreover, that institutionalization also means a shift in mainstream politics to new processes and ones that offer the first steps to the evolution of democratic practices. Social movement societies demand that the rigid and often unproductive distinctions between mainstream and contentious politics be questioned, probed, and investigated. Instead, as Charles Tilly (with Sidney Tarrow 2006) noted in his later conceptualization of contentious politics, they are one means of political struggle on a broader continuum of power relations. Understood in this way, the blurring of social movements and mainstream politics can provoke a fuller understanding of how power is contested.

Ultimately, this revisitation of the SMS thesis has offered an opportunity for us, and hopefully readers of this book, to reconsider political participation in the twenty-first century. All of the chapters have offered insight into unpacking the ironic trend of a decline of mainstream politics and the rise of contentious politics. In a century with unprecedented opportunities for communication, spaces for political engagement, and organizational forms, political participation has also changed.

Thus, although we have reidentified many of the insights first discovered by Meyer and Tarrow (1998), we also believe that by revisiting the SMS thesis we have identified new avenues of exploration and have highlighted how the Canadian case speaks to the broader trend of social movement societies more globally. Although the contributors, like ourselves, have identified dimensions of the SMS thesis in need of refinement we believe that the argument is still useful in unpacking contemporary politics, both mainstream and contentious.

References

Abelson, Donald E. 1995. "From Policy Research to Political Advocacy: The Changing Role of Think Tanks in American Politics." *Canadian Review of American Studies* 25 (1): 93–126. http://dx.doi.org/10.3138/CRAS-025-01-05.

Abrahamian, Atossa Araxia. 2012. "The 'I' in Union." *Dissent* 59: 40–45.

Abreu, Maria, Allessandra Faggian, Roberta Comunian, and Philip McCann. 2012. "Life Is Short, Art Is Long: The Persistent Wage Gap between Bohemian and Non-Bohemian Graduates." *Annals of Regional Science* 49 (2): 305–21. http://dx.doi.org/10.1007/s00168-010-0422-4.

Adut, Ari. 2008. *On Scandal: Moral Disturbances in Society, Politics, and Art.* New York: Cambridge University Press.

AG HRB (Attorney General of British Columbia, Human Rights Branch). 1977–79. Boards of Inquiry list. Acc. 1989-699-05. Human Rights Branch collection (HRB). Ministry of Attorney General (MAG).

–. 1979. Linda J. Brandie to Margaret Strongitharm. 28 August. Acc. 1989-699-05. HRB. MAG.

–. 1981a. Memorandum on Community Organizations. Acc. 1989-700-14. HRB. MAG.

–. 1981b. British Columbia Civil Liberties Association brief on the Human Rights Code. Acc. 1989-700-42. HRB. MAG.

–. n.d. Lists of grants provided by the Human Rights Commission. Acc. 1989-699-27 and Acc. 1989-699-6. HRB. MAG.

Agustoni, Alfredo, and Mara Maretti. 2012. "Energy and Social Change: An Introduction." *International Review of Sociology* 22 (3): 391–404. http://dx.doi.org/10.1080/03906701.2012.730820.

Agyeman, Julian, Robert D. Bullard, and Bob Evans, eds. 2003. *Just Sustainabilities: Development in an Unequal World.* Cambridge, MA: MIT Press.

Aird, John, Charles A. Bowman, and Augustin Frigon. 1929. *Report of the Royal Commission on Radio Broadcasting* [a.k.a. The Aird Report]. Ottawa: Royal Commission on Radio Broadcasting.

Alberta Federation of Labour. 2009. *Lost Down the Pipeline.* Edmonton: Alberta Federation of Labour.

Alexander, Anne McDonald. 1997. *The Antigonish Movement: Moses Coady and Adult Education Today.* Toronto: Thompson Educational.

Alimi, Etian Y., and David S. Meyer. 2011. "Seasons of Change: Arab Spring and Political Opportunities." *Swiss Political Science Review* 17 (4): 475-79.

Amenta, Edwin. 2003. "What We Know about the Development of Social Policy: Comparative and Historical Research in Comparative and Historical Perspective." In *Comparative Historical Analysis in the Social Sciences,* ed. James Mahoney and Dietrich Rueschemeyer, 91–130. Cambridge: Cambridge University Press. http://dx.doi.org/10.1017/CBO9780511803963.004.

Anderson, Benedict. 1991. *Imagined Communities: Reflections on the Origin and Spread of Nationalism.* Rev. ed. London: Verso.

Anderson, Donald. 1986. "The Development of Human Rights Protections in British Columbia." MA thesis, University of Victoria.

Andison, Alan. 2010. Interview by Dominique Clément. 19 August.

Andrew, Merrindahl. 2010. "Women's Movement Institutionalization: The Need for New Approaches." *Politics and Gender* 6 (4): 609–16. http://dx.doi.org/10.1017/S1743923X10000395.

Andrews, Kenneth T. 2001. "Social Movements and Policy Implementation: The Mississippi Civil Rights Movement and the War on Poverty, 1965 to 1971." *American Sociological Review* 66 (1): 71–95. http://dx.doi.org/10.2307/2657394.

–. 2004. *Freedom Is a Constant Struggle.* Chicago: University of Chicago Press.

Anonymous. 1976. *The Rally Story.* Vancouver: Press Gang.

Antrobus, Peggy. 2004. *The Global Women's Movement: Origins, Issues and Strategies.* London: Zed Books.

Armstrong, Robert. 2010. *Broadcasting Policy in Canada.* Toronto: University of Toronto Press.

Assembly of First Nations. 2007. "The United Nations Declaration on the Rights of Indigenous Peoples: What It Says and What It Means for First Nations in Canada." http://www.afn.ca/uploads/files/07-12-4_un_declaration_flyer_fe.pdf.

Aunio, Anna-Liisa, and Suzanne Staggenborg. 2011. "Transnational Linkages and Movement Communities." *Social Compass* 5 (5): 364–75. http://dx.doi.org/10.1111/j.1751-9020.2009.00249.x.

Auyero, Javier, and Débora Alejandra Swistun. 2009. *Flammable: Environmental Suffering in an Argentine Shantytown.* New York: Oxford University Press.

Ayres, Jeffrey M. 1999. "From the Streets to the Internet: The Cyber-Diffusion of Contention." *Annals of the American Academy of Political and Social Science* 566 (1): 132–43. http://dx.doi.org/10.1177/0002716299566001011.

Baczynskyj, Anastasia. 2009. "Learning How to Be Ukrainian: Ukrainian Schools in Toronto and the Formation of Identity, 1947–2009." MA thesis, University of Toronto. https://tspace.library.utoronto.ca/bitstream/1807/18089/1/bazynskyj_anastasia_200911_MA_thesis.pdf.

Baer, Douglas, Edward Grabb, and William A. Johnston. 1990. "The Values of Canadians and Americans: A Critical Analysis and Reassessment." *Social Forces* 68 (3): 693–713. http://dx.doi.org/10.1093/sf/68.3.693.

Bair, Jennifer. 2009. "Taking Aim at the New International Economic Order." In *The Road from Mont Pèlerin: The Making of the Neoliberal Thought Collective*, ed. Philip Mirowski and Dieter Plehwe , 347–85. Cambridge, MA: Harvard University Press.

Bannerji, Himani. 2000. *The Dark Side of the Nation: Essays on Multiculturalism, Nationalism and Gender*. Toronto: Canadian Scholars' Press.

Barclay, Bill. 2009. *Financing Global Warming: Canadian Banks and Fossil Fuels*. San Francisco: Rainforest Action Network.

Barman, Jean. 2007. *The West beyond the West: A History of British Columbia*. 3rd ed. Toronto: University of Toronto Press.

Baron, Ethan. 2011. "Imperial Plays Favourites with Cheap Smokes: Small Mom-and-Pop Shops Pay More to Stock Cigarettes while Big Retailers Enjoy Deep Discounts." *The Province*, 17 February.

Bashevkin, Sylvia. 1996. "Losing Common Ground: Feminists, Conservatives and Public Policy in Canada during the Mulroney Years." *Canadian Journal of Political Science* 29 (2): 211–42. http://dx.doi.org/10.1017/S0008423900007691.

–. 2009. *Women, Power, Politics: The Hidden Story of Canada's Unfinished Democracy*. Don Mills, ON: Oxford University Press Canada.

BC Department of Labour. 1959–63, 1981–82. *Annual Report*. Victoria: Queen's Printer.

–. 1981. "Memorandum from D.H. Cameron to W. Mithchell." G85 168, Acc. 880057-3714, Box 4, f. H-5-L. Department of Labour collection. British Columbia Archives (BCA).

–. 1982a. "SWAG Report on the Human Rights Code." Box 5. G84-079. Department of Labour collection. BCA.

–. 1982b. "Cabinet Submission re the Human Rights Code of British Columbia." 15 May. G85–168, Acc. 880057-3730, Box 20. Department of Labour collection. BCA.

BC Federation of Labour. 1964 to 1969. Submission by the Human Rights Committee of the BC Federation of Labour. MG31 H155, Vol. 16, file 17. Dan Hill collection. Library and Archives Canada (LAC).

–. 1975. *Newsletter*, June.

BC Federation of Labour Human Rights Committee. 1961. Report of the British Columbia Federation of Labour Human Rights Committee. MG28, V75, Vol. 23, file 6. Jewish Labour Committee collection. LAC.

BC Federation of Women. (n.d.). Human rights policy. Vol. 1, file 28. British Columbia Federation of Women Collection. University of British Columbia Rare Books and Special Collections (UBC RBSC).

BC Human Rights Commission. 1983a. "How to Make It Work: A Report of the BC Human Rights Commission on Strengthening the Statutory Protection of Human Rights." Victoria: Queen's Printer for British Columbia.

–. 1983b. "I'm Okay; We're Not So Sure About You: A Report of the BC Human Rights Commission on Extensions to the Code." Victoria: Queen's Printer for British Columbia.

Beasley, Norman, T. Graham, and C. Holmberg. 2000. "Justice Department's Civil Disorder Initiative Addresses Police Training Gap." *Police Chief Magazine*, 1 October, 13–22.

Beaudry, Micheline. 1984. *Les maisons des femmes battues au Québec.* Montréal: Les éditions coopératives Albert Saint-Martin.

Beck, Ulrich. 1992. *Risk Society: Towards a New Modernity.* New Delhi: Sage.

Beckfield, Jason. 2003. "Inequality in the World Polity: The Structure of International Organization." *American Sociological Review* 68 (3): 401–24. http://dx.doi.org/ 10.2307/1519730.

Bélanger, Paul R., and Benoît Lévesque. 1992. "Le mouvement populaire et communautaire: de la revendication au partenariat (1963–1992)." In *Le Québec en jeu. Comprendre les grands défis*, ed. Gérard Daigle, 712–47. Montréal: Presses de l'Université de Montréal.

Benen, Steve. 2011. "High Intensity, Low Turnout in Madison." *Washington Monthly: Political Animal*, 17 April. http://www.washingtonmonthly.com/search2.php? search=high+intensity%2C+low+turnout+in+madison.

Benford, Robert D. 1997. "An Insider's Critique of the Social Movement Framing Perspective." *Sociological Inquiry* 67 (4): 409–30. http://dx.doi.org/10.1111/ j.1475-682X.1997.tb00445.x.

Benford, Robert D., and David A. Snow. 2000. "Framing Processes and Social Movements: An Overview and Assessment." *Annual Review of Sociology* 26 (1): 611–39. http://dx.doi.org/10.1146/annurev.soc.26.1.611.

Beres, Melanie A., Barbara Crow, and Lise Gottell. 2009. "The Perils of Institutionalization in Neoliberal Times: Results of a National Survey of Canadian Sexual Assault and Rape Crisis Centres." *Canadian Journal of Sociology* 34 (1): 135–63.

Berman, Tzeporah, with Mark Leiren-Young. 2011. "The Black Hole: Setting Up Camp in Clayoquot Sound." In *This Crazy Time*, ed. Tzeporah Berman with Mark Leiren-Young, 37–56. Toronto: Knopf Canada.

Berry, Dave. 2010. "The Disobedient Albertans." *Alberta Views*, June.

Berton, Pierre. 1965. *The Comfortable Pew: A Critical Look at Christianity and the Religious Establishment in the New Age.* Toronto: McClelland and Stewart.

Beuchler, Steven M. 2000. *Social Movements in Advanced Capitalism: The Political and Cultural Construction of Social Activism.* New York: Oxford University Press.

Bird, Roger, ed. 1988. *Documents of Canadian Broadcasting.* Ottawa: Carleton University Press.

Black, Bill. 1994. *B.C. Human Rights Review: Report on Human Rights in British Columbia.* Vancouver: Government of British Columbia.

Boltanski, Luc. 1990. *L'amour et la justice comme compétences: trois essais de sociologie de l'action.* Paris: Métailié.

–. 1999. *Distant Suffering: Morality, Media, and Politics.* Trans. Graham Burchell. Cambridge Cultural Social Studies. Cambridge: Cambridge University Press. [1993. *La souffrance à distance: morale humanitaire, médias et politique.* Paris: Métailié] http://dx.doi.org/10.1017/CBO9780511489402.

—. 2004. *La condition fœtale: une sociologie de l'engendrement et de l'avortement.* Paris: Gallimard.

Boltanski, Luc, and Eve Chiapello. 2005. *The New Spirit of Capitalism.* Trans. Gregory Elliott. London: Verso. [1999]. *Le nouvel esprit du capitalisme.* Paris: Gallimard.

Boltanski, Luc, and Elisabeth Claverie. 2007. "Du monde social en tant que scène d'un procès." In *Affaires, scandales et grandes causes: de Socrate à Pinochet,* ed. L. Boltanski, E. Claverie, N. Offenstadt, and S. Van Damme, 395–452. Paris: Stock.

Boltanski, Luc, and Laurent Thévenot. 1999. "The Sociology of Critical Capacity." *European Journal of Social Theory* 2 (3): 359–77. http://dx.doi.org/10.1177/136843199002003010.

—. 2006. *On Justification: Economies of Worth.* Trans. Catherine Porter. Princeton: Princeton University Press. [1991]. *De la justification: les économies de la grandeur.* Paris: Gallimard.

Bonisteel, Mandy, and Linda Green. 2005. "Implications of the Shrinking Space for Feminist Anti-Violence Advocacy." Paper presented at the Canadian Social Welfare Policy Conference, Fredericton. http://www.awcca.ca/pdf/ShrinkingFeminist Space.pdf.

Bornstein, Avram. 2009. "N30 + 10: Global Civil Society, a Decade after the Battle of Seattle." *Dialectical Anthropology* 33 (2): 97–108. http://dx.doi.org/10.1007/s10624-009-9114-9.

Bouchard, Bishop Luc. 2009. "A Pastoral Letter on the Integrity of Creation and the Athabasca Oil Sands." http://oilsandstruth.org/integrity-creation-and-athabasca -tar-sands.

Boudreau, Joseph. 1975. *Alberta, Aberhart, and Social Credit.* Toronto: Holt, Rinehart and Winston of Canada.

Bourdieu, Pierre. 1990. *The Logic of Practice.* Palo Alto, CA: Stanford University Press.

Boven, Joseph. 2011. "Tea Party Ralliers Praise Ryan Budget and Wisconsin Union Busting." *Colorado Independent,* 16 April. http://www.coloradoindependent. com/84399/tea-party-ralliers-praise-ryan-budget-and-wisconsin-union-busting.

Bowen, Paddy. 2006. "Voluntary Sector Awareness Project." http://www.ccsd.ca/ pubs/2003/fm/natini.htm. Accessed 15 September 2014.

Boychuk, Regan. 2010. *Misplaced Generosity: Extraordinary Profits in Alberta's Oil and Gas Industry.* Edmonton: Parkland Institute.

Brennan, Richard J. 2012. "Federal Budget 2012: Changing Old Age Security a 'Bad Idea,' Says Poll." *Toronto Star,* 5 April. http://www.thestar.com/news/canada/ 2012/04/05/federal_budget_2012_changing_old_age_security_a_bad_idea_ says_poll.html.

Breton, Raymond. 2003. "Social Capital and the Civic Participation of Immigrants and Members of Ethno-Cultural Groups." Paper presented at the Conference on the Opportunities and Challenges of Diversity: A Role for Social Capital? Montreal, November.

Brodie, Janine. 2008. "We Are All Equal Now: Contemporary Gender Politics in Canada." *Feminist Theory* 9 (2): 145–64. http://dx.doi.org/10.1177/14647001080 90408.

Brodie, Janine, and Isabella Bakker. 2007. *Canada's Social Policy Regime and Women: An Assessment of the Last Decade.* Ottawa: Status of Women Canada.

Brown, Rosemary. 1979. Briefs and correspondence by the Vancouver Young Women's Christian Association, British Columbia Federation of Labour Women's Rights Committee, and the University of British Columbia Women's Action Group. Vol. 8, file 9. Rosemary Brown collection. UBC RBSC.

–. 1989. *Being Brown: A Very Public Life.* Toronto: Random House.

Brulle, Robert. 2000. *Agency, Democracy and Nature: The U.S. Environmental Movement from a Critical Theory Perspective.* Cambridge, MA: MIT Press.

Brushett, Kevin. 2009. "Making the Shit Disturbers: The Selection and Training of the Company of Young Canadian Volunteers 1965–1970." In *The Sixties in Canada: A Turbulent and Creative Decade,* ed. M. Athena Palaeologu, 246–69. Montreal: Black Rose.

Brym, Robert, Melissa Godbout, Andreas Hoffbauer, Gabe Menard, and Tony Huiquan Zhang. 2014. "Social Media in the 2011 Egyptian Uprising." *British Journal of Sociology* 65 (2): 266–92. http://dx.doi.org/10.1111/1468-4446.12080.

Buček, Jan, and Brian Smith. 2000. "New Approaches to Local Democracy: Direct Democracy, Participation and the 'Third Sector.'" *Environment and Planning. C, Government and Policy* 18 (1): 3–16. http://dx.doi.org/10.1068/c9950.

Burawoy, Michael. 2009. "Challenges for a Global Sociology." *Contexts* 8 (4): 36–41. http://dx.doi.org/10.1525/ctx.2009.8.4.36.

Byfield, Mike. 2007. "Gil McGowan: A Union Vision for the Future Oilpatch." *Oil and Gas Inquirer,* October.

Campanella, David. 2012. *Misplaced Generosity Update 2012: Extraordinary Profits in Alberta's Oil and Gas Industry.* Edmonton: Parkland Institute.

Campbell, John L. 2005. "Where Do We Stand? Common Mechanisms in Organizations and Social Movements Research." In *Social Movements and Organization Theory,* ed. Gerald F. Davis, Doug McAdam, W. Richard Scott, and Mayer N. Zald, 41–68. Cambridge: Cambridge University Press. http://dx.doi.org/10.1017/CBO9780511791000.004.

Canada. Department of Labour. 1960. *Canadian Labour in the Struggle against Employment Discrimination.* Ottawa: Queen's Printer.

Cannavo, Peter F. 2007. *The Working Landscape: Founding, Preservation, and the Politics of Place.* Cambridge, MA: MIT Press.

Carbone, Nick. 2011. "We Are the 99%." *TIME,* 7 December. http://content.time.com/time/specials/packages/article/0,28804,2101344_2100875_2100915,00.html.

Caren, Neal, Raj Andrew Ghoshal, and Vanesa Ribas. 2011. "A Social Movement Generation Cohort and Period Trends in Protest Attendance and Petition Signing." *American Sociological Review* 76 (1): 125–51. http://dx.doi.org/10.1177/0003122410395369.

Carroll, William K. 2003. "Undoing the End of History: Canada-Centred Reflections on the Challenge of Globalization." In *Global Shaping and Its Alternatives,* ed. Y. Atasoy and W.K. Carroll, 33–55. Aurora, ON: Garamond Press.

–. 2007. "Hegemony and Counter-Hegemony in a Global Field." *Studies in Social Justice* 1: 36–66.

–. 2010a. "Crisis, Movements, Counter-Hegemony: In Search of the New." *Interface: A Journal for and about Social Movements* 2 (2): 168–98.

–. 2010b. *The Making of a Transnational Capitalist Class.* London: Zed Books.

–. 2013. "Networks of Cognitive Praxis: Transnational Class Formation from Below?" *Globalizations* 10 (5): 691–710. http://www.tandfonline.com/doi/full/10.1080/14747731.2013.828962#.VOTmHiwYFsZ.

–. 2014. "Alternative Policy Groups and Transnational Counter-Hegemonic Struggle." In *Global Economic Crisis and the Politics of Diversity,* ed. Yildiz Atasoy, 259–84. London and New York: Palgrave Macmillan.

Carroll, William K., and R.S. Ratner. 1996. "Master Framing and Cross-Movement Networking in Contemporary Social Movements." *Sociological Quarterly* 37 (4): 601–25. http://dx.doi.org/10.1111/j.1533-8525.1996.tb01755.x.

–. 2010. "Social Movements and Counter-Hegemony: Lessons from the Field." *New Proposals* 4: 7–22.

Carroll, William K., and J. Sapinski. 2013. "Embedding Post-Capitalist Alternatives? The Global Network of Alternative Knowledge Production and Mobilization." *Journal of World-Systems Research* 19 (2): 211–40.

Carroll, William K., and Murray Shaw. 2001. "Consolidating a Neoliberal Policy Bloc in Canada, 1976 to 1996." *Canadian Public Policy* 27 (2): 195–216. http://dx.doi.org/10.2307/3552197.

Castells, Manuel. 2004. *The Power of Identity.* 2nd ed. Vol. 2, *The Information Age: Economy, Society, and Culture.* Malden, MA: Blackwell.

–. 2012. *Networks of Outrage and Hope: Social Movements in the Internet Age.* Cambridge: Polity Press.

Cattaneo, Claudia. 2008. "Oil Sands Producers Start Web Site to Encourage 'Dialogue.'" *Financial Post,* 23 June. http://www.financialpost.com/story.html?id=608585. Accessed 18 September 2014.

Catungal, John Paul, Deborah Leslie, and Yvonne Hii. 2009. "Geographies of Displacement in the Creative City: The Case of Liberty Village, Toronto." *Urban Studies* 46 (5-6): 1095–114.

CBC News. 2006a. "Cyclist-Driver Clash Photos Spark Online Debate." 31 January. http://www.cbc.ca/canada/story/2006/01/31/toronto-fightphotos060131.html. Accessed 28 September 2010.

–. 2006b. "Your Space: Cyclist-Driver Clash Photos Spark Online Debate." 1 February. http://www.cbc.ca/news/viewpoint/yourspace/cyclist_driver.html. Accessed 28 September 2010.

CBC News. 2010. "'Compassionate Homicide': The Law and Robert Latimer." 6 December. http://www.cbc.ca/news/canada/story/2010/12/06/f-robert-latimer-compassionate-homicide.html. Accessed 28 September 2010.

–. 2011. "Voter Turnout Inches Up to 61.4%." 3 May. http://www.cbc.ca/news/politics/voter-turnout-inches-up-to-61-4-1.997399.

Cha, Nanok. 2009. "Korean Immigrant Women's Lived Experiences in Halifax: Challenging Gender Relations in the Family, Workplace, and Community." MA thesis, Saint Mary's University.

Chatfield, Charles. 1992. *The American Peace Movement: Ideals and Activism.* New York: Twayne.

Chivers, Sally. 2007. "Barrier by Barrier: The Canadian Disability Movement and the Fight for Equal Rights." In *Group Politics and Social Movements in Canada,* ed. Miriam Smith, 159–80. Peterborough, ON: Broadview Press.

Chui, Tina, and Hélène Maheux. 2011. *Visible Minority Women.* Ottawa: Statistics Canada. http://www.statcan.gc.ca/pub/89-503-x/2010001/article/11527-eng.htm.

Chung, Jinhee. 2008. *An Exploration of Korean Immigrant Women's Leisure in Spiritual Settings.* MA thesis, University of Waterloo. https://uwspace.uwaterloo. ca/handle/10012/3675.

Church Investors Group. 2008. *Unconventional Oil: Tar and Shale Sands: A Briefing for Church Investors.* London: Church Investors Group.

Churchill, Ward. 1986. *Pacifism as Pathology.* New York: Primus.

CIC (Citizenship and Immigration Canada). 2011. "Facts and Figures: Immigration Overview: Permanent and Temporary Residents." Ottawa. http://www.cic.gc.ca/ english/resources/statistics/facts2010/permanent/10.asp.

Citynoise. 2006. "Motorist vs Courier." http://citynoise.org/article/2770.

Clark, David. 2004. "Implementing the Third Way: Modernizing Governance and Public Services in Quebec and the UK." *Public Management Review* 6 (4): 493–510. http://dx.doi.org/10.1080/1471903042000303300.

Clarke, Gerard. 1998a. "Nongovernmental Organizations (NGOs) and Politics in the Developing World." *Political Studies* 46 (1): 36–52. http://dx.doi.org/10. 1111/1467-9248.00128.

–. 1998b. *The Politics of NGOs in South-East Asia.* London: Routledge. http://dx. doi.org/10.4324/9780203268681.

Claverie, Elisabeth. 1994. "Procès, affaire, cause. Voltaire et l'innovation critique." *Politix* 7 (26): 76–85. http://dx.doi.org/10.3406/polix.1994.1843.

Clemens, Elisabeth. 1997. *The People's Lobby: Organizational Innovation and the Rise of Interest Group Politics in the United States, 1890–1925.* Chicago: University of Chicago Press.

Clément, Dominique. 2005. "An Exercise in Futility? Regionalism, State Funding and Ideology as Obstacles to the Formation of a National Social Movement Organization in Canada." *BC Studies* 146 (Summer): 63–91.

–. 2008a. *Canada's Rights Revolution: Social Movements and Social Change, 1937–1982.* Vancouver: UBC Press.

–. 2008b. "'I Believe in Human Rights, Not Women's Rights': Women and the Human Rights State, 1969–1984." *Radical History Review* 2008 (101): 107–29. http:// dx.doi.org/10.1215/01636545-2007-040.

–. 2010. "Human Rights Law and Sexual Discrimination in British Columbia, 1953-1984." In *The West and Beyond,* ed. Sara Carter, Alvin Finkel, and Peter Fortna, 297–325. Edmonton: Athabasca University Press.

–. 2012. "Equality Deferred: The Origins of the Newfoundland Human Rights State." *Acadiensis* 41 (1): 102–27.

–. 2014. *Gendered Inequality: The Rise and Fall of British Columbia's Human Rights State, 1953–1984.* Vancouver: UBC Press/Osgoode Society for Canadian Legal History.

Cobban, Alfred. 1965. *France of the Republics, 1871–1962.* Vol. 3, *A History of Modern France.* Harmondsworth, UK: Penguin Books.

Coburn, Elaine. 2010. "Resisting Neoliberal Capitalism: Insights from Marxist Political Economy." In *Relations of Global Power: Neoliberal Order and Disorder,* ed. G. Teeple and S. McBride, 194–226. Toronto: University of Toronto Press.

Le Collectif Clio. 1982. *L'histoire des femmes au Québec depuis quatre siècles.* Montréal: Quinze.

Comeau, Pauline, and Aldo Santin. 1990. *The First Canadians: A Profile of Canada's Native People Today.* Toronto: James Lorimer.

Cook, Peter G., and Myles A. Ruggles. 1992. "Balance and Freedom of Speech: Challenge for Canadian Broadcasting." *Canadian Journal of Communication* 17 (1): 37–59.

Coombs, Gretchen. 2012. "Park(ing) Day." *Contexts* (Summer): 64-65.

Cordero-Guzmán, Héctor R. 2005. "Community-Based Organizations and Migration in New York City." *Journal of Ethnic and Migration Studies* 31 (5): 889–909. http://dx.doi.org/10.1080/13691830500177743.

Cormier, Jeffrey, and D.B. Tindall. 2005. "Wood Frames: Framing the Forests in British Columbia." *Sociological Focus* 38 (1): 1–24. http://dx.doi.org/10.1080/00380237.2005.10571254.

Corrigall-Brown, Catherine. 2012. *Patterns of Protest: Trajectories of Participation in Social Movements.* Palo Alto, CA: Stanford University Press.

Couton, Philippe. 2011. "The Impact of Communal Organizational Density on the Labour Market Integration of Immigrants in Canada." *International Migration* 51 (1): 1–31.

Cox, Robert W. 1987. *Production, Power and World Order.* New York: Columbia University Press.

Coy, Patrick, and Timothy Hedeen. 2005. "A Stage Model of Social Movement Co-optation: Community Mediation in the United States." *Sociological Quarterly* 46 (3): 405–35. http://dx.doi.org/10.1111/j.1533-8525.2005.00020.x.

Cronin, J. Keri. 2011. *Manufacturing National Park Nature: Photography, Ecology, and the Wilderness Industry of Jasper.* Vancouver: UBC Press.

Cronon, William. 1995. "The Trouble with Wilderness, or, Getting Back to the Wrong Nature." In *Uncommon Ground: Toward Reinventing Nature,* ed. W. Cronon, 69–90. New York: W.W. Norton.

Crooks, Ed. 2008. "Investors Warned of Risk to Oil Sands Plans." *Financial Times,* 15 September. http://www.ft.com/cms/s/0/eee600b0-8362-11dd-907e-000077b07658.html.

Crossley, Nick. 2003. "From Reproduction to Transformation: Social Movement Fields and the Radical Habitus." *Theory, Culture and Society* 20 (6): 43–68. http://dx.doi.org/10.1177/0263276403206003.

Dale, Stephen. 1996. *McLuhan's Children: The Greenpeace Message and the Media.* Toronto: Between the Lines.

Dalton, Russell. 2002. *Citizen Politics: Public Opinion and Political Parties in Advanced Industrial Democracies.* 3rd ed. New York: Chatham House Publishers.

Darling, Alan J. 1993. "Public Notice CRTC 1993-78." http://www.crtc.gc.ca/eng/archive/1993/pb93-78.htm.

Daub, Shannon J. 2010. "Negotiating Sustainability: Climate Change Framing in the Communications, Energy and Paperworkers Union." *Symbolic Interaction* 33 (1): 115–40. http://dx.doi.org/10.1525/si.2010.33.1.115.

Davenport, Christian, and Marci Eads. 2001. "Cued to Coerce or Coercing Cues? An Exploration of Dissident Rhetoric and Its Relationship to Political Repression." *Mobilization: An International Quarterly* 6 (2): 151–71.

Davidson, Debra J., and Mike Gismondi. 2011. *Challenging Legitimacy at the Precipice of Energy Calamity.* Berlin: Springer. http://dx.doi.org/10.1007/978-1-4614-0287-9.

Dawson, Michael. 2004. *Selling British Columbia: Tourism and Consumer Culture, 1890–1970.* Vancouver: UBC Press.

Day, Richard F. 2005. *Gramsci Is Dead: Anarchist Currents in the Newest Social Movements.* Toronto: Between the Lines.

De Haas, Hein. 2010. "Migration and Development: A Theoretical Perspective." *International Migration Review* 44 (1): 227–64. http://dx.doi.org/10.1111/j.1747-7379.2009.00804.x.

de Lint, Willem, and Alan Hall. 2009. *Intelligent Control: Developments in Public Order Policing in Canada.* Toronto: University of Toronto Press.

de Sousa Santos, B. 2006. *The Rise of the Global Left: The World Social Forum and Beyond.* London: Zed Books.

–. 2008. "The World Social Forum and the Global Left." *Politics and Society* 36 (2): 247–70. http://dx.doi.org/10.1177/0032329208316571.

della Porta, Donatella, Olivier Fillieule, and Herbert Reiter. 1998. "Policing Protest in France and Italy: From Intimidation to Cooperation." In *The Social Movement Society: Contentious Politics for the New Century,* ed. David S. Meyer and Sidney Tarrow, 111–30. Lanham, MD: Rowman and Littlefield.

della Porta, Donatella, Abby Peterson, and Herbert Reiter. 2006. *The Policing of Transnational Protest.* Aldershot, UK/Burlington, VT: Ashgate.

della Porta, Donatella, and Herbert Reiter, eds. 1998. *Policing Protest: The Control of Mass Demonstrations in Western Democracies.* Minneapolis: University of Minnesota Press.

Dembecki, Greg. 2011. "A Tyee Series: In America's Capital, a Fierce Fight over Oil Sands." *The Tyee,* 14 March. http://thetyee.ca/News/2011/03/14/OilSandsFight/.

Diani, Mario. 1992. "The Concept of Social Movement." *Sociological Review* 40 (1): 1–25. http://dx.doi.org/10.1111/j.1467-954X.1992.tb02943.x.

–. 1997. "Social Movements and Social Capital: A Network Perspective on Movement Outcomes." *Mobilization: An International Quarterly* 2 (2): 129–47.

–. 2003. "Networks and Social Movements: A Research Programme." In *Social Movements and Networks,* ed. Mario Diani and Doug McAdam, 299–319. Oxford: Oxford University Press.

–. 2011. "Social Movements and Collective Action." In *Sage Handbook of Social Network Analysis,* ed. John Scott and Peter Carrington, 223–35. London: Sage.

–. 2012. "Modes of Coordination of Collective Action: What Actors in Policy Making?" In *Networks in Social Policy Problems,* ed. Marco Scotti and Balaz Vedres, 101–23. Cambridge: Cambridge University Press.

–. 2013. "Organizational Fields and Social Movement Dynamics." In *The Future of Social Movement Research,* ed. Jacqueline Van Stekelenburg, Conny Roggeband, and Bert Klandermans, 145–68. Minneapolis: University of Minnesota Press.

Diani, Mario, and Ivano Bison. 2004. "Organizations, Coalitions, and Movements." *Theory and Society* 33 (3/4): 281–309. http://dx.doi.org/10.1023/B:RYSO.000 0038610.00045.07.

Dickerson, Carrie A., and William J. Campbell. 2008. "Strange Bedfellows: Youth Activists, Government Sponsorship, and the Company of Young Canadians (CYC), 1965–1970." *European Journal of American Studies* 3 (2). http://dx.doi. org/10.4000/ejas.2862.

Dillman, Don A., John L. Eltinge, Robert M. Groves, and Roderick J.A. Little. 2002. "Survey Nonresponse in Design, Data Collection, and Analysis." In *Survey Nonresponse,* ed. Robert M. Groves, Don A. Dillman, John L. Eltinge, and Roderick J.A. Little, 3–26. New York: John Wiley and Sons.

DiMaggio, Paul J., and Walter W. Powell. 1983. "The Iron Cage Revisited: Institutional Isomorphism and Collective Rationality in Organizational Fields." *American Sociological Review* 48 (2): 147–60.

Dobrowolsky, Alexandra. 2006. "The Chretien Legacy and Women: Changing Policy Priorities with Little Cause for Celebration." In *The Chretien Legacy: Politics and Public Policy in Canada,* ed. L. Harder and S. Patten, 181–211. Montreal and Kingston: McGill-Queen's University Press.

Dobson, Kyle. 2011. "The Movement Society in Comparative Perspective." *Mobilization: An International Quarterly* 16 (4): 475–94.

Dodaro, Santo, and Leonard Pluta. 2012. *The Big Picture: The Antigonish Movement of Eastern Nova Scotia.* Montreal and Kingston: McGill-Queen's University Press.

Domhoff, G. William. 2006. *Who Rules America? Power, Politics, and Social Change.* New York: McGraw-Hill.

Douglas, Mary. 2005. *Purity and Danger: An Analysis of Concepts of Pollution and Taboo.* London: Routledge.

Dryzek, John, David Downes, Christian Hunold, David Schlosberg, and Hans-Kristian Hernes. 2003. *Green States and Social Movements: Environmentalism in the United States, United Kingdom, Germany and Norway.* Oxford: Oxford University Press. http://dx.doi.org/10.1093/0199249024.001.0001.

Duclos, Nitya. 1993. "Disappearing Women: Racial Minority Women in Human Rights Cases." *Canadian Journal of Women and the Law* 6: 25–51.

Dufour, Pascale, and Isabelle Giraud. 2007a. "The Continuity of Transnational Solidarities in the World March of Women, 2000 and 2005: A Collective Identity-Building Approach." *Mobilization: An International Quarterly* 12: 307–22.

–. 2007b. "Globalization and Political Change in the Women's Movement: The Politics of Scale and Political Empowerment in the World March of Women." *Social Science Quarterly* 88 (5): 1152–73. http://dx.doi.org/10.1111/j.1540-6237. 2007.00496.x.

Dufour, Pascale, Johanne Lachance, et al. 2007. *La mise en oeuvre de la Politique de reconnaissance et de soutien de l'action communautaire dans le champ: Défense collective des droits.* Montréal: CPDS, Université de Montréal. http://www.cpds. umontreal.ca/pdf/Rapport%20d%C3%A9fences%20droits.pdf.

Dumont, Micheline, and Louise Toupin. 2003. *La pensée féministe au Québec.* Montréal: Les Éditions du Remue-Ménage.

Earl, Jennifer. 2011. "Political Repression: Iron Fists, Velvet Gloves, and Diffuse Control." *Annual Review of Sociology* 37: 261-84.

Earl, Jennifer, and Katrina Kimport. 2009. "Movement Societies and Digital Protest: Fan Activism and Other Nonpolitical Protest Online." *Sociological Theory* 27 (3): 220–43. http://dx.doi.org/10.1111/j.1467-9558.2009.01346.x.

–. 2011. *Digitally Enabled Social Change: Activism in the Internet Age.* Cambridge, MA: MIT Press. http://dx.doi.org/10.7551/mitpress/9780262015103.001.0001.

Eberlee, T.M., and D.G. Hill. 1964. "The Ontario Human Rights Code." *University of Toronto Law Journal* 15 (2): 448–55. http://dx.doi.org/10.2307/825295.

Egale Canada. 2011. *In the Supreme Court of Canada,* File no. 29866. http://www.samesexmarriage.ca/docs/scc/agc_factum.pdf.

Eliasoph, Nina. 1998. *How Americans Produce Apathy in Everyday Life.* Cambridge: Cambridge University Press. http://dx.doi.org/10.1017/CBO9780511583391.

–. 1999. "'Everyday Racism' in a Culture of Political Avoidance: Civil Society, Speech, and Taboo." *Social Problems* 46 (4): 479–502. http://dx.doi.org/10.2307/3097072.

Ericson, Richard, and Aaron Doyle. 1999. "Globalization and the Policing of Protest: The Case of APEC 1997." *British Journal of Sociology* 50 (4): 589–608. http://dx.doi.org/10.1111/j.1468-4446.1999.00589.x.

Etzioni, Amitai. 1970. *Demonstration Democracy.* New York: Gordon and Breach.

Evans, P. 2008. "Is an Alternative Globalization Possible?" *Politics and Society* 36 (2): 271–305. http://dx.doi.org/10.1177/0032329208316570.

Eyerman, Ron, and Andrew Jamison. 1991. *Social Movements: A Cognitive Approach.* University Park: Pennsylvania State University Press.

Faassen, Mark. 2011. "A Fine Balance: The Regulation of Canadian Religious Broadcasting." *Queen's Law Journal* 37 (1): 303–37.

Fairlie, Robert W., Julie Zissimopoulos, and Harry Krashinsky. 2010. "The International Asian Business Success Story? A Comparison of Chinese, Indian and Other Asian Businesses in the United States, Canada and United Kingdom." In *International Differences in Entrepreneurship,* ed. Josh Lerner and Antoinette Schoar, 179–208. Chicago: University of Chicago Press. http://dx.doi.org/10.7208/chicago/9780226473109.003.0007.

Ferree, Myra Marx. 2003. "Resonance and Radicalism: Feminist Framing in the Abortion Debates of the United States and Germany." *American Journal of Sociology* 109 (2): 304–44. http://dx.doi.org/10.1086/378343.

Ferree, Myra Marx, William Anthony Gamson, Jürgen Gerhards, and Dieter Rucht. 2002. *Shaping Abortion Discourse: Democracy and the Public Sphere in Germany and the United States.* New York: Cambridge University Press. http://dx.doi.org/10.1017/CBO9780511613685.

Ferree, Myra Marx, and Patricia Yancey Martin. 1995. "Doing the Work of the Movement: Feminist Organizations." In *Feminist Organizations: Harvest of the New Women's Movement,* ed. Myra Marx Ferree and Patricia Yancey Martin, 3–23. Philadelphia: Temple University Press.

Fetner, Tina. 2008. *How the Religious Right Shaped Lesbian and Gay Activism.* Minneapolis: University of Minnesota Press.

Fetner, Tina, and Carrie B. Sanders. 2011. "The Pro-Family Movement in Canada and the United States: Institutional Histories and Barriers to Diffusion." In *Faith, Politics, and Sexual Diversity in Canada and the United States*, ed. David Rayside and Clyde Wilcox, 87–100. Vancouver: UBC Press.

–. 2012. "Similar Strategies, Different Outcomes: Institutional Histories of the Christian Right of Canada and of the United States." In *Strategies in Social Change*, ed. Greg Maney, Rachel Kutz-Flamembaum, Deanna Rohlinger, and Jeff Goodwin, 245–62. Minneapolis: University of Minnesota Press.

Finke, Roger, and Rodney Stark. 2005. *The Churching of America, 1776–2005: Winners and Losers in Our Religious Economy*. New Brunswick, NJ: Rutgers University Press.

Finkel, Alvin. 1989. *The Social Credit Phenomenon in Alberta*. Toronto: University of Toronto Press.

Fleras, Augie, and Jean Leonard Elliott. 1992. *The "Nations Within": Aboriginal-State Relations in Canada, the United States, and New Zealand*. Toronto: Oxford University Press.

Florida, Richard. 2004. *Cities and the Creative Class*. New York: Routledge.

Floris, Vermeulen. 2013. "Mutualism, Resource Competition and Opposing Movements among Turkish Organizations in Amsterdam and Berlin, 1965–2000." *British Journal of Sociology* 64 (3): 453–77.

Fluet, Colette, and Naomi Krogman. 2009. "The Limits of Integrated Resource Management in Alberta for Aboriginal and Environmental Groups: The Northern East Slopes Sustainable Resource and Environmental Management Strategy." In *Environmental Conflict and Democracy in Canada*, ed. L. Adkins, 123–39. Vancouver: UBC Press.

Fluker, Shaun. 2010. "The Case of the 1600 Dead Ducks: The Verdict Is in – Syncrude Guilty under the Migratory Birds Convention Act." http://ablawg.ca/2010/06/30/the-case-of-the-1600-dead-ducks-the-verdict-is-in-syncrude-guilty-under-the-migratory-birds-convention-act.

Fong, Eric, and Emi Ooka. 2002. "The Social Consequences of Participating in the Ethnic Economy." *International Migration Review* 36 (1): 125–46. http://dx.doi.org/10.1111/j.1747-7379.2002.tb00074.x.

Fortner, Robert S. 2005. *Radio, Morality, and Culture: Britain, Canada, and the United States, 1919–1945*. Carbondale: Southern Illinois University Press.

Fotheringham, Allan. 1978. "Column." *Vancouver Sun*, 2 September.

Fournier, Marcel. 2007. *Émile Durkheim: 1858–1917*. Paris: Fayard.

Fox News. 2012. "Tea Party Patriots Leader Defends Group after Co-Founder Leaves Claiming GOP Ties." 3 March. http://www.foxnews.com/politics/2012/03/03/tea-party-patriots-leader-defends-groups-independence-after-co-founder-leaves/#ixzz2d7Had3KK.

Franklin, H. Bruce. 2001. "Pentagon Papers Chase." *Nation*, 9 July.

Fraser, Nancy. 2005. "Reframing Justice in a Globalizing World." *New Left Review* 36: 69–88.

FreedomWorks. 2011. "Key Issues." http://www.freedomworks.org/issues.

Fudge, Judy. 1989. "The Effect of Entrenching a Bill of Rights upon Political Discourse: Feminist Demands and Sexual Violence in Canada." *International Journal of the Sociology of Law* 17: 445–63.

Gailus, Jeff. 2012. *Little Black Lies: Corporate and Political Spin in the Global War for Oil.* Calgary: Rocky Mountain Books.

Galabuzi, Grace Edward. 2006. *Canada's Economic Apartheid: The Social Exclusion of Racialized Groups in the New Century.* Toronto: Canadian Scholars' Press.

Gamson, William A. 1988. "Political Discourse and Collective Action." *International Social Movement Research* 1: 219–44.

–. 1990 [1975]. *The Strategy of Social Protest.* Belmont, CA: Wadsworth.

–. 1992. "The Social Psychology of Collective Action." In *Frontiers in Social Movement Theory,* ed. A.D. Morris and C.M. Mueller, 53–76. New Haven, CT: Yale University Press.

–. 1995. "Constructing Social Protest." In *Social Movements and Culture,* ed. Hank Johnston and Bert Klandermans, 85–106. Minneapolis: University of Minnesota Press.

Gamson, William A., Bruce Fireman, and Steven Rytina. 1982. *Encounters with Unjust Authority.* Homewood, IL: Dorsey Press.

Gans, Herbert. 1979. *Deciding What's News.* Evanston, IL: Northwestern University Press.

Garon, Francis. 2008. *La mise en oeuvre de la Politique de reconnaissance et de soutien de l'action communautaire dans le champ: Environnement.* Montréal: CPDS, Université de Montréal. http://www.cpds.umontreal.ca/pdf/Rapport%20final%20Environnement%2018%20Mai%2008.pdf.

Garon, Francis, Julie Dufresne, and Lorraine Guay. 2006. *La mise en oeuvre de la Politique de reconnaissance et de soutien de l'action communautaire au niveau intersectoriel: Identification des enjeux.* Montréal: CPDS, Université de Montréal. http://www.cpds.umontreal.ca/pdf/Rapport-intersectoriel.pdf.

Garrett, R. Kelly. 2006. "Protest in an Information Society: A Review of Literature on Social Movements and New ICTs." *Information, Communication and Society* 9 (2): 202–24.

Gay, Peter. 1965. *Voltaire's Politics: The Poet as Realist.* New York: Vintage Books.

Gellert, Paul K., and Jon Shefner. 2009. "People, Place, and Time: How Structural Fieldwork Helps World-Systems Analysis." *Journal of World-Systems Research* 15 (2): 193–218.

Germino, Dante L. 1990. *Antonio Gramsci: Architect of a New Politics.* Baton Rouge: Louisiana State University.

Gibbins, Dan. 2010. *Blackened Reputation: A Year of Coverage of Alberta's Oil Sands.* Calgary: Canada West Foundation.

Gibbins, Roger, and Robert Roach. 2010. *Look before You Leap: Oil and Gas, the Western Canadian Economy and National Prosperity.* Calgary: Canada West Foundation.

Gill, Rosalind, and Andy Pratt. 2008. "In the Social Factory? Immaterial Labour, Precariousness, and Cultural Work." *Theory, Culture and Society* 25 (7–8): 1–30. http://dx.doi.org/10.1177/0263276408097794.

Gill, Stephen R. 1995. "Theorizing the Interregnum: The Double Movement of Global Politics in the 1990s." In *International Political Economy: Understanding Global Disorder,* ed. B. Hettne, 65–99. Halifax: Fernwood Books.

Gillham, Patrick F., and John A. Noakes. 2007. "More than a March in a Circle': Transgressive Protests and the Limits of Negotiated Management." *Mobilization: An International Quarterly* 12: 341–57.

Ginsberg, Benjamin, and Martin Shefter. 2002. *Politics by Other Means.* New York: Norton.

Gitlin, Todd. 1981. *The Whole World Is Watching.* Berkeley: University of California Press.

Giugni, Marco. 1998. "Was It Worth the Effort? The Outcomes and Consequences of Social Movements." *Annual Review of Sociology* 24 (1): 371–93. http://dx.doi.org/10.1146/annurev.soc.24.1.371.

Givan, Rebecca Kolins, Kenneth M. Roberts, and Sarah A. Soule, eds. 2010. *The Diffusion of Social Movements: Actors, Mechanisms, and Political Effects.* New York: Cambridge University Press. http://dx.doi.org/10.1017/CBO9780511761638.

Glasius, M., M. Kaldor, and H. Anheier, eds. 2006. *Global Civil Society 2005/6.* London: Sage.

Goffman, Erving. 1971. *Relations in Public: Microstudies of the Public Order.* New York: Harper and Row.

Goldenberg, Suzanne. 2012. "Canada's PM Stephen Harper Faces Revolt by Scientists." *The Guardian,* 8 January. http://www.theguardian.com/environment/2012/jul/09/canada-stephen-harper-revolt-scientists.

Goldstone, Jack A. 2003. "Introduction: Bridging Institutionalized and Non-institutionalized Politics." In *States, Parties and Social Movements,* ed. Jack A. Goldstone, 1–24. Cambridge: Cambridge University Press. http://dx.doi.org/10.1017/CBO9780511625466.002.

–. 2004. "More Social Movements or Fewer? Beyond Political Opportunity Structures to Relational Fields." *Theory and Society* 33 (3/4): 333–65. http://dx.doi.org/10.1023/B:RYSO.0000038611.01350.30.

Gottlieb, Robert. 2005. *Forcing the Spring: The Transformation of the American Environmental Movement.* Washington, DC: Island Press.

Gottlieb, Roger S. 2006. *A Greener Faith: Religious Environmentalism and Our Planet's Future.* Oxford: Oxford University Press. http://dx.doi.org/10.1093/acprof:oso/9780195176483.001.0001.

Gould, Kenneth A., Allan Schnaiberg, and Adam S. Weinberg. 1996. *Local Environmental Struggles: Citizen Activism in the Treadmill of Production.* New York: Cambridge University Press. http://dx.doi.org/10.1017/CBO9780511752759.

Gouvernement du Québec. 2001. *L'action communautaire – Une contribution essentielle à l'exercice de la citoyenneté et au développement social du Québec. Politique gouvernementale.* Direction des communications, Ministère de l'Emploi et de la Solidarité sociale, September. http://www.mess.gouv.qc.ca/sacais/action-communautaire/politique-reconnaissance-soutien.asp.

Graefe, Peter. 2000. "The High Value-Added, Low-Wage Model: Progressive Competitiveness in Quebec from Bourassa to Bouchard." *Studies in Political Economy* 59: 17–60.

–. 2003. "Broadening the Options: Inflecting Quebec's Post-Industrial Strategy." Paper presented at the annual meeting of the Canadian Political Science Association, Halifax, 29 May. http://www.cpsa-acsp.ca/paper-2003/graefe.pdf.

Gramsci, Antonio. 1971. *Selections from the Prison Notebooks of Antonio Gramsci.* New York: International Publishers.

Grant, Peter S., and Grant Buchanan. 2010. *Canadian Broadcasting Regulatory Handbook.* 10th ed. Toronto: McCarthy Tétrault.

Grayson, J. Paul, and Linda Grayson. 1974. "The Social Basis of Interwar Political Unrest in Urban Alberta." *Canadian Journal of Political Science* 7 (02): 289–313. http://dx.doi.org/10.1017/S0008423900038348.

Hackett, Robert A., and Yuezhi Zhao. 1999. *Sustaining Democracy? Journalism and the Politics of Objectivity.* Toronto: University of Toronto Press.

Haines, Herbert H. 1995. *Black Radicals and the Civil Rights Mainstream.* Knoxville: University of Tennessee Press.

Hall, Alan, and Willem de Lint. 2003. "Policing Labour in Canada." *Policing and Society: An International Journal of Research and Policy* 13 (3): 219–34. http://dx.doi.org/10.1080/10439460308035.

Haluza-DeLay, Randolph B. 2008. "A Theory of Practice for Social Movements: Environmentalism and Ecological Habitus." *Mobilization: An International Quarterly* 13 (2): 205–18.

–. 2014. "Assembling Consent in Alberta: Hegemony and the Tar Sands." In *A Line in the Tar Sands: Struggles for Environmental Justice,* ed. Stephen D'Arcy, Toban Black, Tony Weis, and Joshua Kahn Russell, 36-44. Toronto: Between the Lines.

Haluza-DeLay, Randolph B., and Ron Berezan. 2013. "Permaculture in the City: Ecological Habitus and the Distributed Ecovillage." In *Environmental Anthropology Engaging Ecotopia: Bioregionalism, Permaculture, and Ecovillages for a Sustainable Future,* ed. J. Lockyear and J. Veteto, 130–45. New York: Berghahn Books.

Haluza-DeLay, Randolph, and Angela Carter. Forthcoming. "Social Movements Scaling Up: Strategies and Opportunities in Opposing the Oilsands Status Quo." In *Political Ecology and Governance in Alberta,* vol. 1. ed. L. Adkin, B. Miller, and N. Krogman. Toronto: University of Toronto Press.

Haluza-DeLay, Randolph B., Michael Ferber, and Tim Wiebe-Neufeld. 2013. "Watching *Avatar* from 'AvaTarSands' Land." In *Avatar and Nature Spirituality,* ed. B. Taylor, 123–40. Waterloo, ON: Wilfrid Laurier University Press.

Haluza-DeLay, Randolph B., and Heather Fernhout. 2011. "Sustainability and Social Inclusion? Examining the Frames of Canadian English-Speaking Environmental Movement Organizations." *Local Environment: A Journal of Justice and Sustainability* 16 (7): 727–45. http://dx.doi.org/10.1080/13549839.2011.594036.

Hamel, Pierre. 1991. *Action collective et démocratie locale. Les mouvements urbains Montréalais.* Montréal: Presses de l'Université de Montréal.

Han, J.D., and Peter Ibbott. 2005. "Korean Migration to North America: Some Prices That Matter." *Canadian Studies in Population* 32 (2): 155–76.

Harrell, David Edwin Jr. 1985. *Oral Roberts: An American Life.* Bloomington: Indiana University Press.

Harter, John-Henry. 2011. *New Social Movements, Class and the Environment: A Case Study of Greenpeace Canada.* Newcastle, UK: Cambridge Scholars Publishing.

Harvey, D. 2003. *The New Imperialism.* New York: Oxford University Press.

—. 2005. *A Brief History of Neoliberalism.* New York: Oxford University Press.

Herberg, Edward N. 1990. "The Ethno-Racial Socioeconomic Hierarchy in Canada: Theory and Analysis of the New Vertical Mosaic." *International Journal of Comparative Sociology* 31 (3–4): 206–21. http://dx.doi.org/10.1177/002071529 003100305.

Hercus, Cheryl. 2005. *Stepping Out of Line: Becoming and Being a Feminist.* New York: Routledge.

Hewson, Claire. 2008. "Internet-Mediated Research as an Emergent Method and Its Potential Role in Facilitating Mixed Methods Research." In *Handbook of Emergent Methods,* ed. S.N. Hesse-Biber and P. Leavy, 543–70. New York: Guilford Press.

Hine, Christine. 2008. "Internet Research as Emergent Practice." In *Handbook of Emergent Methods,* ed. S.N. Hesse-Biber and P. Leavy, 525–41. New York: Guilford Press.

Hinther, Rhonda L., and Jim Mochoruk, eds. 2011. *Re-imagining Ukrainian Canadians: History, Politics, and Identity.* Toronto: University of Toronto Press.

Hoberg, George, and Jeffrey Phillips. 2011. "Playing Defence: Early Responses to Conflict Expansion in the Oil Sands Policy Subsystem." *Canadian Journal of Political Science/Revue canadienne de science politique* 44 (03): 507–27. http://dx.doi.org/10.1017/S0008423911000473.

Hoekstra, Gordon. 2009. "Propaganda Pipeline." *Prince George Citizen,* 29 May. http://www.sqwalk.com/bc2009/001646.html.

Hoffbauer, Andreas, and Howard Ramos. 2014. "Social and Political Convergence on Environmental Events: The Roles of Simplicity and Visuality in the BP Oil Spill." *Canadian Review of Sociology* 51 (3): 216-38.

Hoffman, Steven M. 2012. "Hijacking Canada: Tar Sands and the Problem of an Effective Opposition." Paper presented at the Petrocultures, Edmonton.

House of Commons. 1976–77a. *Debates.* 30th Parliament, 2nd Session. Vol. 3 (11 February), 2975–3412, 6143–6226. Ottawa: Queen's Printer.

—. 1976–77b. Standing Committee on Justice and Legal Affairs. 30th Parliament, 2nd Session. Issue 4 (10 March), 6A–13A. Ottawa: Queen's Printer.

Howe, R. Brian. 1991. "The Evolution of Human Rights Policy in Ontario." *Canadian Journal of Political Science/Revue canadienne de science politique* 24 (04): 783–802. http://dx.doi.org/10.1017/S0008423900005667.

Howe, R. Brian, and Malcolm J. Andrade. 1994. "The Reputations of Human Rights Commissions in Canada." *Canadian Journal of Law and Society* 9 (02): 1–20. http://dx.doi.org/10.1017/S082932010000363X.

Howe, R. Brian, and David Johnson. 2000. *Restraining Equality: Human Rights Commissions in Canada.* Toronto: University of Toronto Press.

Hume, Stephen. 1979a. "Rights Appointee Involved in Two Violation Cases." *Victoria Times-Colonist,* 11 April.

—. 1979b. "Decision on Quitting Up to Them." *Victoria Times-Colonist,* 13 April.

Inglehart, Ronald. 1990. *Culture Shift in Advanced Industrial Society.* Princeton, NJ: Princeton University Press.

Inglehart, Ronald, and Gabriela Catterberg. 2002. "Trends in Political Action: The Developmental Trend and the Post-Honeymoon Decline." *International Journal of Comparative Sociology* 43 (3–5): 300–16. http://dx.doi.org/10.1177/0020 71520204300305.

Ipsos. 2008. "Canadians Choose the People, Places, Events, Accomplishments and Symbols That Define Canada." Ipsos North America, http://www.ipsos-na.com/news-polls/pressrelease.aspx?id=3984.

Isajiw, Wsevolod. 2010. "The Ukrainian Diaspora." In *The Call of the Homeland: Diaspora Nationalisms, Past and Present,* ed. Allon Gal, Athena S. Leoussi, and Anthony D. Smith, 289–320. Leiden: Brill. http://dx.doi.org/10.1163/ej.978900 4182103.i-402.76.

Isajiw, Wsevolod, Vic Satzewich, and Ewhen Duvalko. 2002. "Fourth Wave Immigrants from Ukraine, 1991-2001: Results of a New Study." Paper presented at the Canadian Ukrainian Immigrant Aid Society seminar, 28 January, Toronto.

Iyer, Nitya. 1993. "Categorical Denials: Equality Rights and the Shaping of Social Identity." *Queen's Law Journal* 19: 179–207.

James, Matt. 2006. *Misrecognized Materialists: Social Movements in Canadian Constitutional Politics.* Vancouver: UBC Press.

Jamison, Andrew, Ron Eyerman, Jacqueline Cramer, and Jeppe Laessoe. 1990. *The Making of a New Environmental Consciousness: A Comparative Study of the Environmental Movements in Sweden, Denmark and the Netherlands.* Edinburgh: Edinburgh University Press.

Jasen, Patricia Jane. 1995. *Wild Things: Nature, Culture, and Tourism in Ontario, 1790–1914.* Toronto: University of Toronto Press.

Jasper, James M. 1992. "The Politics of Abstractions: Instrumental and Moralist Rhetorics in Public Debate." *Social Research* 59 (2): 315-44.

Jenkins, Craig, Michael Wallace, and Andrew S. Fullerton. 2008. "A Social Movement Society? A Cross-National Analysis of Protest Potential." *International Journal of Sociology* 38 (3): 12–35. http://dx.doi.org/10.2753/IJS0020-7659380301.

Jenson, Jane, and Susan D. Phillips. 1996. "Regime Shift: New Citizenship Practices in Canada." *International Journal of Canadian Studies* 14: 111–35.

Jetté, Christian. 2008. *Les organismes communautaires et la transformation de l'État-Providence.* Québec: Presses de l'Université du Québec.

Jeyapal, Daphne. 2013. "'Since When Did We Have 100,000 Tamils?' Media Representations of Race Thinking, Spatiality, and the 2009 Tamil Diaspora Protests." *Canadian Journal of Sociology* 28 (4): 557–79.

Johnston, Elton. 1924. "Canada's Radio Consciousness." *Maclean's,* 15 October, 29.

Johnston, Hank. 2011. *States and Social Movements.* Cambridge: Polity Press.

Johnston, Russell. 1994. "The Early Trials of Protestant Radio: 1922–1938." *Canadian Historical Review* 75 (3): 376–403. http://dx.doi.org/10.3138/CHR-075-03-03.

Juris, Jeffrey S. 2005. "The New Digital Media and Activist Networking within Anti–Corporate Globalization Movements." *Annals of the American Academy of*

Political and Social Science 597 (1): 189–208. http://dx.doi.org/10.1177/00027 16204270338.

Kalifa, Dominique. 2007. "Qu'est-ce qu'une affaire aux XIXe siècle?" In *Affaires, scandales et grandes causes: de Socrate à Pinochet,* ed. L. Boltanski, E. Claverie, N. Offenstadt, and S. Van Damme, 197–211. Paris: Stock.

Kantola, Johanna. 2006. *Feminists Theorize the State.* New York: Palgrave Macmillan. http://dx.doi.org/10.1057/9780230626324.

Katz, Elihu. 1968. "Diffusion (Interpersonal Influence)." In *International Encyclopedia of the Social Sciences,* ed. D. Shils, 78–85. London: Macmillan and Free Press.

Katz, Hagai. 2006. "Gramsci, Hegemony, and Global Civil Society Networks." *Voluntas: International Journal of Voluntary and Nonprofit Organizations* 17 (4): 332–48. http://dx.doi.org/10.1007/s11266-006-9022-4.

Keck, Margaret E., and Kathryn Sikkink. 1998. *Activists beyond Borders: Advocacy Networks in International Politics.* Ithaca, NY: Cornell University Press.

Kellner, Douglas. 2002. "Theorizing Globalization." *Sociological Theory* 20 (3): 285–305. http://dx.doi.org/10.1111/0735-2751.00165.

Kelly, Erin N., David W. Schindler, Peter V. Hodson, Jeffrey W. Short, Roseanna Radmanovich, and Charlene C. Nielsen. 2010. "Oil Sands Development Contributes Elements Toxic at Low Concentrations to the Athabasca River and Its Tributaries." *Proceedings of the National Academy of Sciences of the United States of America* 107 (37): 16178–83. http://dx.doi.org/10.1073/pnas.1008754107.

Kelly, Erin N., Jeffrey W. Short, David W. Schindler, Peter V. Hodson, Mingsheng Ma, Alvin K. Kwan, and Barbra L. Fortin. 2009. "Oil Sands Development Contributes Polycyclic Aromatic Compounds to the Athabasca River and Its Tributaries." *Proceedings of the National Academy of Sciences of the United States of America* 106 (52): 22346–51. http://dx.doi.org/10.1073/pnas.0912050106.

Kelly, James B. 2005. *Governing with the Charter: Legislative and Judicial Activism and Framers' Intent.* Vancouver: UBC Press.

Kertscher, Tom. 2011. "Palin Rallies Madison Tea Party Crowd." *Milwaukee Journal-Sentinel,* 16 April. http://www.jsonline.com/news/statepolitics/119975244.html.

Kim, Kenneth. 2010. "Government of Canada Fails to Address Today's Real Tobacco Issues." Ontario Korean Businessmen's Association press release. Canada Newswire, 21 April. http://www.newswire.ca/en/story/715027/government-of-canada-fails -to-address-today-s-real-tobacco-issues.

King, Leslie. 2007. "Charting a Discursive Field: Environmentalists for U.S. Population Stabilization." *Sociological Inquiry* 77 (3): 301–25. http://dx.doi.org/10.1111/j. 1475-682X.2007.00195.x.

King, Mike, and David Waddington. 2005. "Flashpoints Revisited: A Critical Application to the Policing of Anti-Globalization Protest." *Policing and Society* 15 (3): 255–82. http://dx.doi.org/10.1080/10439460500168584.

Kostiyuk, Sheryi. 2007. *Canada and Saskatchewan through Their Eyes: Survey of Recent Immigrants from Ukraine.* Analytical Report. Kyiv and Saskatoon: Sergius Press.

KOTRA (Korea Trade-Investment Promotion Agency). 2012. "KOTRA." http:// english.kotra.or.kr/html/ebrochure.html?1=1.

Kowalsky, Nathan, and Randolph Haluza-DeLay. 2013. "Homo Energeticus: An Ellulian Analysis of the Alberta Tar Sands." In *Jacques Ellul and the Technological Society in the 21st Century,* ed. H. M. Jeronimo, J.L. Garcia, and C. Mitcham, 159–75. Berlin: Springer. http://dx.doi.org/10.1007/978-94-007-6658-7_12.

Kraetke, Stefan. 2010. "Creative Cities and the Rise of the Dealer Class: A Critique of Richard Florida's Approach to Urban Theory." *International Journal of Urban and Regional Research* 34 (4): 835–53. http://dx.doi.org/10.1111/j.1468-2427.2010.00939.x.

Kraska, Peter B., and Victor E. Kappeler. 1997. "Militarizing American Police: The Rise and Normalization of Paramilitary Units." *Social Problems* 44 (1): 1–18. http://dx.doi.org/10.2307/3096870.

Kutz-Flamenbaum, Rachel, Suzanne Staggenborg, and Brittany Duncan. 2012. "Media Framing of the Pittsburgh G-20 Protests." *Research in Social Movements, Conflicts and Change* 33: 109–35.

Kuumba, M. Bahati. 2001. *Gender and Social Movements.* Walnut Creek, CA: Altamira Press.

Kwak, Min-Jung, and Daniel Hiebert. 2010. "Globalizing Canadian Education from Below: A Case Study of Transnational Immigrant Entrepreneurship between Seoul, Korea and Vancouver, Canada." *Journal of International Migration and Integration* 11 (2): 131–53. http://dx.doi.org/10.1007/s12134-010-0130-z.

Laforest, Rachel, ed. 2009. *The Conservative Federal Policy Agenda and the Voluntary Sector: On the Cutting Edge.* Montreal and Kingston: McGill-Queen's University Press.

–. 2011. *Voluntary Sector Organizations and the State.* Vancouver: UBC Press.

Laforest, Rachel, and Michael Orsini. 2005. "Evidence Based Engagement in the Voluntary Sector: Lessons from Canada." *Social Policy and Administration* 39 (5): 481–97. http://dx.doi.org/10.1111/j.1467-9515.2005.00451.x.

Laforest, Rachel, and Susan Phillips. 2001. "Repenser les relations entre gouvernement et secteur bénévole: à la croisée des chemins au Québec et au Canada." *Politique et Sociétés* 20 (2–3): 37–68. http://dx.doi.org/10.7202/040274ar.

Lambertson, Ross. 2001. "The Dresden Story: Racism, Human Rights, and the Jewish Labour Committee of Canada." *Labour/Le Travail* (Spring): 43–82.

Lamont, Michèle. 1992. *Money, Morals, and Manners: The Culture of the French and American Upper Middle Class.* Chicago: University of Chicago Press. http://dx.doi.org/10.7208/chicago/9780226922591.001.0001.

–. 2012. "Toward a Comparative Sociology of Valuation and Evaluation." *Annual Review of Sociology* 38 (1): 201–21. http://dx.doi.org/10.1146/annurev-soc-070308-120022.

Lamont, Michèle, and Laurent Thévenot, eds. 2000a. *Rethinking Comparative Cultural Sociology: Repertoires of Evaluation in France and the United States.* Cambridge: Cambridge University Press. http://dx.doi.org/10.1017/CBO9780511628108.

–. 2000b. "Introduction: Toward a Renewed Comparative Cultural Sociology." In *Rethinking Comparative Cultural Sociology: Repertoires of Evaluation in France and the United States,* ed. Michèle Lamont and Laurent Thévenot, 1–22. Cambridge: Cambridge University Press. http://dx.doi.org/10.1017/CBO978051162 8108.001.

Landriscina, Mirella. 2006. "A Calmly Disruptive Insider: The Case of an Institutionalized Advocacy Organization at Work." *Qualitative Sociology* 29 (4): 447–66. http://dx.doi.org/10.1007/s11133-006-9034-9.

Langer, Rosanna L. 2007. *Defining Rights and Wrongs: Bureaucracy, Human Rights, and Public Accountability.* Vancouver: UBC Press.

Latour, Bruno. 1993. *We Have Never Been Modern.* Trans. C. Porter. Cambridge, MA: Harvard University Press.

–. 1998. "To Modernise or to Ecologise? That Is the Question." In *Remaking Reality: Nature at the Millennium,* ed. Noel Castree and Bruce Willems-Braun, 220-41. London and New York: Routledge.

–. 2004. *Politics of Nature: How to Bring the Sciences into Democracy.* Trans. C. Porter. Cambridge, MA: Harvard University Press.

Laudati, Ann. 2010. "Ecotourism: The Modern Predator? Implications of Gorilla Tourism on Local Livelihoods in Bwindi Impenetrable National Park, Uganda. Environment and Planning." *Society and Space* 28 (4): 726–43.

Legislature of British Columbia. 1977. *Debates.* 31st Parliament, 1st Session. Vol. 6 (2 August), 4198. Victoria: Queen's Printer.

–. 1983. *Debates.* 33rd Parliament, 1st Session. Vol. 2 (11 August), 769. Victoria: Queen's Printer.

–. 1984. *Debates.* 33rd Parliament, 2nd Session. Vol. 9 (13 May), 4471–72. Victoria: Queen's Printer.

Lepore, Jill. 2010. *The Whites of Their Eyes: The Tea Party's Revolution and the Battle over American History.* Princeton, NJ: Princeton University Press.

Levant, Ezra. 2010. *Ethical Oil: The Case for Canada's Oil Sands.* Toronto: McClelland and Stewart.

Li, Xiaoping. 2007. *Voices Rising: Asian Canadian Cultural Activism.* Vancouver: UBC Press.

Lichterman, Paul. 2002. "Seeing Structure Happen: Theory-Driven Participant-Observation." In *Methods of Social Movement Research,* ed. B. Klandermans and S. Staggenborg, 118–45. Minneapolis: University of Minnesota Press.

Light, I.H., and E. Bonacich. 1988. *Immigrant Entrepreneurs: Koreans in Los Angeles, 1965–1982.* Berkeley: University of California Press.

Lind, Christopher, and Joe Mihevc, eds. 1994. *Coalitions for Justice.* Ottawa: Novalis.

Lindsay, Colin. 2007. "The Korean Community in Canada." Ottawa: Statistics Canada.

Lipset, Seymour M. 1986. "Historical Traditions and National Characteristics: A Comparative Analysis of Canada and the United States." *Canadian Journal of Sociology* 11 (2): 113–55. http://dx.doi.org/10.2307/3340795.

–. 1990. *Continental Divide.* New York: Routledge.

Lipsky, Michael. 1970. *Protest in City Politics.* Chicago: Rand McNally.

Loewen, Royden, and Gerald Friesen. 2009. *Immigrants in Prairie Cities.* Toronto: University of Toronto Press.

Loué, Thomas. 2007. "L'affaire Dreyfus." In *Affaires, scandales et grandes causes: de Socrate à Pinochet,* ed. L. Boltanski, E. Claverie, N. Offenstadt, and S. Van Damme, 213–27. Paris: Stock.

Luke, Timothy W. 1997. *Ecocritique: Contesting the Politics of Nature, Economy, and Culture.* Minneapolis: University of Minnesota Press.

Macartney, H. 2008. "Articulating Particularistic Interests: The Organic Organisers of Hegemony in Germany and France." *British Journal of Politics and International Relations* 10 (3): 429–51. http://dx.doi.org/10.1111/j.1467-856X.2008.00330.x.

MacDonald, L. 1997. *Supporting Civil Society: The Political Role of Nongovernmental Organizations in Central America.* New York: MacMillan.

MacEachern, Alan. 2001. *Natural Selections: National Parks in Atlantic Canada, 1935–1970.* Montreal and Kingston: McGill-Queen's University Press.

Mackay, Fiona, Surya Monro, and Georgina Waylen. 2009. "The Feminist Potential of Sociological Institutionalism." *Politics and Gender* 5 (2): 253–62. http://dx.doi.org/10.1017/S1743923X09000208.

Mackrael, Kim. 2011. "Canadians Tend to View Occupy Protest in Positive Light: Poll." *Globe and Mail,* 8 November. http://www.theglobeandmail.com/news/national/canadians-tend-to-view-occupy-protests-in-positive-light-poll/article2228837/.

Maeckelbergh, Marianne. 2011. "Doing Is Believing: Prefiguration as Strategic Practice in the Alterglobalization Movement." *Social Movement Studies* 10 (1): 1–20. http://dx.doi.org/10.1080/14742837.2011.545223.

Magdoff, F., and J.B. Foster. 2011. *What Every Environmentalist Needs to Know about Capitalism.* New York: Monthly Review Press.

Magnusson, Warren. 1997. "Globalization, Movements and the De-Centred State." In *Organizing Dissent,* 2nd ed., ed. William K. Carroll, 94–113. Toronto: Garamond Press.

Magnusson, Warren, and Karena Shaw, eds. 2002. *A Political Space: Reading the Global through Clayoquot Sound.* Montreal and Kingston: McGill-Queen's University Press.

Mahon, Rianne. 2008. "Varieties of Liberalism: Canadian Social Policy from the 'Golden Age' to the Present." *Social Policy and Administration* 42 (4): 342–61. http://dx.doi.org/10.1111/j.1467-9515.2008.00608.x.

Mancini, Melissa. 2013. "Science Cuts and Muzzling in Canada." *Huffington Post,* 13 September. http://www.huffingtonpost.ca/2013/04/30/science-cuts-muzzling-canada-conservatives_n_3112348.html.

Maney, Gregory M., Lynne M. Woehrle, and Patrick G. Coy. 2005. "Harnessing and Challenging Hegemony: The U.S. Peace Movement after 9/11." *Sociological Perspectives* 48 (3): 357–81. http://dx.doi.org/10.1525/sop.2005.48.3.357.

Manfredi, Christopher. 2004. *Feminist Activism in the Supreme Court: Legal Mobilization and the Women's Legal Education and Action Fund.* Vancouver: UBC Press.

Mansbridge, Jane J., and Aldon Morris. 2001. *Oppositional Consciousness: The Subjective Roots of Social Protest.* Chicago: University of Chicago Press.

References

Maratea, Ray. 2008. "The e-Rise and Fall of Social Problems: The Blogosphere as a Public Arena." *Social Problems* 55 (1): 139–60. http://dx.doi.org/10.1525/sp. 2008.55.1.139.

Martin, Patricia Yancey. 2004. "Gender as Social Institution." *Social Forces* 82 (4): 1249–73.

Marx, Gary T. 1998. "Ethics for the New Surveillance." *Information Society* 14 (3): 171–85.

Marx, Karl. 1844. "Introduction to 'A Contribution to the Critique of Hegel's Philosophy of Right.'" http://www.marxists.org/archive/marx/works/1843/critique-hpr/intro.htm.

Massey, Douglas S. 2009. "Racial Formation in Theory and Practice: The Case of Mexicans in the United States." *Race and Social Problems* 1 (1): 12–26. http://dx.doi.org/10.1007/s12552-009-9005-3.

Masson, Dominique. 1997. "Language, Power, and Politics: Revisiting the Symbolic Challenge of Movements." In *Organizing Dissent: Contemporary Social Movements in Theory and Practice*, ed. William K. Carroll, 57–75. Toronto: Garamond.

–. 1998. "With and despite the State: Doing Women's Movement Politics in Local Service Groups in the 1980s in Quebec." PhD dissertation, Department of Sociology and Anthropology, Carleton University.

–. 1999/2000. "Constituting 'Post-Welfare State' Welfare Arrangements: The Role of Women's Movement Service Groups in Quebec." *Resources for Feminist Research* 27 (3–4): 49–70.

–. 2012. "Changing State Forms, Competing State Projects: Funding Women's Organizations in Quebec." *Studies in Political Economy* 80: 79–103.

Masuda, Jeffrey R., Tara K. McGee, and Theresa D. Garvin. 2008. "Power, Knowledge, and Public Engagement: Constructing 'Citizenship' in Alberta's Industrial Heartland." *Journal of Environmental Policy and Planning* 10 (4): 359–80. http://dx.doi.org/10.1080/15239080802332026.

Mayer, Jane. 2010. "Covert Operations: The Billionaire Brothers Who Are Waging a War against Obama." *New Yorker*, 21 August. http://www.newyorker.com/magazine/2010/08/30/covert-operations.

McAdam, Doug. 1982. *Political Process and the Origins of Black Insurgency.* Chicago: University of Chicago Press.

–. 1989. "The Biographical Consequences of Activism." *American Sociological Review* 54 (5): 744–60. http://dx.doi.org/10.2307/2117751.

–. 1996. "Conceptual Origins, Current Problems, Future Directions." In *Comparative Perspectives on Social Movements*, ed. Doug McAdam, John D. McCarthy, and Mayer N. Zald, 23–40. Cambridge: Cambridge University Press. http://dx.doi.org/10.1017/CBO9780511803987.003.

McAdam, Doug, and Hilary Schaffer Boudet. 2012. *Putting Social Movements in Their Place: Explaining Opposition to Energy Projects in the United States, 2000–2005.* Cambridge: Cambridge University Press. http://dx.doi.org/10.1017/CBO9781139105811.

McAdam, Doug, John D. McCarthy, and Mayer N. Zald. 1996. "Introduction: Opportunities, Mobilizing Structures, and Framing Processes – Towards a Synthetic, Comparative Perspective on Social Movements." In *Comparative*

Perspectives on Social Movements, ed. Doug McAdam, John D. McCarthy, and Mayer N. Zald, 1–20. Cambridge: Cambridge University Press. http://dx.doi.org/10.1017/CBO9780511803987.002.

McAdam, Doug, Robert J. Sampson, Simon Weffer, and Heather MacIndoe. 2005. "'There Will Be Fighting in the Streets': The Distorting Lens of Social Movement Theory." *Mobilization: An International Quarterly* 10 (1): 1–18.

McAdam, Doug, Sidney Tarrow, and Charles Tilly. 2001. *Dynamics of Contention.* Cambridge: Cambridge University Press. http://dx.doi.org/10.1017/CBO9780511805431.

McCarthy, John D. 1996. "Constraints and Opportunities in Adopting, Adapting, and Inventing." In *Comparative Perspectives on Social Movements: Political Opportunities, Mobilizing Structures and Cultural Framings,* ed. Doug McAdam, John D. McCarthy, and Mayer N. Zald, 141–51. Cambridge: Cambridge University Press. http://dx.doi.org/10.1017/CBO9780511803987.008.

McCarthy, John D., and Clark McPhail. 1998. "The Institutionalization of Protest in the United States." In *The Social Movement Society,* ed. D.S. Meyer and S. Tarrow, 83–110. Lanham, MD: Rowman and Littlefield.

McCarthy, John D., Patrick Rafail, and Ashley Gromis. 2013. "Recent Trends in Public Protest in the United States: The Social Movement Society Thesis Revisited." In *The Future of Social Movement Research: Dynamics, Mechanisms, and Processes,* ed. Jacqueline Van Stekelenburg, Conny Roggeband, and Bert Klandermans, 369–96. Minneapolis: University of Minnesota Press.

McCarthy, John D., Jackie Smith, and Mayer N. Zald. 1996. "Accessing Public, Media, Electoral, and Governmental Agendas." In *Comparative Perspectives on Social Movements: Political Opportunities, Mobilizing Structures, and Cultural Framings,* ed. Doug McAdam, John D. McCarthy, and Mayer N. Zald, 291–311. Cambridge: Cambridge University Press. http://dx.doi.org/10.1017/CBO9780511803987.015.

McCarthy, John D., and Mayer N. Zald. 1977. "Resource Mobilization and Social Movements: A Partial Theory." *American Journal of Sociology* 82 (6): 1212–41. http://dx.doi.org/10.1086/226464.

McCarthy, Shawn, and Oliver Moore. 2012. "David Suzuki Laments Tory-Imposed 'Chill' on Green Groups." *Globe and Mail,* 25 April. http://ecestats.theglobeandmail.com/news/politics/david-suzuki-laments-tory-imposed-chill-on-green-groups/article2400300/?service=mobile.

McPhail, Clark, David Schweingruber, and John McCarthy. 1998. "Policing Protest in the United States: 1960–1995." In *Policing Protest: The Control of Mass Demonstrations in Western Democracies,* ed. Donatella della Porta and Herbert Reiter, 49–69. Minneapolis: University of Minnesota Press.

Meyer, David S. 1990. *A Winter of Discontent: The Nuclear Freeze and American Politics.* New York: Praeger.

–. 2002. "Opportunities and Identities: Bridge-Building in the Study of Social Movements." In *Social Movements: Identity, Culture, and the State,* ed. David S. Meyer, Nancy Whittier, and Belinda Robnett, 3–201. New York: Oxford University Press.

–. 2004. "Protest and Political Opportunities." *Annual Review of Sociology* 30 (1): 125–45. http://dx.doi.org/10.1146/annurev.soc.30.012703.110545.

–. 2007. *The Politics of Protest: Social Movements in America*. New York: Oxford University Press.

Meyer, David S., and Steven Boutcher. 2007. "Signals and Spillover: *Brown v. Board of Education* and Other Social Movements." *Perspectives on Politics* 5 (1): 81–93. http://dx.doi.org/10.1017/S1537592707070077.

Meyer, David S., and Catherine Corrigall-Brown. 2005. "Coalitions and Political Context: U.S. Movements against Wars in Iraq." *Mobilization: An International Quarterly* 10 (3): 327–44.

Meyer, David S., and Josh Gamson. 1995. "The Challenge of Cultural Elites: Celebrities and Social Movements." *Sociological Inquiry* 65 (2): 181–206. http://dx.doi.org/10.1111/j.1475-682X.1995.tb00412.x.

Meyer, David S., and Debra C. Minkoff. 2004. "Conceptualizing Political Opportunity." *Social Forces* 82 (4): 1457–92.

Meyer, David S., and Suzanne Staggenborg. 1996. "Movements, Countermovements, and the Structure of Political Opportunity." *American Journal of Sociology* 101 (6): 1628–60. http://dx.doi.org/10.1086/230869.

Meyer, David S., and Sidney Tarrow, eds. 1998. *The Social Movement Society: Contentious Politics for a New Century*. Lanham, MD: Rowman and Littlefield.

Mikisew Cree First Nation. 2007. "Response to the Multi-Stakeholder Committee Phase II Proposed Options for Strategies and Actions and Submission to the Government of Alberta for the Oil Sands Strategy." http://mcfngir.org/Documents_files/MCFN%20Response%20to%20OSS%20-%20FINAL.pdf.

Milbrandt, Tara. 2012. "Visual Irruptions, Mediated Suffering, and the Robert Dziekanski Tragedy: An Inquiry into the Efficacy of the Image." In *Ethics and Images of Pain*, ed. Asbjørn Grønstad and Henrik Gustafsson, 74–92. New York: Routledge.

Min, Pyong Gap. 1998. *Changes and Conflicts: Korean Immigrant Families in New York*. Boston: Allyn and Bacon.

–. 2008. *Ethnic Solidarity for Economic Survival: Korean Greengrocers in New York City*. New York: Russell Sage Foundation.

Minkoff, Debra. 1995. *Organizing for Equality: The Evolution of Women's and Radical Ethnic Organizations in America, 1955–1985*. New Brunswick, NJ: Rutgers University Press.

Mische, Ann. 2003. "Cross-Talk in Movements: Reconceiving the Culture-Network Link." In *Social Movements and Networks: Relational Approaches to Collective Action*, ed. Mario Diani and Doug McAdam, 258–80. Oxford: Oxford University Press. http://dx.doi.org/10.1093/0199251789.003.0011.

Mittelstaedt, Martin. 2010. "Environmentalists Back *Avatar* for Oscar." *Globe and Mail*, 4 March. http://www.theglobeandmail.com/arts/awards-and-festivals/environmentalists-back-avatar-for-oscar/article1209178/.

Mohai, Paul, David Pellow, and Timmons Roberts. 2009. "Environmental Justice." *Annual Review of Environment and Resources* 34 (1): 405–30. http://dx.doi.org/10.1146/annurev-environ-082508-094348.

Mohr, John W. 1998. "Measuring Meaning Structures." *Annual Review of Sociology* 24 (1): 345–70. http://dx.doi.org/10.1146/annurev.soc.24.1.345.

Moody, Michael, and Laurent Thévenot. 2000. "Comparing Models of Strategy, Interests, and the Public Good in French and American Environmental Disputes." In *Rethinking Comparative Cultural Sociology: Repertoires of Evaluation in France and the United States*, ed. Michèle Lamont and Laurent Thévenot, 273–306. Cambridge: Cambridge University Press. http://dx.doi.org/10.1017/CBO9780511628108.010.

Moore, Barrington Jr. 1978. *Injustice: The Social Bases of Obedience and Revolt.* Armonk, NY: M.E. Sharpe.

Moore, Donald S., Jake Kosek, and Anand Pandian, eds. 2003. *Race, Nature, and the Politics of Difference.* Durham, NC: Duke University Press. http://dx.doi.org/10.1215/9780822384656.

Moore, Dorothy Emma. 1980. "Multiculturalism: Ideology or Social Reality?" PhD thesis, Boston University.

Morgan, Rhiannon. 2007. "On Political Institutions and Social Movement Dynamics: The Case of the United Nations and the Global Indigenous Movement." *International Political Science Review* 28 (3): 273–92. http://dx.doi.org/10.1177/0192512107077099.

Morris, Aldon. 1984. *The Origins of the Civil Rights Movement: Black Communities Organizing for Change.* New York: Free Press.

Morris, Aldon, and Suzanne Staggenborg. 2007. "Leadership in Social Movements." In *The Blackwell Companion to Social Movements*, ed. David A. Snow, Sarah A. Soule, and Hanspeter Kriesi, 171–96. Oxford: Blackwell.

Morrow, Marina, Olena Hankivsky, and Coleen Vascoe. 2004. "Women and Violence: The Effects of Dismantling the Welfare State." *Critical Social Policy* 24 (3): 358–84. http://dx.doi.org/10.1177/0261018304044364.

Mortimer-Sandilands, Catriona. 2009. "The Cultural Politics of Ecological Integrity: Nature and Nation in Canada's National Parks, 1885-20." *International Journal of Canadian Studies* (39-40): 161–89. http://dx.doi.org/10.7202/040828ar.

Morton, F.L. and Rainer Knopff. 2000. *The Charter Revolution and the Court Party.* Toronto: University of Toronto Press.

Motyl, Alexander J. 2011. "Ukraine's Orange Blues: The Ukrainian Diaspora and Ukraine." *World Affairs*, 5 September. http://www.worldaffairsjournal.org/blog/alexander-j-motyl/ukrainian-diaspora-and-ukraine.

Muller, E.N., and K. Opp. 1986. "Rational Choice and Rebellious Collective Action." *American Political Science Review* 80 (2): 471–87. http://dx.doi.org/10.2307/1958269.

Murphy, Gillian. 2005. "Coalitions and the Development of the Global Environmental Movements: A Double-Edged Sword." *Mobilization: An International Journal* 10: 235–50.

Murphy, Raymond. 2006. "Environmental Realism: From Apologetics to Substance." *Nature and Culture* 1 (2): 181–204. http://dx.doi.org/10.3167/155860706780608689.

Nash, Roderick Frazier. 2001. *Wilderness and the American Mind.* New Haven, CT: Yale University Press.

Ndegwa, S.N. 1996. *The Two Faces of Civil Society.* West Hartford, CT: Kumarian.

NDP Caucus. 2010. "Small Business Owners Join with NDP to Call on B.C. Liberals to Stop the HST." New Democratic Party, http://bcndpcaucus.ca/news/small-business-owners-join-with-ndp-to-call-on-b-c-liberals-to-stop-the-hst/.

New York Times/CBS News. 2010. "National Survey of Tea Party Supporters." http://documents.nytimes.com/new-york-timescbs-news-poll-national-survey-of-tea-party-supporters.

Newman, Graeme R., and Ronald V. Clarke. 2008. *Policing Terrorism: An Executive's Guide.* Washington, DC: US Department of Justice, Office of Community Oriented Policing Services, Center for Problem-Oriented Policing.

Ng, Roxana. 1990. "State Funding to a Community Employment Centre: Implications for Working with Immigrant Women." In *Community Organization and the Canadian State,* ed. Roxana Ng, Gillian Walker, and Jacob Mueller, 165–83. Toronto: Garamond Press.

Nicholls, Walter J. 2013. "Fragmenting Citizenship: Dynamics of Cooperation and Conflict in France's Immigrant Rights Movement." *Ethnic and Racial Studies* 36 (4): 611–31. http://dx.doi.org/10.1080/01419870.2011.626055.

Nikiforuk, Andrew. 2002. *Saboteurs: Wiebo Ludwig's War against Big Oil.* Toronto: Macfarlane Walter and Ross.

–. 2008. *Tar Sands: Dirty Oil and the Future of a Continent.* Vancouver: Greystone Books.

Noakes, John, and Patrick F. Gillham. 2006. "Aspects of the 'New Penology' in the Police Response to Major Political Protests in the United States, 1999–2000." In *The Policing of Transnational Protest,* ed. Donatella della Porta, Abby Peterson, and Herbert Reiter, 97–116. London: Ashgate Publishing.

–. 2007. "Police and Protester Innovation Since Seattle." *Mobilization* 12 (4): 335–40.

Noakes, John, Brian Klocke, and Patrick F. Gillham. 2005. "Whose Streets? Police and Protesters Struggle over Space in Washington, DC, 29–30 September 2001." *Policing and Society* 15 (3): 235–54. http://dx.doi.org/10.1080/10439460500168576.

Noh, Samuel, and William R. Avison. 1996. "Asian Immigrants and the Stress Process: A Study of Koreans in Canada." *Journal of Health and Social Behavior* 37 (2): 192–206. http://dx.doi.org/10.2307/2137273.

Noh, Samuel, Ann H. Kim, and Marianne S. Noh, eds. 2012. *Korean Immigrants in Canada: Perspectives on Migration, Integration, and the Family.* Toronto: University of Toronto Press.

Nolan, Michael. 1989. "An Infant Industry: Canadian Private Radio 1919–36." *Canadian Historical Review* 70 (4): 496–518. http://dx.doi.org/10.3138/CHR-070-04-02.

Obach, Brian. 2004. *Labor and the Environmental Movement: The Quest for Common Ground.* Cambridge, MA: MIT Press.

Oliver, Joe. 2012. "An Open Letter on Canada's Commitment to Diversify Our Energy Markets and the Need to Further Streamline the Regulatory Process in Order to Advance Canada's National Economic Interest." 9 January. www.nrcan.gc.ca/media-room/news-release/2012/1/1909.

Oliver, Pamela E., and Hank Johnston. 2000. "What a Good Idea! Ideology and Frames in Social Movement Research." *Mobilization: An International Quarterly* 5 (1): 37–54.

Ontario Coalition Against Poverty. 2008. "Victory at Everest! Disabled Activist Receives Public Apology for Discrimination." http://ocap.ca/node/1259.

Opp, Karl-Dieter. 1986. "Soft Incentives and Collective Action: Participation in the Anti-Nuclear Movement." *British Journal of Political Science* 16 (1): 87–112. http://dx.doi.org/10.1017/S0007123400003811.

Ostling, Richard N. 1984. "Evangelical Publishing and Broadcasting." In *Evangelicalism and Modern America,* ed. George M. Marsden, 46–55. Grand Rapids, MI: William B. Eerdmans.

"Ottawa Steps Up Rights Pressure on B.C." 1983. *Vancouver Province,* 17 July.

Pal, Leslie. 1993. *Interests of State: The Politics of Language, Multiculturalism, and Feminism in Canada.* Montreal and Kingston: McGill-Queen's University Press.

Palaeologu, M. Athena. 2009. *The Sixties in Canada: A Turbulent and Creative Decade.* Montreal: Black Rose.

Palmer, Bryan. 1987. *Solidarity: The Rise and Fall of an Opposition in British Columbia.* Vancouver: New Star Books.

Park, Lisa Sun-Hee, and David Naguib Pellow. 2011. *The Slums of Aspen: Immigrants vs. the Environment in America's Eden.* New York: New York University Press.

Parker, Christopher S., and Matt A. Barreto. 2013. *"Change They Can't Believe In": The Tea Party and Reactionary Politics in America.* Princeton, NJ: Princeton University Press.

Parkins, John. 2006. "De-centering Environmental Governance: A Short History and Analysis of Democratic Processes in the Forest Sector of Alberta, Canada." *Policy Sciences* 39 (2): 183–202. http://dx.doi.org/10.1007/s11077-006-9015-6.

Partington, P.J., and Clare Demerse. 2013. "Context for Climate Action in Canada." October. Calgary: Pembina Institute.

Patrias, Carmela. 2006. "Socialists, Jews, and the 1947 Saskatchewan Bill of Rights." *Canadian Historical Review* 87 (2): 265–92. http://dx.doi.org/10.3138/CHR/87.2.265.

Patrias, Carmela, and Ruth A. Frager. 2001. "This Is Our Country, These Are Our Rights': Minorities and the Origins of Ontario's Human Rights Campaigns." *Canadian Historical Review* 82 (1): 1–35. http://dx.doi.org/10.3138/CHR.82.1.1.

Pellow, David Naguib. 2007. *Resisting Global Toxics: Transnational Movements for Environmental Justice.* Cambridge, MA: MIT Press.

PERF (Police Executive Research Forum). 2011. "Managing Major Events: Best Practices from the Field." http://www.policeforum.org/assets/docs/Critical_Issues_Series/managing%20major%20events%20-%20best%20practices%20from%20the%20field%202011.pdf.

Phillips, Susan. 2001. "More than Stakeholders: Reforming State-Voluntary Sector Relations." *Journal of Canadian Studies/Revue d'etudes Canadiennes* 35 (4): 182–202.

Piven, Frances Fox, and Richard A. Cloward. 1979. *Poor People's Movements: Why They Succeed, How They Fail.* New York: Vintage Books.

Pivnenko, Sergiy, and Don J. DeVoretz. 2003. "The Recent Economic Performance of Ukrainian Immigrants in Canada and the U.S." Metropolis Working Papers, October. http://repec.iza.org/dp913.pdf.

Plumwood, Val. 1998. "Wilderness Skepticism and Wilderness Dualism." In *The Great New Wilderness Debate*, ed. J.B. Callicott and M.P. Nelson, 651–90. Athens: University of Georgia Press.

Police Review Commission. 2003. "Information Calendar: Crowd Control Training for BDP." http://www.ci.berkeley.ca.us/citycouncil/2003citycouncil/packet/090903/2003-09-09%20Item%2054-57.pdf.

Polletta, Francesca. 2002. *Freedom Is an Endless Meeting: Democracy in American Social Movements*. Chicago: University of Chicago Press. http://dx.doi.org/10.7208/chicago/9780226924281.001.0001.

–. 2012. "Three Mechanisms by Which Culture Shapes Movement Strategy: Repertoires, Institutional Norms, and Metonymy." In *Strategies for Social Change*, ed. Gregory M. Maney, Rachel V. Kutz-Flamenbaum, Deana A. Rohlinger, and Jeff Goodwin, 43–60. Minneapolis: University of Minnesota Press.

Polletta, Francesca, and James Jasper. 2001. "Collective Identity and Social Movements." *Annual Review of Sociology* 27 (1): 283–305. http://dx.doi.org/10.1146/annurev.soc.27.1.283.

Ponzini, Davide, and U. Rossi. 2010. "Becoming a Creative City: The Entrepreneurial Mayor, Network Politics and the Promise of an Urban Renaissance." *Urban Studies* 47 (5): 1037–57. http://dx.doi.org/10.1177/0042098009353073.

Pothier, Diane. 2001. "Connecting Grounds of Discrimination to Real People's Real Experiences." *Canadian Journal of Women and the Law* 13: 37–73.

Powell, Betsy. 2006. "Many Wade into Toronto Brawl." *Toronto Star* (Ontario ed.), 31 January, A08.

Priest, Gerald L. 2005. "T.T. Shields the Fundamentalist: Man of Controversy." *Detroit Baptist Seminary Journal* 10: 69–101.

Princen, Thomas, and Matthias Finger. 1994. *Environmental NGOs in World Politics*. New York: Routledge. http://dx.doi.org/10.4324/9780203429037.

Pross, Harry. 1992. *Protestgesellschaft. Von der Wirksamkeit des Widerspruchs*. Munich: Artemis.

The Province. 1969. "Human Rights Act Full of Holes – Federation." 10 April.

Putnam, Robert. 2000. *Bowling Alone: The Collapse and Revival of American Community*. New York: Touchstone. http://dx.doi.org/10.1145/358916.361990.

Rafail, Patrick. 2010. "Asymmetry in Protest Control? Comparing Protest Policing Patterns in Montreal, Toronto and Vancouver, 1998–2004." *Mobilization: An International Quarterly* 15 (4): 489–509.

Ramos, Howard. 2004. *Divergent Paths: Aboriginal Mobilization in Canada, 1951–2000*. PhD dissertation, McGill University.

–. 2006. "What Causes Canadian Aboriginal Protest? Examining Resources, Opportunities and Identity, 1951–2000." *Canadian Journal of Sociology* 31 (2): 211–34. http://dx.doi.org/10.2307/20058697.

–. 2008. "Opportunity for Whom? Political Opportunity and Critical Events in Canadian Aboriginal Mobilization, 1951–2000." *Social Forces* 87 (2): 795–823. http://dx.doi.org/10.1353/sof.0.0145.

Rauch, Jonathan. 2010. "How Tea Party Organizes without Leaders." *National Journal*, 11 September. http://www.freerepublic.com/focus/bloggers/2591379/posts.

Reason, Peter. 2011. "Cooperative Inquiry." In *The Participation Reader*, ed. Andrea Cornwall, 99–108. London: Zed Books.

Réaume, Denise G. 2002. "Of Pigeonholes and Principles: A Reconsideration of Discrimination Law." *Osgoode Hall Law Journal* 40: 113–44.

Rebick, Judy. 2005. *Ten Thousand Roses: The Making of a Feminist Revolution.* Toronto: Penguin Canada.

Reed, Maureen G. 2003. *Taking Stands: Gender and the Sustainability of Rural Communities.* Vancouver: UBC Press.

Reese, Ellen, Christopher Chase-Dunn, Kadambari Anantram, Gary Coyne, Matheu Kaneshiro, Ashkey N. Koda, Roy Kwon, and Preeta Saxena. 2008. "Research Note: Surveys of World Social Forum Participants Show Influence of Place and Base in the Global Public Sphere." *Mobilization* 13 (4): 431-45.

Reese, Laura, Jessica Faist, and Gary Sands. 2010. "Measuring the Creative Class: Do We Know It When We See it?" *Journal of Urban Affairs* 32 (3): 345–66. http://dx.doi.org/10.1111/j.1467-9906.2010.00496.x.

Reimer, Sam. 2003. *Evangelicals and the Continental Divide: The Conservative Protestant Subculture in Canada and the United States.* Montreal and Kingston: McGill-Queen's University Press.

Renate Shearer. 1979–83. "Lists of Grants Provided by the Human Rights Commission." Renate Vol.1, file 15. Shearer Collection. UBC RBSC.

Richardson, Ian N., Andrew P. Kakabadse, and Nada K. Kakabadse. 2011. *Bilderberg People: Elite Power and Consensus in Global Affairs.* London: Routledge.

Riger, Stephanie. 1994. "Challenges of Success: Stages of Growth in Feminist Organizations." *Feminist Studies* 20 (2): 275–300. http://dx.doi.org/10.2307/3178153.

Roberts, Lance W., Rodney A. Clifton, Barry Ferguson, Karen Kampen, and Simon Langlois, eds. 2005. *Recent Social Trends in Canada: 1960–2000.* Montreal and Kingston: McGill-Queens University Press.

Robinson, Joanna L., David B. Tindall, Erin Seldat, and Gabriela Pechlaner. 2007. "Support for First Nations' Land Claims amongst Members of the Wilderness Preservation Movement: The Potential for an Environmental Justice Movement in British Columbia." *Local Environment* 12 (6): 579–98. http://dx.doi.org/10.1080/13549830701657307.

Rochon, Thomas R. 1998. *Culture Moves: Ideas, Activism, and Changing Values.* Princeton, NJ: Princeton University Press.

Rodgers, Kathleen, and Melanie Knight. 2011. "'You Just Felt the Collective Wind Being Knocked Out of Us': The Deinstitutionalization of Feminism and the Survival of Women's Organizing in Canada." *Women's Studies International Forum* 34 (6): 570–81. http://dx.doi.org/10.1016/j.wsif.2011.08.004.

Rohrschneider, Robert, and Russell J. Dalton. 2002. "A Global Network? Transnational Cooperation among Environmental Groups." *Journal of Politics* 64 (2): 510–33. http://dx.doi.org/10.1111/1468-2508.00137.

Rootes, Christopher. 2003. *Environmental Protest in Western Europe.* Oxford: Oxford University Press. http://dx.doi.org/10.1093/0199252068.001.0001.

Rose, Fred. 2000. *Coalitions across the Class Divide: Lessons from the Labor, Peace and Environmental Movements.* Ithaca, NY: Cornell University Press.

Rosenstone, Steven, and John Mark Hansen. 1993. *Mobilization, Participation, and Democracy in America.* New York: Macmillan.

Rucht, Dieter. 1996. "The Impact of National Contexts on Social Movement Structures: A Cross-Movement and Cross-National Comparison." In *Comparative Perspectives on Social Movements,* ed. Doug McAdam, John D. McCarthy, and Mayer N. Zald, 185–204. Cambridge: Cambridge University Press. http://dx.doi.org/10.1017/CBO9780511803987.010.

–. 1998. "The Structure and Culture of Collective Protest in Germany since 1950." In *The Social Movement Society,* ed. David S. Meyer and Sidney Tarrow, 29–58. Lanham, MD: Rowman and Littlefield.

–. 1999. "The Impact of Environmental Movements in Western Societies." In *How Social Movements Matter,* ed. Marco Giugni, Doug McAdam, and Charles Tilly, 204–24. Minneapolis: University of Minnesota Press.

Rucht, Dieter, and Friedhelm Neidhardt. 2002. "Towards a 'Movement Society'? On the Possibilities of Institutionalizing Social Movements." *Social Movement Studies* 1 (1): 7–30. http://dx.doi.org/10.1080/14742830120118873.

Ruff, Kathleen. 2010. Interview by Dominique Clément. 14 April.

Rupp, Leila J. 1997. *Worlds of Women: The Making of an International Women's Movement.* Princeton, NJ: Princeton University Press.

Russell, Ian. 1993. "Australia's Human Rights Policy: From Evatt to Evans." In *Australia's Human Rights Diplomacy,* ed. Ian Russell, Peter Van Ness, and Beng-Huat Chua, 3–48. Canberra: Australia Foreign Policy Publications Program.

Ryan, Charlotte. 1991. *Primetime Activism.* Boston: South End Press.

SACAIS (Secrétariat à l'action communautaire autonome et aux initiatives sociales). 2011. *État de situation de l'intervention gouvernementale en matière d'action communautaire, 2010–2011.* Québec: Gouvernement du Québec.

Salaff, Janet W., Arent Greve, Siu-Lun Wong, and Lynn Xu Li Ping. 2003. "Ethnic Entrepreneurship, Social Networks, and the Enclave." In *Approaching Transnationalism: Transnational Societies, Multicultural Contacts, and Imaginings of Home,* ed. Brenda Yeoh, Tong Chee Kiong, and Michael W. Charney, 61–82. Boston: Kluwer Academic Publishers.

Salter, Liora, and Felix N.L. Odartey-Wellington. 2008. *The CRTC and Broadcasting Regulation in Canada.* Toronto: Thomson Carswell.

Sampson, Robert J., Doug McAdam, Heather MacIndoe, and Simón Weffer-Elizondo. 2005. "Civil Society Reconsidered: The Durable Nature and Community Structure of Collective Civic Action." *American Journal of Sociology* 111 (3): 673–714. http://dx.doi.org/10.1086/497351.

Satzewich, Vic. 2002. *The Ukrainian Diaspora.* London: Routledge. http://dx.doi.org/10.4324/9780203217498.

Satzewich, Vic, Wsevolod Isajiw, and Eugene Duvalko. 2006. "Social Networks and the Occupational Settlement Experiences of Recent Immigrants from Ukraine in Toronto." *Journal of Ukrainian Studies* 31: 1–26.

Sawer, Marian. 2010. "Premature Obituaries: How Can We Tell if the Women's Movement Is Over?" *Politics and Gender* 6 (4): 602–9. http://dx.doi.org/10.1017/S1743923X10000383.

Sayad, Abdelmalek. 2006. "L'immigration ou les paradoxes de l'altérité." Vol. 1. *L'illusion du provisoire;* vol. 2, *Les enfants illégitimes.* Paris: Éditions Raisons d'agir.

Schnaiberg, Allan, and Kenneth Alan Gould. 2000. *Environment and Society: The Enduring Conflict.* Caldwell, NJ: Blackburn Press.

Schneider, Keith. 2009. "Oral Roberts, Fiery Preacher, Dies at 91." *New York Times,* 15 December, A1.

Schneider, Richard R. 2002. *Alternative Futures: Alberta's Boreal Forest at the Crossroads.* Edmonton: Federation of Alberta Naturalists.

Schrepfer, Susan R. 2005. *Nature's Altars: Mountains, Gender, and American Environmentalism.* Lawrence: University Press of Kansas.

Schussman, Alan, and Sarah A. Soule. 2005. "Process and Protest: Accounting for Individual Protest Participation." *Social Forces* 84 (2): 1083–108. http://dx.doi.org/10.1353/sof.2006.0034.

Shellenberger, Michael, and Ted Nordhaus. 2004. "The Death of Environmentalism." http://www.thebreakthrough.org/

Sheller, Mimi, and John Urry. 2004. "Places to Play, Places in Play." In *Tourism Mobilities: Places to Play, Places in Play,* ed. M. Sheller and J. Urry, 1–22. London: Routledge.

Siegel, Bernard J. 1970. "Defensive Structuring and Environmental Stress." *American Journal of Sociology* 76 (1): 11–32. http://dx.doi.org/10.1086/224903.

Simon, Alexander. 2003. "A Comparative Historical Explanation of the Environmental Policies of Two Woodworkers' Unions in Canada." *Organization and Environment* 16 (3): 289–305. http://dx.doi.org/10.1177/1086026603251295.

Sisterhood [Newsletter of the NDP Women's Rights Committee]. 1983. Vol. 7, no. 2, August.

Skocpol, Theda. 1992. *Protecting Soldiers and Mothers: The Political Origins of Social Policy in the United States.* Cambridge, MA: Harvard University Press.

Skocpol, Theda, and Vanessa Williamson. 2013. *The Tea Party and the Remaking of Republican Conservatism.* New York: Oxford University Press.

Skolnick, Jerome H. 1969. *The Politics of Protest.* New York: Simon and Schuster.

Smillie, Ian. 1999. "At Sea in a Sieve? Trends and Issues in the Relationship between Northern NGOs and Northern Governments." In *Stakeholders: Government-NGO Partnerships for International Development,* ed. Ian Smillie and Henry Helmich, 7–35. London: Earthscan Publications.

Smith, Dorothy. 1999. *Writing the Social.* Toronto: University of Toronto Press.

Smith, Jackie. 2008. *Social Movements for Global Democracy.* Baltimore: Johns Hopkins University Press.

Smith, Jackie, John McCarthy, Clark McPhail, and Boguslaw Augustyn. 2001. "From Protest to Agenda-Building: Description Bias in Media Coverage of Protest Events in Washington, D.C." *Social Forces* 79 (4): 1397–423. http://dx.doi.org/10.1353/sof.2001.0053.

Smith, Miriam. 1999. *Lesbian and Gay Rights in Canada: Social Movements and Equality-Seeking, 1971–1995.* Toronto: University of Toronto Press.

–. 2005a. *A Civil Society? Collective Actors in Canadian Political Life.* Peterborough, ON: Broadview Press.

–. 2005b. "Diversity and Identity in the Nonprofit Sector: Lessons from LGBT Organizing in Toronto." *Social Policy and Administration* 39 (5): 463–80. http://dx.doi.org/10.1111/j.1467-9515.2005.00450.x.

–. 2007. "Identity and Opportunity: The Lesbian and Gay Rights Movement." In *Group Politics and Social Movements in Canada,* ed. Miriam Smith, 159–80. Peterborough, ON: Broadview Press.

–. ed. 2008. *Group Politics and Social Movements in Canada.* Peterborough, ON: Broadview Press.

–. 2013. "Social Movements and Human Rights: Gender, Sexuality, and the Charter in English-Speaking Canada." In *Taking Liberties: A History of Human Rights in Canada,* ed. Stephen Heathorn and David Goutor, 213–32. Toronto: Oxford University Press.

Snow, David A. 2008. "Elaborating the Discursive Contexts of Framing: Discursive Fields and Spaces." *Studies in Symbolic Interaction* 30: 3–28. http://dx.doi.org/10.1016/S0163-2396(08)30001-5.

Snow, David A., and Robert D. Benford. 1988. "Ideology, Frame Resonance, and Participant Mobilization." *International Social Movement Research* 1: 197–217.

–. 1992. "Master Frames and Cycles of Protest." In *Frontiers in Social Movement Theory,* ed. A.D. Morris and C.M. Mueller, 133–55. New Haven, CT: Yale University Press.

Snow, David A., Burke Rochford Jr., Stephen K. Worden, and Robert D. Benford. 1986. "Frame Alignment Processes, Micromobilization, and Movement Participation." *American Sociological Review* 51 (4): 464–81. http://dx.doi.org/10.2307/2095581.

Snow, David A., Rens Vliegenthart, and Catherine Corrigall-Brown. 2007. "Framing the French Riots: A Comparative Study of Frame Variation." *Social Forces* 86 (2): 385–415. http://dx.doi.org/10.1093/sf/86.2.385.

Sohn, Herbert A. 1975. *Human Rights Legislation in Ontario: A Study of Social Action.* Toronto: Faculty of Social Work, University of Toronto.

Solidarity Coalition. 1984. "Briefs to the People's Commission on Social and Economic Policy Alternatives." Vols. 2 and 5. Solidarity Coalition collection. UBC RBSC.

Soule, Sarah A., and Christian Davenport. 2009. "Velvet Glove, Iron Fist, or Even Hand? Protest Policing in the United States, 1960–1990." *Mobilization: An International Quarterly* 14 (1): 1–22.

Soule, Sarah A., and Jennifer Earl. 2005. "A Social Movement Society Evaluated: Collective Protest in the United States, 1960–1986." *Mobilization: An International Quarterly* 10 (3): 345–65.

Stackhouse, John. 1999 [1993]. *Canadian Evangelicalism in the Twentieth Century: An Introduction to Its Character.* Toronto: University of Toronto Press.

Staggenborg, Suzanne. 1988. "The Consequences of Professionalization and For-malization in the Pro-Choice Movement." *American Sociological Review* 53 (4): 585–605. http://dx.doi.org/10.2307/2095851.

–. 1998. "Social Movement Communities and Cycles of Protest: The Emergence and Maintenance of a Local Women's Movement." *Social Problems* 45 (2): 180–204. http://dx.doi.org/10.2307/3097243.

–. 2008. "The Environmental Movement." In *Social Movements,* ed. Suzanne Staggenborg, 104–22. Don Mills, ON: Oxford University Press.

Staggenborg, Suzanne, and Josée Lecomte. 2009. "Social Movement Campaigns: Mobilization and Outcomes in the Montreal Women's Movement Community." *Mobilization: An International Quarterly* 14:405–22.

Status of Women Action Group. 1972. "Report on Discrimination in the Retail Trades". Vol. 3, file 32. SWAG collection. BCA.

–. 1979. "Human Rights Commission Unfit to Serve." Letter to Membership, 7 April. SWAG collection. University of Victoria Archives.

Steil, Justin Peter, and Ion Bogdan Vasi. 2014. "The New Immigration Contestation: Social Movements and Local Immigration Policy Making in the United States, 2000–2011." *American Journal of Sociology* 119 (4): 1104–55. http://dx.doi.org/10.1086/675301.

Steinberg, Marc W. 1998. "Tilting the Frame: Considerations on Collective Action Framing from a Discursive Turn." *Theory and Society* 27 (6): 845–72. http://dx.doi.org/10.1023/A:1006975321345.

–. 1999. "The Talk and Back Talk of Collective Action: A Dialogic Analysis of Repertoires of Discourse among Nineteenth-Century English Cotton Spinners." *American Journal of Sociology* 105 (3): 736–80. http://dx.doi.org/10.1086/210359.

–. 2002. "Toward a More Dialogic Analysis of Social Movement Culture." In *Social Movements: Identity, Culture and the State,* ed. David S. Meyer, Nancy Whittier, and Belinda Robnett, 208–25. New York: Oxford University Press.

Stephen, M.D. 2009. "Alter-Globalism as Counter-Hegemony: Evaluating the 'Post-modern Prince.'" *Globalizations* 6 (4): 483–98. http://dx.doi.org/10.1080/14747730903298819.

Stewart, James B. 2011. "An Uprising with Plenty of Potential." *New York Times,* 18 November. http://www.nytimes.com/2011/11/19/business/occupy-wall-street-has-plenty-of-potential.html?_r=1&.

Stoddart, Mark C.J. 2012. *Making Meaning out of Mountains: The Political Ecology of Skiing.* Vancouver: UBC Press.

Stoddart, Mark C.J., and David B. Tindall. 2010. "'We've Also Become Quite Good Friends': Environmentalists, Social Networks and Social Comparison in British Columbia, Canada." *Social Movement Studies* 9 (3): 253–71. http://dx.doi.org/10.1080/14742837.2010.493658.

Stoecker, Randy. 2002. "Cyberspace vs. Face-to-Face: Community Organizing in the New Millennium." *Perspectives on Global Development and Technology* 1 (2): 143–64. http://dx.doi.org/10.1163/156915002100419781.

Stone, Diane. 2000. "Think Tank Transnationalization and Non-Profit Analysis and Advocacy." *Global Society* 14 (2): 153–72. http://dx.doi.org/10.1080/1360082 0050008421.

Stromquist, Shelton. 2006. *Reinventing "The People": The Progressive Movement, the Class Problem, and the Origins of Modern Liberalism.* Champaign: University of Illinois Press.

Sullivan, J.L., and H. Hendriks. 2009. "Public Support for Civil Liberties Pre- and Post-9/11." *Annual Review of Law and Social Science* 5 (1): 375–91. http://dx.doi.org/10.1146/annurev.lawsocsci.093008.131525.

Swidler, Ann. 1986. "Culture in Action: Symbols and Strategies." *American Sociological Review* 51 (2): 273–86. http://dx.doi.org/10.2307/2095521.

Swyngedouw, Erik. 2010. "Apocalypse Forever? Post-Political Populism and the Spectre of Climate Change." *Theory, Culture and Society* 27 (2-3): 213–32.

Swyripa, Frances. 1993. *Wedded to the Cause: Ukrainian-Canadian Women and Ethnic Identity, 1891–1991.* Toronto: University of Toronto Press.

–. 1999. "Ukrainians." In *Encyclopedia of Canada's Peoples.* Toronto: Multicultural History Society of Ontario.

Szerszynski, Bronislaw. 2007. "The Post-Ecologist Condition: Irony as Symptom and Cure." *Environmental Politics* 16 (2): 337–55. http://dx.doi.org/10.1080/09644010701211965.

Szymanski, Ann-Marie E. 2003. *Pathways to Prohibition: Radicals, Moderates, and Social Movement Outcomes.* Durham, NC: Duke University Press.

Tarr, Leslie K. 1967. *Shields of Canada: T. T. Shields, 1873–1955.* Grand Rapids, MI: Baker Book House.

Tarrow, Sidney. 1998. *Power in Movement: Social Movements, Collective Action and Politics.* 2nd ed. New York: Cambridge University Press. http://dx.doi.org/10.1017/CBO9780511813245.

–. 2005. *The New Transnational Activism.* New York: Cambridge University Press. http://dx.doi.org/10.1017/CBO9780511791055.

–. 2011. "Global, Conventional and Warring Movements and the Suppression of Contention: Themes in Contentious Politics Research." *Politica & Sociedade* 10 (18): 25–49.

Taylor, Judith. 2007. "Organizational Elaboration as Social Movement Tactic: A Case Study of Strategic Leadership in the First U.S. School Sponsored Program for Gay and Lesbian Youth." *Social Movement Studies* 6 (3): 311-26.

Taylor, Verta, Katrina Kimport, Nella Van Dyke, and Ellen Ann Andersen. 2009. "Culture and Mobilization: Tactical Repertoires, Same-Sex Weddings, and the Impact on Gay Activism." *American Sociological Review* 74 (6): 865–90. http://dx.doi.org/10.1177/000312240907400602.

Teeple, G. 2000. *Globalization and the Decline of Social Reform: Into the Twenty-First Century.* Aurora, ON: Garamond Press.

Tennant, Paul. 1990. *Aboriginal People and Politics: The Indian Land Question in British Columbia, 1849–1989.* Vancouver: UBC Press.

Tetlock, Philip E. 2005. *Expert Political Judgment.* Princeton, NJ: Princeton University Press.

Thévenot, Laurent. 2004. "The French Convention School and the Coordination of Economic Action. Laurent Thévenot Interviewed by Søren Jagd." *Economic Sociology – European Electronic Newsletter* 5 (3): 10–16.

–. 2006. *L'action au pluriel: sociologie des régimes d'engagement.* Paris: Éditions la découverte.

–. 2007. "A Science of Life Together in the World." *European Journal of Social Theory* 10 (2): 233–44. http://dx.doi.org/10.1177/1368431007078889.

Thévenot, Laurent, and Michèle Lamont. 2000. "Conclusion: Exploring the French and the American Polity." In *Rethinking Comparative Cultural Sociology: Repertoires of Evaluation in France and the United States,* ed. Michèle Lamont and Laurent Thévenot, 307–27. Cambridge: Cambridge University Press. http://dx.doi.org/10.1017/CBO9780511628108.011.

Thévenot, Laurent, Michael Moody, and Claudette Lafaye. 2000. "Forms of Valuing Nature: Arguments and Modes of Justification in French and American Environmental Disputes." In *Rethinking Comparative Cultural Sociology: Repertoires of Evaluation in France and the United States,* ed. Michèle Lamont and Laurent Thévenot, 229–72. Cambridge: Cambridge University Press. http://dx.doi.org/10.1017/CBO9780511628108.009.

Thomas, Jim. 1993. *Doing Critical Ethnography.* Newbury Park, CA: Sage Publications.

Thompson, Becky. 2001. *A Promise and a Way of Life: White Antiracist Activism.* Minneapolis: Minnesota University Press.

Thompson, David. 2009. *Green Jobs: It's Time to Build Alberta's Future.* Edmonton: Alberta Federation of Labour, Greenpeace, and Sierra Club.

Tilly, Charles. 1978. *From Mobilization to Revolution.* Reading, MA: Addison-Wesley.

–. 2006a. *Why?* Princeton, NJ: Princeton University Press.

–. 2006b. *Regimes and Repertoires.* Chicago: University of Chicago Press. http://bibliovault.org/BV.landing.epl?ISBN=9780226803500.

–. 2008a. *Contentious Performances.* New York: Cambridge University Press.

–. 2008b. *Credit and Blame.* Princeton, NJ: Princeton University Press.

Tilly, Charles, and Sidney Tarrow. 2006. *Contentious Politics.* Boulder, CO: Paradigm Publishers.

Tilly, Charles, and Lesley J. Wood. 2012. *Social Movements, 1768–2012.* Boulder, CO: Paradigm Press.

Tindall, David B. 2002. "Social Networks, Identification, and Participation in an Environmental Movement: Low-Medium Cost Activism within the British Columbia Wilderness Preservation Movement." *Canadian Review of Sociology and Anthropology/La revue Canadienne de sociologie et d'anthropologie* 39 (4): 413–52. http://dx.doi.org/10.1111/j.1755-618X.2002.tb00628.x.

–. 2004. "Social Movement Participation Over Time: An Ego-Network Approach to Micro-Mobilization." *Sociological Focus* 37 (2): 163–84. http://dx.doi.org/10.1080/00380237.2004.10571240.

Toronto Star. 1961. "Discrimination and the Law." 3 August.

Train, Russell E. 2003. *Politics, Pollution, and Pandas: An Environmental Memoir.* Washington, DC: Island Press.

Turner, Ralph H. 1970. "Determinants of Social Movement Strategies." In *Human Nature and Collective Behavior: Papers in Honor of Herbert Blumer*, ed. S. Tamotsu, 145–64. Englewood Cliffs, NJ: Prentice-Hall.

UCC (Ukrainian Canadian Congress). 2012. "TUF Marks End of 120th Anniversary Celebrations." http://www.ucc.ca/2012/09/28/tuf-marks-end-of-120th-anniversary-celebrations/.

Urry, John. 2008. "Governance, Flows, and the End of the Car System?" *Global Environmental Change* 18 (3): 343–49. http://dx.doi.org/10.1016/j.gloenvcha.2008.04.007.

Van der Pijl, K. 1998. *Transnational Classes and International Relations*. London: Routledge.

Vancouver Rape Relief and Women's Shelter. 2002. "Anniversary of the Universal Declaration of Human Rights." http://rapereliefshelter.bc.ca/learn/news/anniversary-universal-declaration-human-rights.

Vancouver Women's Caucus. 1969. "Brief to the Human Rights Commission." 3 December. File162-3-3-0-4. Frances Wasserlein collection. Simon Fraser University Archives.

Vander Kloet, Marie. 2009. "A Trip to the Co-op: The Production, Consumption and Salvation of Canadian Wilderness." *International Journal of Canadian Studies* (39–40): 231–51. http://dx.doi.org/10.7202/040831ar.

Veldman, Robin Globus, Andy Szasz, and Randolph Haluza-DeLay. 2013. *How the World's Religions Are Responding to Climate Change: Social Science Investigations*. New York: Routledge.

Vickers, Jill, Pauline Rankin, and Christine Appelle. 1993. *Politics as If Women Mattered: A Political Analysis of the National Action Committee on the Status of Women*. Toronto: University of Toronto Press.

Victoria Human Rights Council. 1979. "Victoria Human Rights Council Brief to the Human Rights Commission." MG31 H155. Vol. 16, file 17. Dan Hill collection. Library and Archives Canada (LAC).

Vipond, Mary. 2000. *The Mass Media in Canada*. Toronto: Lorimer.

Vitale, Alex S. 2007. "The Command and Control and the Miami Models at the 2004 Republican National Convention: New Forms of Policing Protests." *Mobilization: An International Quarterly* 12(4): 403–15.

–. 2008. *City of Disorder: How the Quality of Life Campaign Transformed New York Politics*. New York: NYU Press.

VLCHR (Vancouver Labour Committee for Human Rights). 1952. "Report of Progress." Box 5. Vancouver Labour Committee for Human Rights collection. UBC RBSC.

–. 1952–71. "Report on Activities." Box 1. VLCHR collection. UBC RBSC.

–. 1959. "Report on Activities." Box 1. VLCHR collection. UBC RBSC.

–. 1960–71. "Monthly Progress Reports." Box 1. VLCHR collection. UBC RBSC.

–. n.d.a. "Survey of Application Forms." Box 1. VLCHR collection. UBC RBSC.

–. n.d.b. "A Resume of the VLCHR." Box 2. VLCHR collection. UBC RBSC.

VSW (Vancouver Status of Women). 1972. "A Two-Fold Proposal to Improve the Status of Women in British Columbia: Brief Presented to David Barrett." Vol. 13, file 22. Vancouver Status of Women collection. UBC RBSC.

–. 1973. "Brief to the NDP Caucus on the Status of Women." Vol. 13, file 1. VSW collection. UBC RBSC.

–. 1976a. "Kathleen Ruff to Carol Pfeifer." 15 December. Vol. 10, file 2. VSW collection. UBC RBSC.

–. 1976b. "Day of Mourning for the Human Rights Code." Vol. 6, file 15. VSW collection. UBC RBSC.

–. 1978. "Grant Application to the Provincial Secretary of British Columbia." 31 March. Vol. 5, file 1. VSW collection. UBC RBSC.

Waddington, P.A.J. 1994. *Liberty and Order: Public Order Policing in a Capital City.* London: UCL Press.

Wagner, Peter. 1999. "After Justification: Repertoires of Evaluation and the Sociology of Modernity." *European Journal of Social Theory* 2 (3): 341–57. http://dx.doi. org/10.1177/13684319922224572.

Waldie, Paul. 2012. "New Rules in Budget 'Create More Fear' among Politically Active Charities." *Globe and Mail,* 30 March.

Waldinger, R.D. 1994. "The Making of an Immigrant Niche." *International Migration Review* 28 (1): 3–30. http://dx.doi.org/10.2307/2547023.

Walker, Jack L. Jr. 1991. *Mobilizing Interest Groups in America: Patrons, Professions and Social Movements.* Ann Arbor, MI: University of Michigan Press.

Warner, Tom. 2002. *Never Going Back: A History of Queer Activism in Canada.* Toronto: University of Toronto Press.

Warnica, Richard. 2010. "Bishop Assesses Fallout from Letter." *Edmonton Journal,* 28 February.

Watts, Michael J. 2005. "Righteous Oil? Human Rights, the Oil Complex and Corporate Social Responsibility." *Annual Review of Environment and Resources* 30 (1): 373–407. http://dx.doi.org/10.1146/annurev.energy.30.050504.144456.

Waylen, Georgina. 1998. "Gender, Feminism and the State: An Overview." In *Gender, Politics and the State,* ed. Vicky Randall and Georgina Waylen, 1–17. London: Routledge. http://dx.doi.org/10.4324/9780203004890_chapter_1.

White, Deena. 2006. "Governing Advocacy and Dissent in the Partnership State: Canadian Stories." Paper presented at the 7th international conference of the International Society for Third Sector Research, Bangkok, Thailand, 9–12 July.

–. 2008. "Can Advocacy Survive Partnership? Representing the Clients of the Welfare State." Paper presented to the annual meetings of International Sociological Association RC19, Stockholm, September. Retrieved from http://www2.sofi. su.se/RC19/pdfpapers/White_RC19_2008.pdf.

White, Deena, et al. 2008. "La gouvernance intersectorielle à l'épreuve: l'évaluation de la mise en oeuvre de la politique de reconnaissance et de soutien à l'action communautaire." Rapport final, Équipe d'évaluation de la mise en oeuvre de la politique de reconnaissance et de soutien de l'action communautaire, sous la dir. de Deena White. Montréal: CPDS, Université de Montréal. http://www.cpds. umontreal.ca/pdf/WHITE%20RAPPORT%20FINAL-b.pdf.

Willems-Braun, Bruce. 1996–97. "Colonial Vestiges: Representing Forest Landscapes on Canada's West Coast." *BC Studies* (112): 5–39.

Williams, Kristian. 2011. "The Other Side of the COIN: Counterinsurgency and Community Policing." *Interface* 3 (1): 81–117.

Williams, Rhys H. 1995. "Constructing the Public Good: Social Movements and Cultural Resources." *Social Problems* 42 (1): 124–44. http://dx.doi.org/10.2307/3097008.

—. 2004. "The Cultural Contexts of Collective Action: Constraints, Opportunities, and the Symbolic Life of Social Movements." In *The Blackwell Companion to Social Movements,* ed. David A. Snow, Sarah A. Soule, and Hanspeter Kriesi, 91–115. Oxford: Blackwell Publishing. http://dx.doi.org/10.1002/9780470999103.ch5.

Williams, Rhys H., and Timothy J. Kubal. 1999. "Movement Frames and the Cultural Environment: Resonance, Failure, and the Boundaries of the Legitimate." *Research in Social Movements, Conflicts and Change* 21: 225–48.

Wilson, Jeremy. 1998. *Talk and Log: Wilderness Politics in British Columbia, 1965–96.* Vancouver: UBC Press.

Wiseman, Nelson. 2007. "Five Immigrant Waves: Their Ideological Orientations and Their Partisan Reverberations." *Canadian Ethnic Studies* 39 (1–2): 5–30.

Woldoff, Rachael, Travis DeCola, and Robert C. Litchfield. 2011. "The Aspirational Creative Class: Urban Residential Preferences of College Students in Creative Majors." *City, Culture and Society* 2 (2): 75–83.

Worth, O., and K. Buckley. 2009. "The World Social Forum: Postmodern Prince or Court Jester?" *Third World Quarterly* 30 (4): 649–61. http://dx.doi.org/10.1080/01436590902867003.

Yaffe, Barbara. 2008. "'In Fact, Every Canadian Has a Stake in This': Alberta Oilsands Industry Fights a Public Relations War in Advance of a New Energy Policy in the U.S." *Vancouver Sun,* 25 November.

Young, Michael P. 2007. *Bearing Witness against Sin: The Evangelical Birth of the American Social Movement.* Chicago: University of Chicago Press.

Yu, Sherry S., and Catherine A. Murray. 2007. "Ethnic Media under a Multicultural Policy: The Case of the Korean Media in British Columbia." *Canadian Ethnic Studies* 39 (3): 99–124.

Zald, Mayer N. 1996. "Culture, Ideology, and Strategic Framing." In *Comparative Perspectives on Social Movements: Political Opportunities, Mobilizing Structures, and Cultural Framings,* ed. Doug McAdam, John D. McCarthy, and Mayer N. Zald, 261–74. Cambridge: Cambridge University Press. http://dx.doi.org/10.1017/CBO9780511803987.013.

Zelko, Frank. 2013. *Make It a Green Peace!* Oxford: Oxford University Press.

Zetter, Kim. 2011. "*New York Times:* Assange Was a Source, Not Media Partner." *Wired,* 26 January. http://www.wired.com/2011/01/nytimes-and-assange/.

List of Contributors

William K. Carroll is a professor of sociology at the University of Victoria. His research focuses on social movements and social change, the political economy of corporate capitalism, and critical social theory and method. His work has appeared in *International Sociology, Capital and Class, Global Networks, Globalizations, Sociology, Critical Sociology, Journal of World-System Research, Antipode, Sociological Review, Sociological Quarterly, Socialist Register,* and *Media, Culture and Society.*

Dominique Clément is an associate professor in the Department of Sociology at the University of Alberta and an adjunct professor in the Departments of History and Classics and Educational Policy Studies. He is the author of *Canada's Rights Revolution* and *Equality Deferred: Sex Discrimination and British Columbia's Human Rights State, 1953–1984,* and is also co-editor for *Alberta's Human Rights Story* and *Debating Dissent: Canada and the Sixties.* Clément manages HistoryOfRights.ca, a research and teaching portal on the history of human rights and social movements in Canada.

Jim Conley is an associate professor of sociology at Trent University. He works in the areas of social movements, sociological theory, and mobilities. His current research concerns the pragmatic sociology of critical capacities, and urban foot, bicycle, and automobile traffic.

Catherine Corrigall-Brown is an assistant professor of sociology at the University of British Columbia. Her work examines participation in social movements and the role of funding in shaping movement outcomes. Her work has appeared in *Social Forces, Mobilization, Canadian Review of Sociology, Sociological Perspectives,* and the *International Journal of Comparative Sociology.* She is also the author of *Patterns of Protest.*

Philippe Couton is an associate professor of sociology at the University of Ottawa. His research and teaching interests include political sociology, international migration, and immigrant social and political participation. He has published a number of articles in international journals on these topics.

Tina Fetner is an associate professor of sociology at McMaster University. Her research interests include social movements, politics, and sexuality. She has published on conservative politics and is the author of *How the Religious Right Shaped Lesbian and Gay Activism.*

Randolph Haluza-DeLay is an associate professor of sociology at the King's University in Edmonton, Alberta. He has co-edited *Speaking for Ourselves: Environmental Justice in Canada* and *How the World's Religions are Responding to Climate Change: Social Science Investigations.* His research interests revolve around questions of peace, justice, and sustainability. In his spare time, he leads a risky life cycling in the city and watching birds from mountaintops.

Mabel Ho is a PhD student in the Department of Sociology at the University of British Columbia. Her current research centres on the relationship between transnational practices, identity, and belonging. Her work has appeared in *Social Identities: Journal for the Study of Race, Nation and Culture.*

Dominique Masson is a professor at the Institute of Feminist and Gender Studies and the School of Sociological and Anthropological Studies at the University of Ottawa. She has worked on the funding of the Québec women's movement, as well as on its engagement in the politics of regional development. She has recently published a co-edited collection, *Solidarities beyond Borders: Transnationalizing Women's Movements,* and is currently directing a research project on solidarity building and food sovereignty in the World March of Women.

David S. Meyer is a professor of sociology and political science at the University of California, Irvine. His research has focused on the impact of social movements on politics and public policy. He has written extensively on contemporary challenging movements on the left and right in America, and maintains a blog,Politicsoutdoors.com.

Amanda Pullum is a lecturing fellow in the Thompson Writing Program at Duke University and a PhD candidate in the Department of Sociology at the University of California, Irvine. Her current research focuses on social movement strategies and coalitions. She has contributed to several recent books, including *Democratizing Inequalities: Pitfalls and Unrealized Promises of the New Public Participation*, and *Understanding the Tea Party Movement*.

Howard Ramos is an associate professor of sociology at Dalhousie University. He researches issues of social justice. With Karen Stanbridge, he co-authored *Seeing Politics Differently: A Brief Introduction to Political Sociology*, and with Suzanne Staggenborg, *Social Movements* (third Canadian edition).

Joanna L. Robinson is an assistant professor in the Department of Sociology at Glendon College, York University. Her current research examines social movements, environmental politics, labour, and inequality with a focus on how cross-movement coalitions advocate for investment in living-wage jobs in the green economy. She is the author of *Contested Water: The Struggle against Water Privatization in the United States and Canada*.

Kathleen Rodgers is an associate professor of sociology at the University of Ottawa. Her current research areas include political sociology, social movements, and digital media. Her most recent project is focused on Indigenous responses to large-scale mining projects. She is the author of *Welcome to Resisterville: American Dissidents in British Columbia*.

Carrie B. Sanders is an associate professor of criminology at Wilfrid Laurier University. Her theoretical areas of interest are interpretive sociological theories, social shaping of technology, and critical criminology. Her research interests include police culture, policing and family, intelligence-led policing, crime analysis, police technology, and the sociology of work and technological change.

Suzanne Staggenborg is a professor and chair of sociology at the University of Pittsburgh. Her work includes *Social Movements* (third Canadian edition, co-authored with Howard Ramos) and she has published extensively on movement dynamics. Her current research focuses on organization and strategy in the grassroots environmental movement.

Mark C.J. Stoddart is an associate professor in the Department of Sociology at Memorial University. His research interests include the political ecology of nature tourism and outdoor sport, media representations of environmental conflict, and the cultural dynamics of environmental movement participation. He is the author of *Making Meaning Out of Mountains: The Political Ecology of Skiing.* He has published in *Organization and Environment, International Review for the Sociology of Sport, Social Movement Studies,* and the *Canadian Journal of Sociology.*

Allyson Stokes is a Social Sciences and Humanities Research Council postdoctoral fellow in the Department of Sociology at the University of Texas at Austin and a visiting scholar in the Department of Knowledge Integration at the University of Waterloo. Her research interests include the relationship between culture and inequality, especially gender and sexualities. Her current research focuses on fashion design and the intersecting inequalities that shape creative careers in cultural industries.

Judith Taylor is an associate professor at University of Toronto, jointly appointed to the Department of Sociology and the Women and Gender Studies Institute. Her research concerns social movements, community and neighbourhood organizing, and feminist activism.

D.B. Tindall is an associate professor in the Department of Sociology at the University of British Columbia, where he studies and teaches about contention over environmental issues. A major focus of his research has been environmental movements in British Columbia and Canada, and in this context, the interrelationships between social networks, movement identification, and participation. His current research focuses on sociological aspects of contention over climate change in Canada.

Lesley Wood is an associate professor of sociology at York University. Her research on social movements works to understand how ideas travel, how power operates, and how conversations influence practices. Her publications include *Crisis and Control: The Militarization of Protest Policing,* and *Direct Action, Deliberation and Diffusion: Collective Action after the WTO Protests in Seattle.*

Index

Note: ENGOs stands for environmental non-governmental organizations; SMOs stands for social movement organizations; SMS stands for social movement society; TAPGs stands for transnational alternative policy groups

movement, 212; of human rights
state, 75–76; internal and external
processes of, 29–30, 78*n*7, 302; mainstream politics and, 307; of social
movements, 5–6, 61, 69, 80–83, 108,
302–4; sociological conceptualizations of, 96; of state and movements,
84–86, 87, 95–96, 301; of Tea Party
and Occupy movements, 37, 40, 43
International Bible Students Association
(IBSA), 54
International Forum on Globalization
(IFG), 238, 239–40, 242–43, 245,
247, 249
International Organization for a Participatory Society (IOPS), 254*n*9

Jamison, Andrew, 235, 257, 275, 294
Jasper, James, 197
Jenkins, Craig, 11
Jewish Labour Committee (JLC), 64–65,
77
Johnson, David, 71
Johnston, Hank, 63, 73, 75
Johnston, Russell, 57
judgment: cognitive and moral, 200,
203; on justice and injustice, 194,
196, 198, 201, 203, 206; public, 191
Jumbo Pass (BC): media coverage of,
260–61, 263–65; ski resort development, 256, 267–68; as a wilderness
landscape, 257, 262, 266–68, 271
Justice for Jordan Miles, 169
justifications, 200; civic, 201–2. *See also*
injustice; pragmatic sociology of
critique

KAIROS, 281
Kejimkujik National Park, 269
Kensington Market incident, 194, 204–
5; account of incident, 200; public
judgment on, 201–3
King, Mike, 143
Klocke, Brian, 143
knowledge production and mobilization
(KPM), 234; counter-hegemonic,

235, 239; prefigurative, 239–40, 243–
44; of TAPGs, 236, 237, 253, 305
Koch brothers, 33, 34
Korea Trade-Investment Promotion
Agency (KOTRA), 127
Korean Businessmen's Co-op Association
of British Columbia (KBCABC), 126
Korean Canadian Women's Association
(KCWA), 127
Korean immigrants: communal organiz-
ations, 120, 130; gendered divisions,
127–28; small business operations,
122, 125–27, 129, 303
Ktunaxa First Nation, 256, 273*n*1

labour: division of, 127–28; immigrant,
122; left orientation, 177; movement,
64–65; oil sands and, 282–83, 294.
See also entrepreneurship
Langer, Rosanna, 71
Lasn, Kalle, 38, 39
Latimer, Robert, 191–92, 193, 204
Latour, Bruno, 259, 271
left politics: in Germany, 238, 254*n*3;
global, 246, 247; labour, 177; Meyer
and Tarrow on, 27; in North and
South America, 238; women's move-
ment and, 105
lesbian, gay, bisexual, and transgendered
(LGBT), 7–8, 74, 78*n*6
Levant, Ezra, 288
Liberal government: Quebec, 90, 94;
Trudeau era, 104–5; voluntary sector
initiatives, 106–7, 115
Lipset, Seymour M., 7, 48
literature: framing, 195–96, 203, 206; so-
cial movement, 10–12, 87, 211, 227, 302
Local Initiative Program (LIP), 7
local movement communities, 160, 162,
166, 169–72
Loewen, Royden, 132
Ludwig, Wiebo, 278

Maclean's, 54
mainstream media: coverage of environmental conflicts, 259, 260–61, 263–65,

245. *See also* environmental non-
governmental organizations (ENGOs)
Northern Gateway pipeline, 9, 286
Not in My Backyard (NIMBY), 180
Nuclear Freeze, 34
Nunavut, 297

Obama, Barack: Occupy movement
and, 41; Tea Party and, 31–33, 37
Occupy movement: demonstrations
and encampments, 38–40; media
coverage, 39, 297; organizing dilemmas, 40–42; policing, 149–50; politicians and, 41, 304; public opinion
on, 10; resistance to formalization,
43; rise of, 3–4, 13, 38
oil sands: Aboriginal activism, 278–79,
281–82, 286, 287–88, 293–94; Albertan
culture and, 276; counter-responses
to, 286–89, 294; ENGO mobilization,
279–81; health and environmental
impacts of, 277–78; labour organizing
in, 282–83, 294; public perception
of, 289–93; religious groups intervention, 281–82, 294; revenues
from, 274, 276–77; transnational
campaigns against, 283–86
old-growth forests, 268–69
Oliver, Joe, 286
Ontario Coalition Against Poverty
(OCAP), 72
Ontario Korean Businessmen's
Association (OKBA), 125–26
open spaces, 243–44
Opportunities for Youth (OFY): function
of, 7
organizations, formal, 25–26; scholarship on, 46
Oxfam, 166, 168

Palin, Sarah, 34
Parkland Institute, 276, 280, 282
Parti Québécois, 89, 91–92, 94–95,
97n4, 163
Paul, Ron, 37
Pembina Institute, 277–78, 280, 287, 291

People's Plan Study Group (PPSG), 238,
245
Peterson, Abby, 143
Phillips, Jeffrey, 286
pipeline disputes, 285–86
Pittsburgh G-20 Resistance Project
(PGRP), 166, 169; People's Uprising
event, 167–68
Pittsburgh Organizing Group (POG),
168–69
Pittsburgh Principles, 169–70
Pivnenko, Sergiy, 133–34
Plumwood, Val, 272
policing protest: dual model of, 15, 142–
44, 147–51, 158; intelligence-led, 146;
interactive and interpretive processes
in, 148–49; militarized tactics, 138–39,
142, 149–51, 158–59; negotiated management strategy, 26, 139–41, 143, 158,
304; non/cooperation, 138, 146–47,
149–52; at Occupy movement, 41, 150;
at Pittsburgh G-20 Summit, 167–68,
169; routinized interactions in, 139, 158;
strategies, 144–46; training, 141–42
Policy for the Recognition and Support
of Community Action, 92–93
policy groups. *See* transnational alternative policy groups (TAPGs)
political engagement, 305–7; of immigrants, 120, 124; social psychology
of, 174–75, 189. *See also* Clean Train
Coalition (CTC)
political process theory, 102
polity model, 25, 27
populism, 30, 33–34, 36
poverty, 91, 163–64, 171
pragmatic sociology of critique, 16, 196–99
Pratt, Andy, 176
professionalization, 255, 295; financial
resources and, 26; of SMOs, 62, 69,
74, 76, 108, 157; of TAPGs, 253; of
women's services, 86
Programme de soutien aux organismes
communautaires (PSOC), 85–86,
89–91, 93
prostitution, 72

Printed and bound in Canada by Friesens

Set in Segoe and Warnock by Artegraphica Design Co. Ltd.

Copy editor: Francis Chow

Proofreader: Helen Godolphin

Indexer: Celia Braves